# Mary

Art, Culture,
and Religion
through the Ages

CAROLINE H. EBERTSHÄUSER
HERBERT HAAG
JOE H. KIRCHBERGER
DOROTHEE SÖLLE

# Mary

## Art, Culture, and Religion through the Ages

*Translated by Peter Heinegg*

*A Crossroad Herder Book*
The Crossroad Publishing Company
New York

The Crossroad Publishing Company
370 Lexington Avenue, New York,
NY 10017

A production of EMB-Service for Publishers
Lucerne, Switzerland

© 1997 by EMB-Service for Publishers
Lucerne, Switzerland

English translation copyright
© 1998 by The Crossroad Publishing Company
From the German edition, Maria: Kunst,
Brauchtum und Religion in Bild und Text
© 1997 by Verlag Herder,
Freiburg – Basel – Wien

Printed in Switzerland

Concept and design:
Franz Gisler, Lucerne

Typesetting: CS Publishing, Freiburg i.Br.
Photolithos: Job Color srl, Gorle (Bergamo)
Printing: Basler Druck & Verlag AG, Basel
Binding: Buchbinderei Schumacher
Schmitten/Berne

Library of Congress
Cataloging-in-Publication Data
Maria. English
    Mary: art, culture, and religion through the
ages / Caroline H. Ebertshäuser ... [et al.] ;
translated by Peter Heinegg.
        p. cm.
    "A Crossroad Herder book."
    Includes index.
    ISBN 0-8245-1760-1
    1. Mary, Blessed Virgin, Saint.  2. Mary, Blessed
Virgin, Saint--Art.  3. Mary, Blessed Virgin,
Saint--In literature.  4. Mary, Blessed Virgin,
Saint--Theology.  5. Mary, Blessed Virgin,
Saint--Cult.  I. Ebertshäuser, Caroline H.
II. Heinegg, Peter.  III. Title.
BT602.M35413  1998
232.91--dc21                              98-15608
                                              CIP

Captions: Caroline H. Ebertshäuser

*Cover:* Leonardo da Vinci, *Madonna of the Rocks*. Detail. Erich Lessing/Art Resources, New York.

*Page 2:* Emil Nolde (1867–1956), *Madonna and Dahlias*, 1920. Among the many religious themes in Nolde's work is this still life from 1920, which shows a Madonna figure alongside flowers. The Marian symbol of the unicorn (purity) is woven into the ornamentation on the table cloth.

*Right:* Carlos Schwabe, *The Madonna with the Lilies*, 1899, Van Gogh Museum, Amsterdam. This aquarelle symbolically shows Mary's way as a path of lilies, which in Marian iconography is the flower of the Annunciation and the symbol of purity.

# CONTENTS

*The great helper in birth and death spreads her mantle of protection against fear and need.*

6

# THE IMAGE OF MARY

Herbert Haag

I am happy to contribute a foreword to this book. It is designed not just to enrich the Christian image of Mary, but, in several crucial areas, to correct it. From the beginning Mary has played a major role in theology and popular piety. But every period built up its own image of her, so that in each image of Mary we see the reflection of the individual epochs of religious faith.

Certainly the legend of Mary showed its power as far back as the oldest depictions of her. From the outset a woman who was so closely bound up with the history of salvation had to have something special about her. Hence in three of the four Gospels we can already find traces of legend formation. While the earliest evangelist, Mark, reports only about the later public activities of Jesus, the Gospels of Matthew and Luke ten years later contain the story of Jesus' infancy, in which Mary has a significant place. John, by contrast, is less concerned with Mary's story than with its theological meaning.

Of course, the first mention of the mother of Jesus is not in the Gospels. Around the year 55 the Apostle Paul writes in his Letter to the Galatians: "When the time had fully come, God sent forth his Son, born of woman, to redeem those who were under the law, so that we might receive adoption as sons" (4.4). Paul, who preached the gospel in Galatia (Asia Minor), later warns that community about backsliding into circumcision and legalism. He stresses that God has sent his Son into the world in order to devote himself to humans in a new way and to grant them a freedom that they never knew before. This was an historical event, but it would not have been possible without a woman. Her name is not mentioned. The importance of Mary could not be expressed more soberly: she was the gate through which Jesus came into this world as our brother.

The first two chapters of both Matthew and Luke, which contain the story of the birth and childhood of Jesus, are not original components of these Gospels. They go back to independent Palestinian traditions; they were borrowed by the two evangelists and worked up, each in his own way, as a kind of prologue to their Gospels. Their theme is not Mary but Jesus, although Mary does play a major role in them.

In the ancient world it was customary to embellish the circumstances of the birth of great men (e.g., Buddha or Cyrus of Persia) with legends. Thus we find the infancy narrative of Jesus taking the form of a theological legend. It begins with the annunciation of his birth by the angel Gabriel—a scene that has its prototypes in the Old Testament, namely, in the announcement of the birth of Samson (Judges 13) and Samuel (1 Samuel 1). But, despite its legendary form, the story wins us over by its style. The narrative emphasizes Mary's chosenness ("Hail, O favored one, the Lord is with you," "You have found favor with God" [Luke 1.28, 30]), her prudence and thoughtfulness (v. 29), her ready tongue (she raises objections and then lets herself be convinced, vv. 34–35), and above all her faith ("Let it be to me according to your word," v. 36). She summons up this faith because she sees herself as the "handmaid of the Lord": unconditionally open to him and ready for him—an attitude that the gospel tradition has sought to capture with the term "virgin."

Surprisingly we learn nothing in the Gospels about Mary's outer appearance. Christian hymns like to praise her as the "fairest of women," and there is nothing to disprove the notion that she was a beautiful young woman. In the Old Testament, however, the text explicitly says of at least a dozen women that they were beautiful, very beautiful in fact (Sarah or Rebekah, for instance, Rachel, Abigail, Esther, etc.), and in the Song of Solomon the beauty of the Beloved is described in all its particulars. Yet in the New Testament we hear no woman, not even Mary, being called beautiful. Only later did artists attempt to make of her the fairest of the fair.

While the scene of the Annunciation primarily stresses Mary's faith, she shows courage and decisiveness on the trip she takes to visit Elizabeth in the hill country of Judea (Luke 1.39–50). To be sure, a young woman would not make this sort of three-day journey alone; she would have joined a caravan. Still, Mary "hastens," although caravans as a rule don't work under time constraints. The narrator wants to show how intent she is to pass on, from the first moment, as it were, the salvation of Israel that has been entrusted to her. That is how Elizabeth sees it: "Blessed is she who believed that there would be a fulfillment of what was spoken to her from the Lord" (v. 45). And then the evangelist puts a psalm into Mary's mouth, stitched together from many biblical quotations and known as the "Magnificat" from its first word in

Latin. In it Mary not only sings about her own chosenness ("Henceforth all generations will call me blessed," v. 48), but she shows a striking awareness of history, of the old and new people of God. Of course, in reality it is not Mary who is speaking. Rather it is the young Church already singing Mary's praises.

Once again Mary's faith is stressed in the account of the birth of Jesus in Bethlehem (Luke 2.1–20). There is no way to harmonize this description with the historical facts. It is a romanticized treatment (later heightened by generations of Christians to an unbearable level), but within it we hear the simple words relating to the birth itself: "She gave birth to her first-born son and wrapped him in swaddling cloths, and laid him in a manger" (v. 7). Mary appears as a woman like any other—and yet different. It is important to the narrator that the birth of the child is a "great joy" for the world (v. 10). And although it is impossible for any woman who has just given birth to grasp what has happened, how could Mary not have "kept all these things, pondering them in her heart" (v. 19)? There was a domain here that she could make her own only by meditative consent.

This incomprehension will continue through all the rest of Mary's dealings with her Son. Amid the jubilation of the aged Simeon and Anna at the presentation of Jesus in the temple the text already speaks of a sword that "will pierce through your own soul" (v. 3). When the twelve-year-old Jesus, unbeknownst to his parents, stays behind in the Temple, he coolly replies to his mother's reproachful question, "Son, why have you treated us so?" with "How is it that you sought me?" She must realize now that Jesus is breaking away from her in a manner different from that in which growing sons usually separate from their mothers. Jesus explains his behavior by remarking, "Did you not know that I must be in my Father's house?" (v. 49). Jesus knows that he does not belong to his biological parents, but to another Father. This must have deeply unsettled and shaken both of them, even though Jesus now returns with them to Nazareth and is "obedient" to them (v. 50). The evangelist then notes for a second time, and with renewed emphasis, that "his mother kept all these things in her heart" (v. 51). It was, basically, rude of Jesus to let his parents leave the city without telling them what he was doing. Mary must have found it no less difficult than we do to see the will of God in this. But here too the evangelist is pursuing a theological concern. The alienation between Jesus and his closest relatives, especially Mary, that begins in this scene will

grow deeper during his "public life." Jesus' family does not by any means bask in the glow of his popularity with the crowds and his miracles. On the contrary, Jesus brings his family embarrassment and a bad name. In Nazareth the family's reputation seems not to have been the best anyhow. When Jesus appears in the village synagogue, people object: "Is not this the carpenter, the son of Mary and brother of James and Joses and Judas and Simon, and are not his sisters here with us?" (Mark 6.3). We cannot miss the undertone of skepticism, rejection, and even scorn here.

But, from his family's point of view, what Jesus now "went and did" in broad daylight, claiming to be a prophet sent by God, was downright intolerable. Things got so much out of hand that some of them thought he was "beside himself" and tried to "seize hold" of him, that is, get him to disappear, tie him down, and fit him back into the solid space of the clan. His mother took part in this attempted surprise, which demonstrates how bold she was, but also how far the alienation between her and her son had gone.

"And his mother and his brothers came," we are told. Since Jesus is surrounded by the people, his relatives cannot get through to him, and besides they want to avoid causing a sensation. And so they have Jesus summoned to them. He is told: "Your mother and your brothers are outside, asking for you." But Jesus does not take the bait. "And looking around on those who sat about him, he said, 'Here are my mother and my brothers! Whoever does the will of God is my brother, and sister, and mother' (Mark 3.31–35). Jesus had long since bidden farewell to his biological family; he had decided in favor of a new family without boundaries of clan, language, or people. So it was understandable that early Christians would call one another "brother" and "sister".

According to the Synoptic Gospels, this episode is the only one in which Mary appears in the public life of Jesus. On the other hand, in John, who has nothing to tell us about Jesus' infancy, she stands as an interpretive sign at the beginning and end of Jesus' ministry. First there is the miracle of the wine at the marriage feast of Cana (John 2.1–11). It is important to the Fourth Gospel to ground the liturgy, as celebrated around the year 100 by the Christian community, in the life of Jesus. Baptism and the eucharist are at the center of all this. Thus, in the wine that Jesus provides for the wedding guests the evangelist envisions the eucharist, where Jesus as the host serves the wine to his disciples for the sacred meal.

Marc Chagall (1887–1985), *Madonna and Child*, 1911, Art Museum, Bern. Religious themes are deeply rooted in Chagall's mythic-imaginary world. The artist links classical religious motifs, such as the Madonna, to new forms of artistic expression, such as the Expressionist language of color and the free structuring of space.

Mary is the one who prompts the miracle by observing, "They have no wine." Jesus' answer is disconcertingly aloof and once again matches the acknowledged distance between him and his mother: "O woman, what have you to do with me?" Nowadays we would likely say, "What's that got to do with me?" It is a refusal, though naturally an ambiguous one, which leaves room for expectation. That is why Mary instructs the servants, "Do whatever he tells you." After the miracle the evangelist notes: "His disciples believed in him." Mary believed even before the miracle. The Church's veneration of Mary as the mediator between Jesus and his disciples has its biblical anchor here.

Our last glimpse of Mary in the Gospel of John is beneath the cross: "Standing by the cross of Jesus were his mother, and his mother's sister … and Mary Magdalene" (19.25). We have problems with this statement, because in the Synoptic Gospels several women are named as "looking on from afar" at the crucifixion of Jesus. But among them the mother of Jesus is not mentioned (cf. Mark 15.40; Matthew 27.56). In John, by contrast, all the author's interest is focused on the mother of Jesus and the "disciple whom Jesus loved" alongside her (19.26–27). In the community in which the Fourth Gospel was composed, both of them must have been greatly beloved; and it seemed natural to understand their meaning for the community as a togetherness that Jesus wanted. Thus the description has a deeply symbolic content. The disciple "whom Jesus loved" represents the Church, which cannot, however, exist without fellowship with Mary.

We get the same image in the final mention of Mary in the New Testament. Jesus does not appear to her after his resurrection, as we are told in particular of Mary Magdalene (Matthew 18.1, 9–10; John 20. 14–18). But when, after the ascension of Jesus, the Eleven, the women, and the "brothers of Jesus" gather, Mary, the mother of Jesus, is in their midst (Acts 1.14). Apart from the Eleven she is the only one mentioned by name. The community gathered here is the first Church, which now enters upon its path into the world. It can only do so with Mary in its midst. That is how the author of the Acts of the Apostles sees it. This is the same Luke to whom we owe the story of Christmas. If the young mother in that story is the childlike believer, here we have the mature woman who points the way.

When Mary was born, her country, Israel, already had a long and varied history behind it.

Israel had been a major power only once, almost a thousand years before, under its kings David and Solomon. But this heyday did not last long. After Solomon's death the nation was divided; and both parts, the larger northern

than with recreating Israel's religious life in accordance with the law of Moses. Around this time the temple destroyed by the Babylonians was rebuilt in Jerusalem. The place of the old Israelite prophets was now taken by the scribes, who together with the priests of Yahweh gained more and more influence over the people.

# Mary's Life

*Below:* Joachim and Anne: The Immaculate Conception, a miniature from the Book of Hours of Catherine of Cleves (ca. 1440), Pierpont Morgan Library, New York. This work is one of the great masterpieces of Dutch miniature painting.

Joe H. Kirchberger

kingdom of Israel and the smaller southern kingdom of Judah, soon became dependencies of the great Near Eastern powers surrounding it, Assyria and Babylon in the north, Egypt in the south.

The northern kingdom was overthrown (722 B.C.) by the Assyrians, who carried off many of the inhabitants to Mesopotamia, while the remaining population mingled with the surrounding pagan tribes. This gave rise to the mixed race of the Samaritans whom authentic Israelites thought of as unclean and renegades.

Little Judah held out for almost 150 years longer, though only in complete dependency, first upon the Assyrians, then the Babylonians. When the Babylonian King Nebuchadnezzar conquered and destroyed Jerusalem, he took large groups of the population back with him. Granted, this so-called Babylonian Captivity of Israel lasted only a few decades—Cyrus, the king of Persia, conquered Babylon in the year 538 B.C. and granted some of the exiled people the right to return to Jerusalem. But the small group that returned remained the vassals of Babylon. Among the nation's most important leaders were Ezra, a priest and scribe, and Nehemiah, once a high official at the Persian court. They were less concerned with the formation of a political state

Around 330 B.C., when Alexander the Great conquered the Persian empire, Israel too, along with the rest of the Middle East, came under Greek hegemony, which persisted under Alexander's successors—first the Ptolemaic dynasty in Egypt, then the Seleucids, who ruled in Syria.

At this time the Jews lived scattered all over the Middle East, and they increasingly fell under the sway of Hellenistic culture. The Old Testament was translated into Greek (the Septuagint), and outside the land of Israel, in the so-called Diaspora, synagogue services were widely conducted in Greek. There was even a philo-Hellenic party in Jerusalem.

But a reaction to this was not long in coming. The Seleucid King Antiochus IV tried to make the Jews give up their old faith. He profaned the Holy of Holies, ordered the walls of Jerusalem razed, had lawbreakers burned at the stake and a fortress constructed in Jerusalem. At first the high priest and many other Jews complied: they offered sacrifices on the newly-built pagan altars. But then a revolt broke out among the old believers in the rural population. It was aimed not just at the foreign rulers, but also against the Hellenized city dwellers. Under the leadership of the high priest Mattathias and his sons Judas, known as Maccabeus ("the ham-

mer"), Simeon, and Jonathan, the Seleucids were beaten. The cult of Yahweh was restored throughout the country, and under the house of the Hasmoneans (Maccabees) Israel once again became an autonomous state, whose boundaries approached those of the old kingdom of David. But the new kingdom displeased the truly pious Jews. Two parties were formed: the Pharisees—who strove for a pure priestly rule, intent only on looking after religious regulations and interests—and the Sadducees—who wanted to recover political power for the state of Israel.

The masses supported the Pharisees; the nobility and the semi-Hellenized intelligentsia backed the Sadducees. The latter had some early successes: under the later Hasmoneans, especially Alexander Jannaeus, parts of East Jordan and several coastal cities were acquired.

But then the Romans intervened, having already occupied Syria. On the occasion of a dynastic dispute in the house of the Maccabees the Romans were called in as mediators; and their general, Pompey, took the Temple of Jerusalem by storm in 63 B.C. After the collapse of the Seleucid empire Pompey undertook a restructuring of the Middle East. The Jewish priest Hyrcanus was stripped of all secular power, and most of the conquests of the Hasmoneans were taken back from the Jews. Theocracy, a "divine state" with no external power, was restored—but again it was short-lived. The minister governing for Hyrcanus, Antipatros, sided with the Romans in their Middle Eastern campaign and helped Julius Caesar, who had fallen into a dangerous situation after his victory over Pompey in Egypt. Out of gratitude Caesar allowed the Jewish state to undergo a broad-based restoration. Antipatros was an Idumaean, meaning that he came from Edom, to the south of the Dead Sea. The population of Edom traced its origins back to Jacob's twin brother Esau and was just as despised by the orthodox Jews as the Samaritans were. Hence the religious fanatics and the Sanhedrin in Jerusalem fought their own government no less than they did the Romans and their favorites. Finally they forced the weak Hyrcanus to send Herod, the son of Antipatros, who had defeated the rebels, into exile.

But Herod was an even more skilled diplomat than his father. He joined the Roman army and managed to curry favor first with Caesar, then, after his assassination, with the republicans Brutus and Cassius, then with Mark Antony, who had conquered Caesar's murderers, and finally with Octavian/Augustus after his defeat of Antony. But he also knew how to get along with Hyrcanus, whose granddaughter he married. Thus he was appointed first the procurator, then the king of Judea. For strictly religious Jews he always remained an outsider, though he did all he could to promote Israel's position in the world. He maintained a balance between orthodox Judaism on the one hand and Greeks and Romans on the other. He was a committed Jew and spent enormous sums on the Temple in Jerusalem, but had his sons brought up in Rome. With all this, he was a completely ruthless autocrat and despot; he unscrupulously executed his competitors, even in his own family, including his wife Mariamne. Having married ten times, he was surrounded by numerous sons and daughters; and the court intrigues never stopped. The house of the Hasmoneans, which had made itself unpopular in Rome through its alliance with the Parthians, who repeatedly invaded Roman territory, was annihilated by Herod with the permission of the Romans.

When Herod, known as "the Great," died in 4 B.C., he had already divided his kingdom into three parts, which were ruled by his sons. Galilee and the region of the Transjordan were controlled by Herod Antipas, the area south of Damascus by Philip. Both held the title of tetrarch. The princedoms were later united and stayed that way until the end of the century. The southern territories of Judah, Samaria, and Idumea were given, along with the title of king, to Herod's son Archelaus. But he was so hated by his people that the Emperor Augustus deposed him in 6 A.D. His country was placed under direct Ro-

*You bore a child as a virgin, the noblest child in the world.*
*You are like the sun, risen from Nazareth, the glory of Jerusalem,*
*the joy of Israel, Sancta Maria.*

Hymn to Mary from Melk (Austria), before 1150

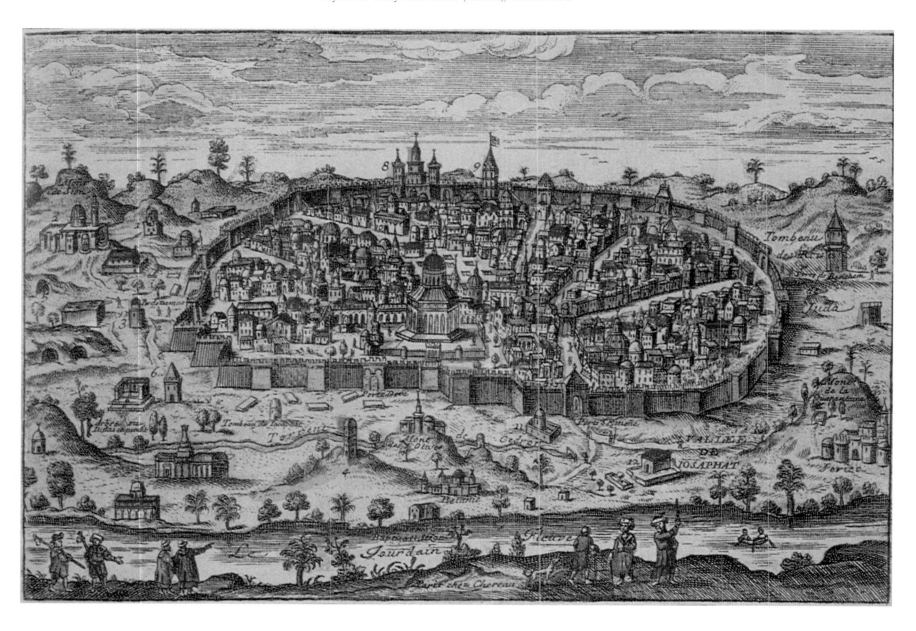

man control and remained a Roman province from then on.

During this time the High Council, called the Sanhedrin, was the ultimate Jewish spiritual and secular authority; at the same time it was also the supreme court. It was subject to the high priest, and the Romans gave it broad freedom of action. Its death sentences, however, had to be confirmed by the procurator.

The Jews had long ago stopped speaking Hebrew; their language was now Aramaic, a Semitic sister language of Hebrew. It was spoken in Syria and was gradually adopted by the Jews who returned from Babylon. Aramaic remained the lingua franca of the Middle East—along with Greek—even during the Hellenistic period, until it was later ousted by Arabic.

Despite the internal division of Judaism into Pharisaism and Sadduceeism, despite the massive penetration of the Hellenistic world, and despite the long regime of the outsider Herod, the Jews as a whole had maintained their unity essentially intact thanks to their inherent sense of national and religious solidarity. Whether they obeyed the Seleucids, the Romans, the Parthians, or Herod, whether in their highest circles they spoke Greek, Latin, or Aramaic, whether their supreme authorities had been given more or less freedom of action by the real dictators, made little difference to most of the Jews of Palestine. The contributions they had to make every year to the Temple were paid more regularly than their taxes were to the state. And even the Jewish

intellectuals who, like Philo of Alexandria, thought they had long broken free of their religion, fundamentally still held on to the old faith in Yahweh. The Jewish people resisted all the pressures from the outside with incredible toughness. The rulers in Rome, especially Augustus, took this into consideration; and, in the East at any rate, if not in the Italian Diaspora, they allowed the Jews many privileges, such as freedom from military service. Nevertheless the great conflict between Rome and Judah could not be avoided, although it did not break out until the year 66, long after the deaths of Jesus and Mary.

Thus Mary was born under Herod the Great. Later his son, Herod Antipas, was the ruler of her country. He offended his people by marrying his sis-

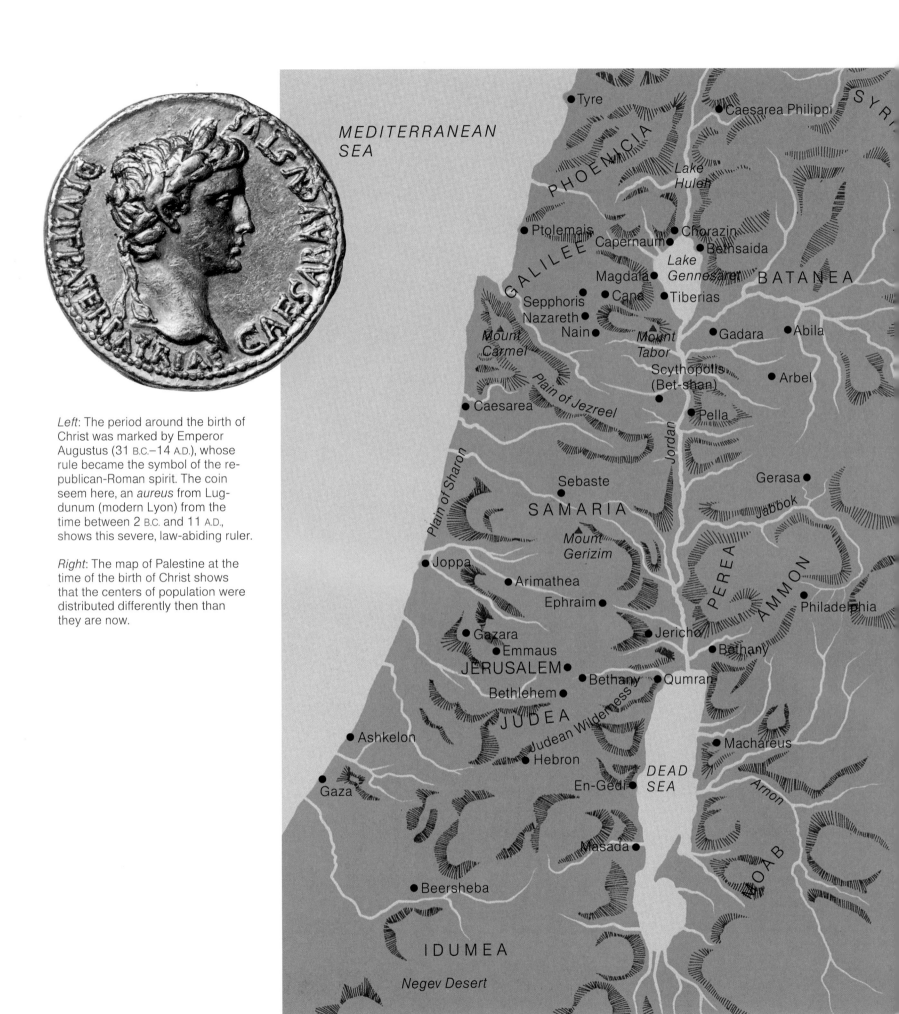

*Left*: The period around the birth of Christ was marked by Emperor Augustus (31 B.C.–14 A.D.), whose rule became the symbol of the republican-Roman spirit. The coin seem here, an *aureus* from Lugdunum (modern Lyon) from the time between 2 B.C. and 11 A.D., shows this severe, law-abiding ruler.

*Right*: The map of Palestine at the time of the birth of Christ shows that the centers of population were distributed differently then than they are now.

MEDITERRANEAN SEA

Tyre

Caesarea Philippi

SYR.

PHOENICIA

Lake Huleh

Ptolemais

Chorazin

Capernaum

Bethsaida

GALILEE

Magdala

Lake Gennesaret

BATANEA

Sepphoris

Cana

Tiberias

Nazareth

Gadara

Abila

Nain

Mount Tabor

Mount Carmel

Scythopolis (Bet-shan)

Arbel

Caesarea

Plain of Jezreel

Pella

Jordan

Plain of Sharon

Sebaste

Gerasa

SAMARIA

Jabbok

Joppa

Mount Gerizim

Arimathea

PEREA

AMMON

Ephraim

Philadelphia

Gazara

Jericho

Emmaus

Bethany

JERUSALEM

Bethany

Qumran

Bethlehem

JUDEA

Judean Wilderness

Ashkelon

Machaerus

Hebron

DEAD SEA

Gaza

En-Gedi

Arnon

Masada

MOAB

IDUMEA

Negev Desert

14

*But when Herod died, behold, an angel of the Lord appeared in a dream to Joseph, saying,*
*"Rise, take the child and his mother, and go to the land of Israel, for those who sought the child's life are dead."*
*And he rose and took the child and his mother, and went to the land of Israel.*

Gospel of Matthew 2.19–21

ter-in-law and niece, Herodias. John the Baptist attacked Herod Antipas in his sermons, was imprisoned by him and, at the urging of Herodias, executed. Herod founded a new capital, named Tiberias after the new emperor in Rome. Herod's ambition finally proved his ruin. Instead of making him king, Emperor Caligula exiled him and his wife to Lugdunum, now Lyon, in Gaul.

What do we know about Nazareth, the place where Mary was born and spent most of her life? In her day Nazareth was a small village; it is mentioned neither by the Jewish historian Flavius Josephus nor in the Talmud, which cites sixty-three localities in Israel. In contrast to Bethlehem, which is mentioned as far back as the 14th century B.C., it was probably a little old settlement. Its location is hard to specify, since modern Nazareth, En-Nasira, which has over 3,200 inhabitants, makes it hard to conduct archeological digs. In any event the place lies in a hollow, around twelve miles northeast of the Sea of Galilee (Lake Gennesaret) and around 1200–1500 feet above sea level. The basin lay open only toward the southeast, which guaranteed a mild climate. But there was only one well, now called Ain Maryam, Mary's Well. No trade route led through the place, but several crisscrossed the Plain of Jezreel, which lay beneath the basin. The whole region at that time must have been much more heavily wooded and more fertile than it is today. Nazareth's inhabitants got their livelihood from farming, and perhaps some occasional trading. Its reputation in the land of Israel was not very impressive—"Can anything good come out of Nazareth?" we read in the New Testament. In the Middle Ages it suffered greatly under Muslim rule, which destroyed or let go to ruin all Christian sites. Not until the 18th century did the town begin to revive again.

*Left:* The animated, linear pictorial language of Romanesque cathedral sculpture underscores the emotions of the subject matter, Herod Antipas and Salome. With rich ornamentation the relationship between the figures is depicted with just a few gestures. As a reward for her dance Salome, on the advice of her mother, asks for the head of John the Baptist. This story has fascinated Western artists for many centuries. The relief is located in Sens, France.

*Right:* The *Slaughter of the Innocents* from the Ingeborg Psalter (ca. 1200) in France shows in the center Herod on his throne. The murder of the children is done at his bidding. Note the remarkable expression of despair on the face of the soldier (right) over the cruelty of the order he has to carry out. Early Gothic stylistic elements are prominent here. The Psalter is named after the French queen Ingeborg, who was its first owner. It is one of the most important early documents in the representation of Mary's life.

# MARY'S LIFE: THE SOURCES

*T*he oldest and most important sources for the story of Mary are to be found in the New Testament. Mary is mentioned by all four evangelists, as well as in the Acts of the Apostles, Paul's Letter to the Galatians, and allusively in his Letter to the Romans. Some of these references are very brief; none is particularly detailed.

Even today expert opinions differ on the issue of the relationship of the evangelists to one another. As far as their chronological order goes, the Church long taught that the order given in the New Testament is historically correct. That would make Matthew the oldest evangelist, followed by Mark, Luke, and John. But nowadays scholars are practically unanimous that Mark is the first evangelist, while both Matthew and Luke have borrowed a great deal from him. Some commentators argue, however, that Matthew originally wrote his account not in Greek but in Aramaic, and did so in fact *before* Mark, and that only the Greek translation of his Gospel came into existence after Mark. Most interpreters of the New Testament are also agreed that both Matthew and Luke, who have the most to report about Mary, later appended the chapters about Jesus' infancy, in which Mary makes the majority of her appearances. Most likely they did so to underpin faith in Jesus' divine sonship through their accounts of his miraculous birth.

On the whole scholars agree about the dates of composition of the biblical sources. The Gospel of Mark is thought to have been written around 70 A.D., hence at about the time of the destruction of Jerusalem by Titus, who later became emperor. The Gospel of Matthew dates to around 75–80 (others would say 80–85), Luke slightly later, and John to around the year 100.

Luke's Acts of the Apostles must have been written immediately after his Gospel, as its continuation. The earliest New Testament sources, therefore, are not the Gospels, but the Letters of the Apostle Paul, which must have been composed roughly between 48 and 55 A.D. Thus none of the biblical sources was drawn up until decades after the events they describe, because the death

of Jesus must have occurred between 30 and 35 A.D.

What do we know now about these New Testament writers? Not much is known for sure about Mark, the author of the oldest and shortest Gospel. He may be the same man as John Mark, who is mentioned in Acts as the companion of Paul. He is said to have received much of his material from Peter himself, to have founded the church in Alexandria, and to have died there as a martyr. It has also been speculated that he was the young man who stayed with Jesus at the time of his arrest, but then was assaulted and had to flee naked—a detail mentioned only in the Gospel of Mark. Mark has nothing to report about Jesus' descent, birth, and childhood, but begins with the activity of John the Baptist. He does not offer a biography of Jesus, but shows him as the Son of God, as a powerful speaker, prophet, and miracle-worker.

Matthew's name does not occur in the Gospel ascribed to him, and is not mentioned until the 2nd century. It is considered highly unlikely that the author of this Gospel was identical to the disciple of Jesus with the same name. In any case his account is written for Jewish Christians. It contains more references to the Old Testament than the other Gospels and makes an effort to prove that Jesus is the Messiah announced in the Hebrew Bible. Particularly interesting is his allusion to Isaiah 7.14 ("Behold a virgin shall conceive and bear a son," cf. Mt. 1.23)—though it must be noted that "virgin" is an inaccurate translation of the Hebrew word in Isaiah, *almah*, which actually means "young woman."

Matthew's first two chapters, a later addition, contain precise information about Jesus' ancestry, which is traced from Abraham through David down to Joseph, Mary's husband. According to accounts from the 2nd century, Matthew is supposed to have died a martyr's death under the Emperor Nero.

Luke, to whom are attributed both the Gospel bearing his name and the Acts of the Apostles, was probably not a Jew and wrote for pagans (i.e., non-Jews) or former pagans. Paul calls Luke

*Below*: The antependium (altarcloth) shown here comes from the 12th century and is to be found in Siena. Christ, enthroned as the Logos, is conceived as a cosmic entity. The mandorla surrounding him is a wreath of stars that encloses the angels as well. Christ is flanked in the corners by the four evangelists, reproduced here only in the form of their symbols: a man (for Matthew), a bull (for Luke), a lion (for Mark), and an eagle (for John). Behind

these representations of the evangelists, as well as the number four, lies an archetypical symbolic language ("The four directions are like the four winds … and the Church, spread over the entire earth. The Church rests on the four pillars of the four Gospels, which are held together by the one Spirit." Irenaeus of Lyon, 2nd century).

*Page 16*: Jacob Jordaens (1593–1673) in Antwerp worked in the great studio of Peter Paul Rubens as one of his most important disciples. His independent work, *The Four Evangelists*, dating from 1625–30, is located in the Louvre. Jordaens conceives the subject in lively Baroque formal terms as an unconventional group composition. In earlier centuries the four Apostles were clearly distinguished through their attributes and the order of composition. But in this picture the differences are expressed only by the heads of the characters. What stands out is the unifying factor of their common work; their unanimity shows itself in the tight formation of the group, which is full of earthly presence.

the "beloved physician," but tradition maintains that he was also a painter and frequently portrayed Mary. He too made use of Mark's Gospel, although to a lesser extent than Matthew. He is considered the most stylistically elegant evangelist. Acts of the Apostles recounts that he accompanied Paul on his second missionary journey and traveled

with him to Rome. He evidently came from Antioch. According to tradition he too suffered a martyr's death in his old age.

John, the fourth evangelist, cannot be the same person as Jesus' beloved disciple, as was long assumed—since his Gospel was not composed until around 100 A.D. Nor can he be the John of Revelation, the last book of the New Testament. He differs considerably from the other three evangelists, the so-called Synoptics, although he was probably familiar with their work. He presents Jesus in relation to God's plan, which existed even before creation, and combines ideas from Greek culture with Judaism much more extensively than the Synoptics. Only in John do we find any evidence that Jesus conceived of himself as divine. The famous open-ing of his Gospel, "In the beginning was the Word, and the Word was with God, and the Word was God," points to his completely different philosophical approach. One might say that his Gospel was less a repository of oral traditions about Jesus than a book of religious teachings.

The four evangelists give us a few

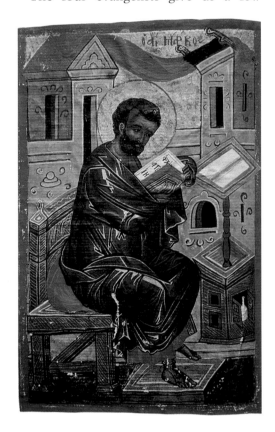

essential hints about the earthly life of Mary, but they contain no references to one of the greatest catastrophes that ever struck the Jewish world. This was the great insurrection against Roman rule that began in the year 66 and led to the siege and conquest of Jerusalem and the destruction of the Temple.

As for Mary herself, there is no discussion of her origins, family, birth, or of how she met Joseph. Concerning her life in the years of Jesus' public life, tradition speaks only of her taking part in the marriage at Cana, and Jesus' repeated hostile answers, when she had him summoned. Even in connection with Jesus' death and burial she is mentioned only briefly in John. Nothing is said about the rest of her life, her death, or her assumption into heaven, except that after Jesus' ascension she was to-gether with his brothers and the apostles, and that John, Jesus' beloved disciple, took her in. After his death Jesus did not appear to her, as he did to many others.

Nowhere does the New Testament suggest that Mary was anything more than an earthly creature—except in the one decisive point that she bore a child without having "known" a man. Nothing is said about her relationship to Joseph. Was he much older than she? No mention is made of him after the years of Jesus' childhood. Was he still living at the time of the marriage feast at Cana?

Apart from these and other gaps, the New Testament texts give rise to many questions and problems:

Mary's most detailed statement (Luke 1.46–55) is full of references to the Old Testament. Could she, a simple Jewish girl, have been so familiar with the Scriptures? Both Matthew in his first chapter and Luke in his third make an effort to establish Joseph's direct descent from Abraham (Luke goes all the way back to Adam). But Joseph was *not* Jesus' biological father, was he?

A further difficulty arises from the fact that Jesus' four brothers are mentioned several times. Mark and Matthew even give them names; and Mark also talks about Jesus' sisters. How does that square with Mary's virginity? The various attempts to solve this problem will be discussed later.

Was Mary, when she got engaged to Joseph, only fifteen or sixteen years old, as was the custom then in Palestine? And did the annunciation by the angel take place during the one year that, according to the custom of the time, had to pass between the engagement and the marriage? (During this time the man already had all the rights of a husband, except he was not allowed to physically touch his fiancée.) The New Testament leaves this question open.

Finally there is the mystery of the slaughter of the innocents in Bethlehem, reported by Matthew (2.16) and only Matthew, perhaps alluding to Jeremiah 31.15 ("Rachel weeping for her children"). One would think that the murder of dozens, perhaps hundreds,

of innocent children would be noteworthy enough to be reported by the other evangelists, but that is not the case. The account also seems dubious, because on his own authority Herod disposes of many human lives, while at Jesus' trial his successor needs the consent of the Roman governor, Pontius Pilate, to condemn a single person to death. But, above all, one wonders how, if such a slaughter took place, the young John, later called the Baptist, as well as Jesus' brothers and sisters, survived it. Because only Jesus accompanied Mary and Joseph on the flight into Egypt.

It is clear that the Christian interpreters of the postbiblical period were intent on filling the gaps pointed out here and on solving the problems in the New Testament accounts.

This was done in the so-called Apoc-rypha, whose reports provided the later literary and artistic portrayals of Mary with a much broader foundation than the New Testament, and which prepared the way for Mary's ever greater significance in both popular consciousness and in the Church's official teaching.

"Apocryphal" means "hidden" or "secret," but that does not fit the books and writings referred to here. Their common feature is that they are related to the Bible in one way or another but were not accepted into the official biblical canon, in our case the New Testament. They were all composed in the first centuries after the birth of Christ in Greek, Latin, Armenian, or Arabic. They are all designed somehow to complete, embellish, or reinterpret the Gospels. Some of the most important come

*Left*: These pages from the Protevangelium of James describe the birth of Mary. The document, written on papyrus, is dated from the 2nd century. "Protevangelium" means first gospel, because it tells stories that are prior to those reported in the four Gospels. The Protevangelium also recounts the early history of Mary up to her adolescence. The original is in the Bibliotheca Bodmeriana in Cologny, near Geneva.

*Right*: Likewise in the Bibliotheca Bodmeriana is the papyrus (Bodmer X) containing correspondence between the Apostle Paul and the Corinthians that deals with the issue of Mary's divine motherhood.

under the rubric of "Pseudepigrapha," which means that they are falsely ascribed to one biblical personality or other. The number is almost unlimited: a few were not discovered until recently, in some cases very recently. Many of them contradict the teachings of the Bible. Many in particular have been strongly influenced by the ideas of Gnosticism, a 2nd- and 3rd-century movement that sought to involve Christianity in syncretism and make it over into a mystery religion. It drew a line between God the creator, or Demiurge, and God the redeemer, who was proclaimed for the first time by Christ. With their mystical speculations about God and matter, their acceptance of ancient Oriental ideas, and their strict reduction of the world to a good and an evil principle, gnostic thinkers greatly distanced themselves from the Christian faith of the New Testament.

Meanwhile the boundary between the officially recognized Scriptures and the Apocrypha was for a long time a wavering one. For a while the Gospel of John was in danger of being excluded from the canon. On the other hand, as late as the 3rd or 4th century Fathers of the Church invoked the authority of writings that were later removed from

the canon. The definitive fixing of the New Testament canon did not occur until 691. But as far back as the early 4th century the main criteria for selection had already been decided upon. The official determination of the books of the New Testament was earlier attributed to Pope Gelasius (492–496), but apparently it was not made until a century later by a subordinate cleric.

Over the course of history the apocryphal books have been rated very differently. Voltaire claimed that the Apocrypha were closer to ancient tradition than the canonical Scriptures. St. Jerome, by contrast, speaks of "the ravings of the Apocrypha" (*deliramenta apocryphiana*). At any rate some of them played a vital role in shaping the cult and image of Mary.

The most influential of the apocryphal books dealing with Mary are undoubtedly the *Protevangelium of James* and the narrative of Pseudo-Melito. The first describes the birth, the second the death, of Mary.

The Protevangelium of James was widely viewed, especially in the East, as authentic; and the Church Father Origen (185–254) cited it as proof of Mary's virgin birth. However, its many references to the Old Testament show

that it is not an eye-witness report, but a later construct. "Protevangelium" means "first gospel" because it tells stories that precede the accounts by the recognized evangelists. Here for the first time we find descriptions of the prehistory, birth, and education of Mary. The narrator calls himself James, clearly hoping to be taken for the brother of Jesus, mentioned in Mark (6.3). But that is historically impossible, because the text was composed around 150 A.D., hence at least 160 years after Mary's birth. It contains the beginnings of the cult of Mary, and it prompted further embellishments by many later writers in various Oriental languages. The Protevangelium was probably first composed in Greek, but it contains many Hebraisms and allusions to Old Testament episodes. The story of Mary's parents, who despite their advanced age bring a child into the world, is reminiscent of the story of Abraham and Sarah, and of Hannah, the mother of Samuel, the last "judge" in Israel.

In the 5th century, after Mary was given the title "Mother of God" at the Council of Ephesus, legends arose about her death and assumption into heaven. They emerge in different languages and with major variations. Al-

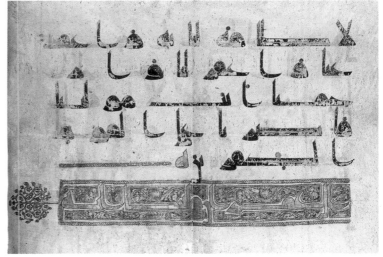

most all of them describe Mary's burial in great detail. But she does not remain in the grave; she is swept up, body and soul, to heavenly glory. The best-known description of her "falling asleep" and assumption into heaven—in Greek *koimesis* and *metastasis*, in Latin *dormitio* or *transitus*—is probably the "Gospel of the Passing Away of the Blessed Mary," composed around 500. It is the Latin version of a Greek text, also known under the name of "Pseudo-Melito," because the author introduces himself as Melito, bishop of Sardis (an actual person, but one who lived in the 2nd century). The author surely wanted to give his work greater legitimacy, because Melito is supposed to have been personally acquainted with the Apostle John. In any case his description has more clarity and terseness than any other that has come down to us.

The Qur'an too can, in a sense, be viewed as a source for Mary's life. The sacred scripture of Muslims consists of the revelations of God (Allah) to the prophet Muhammad through the angel Gabriel, as taken down by Muhammad's scribes and collected by Caliph Othman around 651–653. In the 114 chapters (surahs) of the Qur'an the 19th concerns Mary. It tells first of the birth

of John and then mentions Mary, who left her family and went to a village in the East, where she was visited by a spirit of God, the envoy of the All-Compassionate, who was to give her a pure child. When the birthpangs came upon her beneath the trunk of a palm tree, a little brook sprang up for her, and the palm dropped down fresh dates. But thereafter she is characterized as the sister of Aaron: the text obviously confuses her with the Miriam of Exodus.

The Qur'an is hardly concerned with new, original information about Mary, since all of the material is taken from the New Testament, the Apocrypha, or oral tradition. Still, its statements are of great importance; because the Qur'an is, after the Bible, the most widely disseminated book in history, and so has made the name of Mary known all over the world.

But what do the New Testament and apocryphal sources tell us about the particulars of the earthly life of the Virgin Mary?

*Left*: The depiction of Mary as the "woman clothed with the sun" of Revelation. Alongside Mary stands John as the proclaimer of Revelation. This is an important example of Upper Rhenish illuminated manuscripts (early 14th century) from the monastery of Katharinental in Switzerland.

*Right*: A fragment from the Qur'an (surah 19) on parchment in kufic script (8th–9th century). Metropolitan Museum of Art, New York.

21

## MARY'S PARENTS AND
## THE ANNUNCIATION TO ANNE

*Left*: The picture shows the warm embrace of Joachim and Anne at the Golden Gate. It was painted between 1460 and 1465 and is found today in the Alte Pinakothek in Munich. The painter, the so-called Master of the Life of Mary, got his appellation from the eight panels he did with scenes from Mary's life, a cycle that may be found in the church of St. Ursula in Cologne. The architecture in the background is richly decorative in the spirit of the Late Gothic.

*Above right*: The annunciation by the angel that Anna will bear a child, namely, Mary the Mother of God, is depicted here in a *Speculum humanae salvationis* (mirror of human salvation) from 1340 in the tender Early Gothic manner. Cathedral chapter of Kremsmünster, Austria.

*Below right:* The meeting of Joachim and Anne at the Golden Gate as a motif from a stained-glass window of the Cathedral of Chartres. Here for the first time the richly fashioned windows played an important role in the "total work of art" that was the cathedral. The portrayal of Mary's life is the distinctive feature of the church windows of Chartres.

Since the New Testament tells us nothing about Mary's family, birth, or childhood, we have to rely on the Protevangelium of James. (All quotations from the Protevangelium of James taken from Willis Barnstone, ed., The Other Bible [San Francisco: Harper & Row, 1984], pp. 385ff.) There we read:
(1.1–2.4): *Joachim was a very wealthy man. He brought his offerings twofold to the Lord, saying to himself, "This from my abundance will be for all the people, and this which I owe as a sin offering will be for the Lord God as a propitiation for me." Now the great day of the Lord drew near, and the children of Israel brought their offerings. Reuben stood up against Joachim, saying: "It is not permissible for you to bring your offerings first, for you did not produce offspring in Israel."...Joachim was very sorrowful; he did not appear to his wife, but betook himself into the desert and pitched his tent there. Then he fasted forty days and forty nights, saying to himself, "I will not return, either for food or drink, until the Lord my God considers me. Prayer will be my food and drink."*

(2.1–4): *Now his wife, Anne, sang two dirges and beat her breast in a twofold lament, "I will mourn my widowhood, and I will mourn my barrenness." The great day* of the Lord drew near and Euthine, her maid, said to her, *"How long will you humble your soul? Behold the great day of the Lord has come, and it is not proper for you to mourn... What am I to you, since you do not listen to my voice? The Lord God has closed your womb in order not to grant you fruit in Israel." Anne was very grieved, and she took off her mourning garments and cleansed her head and put on her bridal garments. About the ninth hour she went down into her garden to walk.*

(3.1–2): *Anne looked up toward Heaven and saw a nest of sparrows in the laurel tree; and she sang a dirge to herself, saying, "Woe is me! Who gave me birth? What sort of womb brought me forth? For I was born a curse among the children of Israel, I was made a reproach, and they derided me and banished me out of the Temple of the Lord my God. Woe is me! To what am I likened? I am not likened to the birds of heaven, for even the birds of heaven are fruitful before you, O Lord."*

There follows the annunciation to Anne:
(4.1–2): *And behold, an angel of the Lord appeared, saying, "Anne, Anne, the Lord God heard your prayer, and you will conceive and give birth, and your offspring shall be spoken of in the whole inhabited world."*

Anne said, *"As the Lord my God lives, if I give birth, whether male or female, I will present it as a gift to the Lord my God, and it shall be a ministering servant all the days of its life." And behold, two angels came, saying to her, "Behold, your husband Joachim is coming with his flocks." Now an angel of the Lord had come down to Joachim, saying, "Joachim, Joachim, the Lord God heard your payer. Go down from here; for behold, your wife Anne is pregnant."*

(4.4): *And behold, Joachim came with his flocks, and Anne stood at the door and saw Joachim coming with his flocks. Anne ran and threw her arms around his neck, saying, "Now I know that the Lord God has blessed me very greatly, for behold, the widow is no longer a widow, and she who was barren has conceived!"*

This text seems to be saying that in the case of Anne—unlike Mary, later on—there was no notion of a virgin birth. When the angel gives Joachim the good news, the act of generation has evidently already taken place. On the other hand, some interpreters, such as Origen, have cited this same account as proof of the virgin birth of Mary.

*Left*: The episodes of Mary's life come from the pictures flanking the *Madonna Enthroned* from San Martino in Pisa (ca. 1280). The work is painted in the *maniera greca,* i.e., still entirely in the Byzantine style. The scenes depicted from upper left to right: The Annunciation to Mary. / Joachim's sacrifice in the Temple is rejected. / Joachim distributes alms. / Anne prays for a child; the angel appears to her over the tree with the nest of birds and promises that her prayer will be heard; Anne and her maid. / The angel orders Joachim to return to Anne./ At the angel's behest Joachim offers a sacrifice to the Lord. / The angel announces to Joachim in a dream that his prayer has been heard; Joachim tells this to the shepherds. / Joachim heads back to Jerusalem. / The angel tells Anne to meet Joachim; the meeting at the Golden Gate. / Mary's birth. / Mary goes to the Temple. / Peter, Paul, James, and John the Baptist; under the throne of St. Martin.

*Right*: The meeting at the Golden Gate is also the subject of this Russian icon from the 16th century, Recklinghausen, Germany.

*O*nce again our source is the Protevangelium of James:

(5.2): *Now her time was fulfilled, and in the ninth month Anne gave birth. She said to the midwife, "What have I borne?" The midwife said, "A girl." Then Anne said, "My soul is exalted this day"; and she laid herself down. When the required days were completed, Anne cleansed herself of the impurity of childbirth, and gave her breast to the child. She called her name Mary.*

The origin and meaning of the name Mary have not been satisfactorily explained. In the New Testament she is called "Mariam" twelve times and "Maria" (Mary) seven times. "Mariam" is the same as the Hebrew "Miriam," the name of Moses' sister. The word has been derived from the Hebrew word for "myrrh," and from the word for "bearer of light." St. Jerome interpreted Mary to mean *stilla maris*, a "drop of the sea," which then turned into *stella maris*, the "star of the sea." The name has also been connected with Marah, the place where, according to Exodus 15.23, the people of Israel found bitter water, which they could not drink. Other etymologies would have the word mean "stubborn" or even "portly." At any rate

*Top*: The mosaic in the monastery church in Daphne near Athens, dating from ca. 1100, shows the *Birth of the Mother of God*. St. Anne lies on a richly furnished bed. The influence of antiquity in the arrangement of the clothes is clearly visible.

*Above*: The *Birth of Mary* by Domenico Ghirlandaio (1449–1494) in a fresco of the church of Santa Maria Novella in Florence shows the artist's monumental narrative art and generous use of figures.

*Right*: The depiction of the birth of Mary by Wolf Huber (1485–1553) on the St. Anne altar in Feldkirch near Bregenz shows the event in the spirit of the Northern Renaissance with deep perspectivist space and dramatic movement.

24

the name occurs very often in the New Testament, so often that in many cases it is difficult to distinguish among the various Marys.

The Protevangelium of James reports the following about Mary's childhood and presentation in the Temple:

(6.1–3): *Day by day the child grew strong. When she was six months old her mother stood her on the ground to see if she could stand. Walking seven steps she came to her mother's bosom... Now the child came to be a year old, and Joachim gave a great feast; he invited the high priests, the priests, the scribes, the elders of the council, and all the*

*the Lord my God gave me a fruit of his righteousness, one yet manifold before him. Who will report to the sons of Reuben that Anne gives suck?"*

(8.1–3): *Now Mary was in the Temple of the Lord like a dove being fed, and she received food from the hand of an angel. When she was twelve years old there took place a conference of the priests, saying, "Behold, Mary has become twelve years old in the Temple of the Lord our God. What, therefore, shall we do with her, lest she defile the sanctuary of the Lord?"... The priest entered the Holy of Holies, taking the vestment with the twelve bells, and he prayed*

*Top*: One of the topoi of Mary's childhood is the *Instruction of Mary*, also called Mary's education, as seen here on an oil painting in the parish church of St. Martin in Tannau, Germany.

*Above*: Joachim and Anne caress their child, Mary—a further theme from Mary's childhood, as shown in a mosaic in the Chora Church (Kariye Camii) in Istanbul (1315–20).

*Right*: Mary goes to the Temple, a stone relief from the choir barrier of the Gothic cathedral of Chartres.

*people of Israel. Joachim brought the child to the priests and they blessed her saying, "O God of our fathers, bless this child, and give her a name famous forever in all generations." All the people responded, "So let it be. Amen." Then he brought her to the high priests and they blessed her, saying, "O God of the high places, look upon this child, and bless her with the highest blessing which has no successor."... Then Anne sang a hymn to the Lord God, saying, "I will sing a sacred song to the Lord my God, because he considered me and took away from me the reproach of my enemies. And*

*concerning her. And behold, an angel of the Lord appeared, saying: "Zacharias, Zacharias, go out and call together the widowers of the people, and let each of them bring a rod, and to whomever the Lord God shows a sign, to this one shall she be wife."*

Anna's song of praise (6.3) is reminiscent, like Mary's Magnificat, of Hannah's song of praise in 1 Samuel 2.

# THE ENGAGEMENT TO JOSEPH

We read about this in the Protevangelium (9.1–3): *Now Joseph, casting down his adze, came himself into their meeting. When they were all gathered together, they came to the priest, taking the rods.... Joseph received the last rod, and behold, a dove came forth from the rod and settled on Joseph's head. Then the priest said, "Joseph, Joseph, you have been designated by lot to receive the virgin of the Lord as your ward." Joseph refused, saying, "I have sons, and I am an old man, but she is a young maiden—lest I be a laughing stock to the children of Israel." The priest said, "Joseph, fear the* Lord, your God..." *Joseph, frightened, received her as his ward; and Joseph said to her, "Mary, I have received you from the Temple of the Lord. Now I am leaving you behind in my house, and I am going away to build houses; later I will return to you. The Lord will guard you."*

On the origins of Joseph, who is introduced here in a quite unspectacular fashion, the Protevangelium says nothing. But the New Testament has a number of things to say: Matthew begins his Gospel with a detailed genealogy of Joseph, which is traced from Abraham to Jesse, David, and Solomon, down to Jacob, the father of Joseph. Then the text says simply: "And Jacob [was] the father of Joseph the husband of Mary, of whom Jesus was born, who is called Christ."

Thus, while there is no question here of a direct descent of Jesus from Abraham and David—since Joseph is not Jesus' biological father—the oldest New Testament source, written around fifteen years before the first Gospel, says something different. In the Letter to the Romans (1.1–4), written around

*Left*: The subject of Mary's marriage has been interpreted differently over the centuries. Thus, for example, *The Wedding of Mary* by an unknown master (Pinakothek, Munich) is staged here in a church interior with a late Gothic flavor.

*Upper right*: This scene of the *Election of Joseph* comes from the Book of Hours of Catherine of Cleves (ca. 1440).

*Lower Right*: The painting by Raphael (1504) in the Brera, Milan, links the marriage of Mary with an ideal Renaissance edifice, the circular temple, and hence is a symbol of the combination of Christian faith, idealized ancient architecture, and perspectivist treatment of space.

26

55 A.D., Paul writes:

*Paul, a servant of Jesus Christ, called to be an apostle, set apart for the gospel of God which he promised beforehand through his prophets in the holy scriptures, the gospel concerning his Son, who was descended from David according to the flesh and designated Son of God in power according to the Spirit of holiness by his resurrection from the dead, Jesus Christ our Lord...*

A further episode from the time when Mary was already living in Joseph's house is reported by the Protevangelium. Here Mary is described as descended from the house of David:

(10.1–2): *There took place a council of the priests, saying, "Let us make a veil for the Temple of the Lord." The priest said, "Call the undefiled virgins from the tribe of David." The attendants went out and sought them, and they found seven. Then the priest remembered the child Mary, that she was of the tribe of David and was pure before God; and the attendants went forth and brought her. Then they brought them into the Temple of the Lord. And the priest said, "Assign by lot for me here someone who will spin the gold thread, and the white and the linen and the silk and the hyacinth blue and the scarlet and the genuine purple." The genuine purple and the scarlet were assigned by lot to Mary, and taking them she went into her house.*

It is clear that around this time Mary was already looked upon as Joseph's betrothed, and that he had not touched her.

# ANNUNCIATION AND VISITATION

*T*he most detailed account comes from the Gospel of Luke (1.26–45):

*In the sixth month the angel Gabriel was sent from God to a city of Galilee named Nazareth, to a virgin betrothed to a man whose name was Joseph, of the house of David; and the virgin's name was Mary. And he came to her and said, "Hail, O favored one, the Lord is with you!" But she was greatly troubled at the saying, and considered in her mind what sort of greeting this might be. And the angel said to her, "Do not be afraid, Mary, for you have found favor with God. And behold, you will conceive in your womb and bear a son, and you shall call his name Jesus. He will be great, and will be called the Son of the Most High; and the Lord God will give to him the throne of his father David, and he will reign over the house of Jacob for ever; and of his kingdom there will be no end." And Mary said to the angel, "How shall this be, since I have no husband?" And the angel said to her, "The Holy Spirit will come upon you, and the power of the Most High will overshadow you; therefore the child to be born will be called holy, the Son of God. And behold, your kinswoman Elizabeth in her old age has also conceived a son; and this is the sixth month with her who was called barren. For with God nothing will be impossible." And Mary said, "Behold, I am the handmaid of the Lord; let it be to me according to your word." And the angel departed from her.*

*In those days Mary arose and went with haste into the hill country, to a city of Judah, and she entered the house of Zechariah and greeted Elizabeth. And when Elizabeth heard the greeting of Mary, the babe leaped in her womb; and Elizabeth was filled with the Holy Spirit and she exclaimed with a loud cry, "Blessed are you among women, and blessed is the fruit of your womb! And why is this granted me, that the mother of my Lord should come to me? For behold, when the voice of your greeting came to my ears, the babe in my womb leaped for joy. And blessed is she who believed that there*

*Left*: The *Annunciation to Mary* by the Italian sculptor Benedetto da Maiano (1442–1497) is the centerpiece of a marble altar of the church of St. Anne in Naples. Benedetto da Maiano is one of the most important artists of the early Florentine Renaissance and specialized in marble altars.

*Center*: A variation on the Annunciation theme shows the angel and Mary with a water jug, a symbol of the water of life. The picture comes from a 17th-century Armenian manuscript (British Museum, London).

*Upper right*: Christian scenes such as the Annunciation were also depicted on the lids of jewelry boxes and cameos. This example is an 11th-century sardonyx cameo from Constantinople.

*Right*: An Annunciation of metal, precious stones, and pearls from a 13th-century Venetian diptych, Chilandar monastery.

*Lower right*: The *Annunciation* by Ann Raymo, a contemporary American artist, centers the meeting between Mary and the Holy Spirit, symbolized as a dove, in eye contact between the two.

*would be a fulfillment of what was spoken to her from the Lord."*

And now (Luke 1.46–55) Mary recites her song of praise, the famous Magnificat, which is modeled on Hannah's song of praise in the Old Testament (1 Samuel 2):

*Mary said, "My soul magnifies the Lord, and my spirit rejoices in God my Savior, for he has regarded the low estate of his handmaiden. For behold, henceforth all generations will call me blessed; for he who is mighty has done great things for me, and holy is his name. And his mercy is on those who fear him from generation to generation. He has shown strength with his arm,*

*Left*: The *Annunciation* by Jan van Eyck (1390–1441) in the National Gallery of Art, Washington, D.C., is considered one of the most important works of the Late Gothic period. It also contains, as in a sort of summary, the most essential iconographical material about Mary. Here she is in a church interior, which points to her later role as an archetype of the Church. The lily (purity) in the vase and the bull's eye window panes recall the living accommodations in which Mary is often shown at this time. The angel of the Annunciation wears a brilliant silken, pearl-encrusted mantle, whose beauty was thought to be an expression of divine harmony.

29

The "visitation" that Luke reports describes the visit of Mary with Elizabeth. Both are pregnant. Elizabeth will shortly give birth to John the Baptist. The scene is depicted as the embrace of the two women. It is one of the most moving and tender themes in all Christian art from its origins to the present. *Left*: Mary and Elizabeth on a 15th-century ivory panel from the National Museum, Munich. *Right*: Raphael (1483–1520) paints the intimate scene in a wide open landscape. A very pregnant Mary appears lost in thought, while the older Elizabeth rushes up to her, as if taking part in the coming fateful events (the Prado, Madrid).

he has scattered the proud in the imagination of their hearts, he has put down the mighty from their thrones, and exalted those of low degree; he has filled the hungry with good things, and the rich he has sent away empty. He has helped his servant Israel, in remembrance of his mercy, as he spoke to our fathers, to Abraham and to his posterity forever." And Mary remained with her about three months, and returned to her home.

In the very brief description of the Protevangelium, which is based on Luke, the text says only:
(11.1–2): *She took her pitcher and went out to fill it full of water; and behold there came a voice saying, "Hail, highly favored one! The Lord is with you; you are blessed among women" [Luke 1.28]. Mary looked about, to*

the right and to the left, to see whence this voice might be coming to her. Filled with trembling she went into her house; and putting down the pitcher, she took the purple and sat down on a chair and drew out the purple thread. Behold, an angel of the Lord stood before her, saying, "Do not fear, Mary, for you have found favor before the Lord of all, and you will conceive by his Word" (Luke 1.30–31).*

There are some apocryphal variants. Thus an Armenian text reads:
*At the time when the holy virgin spoke thus [to the angel], the word of God penetrated her through her ear, and the nature of her body was sanctified and all her senses purified like gold in the fire. She was made into the temple of holiness, spotless and the abode of the Divine Word. Around this*

time she became pregnant. But the angel brought the good news to Maria on the 15th of Nisan, that is, the 6th of April, at the third hour of the day.*

In an Arabic text the virgin birth is even predicted in the time of Moses:
*In the days of the prophet Moses there lived a man named Zaradyst [Zoroaster], the founder of a secret teaching. One day, as he was sitting by a spring, instructing his disciples about the secret teaching, he interrupted himself and told them: "Behold, a virgin will conceive without knowing a man. She will bear a child, yet the seal of her virginity will remain intact, and the good news will be known in the seven regions of the earth. The Jews will crucify this child in the holy city, which was founded by Melchisedech."*

# JOSEPH'S DOUBTS

*Right*: The subject of Joseph's doubts and Mary with the spinning thread appears on the ivory triptych of Maximilian as the "the test of the bitter water" (Archiepiscopal Museum in Ravenna).

**W**e read in the Protevangelium: (13.1–3): *It came to be the sixth month for her, and behold, Joseph came from his buildings; and he came into his house and found her pregnant. He struck his face and threw himself to the ground on the sack-cloth and wept bitterly, saying, "With what sort of countenance shall I look to the Lord God? What shall I pray concerning this maiden? For I received her a virgin from the Temple of the Lord God, and I did not guard her. Who is he who has deceived me?...Joseph arose from the sackcloth and called Mary and said to her, "Having been cared for by God, why did you do this,*

*for that which is in her is from the Holy Spirit. She will bear a son, and you shall call his name Jesus..."*

(15.2): *The priest said to him, "Joseph why did you do this?"... But Joseph said, "As the Lord God lives, I am pure regarding her." Then the priest said, "Do not bear false witness, but tell the truth. You married her secretly and did not reveal it to the children of Israel; you did not incline your head beneath the Mighty Hand so that your seed might be blessed."*

(16.1–2): *Joseph began to weep. The priest went on, "I will give you to drink the water of the Lord's testing, and it will make your*

*Holy Spirit; and her husband Joseph, being a just man and unwilling to put her to shame, resolved to divorce her quietly. But as he considered this, behold, an angel of the Lord appeared to him in a dream, saying, "Joseph, son of David, do not fear to take Mary your wife, for that which is conceived in her is of the Holy Spirit; she will bear a son, and you shall call his name Jesus, for he will save his people from their sins."... When Joseph woke from sleep, he did as the angel of the Lord commanded him; he took his wife, but knew her not until she had borne a son; and he called his name Jesus.*

*forgetting the Lord your God?..." She wept bitterly, saying, "I am pure, and I do not know a man." [Luke 1.34] Joseph said to her, "Whence then is this which is in your womb?" She said, "As the Lord my God lives, I do not know whence it came to me."*

(14.1–2): *Then Joseph feared greatly and stopped talking with her, considering what he would do with her. Joseph said, "If I should hide her sin, I will be found disputing with the law of the Lord; if I show her to the children of Israel, I am afraid lest that which is in her is angelic and I shall be found delivering innocent blood to the judgment of death. What therefore shall I do with her? Shall I put her secretly away from me?" [Matthew 1.19] Night came upon him; behold an angel of the Lord appeared to him in a dream, saying, "Do not fear this child,*

*sins manifest in your eyes." Taking it, the priest gave Joseph to drink and sent him into the desert, and he came back whole. He also gave Mary to drink and sent her into the desert; she also returned whole. And all the people wondered, since their sin did not appear in them.*

*The priest said, "If the Lord God did not make your sin manifest, neither will I judge you"; and he released them. Then Joseph took Mary and went into his house, glorifying the God of Israel.*

In Matthew, on the other hand, the angel does not appear to Mary, but to Joseph (1.18–21, 24–25): *Now the birth of Jesus Christ took place in this way. When his mother Mary had been betrothed to Joseph, before they came together she was found to be with child of the*

*Left*: This depiction of *Joseph's Dream* shows Joseph doubting Mary, then informed by the angel that Mary, overshadowed by the Holy Spirit, will bear the Son of God. In this picture from Milan (1630) the painter Daniele Crespi (1575–1633) shows Joseph sleeping at his workbench.

*Center*: This *Maria Platytera* (Greek, "rather broad Mary") from northern Germany, a panel painting from around 1400 (wood, Dahlem Museum, Berlin), is an example of the soft style of the High Gothic. In her hand she has a spindle with the crimson thread for the veil of the Temple in Jerusalem. The miracle of the Incarnation of God in Mary is revealed to Joseph here as he sits doubting at the window.

## THE BIRTH OF JESUS

*Below*: Detail from the ivory throne of Maximilian (6th-century, Constantinople) connects Joseph's dream and the road to Bethlehem in a single panel (Archiepiscopal Museum, Ravenna).

*T*he second chapter of Luke tells of the birth of Jesus and the visit of the shepherds to the manger (2.1, 4–7, 16–19):

*In those days a decree went out from Caesar Augustus that all the world should be enrolled... And Joseph also went up from Galilee, from the city of Nazareth, to Judea, to the city of David, which is called Bethlehem, because he was of the house and lineage of David, to be enrolled with Mary, his betrothed, who was with child. And while they were there, the time came for her to be delivered. And she gave birth to her firstborn son and wrapped him in swaddling clothes, and laid him in a manger, because there was no place for them in the inn...*

*And [the shepherds] went with haste, and found Mary, and Joseph, and the babe lying in a manger. And when they saw it they made known the saying which had been told them concerning this child; and all who heard it wondered at what the shepherds told them. But Mary kept all those things, pondering them in her heart.*

In the Protevangelium Jesus is born, not in a stable but in a cave:

(17.1–2): *Now there came an order from Augustus the emperor for all who were in Bethlehem of Judea to be enrolled [Luke 2.1]. Joseph said, "I will enroll my sons, but this child—what shall I do with her? How shall I enroll her? As my wife? I am*

*ashamed to do so..."*

*He saddled his donkey and set her upon it; his son led, and Samuel followed. They drew near to Bethlehem—they were three miles distant—and Joseph turned and saw Mary looking gloomy, and he said, "Probably that which is in her is distressing her." Once again Joseph turned and saw her laughing, and he said, "Mary, how is it that I see your face at one moment laughing and at another time gloomy?" She said to Joseph, "It is because I see two peoples with my eyes, the one weeping and mourning, the other rejoicing and glad." (The two peoples obviously refer to those who reject or accept the Redeemer.)*

*(18.1; 19.2–3): He found there a cave, and he brought her in and placed his sons beside her. Then he went out to seek a Hebrew midwife in the country at Bethlehem... They stood in the place of the cave, and a dark cloud was overshadowing the cave. The midwife said, "My soul is magnified today, for my eyes have seen a mystery: a Savior has been born to Israel!" And immediately the cloud withdrew from the cave, and a great light appeared in the cave so that their eyes could not bear it...*

*And the midwife came out of the cave and there met Salome. And she spoke to her: "Salome, Salome, I speak to you of a spectacle that has never happened before. A virgin has given birth, which is not permitted by*

*Below:* This early 14th-century book miniature from Lake Constance shows the birth of Christ.

*nature.*" And Salome spoke: "*As the Lord my God lives, I will not believe that a virgin has given birth unless I put forth my finger and investigate her condition.*"

(20.1, 3): *The midwife went in and said, "Mary, get yourself in position, for a great deal of controversy surrounds you." Then Salome tested her virginal nature with her finger, and Salome cried out and said, "Woe is my lawlessness and my faithlessness, for I have tempted the living God. And behold, my hand falls away from me in fire."... And, behold, an angel of the Lord appeared, saying to Salome, "The Lord heard your prayer. Bring your hand near to the child and take*

*came into the grotto and took the child in her arms, and began to caress it and embrace it with all tenderness.... She laid it back in the manger...and left the cave. And suddenly she saw a woman named Salome, who had come from the city of Jerusalem. And Mother Eve went to her and said: "I bring you good news: A young girl, who has never known a man, has in this cave brought a child into the world."*

Once again the story is told differently in the "Martyrdom and Ascension of Isaiah," which represents a combination of the Old Testament and New Testament Apocrypha. It was com-

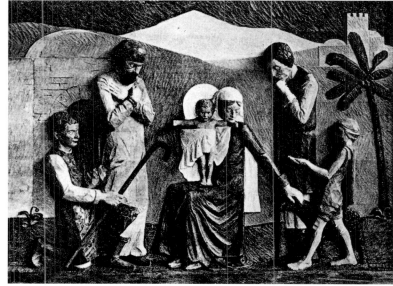

*Above:* A ceiling painting in the popular style from Al in the Hallingdal (Norway) represents the birth of Christ and the adoration of the shepherds, both scenes framed by arches.

*Right:* Modern artist Maja Refsum's severely simple conception of the adoration by the shepherds.

*Page 32, left:* The mosaic in the church of Chora (Kariye Camii, Istanbul, early 14th century) depicts the scene in which St. Joseph has Mary, along with his sons, registered in Bethlehem.

*Page 32, lower right:* In his painting (1558) of Mary and Joseph's search for an inn, Jan Massys (1509–1575) shows both being turned away (Fine Arts Museum, Antwerp).

*him up, and it will be to you salvation and joy."... Immediately Salome was healed.*"

The scene of Jesus' birth in the cave is described somewhat differently in the Armenian "Book of the Childhood" (of Jesus), through its inclusion of Eve: *Joseph and the mother of our race [Eve]... fell down, thanked God in a loud voice, praised him, and said, "Blessed be you, God of our fathers, God of Israel; for on this day you have redeemed mankind by appearing. You have renewed me and exalted me, and again lifted me up to what I originally was. Now my soul feels strong." And, having spoken, Eve, the mother of our race, saw a cloud rising over the grotto to heaven. And from the other side appeared a bright light that came to rest over the manger. And the child sought its mother's breast and her milk; then he went back to his place and stayed there.... And the mother of humanity*

posed at a time when Christians were being persecuted, perhaps as early as the 2nd century, and is clearly attested by the 4th century. It describes the martyrdom of the Jewish prophet Isaiah under Kings Hezekiah and Manasseh. Before his death and rapture Isaiah has visions, of which one is:

*And I saw from the house of David, the prophet, a woman with the name of Mary, who was a virgin and betrothed to a man named Joseph, a carpenter, and he too was from the seed and house of the just David from Bethlehem in Judah... And when he was betrothed, she was found to be with child, and Joseph the carpenter wanted to leave her. But the angel of the Spirit appeared in this world, and thereafter Joseph did not leave Mary, but guarded her; but he revealed this matter to no one. And he did not approach Mary, but guarded her as one*

If one compares these two scenes of Christ's birth in the stable at Bethlehem—the painting by Hans Memling (1433–1494) from the Wallraf-Richartz Museum in Cologne (*right*) and the one by Federico Barocchi (1528–1615) in Milan (*left*)—the path from Memling's strictly Gothic conception, full of pious devotion, to the more personal and realistic treatment by Barocchi, a century later, becomes especially clear. In Memling the figures pay no attention to one another; they remain wrapped up in themselves, absorbed in prayer. With Barocchi it is precisely the free language of gesture that expresses the contents of the painting.

*would a holy virgin, even though with child. And for another two months he did not dwell with her. And after two months, when Joseph was in his house and saw Mary, his wife—but they both were alone—then it happened, while they were alone, that Mary looked with her eyes and saw a little child, and she was filled with consternation. And when the consternation gave way, her womb was as it had been before she was pregnant. And when her husband Joseph said to her, "What fills you with consternation?" his eyes were opened, and he saw the child and praised God, that the Lord was come to his portion. And a voice came to them, "Tell this vision to no one." But the rumors about the child spread in Bethlehem. Some said: "The Virgin Mary has given birth, before she was two months married," and many said, "She has not given birth, and the midwife did not go up to her, and we heard no cries of pain." And they were all in the dark about him; they all knew about him, but no one knew from whence he came.*

A highly fantastical description of the virgin birth may be found in the so-called Christian Sibylline Oracles. In Roman mythology the Sibylline books contained mysterious sayings and prophecies. The Sibyl of Cumae, offered them to the (legendary) Roman king Tarquinius for a very high price. When Tarquinius refused, she burned three of the books and offered him the rest for the same price. Again he refused, but when she burned another three books, he changed his mind and bought the remaining three books. They were kept in the Capitoline Temple until 83 B.C. when they were destroyed by fire. Meanwhile, many "Sibylline" writings were composed on the model of the old books, at first by Romans, but then by Jews as well, whence they made their way into Christian literature. In one of them (VIII, 456–79) we read:

*But in the last times he [the angel Gabriel] went down on earth and appeared very small, and came forth from the womb of the Virgin Mary as a new light, and coming from heaven, he took on human form. At*

*Left* In this tender watercolor Salvador Dali (1904–1989) dissolves the scene of Jesus' birth into a purely chromatic composition. Joseph stands behind Mary and, like her, looks down at the newborn Christ child. Both the message of salvation, as in most images of Christmas, and the darkness of the coming Passion are included in this picture.

*Right*: The depiction of the Sibyls by Michelangelo in the Sistine Chapel of the Vatican likewise revolves around the virgin birth and the prophecies concerning it. Michelangelo (1475–1564) did the painting in 1509. The Sibyl of Cumae shown here is said to have prophesied, before the Christian era, the virgin birth and the Incarnation of Christ.

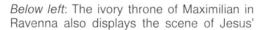

*Below left*: The ivory throne of Maximilian in Ravenna also displays the scene of Jesus' birth. It takes its motifs from the Apocrypha (Salome showing Mary her withered hand).

*first Gabriel showed his powerful, holy form, then the archangel addressed the virgin with these words: "Accept God in your spotless womb, O virgin." Speaking thus, God breathed grace into the holy maiden. But she was seized by confusion and amazement at once, when she heard it, and she stood there trembling; her mind was dazed, her heart trembled from the unheard-of news. But soon she rejoiced, and her heart grew warm from the voice, and she smiled like a bride. Her cheek blushed, joy delighted her, shame enchanted her mind, and her courage returned. But the word flew into her body, and with time became flesh, and taking on life in the womb, it acquired human form, and became a young boy through the virgin birth. This indeed is a great miracle to men, but nothing is a great miracle for God the Father and God the Son. But when the child was born, the earth stretched itself toward him, the heavenly throne laughed, and the world rejoiced. But the newly risen star, the divine star, was worshipped by the Magi. The child in swaddling clothes was shown in the manger to the pious oxherds and goatherds and shepherds, and Bethlehem was named as the divinely chosen home of the Word.* (The last words allude to the beginning of John's Gospel: "In the beginning was the Word...")

In non-Christian circles Jesus' origin was likewise given an entirely different interpretation: The Church Father Origen attacks a rumor, which had spread among Jews and pagans, that Jesus was the son of a Roman centurion named Pantherus. In Alexandria it was even claimed that Mary had had incestuous relations with her own brother. Christians countered the Pantherus rumor with the argument that Pandera (as he is called in the Talmud) was not a personal name but a term for a pimp. That claim, however, does not hold water, because Pandaros appears as the personal name of a warrior in both Homer and Virgil, and only became a synonym for procurer through Boccaccio, Chaucer, and then Shakespeare (*Troilus and Cressida*).

# THE VISIT OF THE WISE MEN FROM THE EAST

*I*n the New Testament only Matthew reports this episode. He calls them "Magoi", or wise men, but never says that they were three in number:
(Mt. 2.11): *Going into the house they saw the child with Mary his mother, and they fell down and worshipped him. Then, opening their treasures, they offered him gifts, gold and frankincense and myrrh.*

In the Protevangelium the story is told in a manner similar to Matthew's. But in an Armenian apocryphal text we find the number three and the names of the wise men, who now have become kings:
*And the angel of the Lord came in great haste to the land of Persia, to guide the Magi kings, who had set out to adore the newborn king. And when the star had led them for*

*Joseph, and the child.... They adored the child and gave him their presents ... And Joseph and Mary were amazed to see three sons of kings, bearing their crowns and kneeling down in adoration, even before they had asked who the newborn child was. Mary and Joseph asked them: "Where do you come from?" And they answered: "We come from Persia." Joseph and Mary said: "When did you leave Persia?" The kings answered: "Yesterday evening we celebrated a feast. And after the feast one of our gods told us: 'Arise and go with presents to the king who was born In Judah'."*

*And Mary took one of the cloths, in which Jesus was wrapped, and gave it to them. And they took it from her hands as a most precious gift....*

*All of Persia was glad at their return... and*

*Above*: The Ratschis altar from the 8th century in Cividali del Friuli, Italy, interprets the topic of the "adoration of the kings" quite superficially, in the ornamental-heraldic style, and radiates the naive warmth of early Christianity.

*nine months, their journey came to an end. At that time the kingdom of Persia ruled over all the kings of the Orient. The Magi kings were three brothers. The first was Melkon (Melchior), who ruled over the Persians; the second, Balthazar, ruled over the Indians; and the third, Caspar, was lord of the Arabs... they arrived just when the virgin had become a mother...*

In a Syrian manuscript, by contrast, the text says:
*They entered the cave and found Mary,*

*then they showed them the wrappings that Mary had given them. In the manner of the Magi they began a great feast and lit a great fire. They threw the cloth into the fire and adored it.... Then the fire was extinguished, and they pulled out the cloth, whiter than snow and stronger than before. And after pulling it out, they kissed it....*

*Center left*: Edward Burne-Jones (1833–1898) and William Morris (1834–1896) treat the "Adoration of the Three Holy Kings" in a wall hanging. Several copies of the tapestry were made. The one shown here is at Exeter College, Oxford.

*Center right*: *The Adoration of the Kings* by Albrecht Dürer (1471–1528), 1504, oil on wood (Uffizi, Florence). The celebrated middle panel of the Jabachsen altar was painted with impressions of Italy fresh in the artist's mind. But the joy in the rich details shows Dürer's northern roots.

# THE FLIGHT INTO EGYPT

*I*n Matthew the Magi tell Herod about the newborn king of the Jews. Herod takes fright and plans to have all the baby boys killed (2.13–14, 19–21):
*Now when they [the Magi] had departed, an angel of the Lord appeared to Joseph in a dream and said, "Rise, take the child and his mother, and flee to Egypt, and remain there till I tell you; for Herod is about to search for the child, to destroy him." And he rose and took the child and his mother by night, and departed to Egypt…. But when Herod died, behold, an angel of the Lord appeared in a dream to Joseph in Egypt, saying, "Rise, take the child and his mother, and go to the land of Israel, for those who sought the child's life are dead." And he rose and took the child and his mother, and went to the land of Israel.*

The Protevangelium says only (22.2): *Mary, hearing that they were killing the babies, was frightened, and she took the child and wrapped him and placed him in a cow stable.*

In a further section (22.3) the Protevangelium tries to provide an explanation for the survival of John the Baptist:
*Now Elizabeth, hearing that Herod sought John, took him and went up into the mountain. She looked around for a place where she might hide him…And immediately the mountain opened up and it received her. That mountain appeared to her as a light, for the angel of the Lord was with them, protecting them.*

The most extensive account of the Egyptian episode comes from one of the Latin Apocrypha, the so-called Gospel of Pseudo-Matthew, which in the form handed down to us comes from the 8th or 9th century. It joins together the descriptions of the Protevangelium and the Gospel of Thomas, and then adds legends about the flight of the Holy Family. These were very popular in the Middle Ages and were used, for example, by Roswitha of Gandersheim as a source. The title of the work, which purports to be by Matthew, is: "On the Birth of the Blessed Mary and the Childhood of the Redeemer":
(18): *When they came to a certain cave and wanted to rest in it, Mary got down from the pack mule, and, sitting down, held Jesus in her lap. There were three boys traveling with Joseph and a girl with Mary. And be-*

*Left*: The relief *Flight into Egypt* (ca. 1130) comes from the Cathedral of Autun and is thought to be one of the most important Romanesque works of art. Its feeling for detailed decorative effect is shown in the fine ornamentation of the edging and the fall of the folds. At the same time the simple depiction, which concentrates on the essentials, radiates the profound religious sensibility of the time.

*Left:* Depictions of the Flight into Egypt often show the miracle with the fig tree that, at the request of the Christ child ("Bend your branches down and refresh my mother with your fruit"), bent its branches so low that they all could be fed with its fruit. This miniature

comes from the *Très Riches Heures* of Jean, the Duke of Berry, in the Condé Museum, Chantilly, and is painted in opaque water color on parchment.

*Above right and center:* A further legend of the Flight into Egypt tells of the "toppling of the pagan idols," when Mary with the child Jesus entered a temple. The picture above shows that scene in a relief in the Church of Saint Pierre in Moissac. The one below comes from the Book of Hours of the Duke of Bedford (Austrian National Library, Vienna).

*hold, suddenly, many dragons came out of the cave. When the boys saw them in front of them they shouted with great fear. Then Jesus got down from his mother's lap, and stood on his feet before the dragons. They, however, worshipped him, and, while they worshipped, they backed away...Mary and Joseph were very afraid lest the child be harmed by the dragons. Jesus said to them, "Do not be afraid, nor consider me a child; I have always been a perfect man and am so now; it is necessary that all the wild beasts of the forest be tame before me."*

*(19): Similarly, lions and leopards worshipped him and accompanied him in the desert. Wherever Mary and Joseph went, they preceded them; showing the way and inclining their heads, they worshipped Jesus. However, the first time that Mary saw the lions and other types of wild beasts around her, she was very frightened... The lions traveled with them and with the oxen*

*and donkeys and the pack animals which carried their necessities, and they hurt none of them while they remained.*

*(20): It happened that, on the third day after their departure, Mary was fatigued by the excessive heat of the sun in the desert and, seeing a palm tree, said to Joseph, "I want to rest a bit under the shadow." Joseph quickly led her to the palm and let her get down from the animal. While Mary sat, she looked at the top of the palm and saw it full of fruit. She said to Joseph, "I wish, if it is possible, that I may have some fruit from this palm." Joseph said to her, "I am astonished that you say this, when you see how high the palm is, that you think to eat from the fruit of the palm. I think more of*

*the lack of water, which already fails us in the water bags; we now having nothing by which we can refresh ourselves and the animals." Then the infant Jesus, who was resting with smiling face at his mother's bosom, said to the palm, "Bend down, tree, and refresh my mother with your fruit." And immediately, at this voice, the palm tree bent down its head to the feet of Mary, and they gathered the fruit from it by which all were refreshed. After they had gathered all its fruit, it remained bent down, waiting so that it should rise up at the command of him who had commanded it to bend. Then Jesus said to it, "Rise up, palm, and be strong, and be a companion to the trees which are in my Father's Paradise. Open a water course beneath your roots which is hidden in the earth, and from it let flow waters to satisfy us." And the palm raised itself at once, and fountains of water, very clear and cold and sweet, began to pour out through the roots.*

Adam Elsheimer (1578–1610), *The Flight into Egypt,* 1609, oil on copper, Alte Pinakothek, Munich. This picture was the basis for Elsheimer's fame. While earlier depictions of the Flight into Egypt showed the group around Mary in the center, Elsheimer conceives of the event in a grand cosmic context and places the fleeing family in a broad, nighttime landscape. The night conceals and protects the refugees, and the bright moon is reflected in the water as a symbol of the reciprocal relations of the divine and earthly world. It also alludes to the light that Christ will bring into the dark world. In this image Elsheimer links the tradition of pure landscape painting with religious motifs.

(22.2): *Rejoicing and exulting they came to the region of Heliopolis, and went into one of the Egyptian cities called Sotinen. Since they knew no one in it from whom they could ask hospitality, they went into the temple which was called the "Capitolium of Egypt." There had been placed in this temple three hundred and sixty-five idols, to which, on appointed days, divine honor was given in sacrilegious ceremonies...*

(23): *It happened that when the most blessed Mary, with her child, had entered the temple, all the idols were thrown to the ground, so that they all lay flat, convulsed and with their faces shattered.*

Another episode from the Flight into Egypt appears in an apocryphal Arabic source:

*[They came]... into a wilderness, and when they heard that it was full of robbers, they thought of crossing it by night. But as they were going through, they saw that two robbers lay in wait for them, and with them was a group of other robbers who were sleeping. The two robbers waiting for them were Titus and Dumachus. And Titus said to Dumachus: "I beg you, let these people through, so that our comrades do not notice them." When Dumachus refused, Titus said: "Take forty drachmas and promise me." And he held his belt against him so that he could not open his mouth. And when our Lady Mary saw that the robber was well disposed to them, she said to him: "The Lord God will support you with his right hand and grant you forgiveness for your sins." And Jesus the Lord said to his mother: "Thirty years from now, O my mother, the Jews will crucify me in Jerusalem, and the two robbers will be hung up on the cross with me, Titus on my right and Dumachus on my left, and on that day Titus will go before me into Paradise." And she said: "May God spare you this, my son" (The Other Bible, pp. 394–97).*

This episode is to some extent a later embellishment of a passage from Luke (23.39–43). There one of the two nameless thieves who are being crucified with Jesus recognizes that Jesus is innocent, and asks him to remember him in the Kingdom of God. Jesus promises him that he will.

*Tell us, Simeon,*
*whom do you bear in your arms*
*in the Temple,*
*whom do you rejoice over?*
*To whom do you raise your voice*
*and call: Now I am set free,*
*for I have seen my Redeemer?*
*This is he:*
*The one born of the Virgin.*

From the hymns for Candlemas (February 2)

*L*uke describes the presentation of Jesus:

*And when the time came for their purification according to the law of Moses, they brought him up to Jerusalem to present him to the Lord... Now there was a man in Jerusalem, whose name was Simeon, and this man was righteous and devout, looking for the consolation of Israel, and the Holy Spirit was upon him... And inspired by the Spirit he came into the temple; and when the parents brought in the child Jesus, to do for him according to the custom of the law, he took him up in his arms and blessed God and said, "Lord, now lettest thou thy servant depart in peace, according to thy word; for mine eyes have seen thy salvation..." And his father and his mother marveled at what was said about him, and Simeon blessed them and said to Mary, his mother, "Behold, this child is set for the fall and rising of many in Israel, and for a sign that is spoken against (and a sword will pierce through your own soul also) that thoughts out of many hearts*

Over the centuries the "Presentation in the Temple" is conceived in increasingly rich and splendid forms. Mary gives the child to Simeon, who breaks out into the *Nunc Dimittis*: "Lord, now lettest thou thy servant depart in peace, according to thy word; for mine eyes have seen thy salvation" (Luke 2.29–32). Behind him appears the prophetess Anna.

*Left*: Etching by C. Galle from the 18th century shows the scene in the Temple with Mary, in whose breast the sword of the Sorrowful Mother has already been plunged, pointing toward her future suffering.

*Right*: Hans Memling (1433–1494), *Presentation in the Temple,* around 1470, oil on wood. This is a wing of the triptych with the *Adoration of the Magi* (the Prado, Madrid).

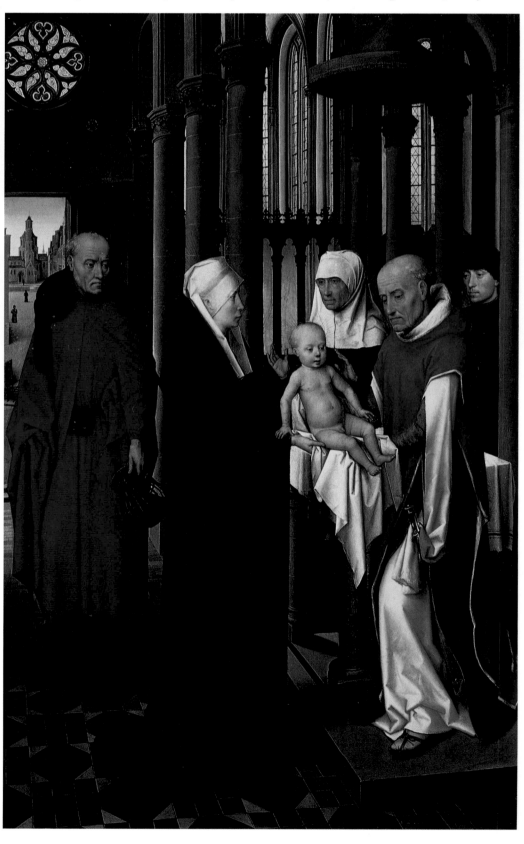

*may be revealed"*(Lk 2.22–35).

Luke also reports the episode of the twelve-year-old Jesus in the Temple (2.41–51):

*Now his parents went to Jerusalem every year at the feast of the Passover. And when he was twelve years old, they went up according to custom; and when the feast was ended, as they were returning, the boy Jesus stayed behind in Jerusalem. His parents did not know it, but supposing him to be in the company they went a day's journey, and*

*stand the saying which he spoke to them. And he went down with them and came to Nazareth, and was obedient to them; and his mother kept all these things in her heart.*

The next period in Mary's life is treated in the Childhood Gospel of Thomas, which deals with the five-to-twelve-year-old Jesus. It was strongly influenced by Gnosticism, and it presents Jesus as a supernatural being. The boy Jesus often appears here in an extremely unflattering light, as he terror-

*they sought him among their kinsfolk and acquaintances; and when they did not find him, they returned to Jerusalem seeking him. After three days they found him in the temple, sitting among the teachers, listening to them and asking them questions; and all who heard him were amazed at his understanding and his answers. And when they saw him they were astonished; and his mother said to him, "Son, why have you treated us so? Behold, your father and I have been looking for you anxiously." And he said to them, "How is it that you sought me? Did you not know that I must be in my Father's house?" And they did not under-*

The last images relating to the youthful life of Christ show the twelve-year-old Jesus in the Temple. Jesus usually sits on a thronelike speaker's chair in the center. Around him are opened books and priests with gestures of embarrassment. On the edge of the picture one sees Mary and Joseph, the parents in search of the child.

*Left*: Simone Martini's (1284–1344) *The Twelve-Year-Old Jesus in the Temple* from 1342 (tempera on wood) hangs today in the

Walker Art Gallery in Liverpool. The scene captures the moment in which Christ answers the reproaches of his parents: "Did you not know that I must be in my Father's house?"

*Right*: The classical form of the depiction of *Christ in the Temple* is seen impressively here in the Mosan Psalter fragment from the 12th century (Kupferstichkabinett, Berlin).

izes everyone around him and then calls upon the powers granted him by his heavenly Father. This gospel shows little concern for Jesus' parents. But it suggests interesting parallels with other religions: Similar stories are told about Buddha and Krishna in India and Osiris and Harpocrates in Egypt.

(11): *When he was six, his mother sent him to draw water and to bring it into the house, giving him a pitcher. But in the crowd he had a collision; the water jug was broken. Jesus spread out the garment he had on, filled it with water, and bore it to his mother. When his mother saw the miracle she kissed him, and she kept to herself the mysteries which she saw him do. (The Other Bible, p. 401.)*

In the 19th chapter the story of the twelve-year-old Jesus in the Temple (Luke 2.41–52) is retold, and the following is added to it:

*The scribes and Pharisees said, "Are you the mother of this child?" She said, "I am." They said to her, "You are blessed among women, because God has blessed the fruit of your womb. We have never before seen or heard such excellence or wisdom."(The Other Bible, p. 402.)*

An Arabic childhood gospel reports this miraculous cure by the boy Jesus: *Another woman had two sons who fell sick; one of them died, the other one was still alive. His mother took him and brought him weeping to our Lady Mary... and said: "Lord, ... you gave me two sons, but, since you have taken one from me, let me at least have this one." To which Mary said: "...Lay your son in my son's bed and cover him with his clothes." And when she had laid him in the bed where Christ lay, he was already dead and had closed his eyes. But as the fragrance of the clothing of our Lord Jesus Christ reached him, he opened his eyes, called out in a loud voice for his mother and*

*Left*: One of the legends that wove themselves around Christ's childhood was the tale from an apocryphal Arabic childhood gospel about "the bringing to life of the clay birds." This is reproduced here on a wooden ceiling from the early Romanesque church of St. Martin in Zillis, Germany.

*Right*: Wolf Huber (1485–1553) shows the end of Christ's childhood in his painting, *Christ Leaving His Mother* from 1519 (Kunsthistorisches Museum, Vienna). In the broad landscape of the Danube School, of which Huber is the chief representative, one sees Mary bent over in grief at the departure, surrounded by women and looking at the Christ who stands before her.

*demanded bread, which he consumed immediately. Then his mother said: "Oh, Lady Mary, now I know that God's power rests in you."... The son who was healed this way is the one who is named in the Gospel of Bartholomew.*

Mary the concerned mother is presented in an Armenian childhood gospel:

(Mary said to Jesus): *I am so overcome with evil premonitions that I don't know what I should do." Jesus asked: "What are you planning for me?" Mary answered: "We have tried to teach you many things during your childhood, and you have ignored our instructions... And now that you have gotten older, what will you do? How will you be able to live?" When Jesus heard these words, he became angry and said to his mother: "You speak thoughtlessly. Do you not understand the signs and wonders that I have done before you?... Think of everything that I have done, and be patient a little while longer. You will see how my work is fulfilled; but my time has not yet come. Only continue to trust me." After saying this, Jesus left his house in haste.*

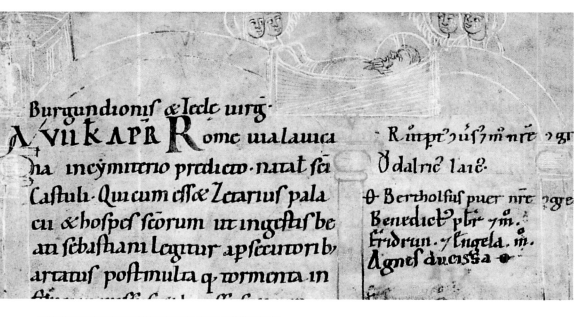

## The Death of Joseph

Some time later Joseph must have died. An Arabic story about Joseph the carpenter relates:

(Jesus speaks): *"My mother, the spotless virgin, arose, came to me, and said: 'O my beloved son, Joseph, the pious old man, lies on his deathbed.' And I answered: '...You too, my virginal mother, must await the end of your life, as must all other mortals. Meanwhile, your death, like that of this pious man, is no death, but eternal life. But my duty is to die, as befits the body that I have received from you.'"* (Then Jesus prays to his Father and asks him to send the archangels Gabriel and Michael, who then wrap the soul of Joseph and guard it from the demons of darkness.)

An Egyptian story about the death of Joseph reports his death in the following way (again it is Jesus who is speaking):

*"...Death itself, however, could not lay hold of my dear father Joseph's body in order to separate it from his soul, because the Angel of Death, who was looking into the room, saw me sit at the end of the bed and he saw that I was stroking his brow.... I crossed the room and saw Death waiting outside, filled with fear. I said to him: 'Come in quickly and do the will of my Father. But keep Joseph as the apple of your eye, for he is my father in the flesh...and was my teacher....' Of all those who were near him, none knew that he was dead. Even Mary, my mother, knew no more than the others. I commanded Michael and Gabriel to guard the corpse of my Father, for outside there were robbers."*

John mentions Mary for the first time in the episode of the marriage feast at Cana, where Jesus turns water into wine (2.1–5, 12):
*On the third day there was a marriage at Cana in Galilee, and the mother of Jesus was there; Jesus also was invited to the marriage, with his disciples. When the wine gave out, the mother of Jesus said to him, "They have no wine." And Jesus said to her,*

*"O woman, what have you to do with me? My hour has not yet come." His mother said to the servants, "Do whatever he tells you."...After this he went down to Capernaum, with his mother and his brothers and his disciples; and there they stayed for a few days.*

The only two passages in Mark that mention Mary relate to Jesus' time as a preacher. Here, in 3.31–35, Jesus has just responded to the invective of the Pharisees: *And his mother and his brothers came; and standing outside they sent to him and called him. And a crowd was sitting about him; and they said to him, "Your mother and your brothers are outside, asking for you." And he replied, "Who are my mother and my brothers?" And looking around on those who sat about him, he said, "Here are my mother and my brothers!*

*Whoever does the will of God is my brother, and sister, and mother."*

Later on we are told that when Jesus preached in his home town, the people said among themselves (Mark 6.3–4): *"Is not this the carpenter, the son of Mary and brother of James and Joses and Judas and Simon, and are not his sisters here with us?" And they took offense at him. And Jesus said to them, "A prophet is not without honor,*

(114): *Simon Peter said: "Let Mary leave us! Women are not of the (higher) life." Jesus said: "I myself shall lead her, so that she too may become a living spirit resembling you males. For every woman who will make herself male will enter the Kingdom of Heaven." (The Other Bible, pp. 300–307).*

*except in his own country, and among his own kin, and in his own house."*

Finally, Matthew reports (12.46–50) yet another scene, in which Jesus, after preaching a sermon, hears that his mother and brothers wish to speak with him, he turns them down. The scene is taken almost verbatim from the third chapter of Mark quoted above.

Luke too (8.19–21) mentions Jesus' mother and brothers briefly yet one more time, when after a sermon he rejects them, in a passage similar to the ones we have already seen in Mark and Matthew.

Not very long ago a collection of sayings by Jesus was unearthed at Nag Hammadi in Upper Egypt. It has since become known as the "Second Gospel of Thomas." Originally composed in Greek, it has been preserved in Coptic, probably goes back to the 2nd century A.D., and once again has a strongly gnostic coloring. The form of the loosely strung together sayings and anecdotes is the first historically demonstrable ex-

ample of a genre that may have served the authors of Matthew and Luke as a background for their speeches and parables. Some of Jesus' sayings may be preserved here in a more original form than in the Gospels. Others sound quite disconcerting because they attest to a decidedly misogynistic spirit and stand in glaring contradiction to the New Testament. This is especially true of the handful of sayings that deal with Mary. Jesus says:

(15): *When you see one who has not been born of woman, prostrate yourselves on your faces and adore him. That one is your Father.*

(55): *Whoever does not hate his father and his mother cannot become a disciple to me.*

(79): *... There will be days on which you will say: "Blessed are the womb which has not conceived and the breasts which have not given milk."* (See Luke 21.23.)

(101:) *Whoever does not hate his father and his mother as I do cannot become a disciple to me. For my mother gave me falsehood, but my true mother gave me life.*

The "Marriage Feast at Cana" was one of the favorite subjects of Renaissance and Baroque painters, offering many possibilities for embellishment and decorative genre details.

*Center left*: In a semicircular painting Gerard David (Bruges, 1460–1523) treats the *Marriage Feast at Cana*. The calm manner of the persons in the background contrasts with the animated gestures of the servants filling the vessels.

*Center right:* This illustration from a Luther Bible portrays the moment in which Christ, standing before the jars, changes the water into wine.

*Page 46:* This painting by Giotto (1266–1337) forms part of the cycle of frescoes painted between 1303 and 1310 in the Capella degli Scrovegni, the so-called Arena Chapel in Padua.

*Page 48 left*: The *Descent from the Cross* and the *Lamentation over Christ* come from a tetraptych (painting composed of four sections), tempera on wood, Constantinople, second half of the 14th century. The main figures, John and Mary, mourn the death of Christ.

## AT THE CRUCIFIXION AND
## RESURRECTION OF HER SON

*T*he last time that John speaks of Mary is the crucifixion scene (19.25–27):
*Standing by the cross of Jesus were his mother, and his mother's sister, Mary the wife of Clopas, and Mary Magdalene. When Jesus saw his mother, and the disciple whom he loved, standing near, he said to his mother, "Woman, behold your son!" Then he said to the disciple, "Behold your mother!" And from that hour the disciple took her to his own house.*

In Luke's Acts of the Apostles Mary is mentioned briefly, right after Christ's ascension (Acts 1.12–14):
*Then they returned to Jerusalem from the mount called Olivet, which is near Jerusalem, a sabbath's day journey away; and, when they had entered, they went up to the upper room, where they were staying, Peter and John and James and Andrew, Philip and Thomas, Bartholomew and Matthew, James the son of Alphaeus and Simon the Zealot and Judas the son of James. All these with one accord devoted themselves to prayer, together with the women and Mary the mother of Jesus, and with his brothers.*

Similarly a "Gospel of Mary" from the early 5th century, discovered in Nag Hammadi, tells about the day when the

risen Jesus leaves his disciples and Mary and goes off to heaven:
(Jesus said): *Go then and teach the Gospel of the Kingdom of Heaven. Lay down no rules beyond what I have taught you..."* When he had said that, he went away.

*But they [the apostles] mourned, wept and said: "How shall we go to the heathens and preach the Gospel of the Son of Man? They have not spared him, how should they spare us?"*

*Then Mary stood up, greeted them all, and said her brothers: "Do not weep, do not mourn, and do not waver, for his grace will be with you completely and will safeguard you. But let us praise his greatness, for he has prepared us and made us men." When Mary said this, they turned their hearts to goodness, and they began to speak about the words of the Redeemer.*

*Peter said to Mary: "We know that the Redeemer loved you more than all other women. Let us hear the words of the Savior that you remember and we do not, or that we have not heard."*

*Mary replied and said: "What has been hidden from you I shall inform you of..." I saw the Lord in a vision and said to him: "Lord, I have seen you today in a vision." And he answered: "Blessed be you, for you*

*Above right*: In the Book of Hours, *Les très riches heures du Duc de Berry* (Condé Museum, Chantilly), the farewell to Mary of individual groups of apostles is shown amid a wide landscape.

*Lower right*: The apparition of the risen Christ to Mary is depicted on a side panel of a Mary altar by Rogier van der Weyden (1400–1464), tempera on wood, Metropolitan Museum of Art, New York. The niche, reminiscent of portal architecture, where Mary and Jesus are shown, is an allusion to Mary as an image of the Church, *Ecclesia*.

48

*did not waver when you saw me. For where the thoughts are, there is the treasure."* I said: *"Lord, does one who sees a vision see it through his soul or through the Spirit?"* And he answered: *"He sees it neither through the soul nor through the Spirit, for the thoughts lie between these two..."* (There are four manuscript pages missing here.)

*"... When the soul had overwhelmed the third power, she climbed up and saw the fourth power, which appeared in seven forms. The first is darkness, the second desire, the third ignorance, the fourth disturbance over death, the fifth the kingdom of the flesh, the sixth the foolish wisdom of the flesh, and the seventh wrathful wisdom... These asked the soul: "Where do you come from, killer of humans, and where are you going, conqueror of space?" The soul answered: "What binds me was struck down, what turns me around has been overcome, my desire is ended and ignorance dead... From now on I shall come to what is left over from time, seasons, eons, in silence."*

*When Mary had said that, she fell silent, for up to this point the Redeemer had spoken with her. But Andrew answered and said to his brothers: "Tell us what you want about what she has said. I at least do not believe that the Redeemer said that. For these teachings are surely very strange."* Peter answered and spoke about these matters. Then he asked her about the Redeemer: *"Did he really speak in confidence to a woman, but not freely to us? Are we to turn around and listen to her? Did he prefer her to us?"*

*Then Mary wept and said to Peter: "Brother Peter, what are you thinking? Do you believe that I made up all this in my heart and that I am telling lies about the Redeemer?"* Levi answered and said to Peter: *"Peter, you have always been a hothead. Now I see you attacking a woman as if she were an enemy. But if the Redeemer has found her worthy, who are you to reject her? Surely the Redeemer knows her very well, that is why he loved her more than us. We should rather be ashamed..., [let us] part,* as he bade us, and preach the Gospel without setting up new rules, which go beyond those of the Redeemer."... And they went forth to preach and to pray.

A further address by Mary, to the newly risen Christ, is reported in the "Pistis-Sophia," a gnostic book of mysteries from the 3rd century. This legend seeks to equate Christ with the Holy Spirit:

*"Since you were small, before the Spirit came over you, while you were with Joseph in the vineyard, the Spirit came out of the heavens and came to me in my house, like unto you, and I had not recognized him, and thought he was you. And the Spirit said to me: 'Where is Jesus, my brother, that I may meet him?' And when he said that to me, I fell into confusion and thought it was a ghost, to tempt me. But I took him and tied him to the foot of the bed, the one in my house, until I went out to you and Joseph in* the field and found you in the vineyard, where Joseph was fencing it round. But even as you heard the Word speaking to Joseph, you grasped the Word, you rejoiced and said: 'Where is he, that I may see him, else I shall wait for him in this place.' But it came to pass that Joseph heard you saying these words, and he was filled with consternation, and we went up together and entered the house and found the Spirit tied to the bed. And we looked at you and him, and found that you were like unto him; and the one bound to the bed was set free, and he embraced and kissed you, and you kissed him, and you two became one."*

Concerning the time after Jesus' ascent into heaven Syrian apocrypha report that Mary prayed every day at his tomb and begged to be allowed to die so that she could be united again with him. But the Jews, who persecuted all followers of Jesus, planned to stone Mary; and Sabinus, the governor of Jerusalem, gave them permission to do so. Meanwhile the Holy Spirit surrounded Mary with a wonderful cloud of invisibility. She escaped and returned to her house in Bethlehem, where she then lived with three virgins.

In the first centuries after Jesus' death people obviously gave little thought to

Mary's later life. The question of her death and burial site did arise, however. The fact that Jesus' beloved disciple John had taken Mary into his care could already be found in the Gospel of John. But the question arose whether she had died and been buried near Jerusalem or in Ephesus. In the first three Christian centuries there was no mention of her having been assumed into heaven.

In the 2nd century interest in the relics of the martyrs was strong, but most people agreed that there were no mortal remains of the Virgin. As early as the 4th century St. Epiphanius

*Left:* The Intercessor for the Poor Souls in Purgatory *after an engraving by J.C. Gutwein (Regensburg, ca. 1700). Mary moves even those souls who have not yet come to the beatific vision of God and who find redemption only through her prayers.*

*Top:* A woodcut from Thomas Murner's rabble-rousing treatise, "The Dishonoring of Mary by the Jews," comes from Matthias Hupfuff (1515).

*Right:* The Spanish artist Bartolomé Esteban Murillo (1618–1682) shows Mary entirely resigned to the announcement of her imminent death.

# ANNOUNCEMENT OF DEATH, DEATH, BURIAL, ASSUMPTION INTO HEAVEN, AND CORONATION

(315–403), a great promoter of monasticism, disputed the possibility of the burial and corruption of the Holy Virgin's body:

*Scripture is completely silent about this, because it is a great miracle, and in order not to stir up people's feelings needlessly. As for myself, I do not dare to speak about [the miracle] and will keep my thoughts to myself... Perhaps we have discovered enough about the holy and blessed woman to be able to say that it is impossible to know whether she died... Holy Scripture leaves the question open out of reverence for the incomparable Virgin, and to put an end to all unworthy and earthly thoughts on this topic... It is possible that she is still alive; for with God nothing is impossible.*

Some of the Eastern apocrypha tell of a further episode in Mary's life: her descent into hell. This event still belongs to her earthly life, because in most of these narratives Mary prays before her death on Golgotha. Then the archangel Michael appears and carries her off to hell, where she has to witness the dreadful agonies and tortures of the murderers, adulterers, usurers, and other sinners, as Dante describes in the first part of his *Divine Comedy*. Mary is horrified and begs Jesus' grace for the tormented souls. At first Jesus angrily points to his own wounds, inflicted on him by sinful humanity. But later he relents and allows the poor souls a respite during the season of Pentecost.

This legend may be found in several Greek manuscripts, none of which is older than the 9th century. The manuscript of an Irish legend about St. Brendan is probably a bit older than that. Brendan meets Judas cooling his feet on a rock in the waves in the middle of the Atlantic Ocean. Judas explains to the saint that he is freed from his tortures in hell on weekends, as well as during the time between Christmas and Epiphany, between Easter and Pentecost, and on two feast days dedicated to the holy Virgin.

*T*he following account by Pseudo-Melito ties in directly to the Gospel of John (19.27):

(2): *... From this hour on the most blessed Mother of God remained, for as long as she lived, entrusted to the special care of John. And when the apostles had drawn lots to see which regions they should set out for, to proclaim the teaching, she remained in her parents' house near the Mount of Olives.*

(3): *In the twenty-second year after Jesus had conquered death and gone to heaven, Mary spent one day in a remote corner of her house, enflamed by the wish to see the Redeemer again and weeping; behold, an angel appeared to her in gleaming light, greeted*

her, and said: *"I greet you, blessed by the Lord; receive the greeting of him who offered Jacob his greeting through the prophets; behold, I bring you a palm branch from God's Paradise; let it be carried before your coffin, when in three days you will be transported to heaven in your body. For your Son awaits you with the Thrones and with the angels and with all the Powers of heaven."* Then Mary said to the angel: *"I pray you, let all the apostles of my Lord Jesus Christ gather around me."* The angel answered her: *"All the apostles will be brought here today*

through the power of Jesus Christ." Then Mary put on new clothes, grasped the palm branch that she had received from the hand of the angel, and she went to the Mount of Olives to pray.

(4): *When now the most blessed John was preaching on the day of the Lord in Ephesus, behold, there was a great earthquake, and a cloud carried him off in the sight of everyone. It brought him before the door of the house where the Virgin Mary, the Mother of God, was staying. He opened the door and entered in at once. When the most blessed Virgin looked upon him, she said joyfully: "... In three days I shall leave this body, and I heard that the Jews have taken*

Duccio di Buoninsegna (1255–1319), *An Angel Announces her Death to Mary,* tempera on wood, Cathedral Museum, Siena. As at the Annunciation Mary sits in front of a book and receives a message from an angel. But whereas at the Annunciation she had turned away in terror at the task before her, in pictures of the announcement of her death she receives the angel serenely and with open arms.

*Below*: On this coin one can make out Mary's death and Assumption, though in a highly stylized form.

counsel and said: 'Let us wait for the day when the woman who bore that deceiver in her womb will die; then let us burn her body...'"

(5): *Then suddenly at God's command all the apostles were carried off in a cloud from the places where they were preaching the word of God and set down before the door of the house where Mary, the Mother of the Redeemer, dwelled. Full of amazement they greeted one another and said: "Why has the Lord gathered us all together in this place?"*

*Paul too had come, he whom the Lord had chosen to preach the Gospel to the pagans. And a pious dispute arose between*

appears and I shall leave this body."

(7): *They sat down and comforted her and spent three days in praising God; but on the third day sleep came over everyone in the house, and none could remain awake, except for the apostles and the three virgins, the companions of the Blessed Virgin. And behold, all at once the Lord Jesus appeared with a great band of angels in shining glory, and the angels sang hymns of praise to the Lord. And the Lord spoke: "Come, you chosen one, most precious pearl, enter into the dwelling of eternal life."*

(8): *Then Mary threw herself on the ground and prayed to the Lord... "Receive*

them over which of them would be the first to pray to the Lord to reveal to them the cause of this event, and Peter asked Paul to pray first. Paul replied: "Does not this duty fall to you, since you were chosen by God to be the pillar of the Church, and since you preside over all the other apostles? I am only the least among you, and I cannot claim to be your equal; yet through God's grace I am what I am."

(6): *They entered the house and greeted her...She said: "The Lord has brought you here to comfort me in the fears that are to come over me. I beg you all to watch unceasingly with me until the hour when the Lord*

your maidservant, O Lord, and redeem me from the power of darkness, so that Satan may not assault me and that I may not see the frightful spirits around me." The Savior replied: "When I was sent by my Father to redeem the world and hung on the cross, the prince of darkness came upon me; but when he could discover in me no traces of his work, he withdrew defeated and despised. I saw him and you shall see him, as the general law of the human race demands, to which you are subject in dying; he will not be able to hurt you.... Come then in peace, for the heavenly hosts await you, so that I may lead you into the joys of Paradise."

*Left*: The death of Mary and her raising up to heaven are depicted here on the west portal of the Cathedral of Notre Dame de Senlis (ca. 1170). Angels bend over Mary and carry her out of the grave into heaven.

*Right*: *The Dormition of the Mother of God*, iconostasis curtain, 1510, Putna Monastery, Moldavia. A frequently recurring theme of Byzantine art is Christ surrounded by angels and apostles, receiving the soul of Mary after her death. Christ often bears Mary's soul, depicted as a little child, in his arms—as seen here.

*Left*: Several "stations" of the death of Mary are joined here on the painting by André Beauneveu (ca. 1330–1403/13), the Louvre, Paris. In the lower portion Mary rests, surrounded by apostles, on a bier. In the upper portion she receives her coronation from the Trinity.

*Right*: Andrea Mantegna (1430–1506) treated the subject of *The Death of the Madonna* (Prado, Madrid) in the strictly perspectivist space and earthly presence of the Renaissance. In the background the view opens out onto a very wide landscape. The dignified architecture is reminiscent of a triumphal arch, as it often appears in Italian art.

*Top:* In the village church of Ratzenried in the Bavarian Alps Mary is depicted on her death-bed like a Late Gothic merchant's wife in a canopy bed, surrounded by the apostles.

*Above:* The death and Assumption of Mary are treated in this illumination from the Pericope Book of Emperor Henry II from 1010 (School of Reichenau; Bavarian State Library, Munich). Christ appears strictly centered in the mandorla over Mary's deathbed with Mary now resurrected and carried by angels.

*Page 55:* Peter Paul Rubens (1577–1640), *Mary's Assumption into Heaven* (Kunsthistorisches Museum, Vienna). Rubens painted the Assumption more than twelve times. This picture, now in Vienna, is surely one of the most beautiful variations on the theme. The scene follows the *Legenda Aurea* ("Golden Legend"). The subject of the Assumption fits in very well with Baroque pathos and the sweeping gestures of the lively figures: Death is overcome, Mary is carried aloft by a jubilant cloud of angels.

*And when the Lord had spoken these words, the Virgin arose, stretched out on her bed and gave up the ghost, thanking God. Then the apostles saw such a burst of glory that no human tongue can describe, for it surpassed the whiteness of snow and the brightness of silver.*

Pseudo-Melito continues:

(9): *And the Redeemer of the world said: "Arise, Peter, with the other apostles, take the body of my much-loved Mary and bear her to the right side, toward the East...." When the Lord had spoken these words, he handed over the soul of his most holy Mother Mary to the archangel Michael, who is the guardian of Paradise and the prince of the Hebrew people, and at the same time with him the archangel Gabriel; then the Lord returned with the other angels to heaven.*

(10): *The three virgins there took the body of Mary and washed it, as is the custom at burials. And when they had unclothed it, this holy body shone with such splendor that only through God's goodness could one touch it; it was wholly pure and quite without stain...*

(11): *The apostles laid the holy body in the coffin and said to one another: "Who shall carry the palm branch before the coffin?" Then John said to Peter: "You who as an apostle stand over us; it is also fitting for you to carry this palm branch." Peter replied: "You are the only one among us who has remained intact, and you have found such grace with the Lord, that you rested in his bosom. Moreover, as he hung on the cross, he entrusted his mother to you. Thus you must carry the palm branch; but I shall bear this holy body to the grave." And Paul said: "I am the youngest of all of you, I will bear it with you." When they had thus agreed, Peter lifted up the coffin and began to sing the words, "When Israel went forth from Egypt." And Paul helped Peter bear the holy body, and John walked ahead with the shining palm branch, and the other apostles sang with most harmonious voices.*

(12): *And behold, another miracle occurred. For a large garland of clouds appeared over the coffin, like the great ring that is wont to surround the shining moon... And the people, fifteen thousand in number, came out of the city and said: "What do these melodious sounds mean?"...Then one of them, who was the high priest of the Jews,*

*flew into a rage and said: "Look what honors are given to the mother of that man who stirred up such unrest among your people!" And he approached the coffin and tried to overturn it. But at once his arms withered from the elbows down and remained fastened to the coffin, while he suffered dreadful pains. Meanwhile the apostles moved on and sang. But the angels in the cloud struck the people with blindness.*

(13): *And he cried out and said: "I beg you, Peter, you whom God loves, do not leave me in such great distress, for I feel terrible torments. Remember that I defended you and put in a good word for you when the maidservant recognized you at the courthouse."*

(14): *Then Peter ordered the coffin to halt and said to the priest: "If you believe in the Lord with your whole heart, may your hands become free again." And when the priest said, "I believe," his hands were released at once from the coffin, but his arms remained paralyzed and his pains did not abate. And Peter said to him: "Come near, kiss the coffin and say: 'I believe in God and the Son of God, Jesus Christ, whom Mary bore in her womb, and I believe everything that Peter, God's apostle, has told me.'" Then the priest came up and kissed the coffin; at once he felt no more pain, and his arms were healed.*

(16): *The apostles bore the corpse of Mary and came into the valley of Jehosaphat, which the Lord had pointed out to them. And they laid the body in a new tomb and shut it. Then they sat down in front of it, as God had bidden them.*

*And behold, suddenly the Lord Jesus appeared with a countless host of angels who shone in great splendor. He spoke to the apostles: "My Father's command chose Mary from among the tribes of Israel, that I should dwell in her. What, then, do you wish to be done with her?" And Peter and the other apostles said: "... It seems right to your servants, that, just as you yourself reign in heaven after conquering death, you should awaken the body of Mary and lead her, the joyous one, into heaven."*

(17): *Then the Redeemer said: "Let it be according to your words." And he ordered the archangel Michael to bring Mary's holy soul. And at once the archangel Gabriel removed the stone that sealed the grave, and the Lord said: "Rise up, my friend. You have*

*not touched man and thus tasted corruption; hence you shall also not suffer the corruption of the body in the grave." And immediately Mary arose and praised the Lord; then she fell at his feet, adored him, and said: "I cannot thank you properly, O Lord, for the favors that you have been pleased to do your maidservant. Redeemer of the world, God of Israel, may your name be blessed to all eternity."*

(18): *Then the Lord kissed her and handed her over to his angels, to take her to Paradise... After these words the Lord went up into heaven on a cloud; but the angels accompanied him and bore the most blessed Mary, the Mother of God, into God's Paradise. And the apostles were brought back on clouds, each to the place where he had been preaching the Gospel...*

The Arabic "Book of the Dying of the

Blessed Virgin Mary" adds the following episode:

*And the immaculate Virgin was borne up in triumph in a chariot of light. Then a cloud covered everyone who was standing about. Only the apostles remained, praying for three days. And when they were still together, Thomas, one of the Twelve, came on a cloud... And when he came to the other apostles, who were still praying, Peter asked Thomas: "Brother, what kept you, that you were absent when the mother of our Lord Jesus departed? You did not see the great miracles that were done in her honor. You did not receive her blessing." And Thomas answered: "My duties in the service of the Lord made it impossible for me... I was preaching in India and baptizing the nephew of King Golodius. Now tell me, where you have placed the body of our Lady." They answered: "In this tomb." And he said: "I wish to see her and to be blessed by her. Then I can see confirmed that what you have told me is true." Then the apostles cried out: "You always distrust what we tell you..." Whereupon Thomas replied: "You know that I am Thomas. I will not rest until I have seen the grave in which Mary was buried. Otherwise I will not believe."*

*Peter rose up quickly and angrily, and with the help of the others he shoved aside the gravestone. Then they found the tomb empty, and they were amazed and cried out: "When we were away, the Jews came and took away the body to do with it what they want."*

*But Thomas said: "Fear not, my brothers; for when I was borne here from India on a cloud, I saw the holy body surrounded by a great band of angels. She has been carried up on high in triumph. I begged her aloud to bless me, and she gave me this scarf."*

This Arabic text has further information about Mary after her Assumption into heaven:

*Now Jesus said to the blessed Virgin: "See now the glory to which you have been exalted." She looked up and saw greater glory than the human eye can bear. And behold, Enoch, Elijah, Moses and all the prophets and patriarchs and the elect came and adored the Lord and blessed Mary. And then they withdrew...*

*And the Lord made the sun stop before the gates of heaven... The Lord sat above the sun in a chariot of light. And Mary saw the great* gate of Jerusalem and rejoiced that the names of the just were written there, the names of Abraham, Isaac, Jacob, David, and all the prophets since Adam's day... And holy Mary heard with great joy how the just were praised; but when she learned what the fate of sinners was, she was seized with grief. And she asked the Lord to have pity on sinners, to be kind to them, since man is weak. And the Lord promised to do so.

And behold, many letters were sent to the Apostles in Rome,... wishing to know what had happened to Mary. And therefore the miracles that Mary had wrought were made known:

Ninety-two ships were out at sea and threatened by strong winds and waves. The sailors prayed to Mary, and after she had shown herself to them, not one ship was lost...

Some travelers who feared that robbers would plunder them called upon Mary. She appeared, and had the robbers blinded, as if they had been struck by lightning... A wild monster came out of a cave and threatened two women who were on a journey. It plunged forward to devour them, but they called upon Mary and cried: "Save us!" The holy Virgin appeared at once and struck the dragon on the jaws. His head split off...

A merchant had borrowed a thousand florins to buy goods, but he lost his wallet on the trip. He did not notice it until he was far away from the spot, then he beat himself in the face, tore his hair, and cried out: "Holy Virgin, help me!" She appeared and said: "Follow me, and do not be concerned." He followed her, and she led him to the place where the wallet was. He picked it up with joy...

...in remembrance of Mary the Apostles instituted a feast on the second day after Christmas so that all the locusts hidden away in the earth should be destroyed, so that the harvests would be good, and the rulers would enjoy Mary's protection and keep the peace between one another...

The years that the Virgin, the Mother of God, spent on earth were fifty-nine. There were three until her entrance into the Temple, where she stayed eleven years and three months. She bore the Lord Jesus in her womb for three months and spent thirty-three years with him while he was on earth. After his ascension she lived on earth for eleven years.

\* \* \*

All the Apocrypha confirm that Mary was buried in or near Jerusalem in the Valley of Jehosaphat. Around 450 the Empress Pulcheria in Constantinople asked the patriarch of Jerusalem to send Mary's body to Constantinople so that it could be venerated in the Blachernae Palace. The patriarch replied that unfortunately this was impossible, because Mary's body had disappeared from the tomb; so he sent Mary's veil instead. The empty tomb was still visited by pilgrims as late as the 6th and 7th centuries. Even after Jerusalem had fallen to the Arabs in 638, and veneration of the saints had suffered a severe setback through the Iconoclast emperors, Mary's gravesite in Jerusalem was acknowledged again and again by the

*Page 56*: Nanni di Banco (1374–1421, Florence), *The Ascension of Mary and the Donation of the Girdle,* pediment relief at the Porta della Mandorla of the Cathedral of Florence. Mary gives doubting Thomas her girdle as a proof of her resurrection. Nanni di Banco was the son of the sculptor Antonio di Banco, one of the early Renaissance sculptors who most admired the ancient world and who influenced the development of Renaissance sculpture. In the late work shown here, however, he went back to Gothic stylistic elements, such as the mandorla.

*Above*: The early ivory hinge from the Cathedral Chapter Library of St. Gall, carved around 900, shows Mary's Assumption. Now raised from the dead, she is depicted in the posture of a worshipper, borne aloft by the angels standing alongside her.

Church Fathers of the 8th century—Germanus, Andreas of Crete, John Damascene. Still, this view was never without controversy. An old tradition maintained that John, whom Jesus had charged to take care of Mary, lived and died in Ephesus. Thus Mary too had to be buried there. This version received an astonishing confirmation in the early 19th century through the visions of Anna Katharina Emmerich.

When we try to take ancient sources, cited here in excerpts, and reshape them into a coherent picture of Mary, our goal cannot be a historically attested, unambiguous biography. As we have seen, the New Testament sources about Mary are quite scanty and were drawn up thirty-five to forty years after Jesus' death. The apocryphal accounts are later still and of far more dubious authority. They also have in view goals that, for the most part, are completely different from that of a factual account of Mary's life. We can only piece together a picture of Mary's life as it was gradually shaped in the general consciousness of the Christian world and the Church. This picture then provided the basis for the myth of Mary and the enormous wealth of material in the fine arts, literature, and theological speculation in the centuries that followed.

That picture would look something like this:

Joachim and Anne, a rich, pious couple, remain childless and are therefore despised by the community. He goes off to the wilderness to do penance, and both he and Anne are visited by an angel who proclaims to them that Anne is pregnant—it is not quite clear whether this is a virginal conception, as later with Mary, or if Joachim was the biological father.

Mary is born in the seventh month; the high priest blesses her and accepts her into the Temple, where she is fed by an angel. When she is twelve years old, an angel orders the high priest to gather together the widowers of Israel. Joseph is chosen from among them as Mary's spouse by the miracle of the dove and the staff. Joseph's ancestry is traced back all the way to Abraham. The angel Gabriel announces to Mary the birth of Jesus. She visits her relative Elizabeth, the future mother of John the Baptist. In Mary's prayer of thanks (the Magnificat) the child is not mentioned. When Joseph comes back from a journey and finds Mary pregnant by the Holy Spirit, doubts arise in his mind; but they are eased by an angel in a dream. Mary declares her innocence, and the doubts of the high priest are removed by the test of the "water of bitterness."

Mary and Joseph betake themselves to Bethlehem for the census; there Jesus is born in an inn—or a cave. The unbelieving Salome is punished, then healed. Eve, too, the mother of the human race, is said to have been in the cave.

Shepherds from thereabouts visit Mary and Joseph and adore the child lying in a manger. The wise men from the East, later known as the holy three kings, are led by a star to Bethlehem. From them King Herod learns about the holy Child. Since the Christ child is threatened by Herod, the angel warns Joseph to flee with Mary and the child to Egypt. During the flight the little boy works many miracles. After Herod's death the angel advises Joseph to return to Israel.

Jesus is brought by his parents to the Temple of Jerusalem to be circumcised; there he is recognized by Simeon as the Messiah. The growing boy performs various miracles. On a trip to Jerusalem Mary and Joseph lose sight of the twelve-year-old Jesus and finally discover him in the Temple, where he astonishes his listeners. Once he has grown up, he accompanies his mother to Cana for a wedding, where he turns water into wine. He begins to preach, and his mother (and brothers) send for him, but he brusquely rejects them. After Joseph's death Jesus has his corpse guarded by angels.

Mary is present at the crucifixion, and Jesus entrusts her to the protection of John, his beloved disciple. After Jesus' ascension Maria meets with his brothers and apostles and prays. Mary tells the disciples of a vision in which the Lord communicated mysterious things to her. Afterward she is threatened by Jews and protected by the Holy Spirit. According to some reports she lives twenty-two years (others say eleven) after Jesus' ascension into heaven, in or near Jerusalem (or else in Ephesus with John). While still alive she is said to have gone down into hell with the archangel Michael, where she sees the torments of the damned and begs Jesus to relieve their suffering.

Then an angel appears to her to announce her imminent death. She asks that all the apostles gather round her. They are all brought to Mary on clouds from the places where they were preaching. After three days Jesus appears with many angels and comforts Mary as she dies.

When the disciples carry away her coffin, many people gather and the high priest tries to overturn her coffin; but his arms wither and remain stuck to the coffin. Peter prays for him, he is converted and healed. Doubting Thomas appears too late and demands to see Mary's body, but the tomb is empty. Then he confesses that he has seen Mary on the way to heaven, borne aloft by angels.

Mary is buried by the apostles in the valley of Jehosaphat. The Redeemer appears yet one more time, awakens Mary from the dead, and has her carried by angels into Paradise. There she is highly honored.

*Page 58: The Apparition of the Virgin* in the Blachernae Chapel in Istanbul. The Mother of God spreads out her veil as a sign of her protection over the people assembled in the church. This 17th-century Russian icon is part of a triptych.

# Mary
# in Literature

Joe H. Kirchberger

Not until the Council of Ephesus (431), which officially gave her the title of *Mother of God* (Theotokos), did the veneration of Mary actually "take off" in the consciousness of the Christian West and Asia Minor, as reflected in Latin, Greek, and Near Eastern literature. But hymns and prayers from the time before the Council have come down to us. They contain songs of praise, greetings, and petitions. Some also reflect on the mother-son relationship between Mary and Jesus. Sometimes the authors have Mary herself speak.

One of the oldest lyrics of this sort is a *Latin prayer,* the core of which is contained in a papyrus of the 3rd or 4th century and was expanded on in the Middle Ages:

*Beneath your protective shelter
we flee, holy Mother of God.
Scorn not our prayer in our distress,
save us ever from all dangers,
O glorious and blessed Virgin,
our dear Lady, our mediator, our advocate.
Lead us to your Son,
recommend us to your Son,
present us to your Son.*

The following Greek hymn can scarcely have been composed much later. Its author is *Gregorios,* who is called "the wonderworker" ("thaumaturgos") because of the legends that later grew up around him. Born into a pagan family, he was a pupil of the famous Church Father Origen and became bishop of Neo-Caesarea. He died around 275.

*O reflection of the light
in the lofty kingdom of the spirit,
in you is the Father glorified,*
*who has no beginning
and whose might overshadowed you.
In you is the Son adored,
whom you bore in your womb, according
   to the flesh.
In you is the Holy Spirit celebrated,
who in your body
brought the Great King to birth.
Through you, O Blessed one,
the holy Trinity, all of the same essence,
could be known to the world.*

One important and especially eloquent praiser of Mary was *Ephrem the Syrian,* whose hymns to Mary were translated from the Syriac and disseminated everywhere. He died in 373. He is considered to be the author of the first of "Mary's complaints." In his hymns about the Nativity he also touches on the mother-son problem. He has Mary say:

*More than all whom he healed,
he has brought joy to me,
because I bore him.
I will enter his Paradise of life,
and there, where Eve was defeated,
I will praise him,
for he was well pleased with me
above all other women created,
that I should be his mother,
because he willed it so
and he, my child,...
The day that Gabriel came to my house,
poor as I am,
has made me all at once
both mistress and servant,
for I am the maidservant of your divinity,
but a mother too,
mother of your humanity, O Lord and
   Son!...
How am I to nurture you,
O Nurturer of the universe?
How am I to sew you swaddling cloths,
you who are shimmering with light?*

This is how Ephrem describes the way Christ made himself small in order to be born from Mary:

*Lest he confuse the onlookers
by his greatness,
he reduced himself,
from the universe into the land of the
   Hebrews,
and from this country to Judea, and from
   there to Bethlehem,
till he filled only the little womb [of
   Mary].*

Christmas as depicted in the Etschmiadzin Gospel Book that is now kept in Erevan, Armenia (6th century). The "Madonna Platytera" holds in her lap the Christ child in a mandorla—the symbol of the Logos in the material world.

*Rejoice, O Blessed one,
The Lord is with you.
Rejoice, O Blessed one,
you radiant heaven.
Rejoice, O Blessed one,
you virgin rich in virtue,
you golden vessel
for the divine manna.
Rejoice, O Blessed one,
you slake every thirst
with the water
of an inexhaustible spring.
Rejoice, immaculate mother,
you have borne Him
who was before you.*

*Rejoice, purple garment,
you have clothed
the King of heaven and earth.
Rejoice, mysterious book,
you let the world read
the divine Word,
the Son of the Father.*

Epiphanius, "Hymn to Mary"

*Above:* Devotional ampulla for holy water or oil for anointing. It served pilgrims in the time of Gregory the Great (ca. 600). The design shows a Madonna Platytera (Cathedral Museum, Monza).

*And as he became the mustard seed in our garden
and the little beam for our eye,
he went up, he spread himself out
and filled the world.*

Of somewhat more recent origin is the "Rejoice" hymn to Mary (*), ascribed to Epiphanius of Salamina. He was born in Palestine, lived for a long time as a monk in Egypt, then spent thirty years as the abbot of a monastery in Palestine, and finally was metropolitan in Constantia (Salamis) on Cyprus. He was a zealous promoter of monasticism and a fanatical opponent of all heresies. He died in the year 403.

One of the most outstanding poets of the old Latin Church was Aurelius Clemens *Prudentius,* born in Spain in 348. He held high government posts in the imperial court but spent his last years in ascetical seclusion. He died some time after 405. We print here an excerpt from his *Dittochaeon* ("Twofold Feeding"), which consists of forty-eight epigrams:

*When God was ready to appear, Gabriel, the messenger, came down from the high throne of the Father and suddenly entered the virgin's dwelling....*

*He said: "The Holy Spirit will fill you, Mary, and you will bring forth the Christ, holy virgin." Here the wise men bring gifts for the Christ child at the virgin's breast: myrrh, frankincense, and gold.... The mother stands amazed at the great honor and that she has borne God, who is both man and the highest king....*

The next significant contribution to the literature on Mary comes from the time of the Council of Ephesus. At the Council *Cyril,* the patriarch of Alexandria—evidently a great orator and as ambitious as he was domineering—prevailed against Nestorius and his followers in Constantinople and Antioch. This subsequently caused the splitting off of the Nestorian Church from the Imperial Church. In this dispute it developed that the population had already begun to take a lively interest in the person and position of Mary. In Ephesus there were large demonstrations, in which cries of "Hail to the Mother of God" (Theotokos) and "Long live Cyril" thundered out. Cyril's prayer at the conclusion of the Council became famous (*).

After the Council of Ephesus the hymns and prayers to Mary began to accumulate. This was especially true for the Christian East. An interesting example is the Ethiopian manuscript called *Weddase Maryam* ("Book of the Praise of Mary"), which must have been written at some time between the Councils of Ephesus and Chalcedon. The text is made up of prayers to Mary for the thirty-two feast days in her honor.

Around 450 *Caelius Sedulius* composed a *Paschale Carmen* (Easter poem) in hexameters. He is probably the source of the phrase "alone of all women," which was often used later:

*Hail, holy Mother, you have borne the king
who rules heaven and earth throughout the ages,
whose reign embraces the universe, a kingdom without end.
Your blessed womb united the joys of the mother
with the spotless honor of the virgin.
There was none like you
and none like you shall be in time to come,
for you found favor with Christ, alone of all women.*

Here is another Latin hymn to Mary by Sedulius (*Martin Luther* later translated it into German):

*Divine grace from heaven great
Overflowed into the chaste mother,
a maiden bore a secret pledge,*

Devotional objects from the earliest period of Marian hymns and prayers:

*Left:* A terra cotta panel from Carthage (5th century).

*Center:* Gold medallion with a Platytera Theotokos (Constantinople, late 6th century), which was worn by a bishop (Dumbarton Oaks Collection, Washington, D.C.).

*Right:* A gilded Roman glass bowl from the 4th century shows Mary in the worshipping posture of antiquity, thus linking Christian and classical prayer (Vatican Museums).

*unknown to nature.*
*The tender, chaste house of the heart*
*soon became a temple of God,*
*whom no man touched or knew,*
*found pregnant by God's word.*
*The noble mother has given birth,*
*to the one whom Gabriel promised,*

*We greet you, Mary, Mother of God, you venerable treasure of the whole world,*
*you inextinguishable lamp, crown of virginity,*
*scepter of orthodox doctrine, everlasting temple,*
*dwelling of him whom no dwelling can contain!*
*Mother and virgin, we greet you!—*
*you who in your virginal womb enclosed*
*the Measureless and Incomprehensible,*
*through whom the Holy Trinity was glorified and adored,*
*the precious cross of the Savior exalted and revered;*
*through whom heaven triumphs, the angels and archangels rejoice,*
*the devils are driven out;*
*through whom the Tempter is overcome*
*and the fallen creature is lifted up to the heavens.*

Cyril's prayer at the conclusion of the Council of Ephesus (431)

*whom St. John welcomed with a leap*
*while still within his mother's womb.*
*He lay in the hay with great poverty,*
*the hard manger did not put him off;*
*a little milk was his food,*
*for him who never let the little birds go*
*hungry.*
*The heavenly choirs rejoice above*
*and the angels sing God's praise,*
*to the poor shepherds is announced*
*the shepherd and creator of all the world.*
*Praise, honor, thanks be unto you,*
*Christ, born of the pure maid,*
*with the Father and the Holy Ghost*
*from now to all eternity.*
A contemporary of Sedulius was *Peter,* bishop of Ravenna, who died around 458. Because of his eloquence he was called *Chrysologos* (the golden

*You are the golden lampstand, who bore the bright lamp,*
*for all time the light of the world...*
*You are the sweetly fragrant flower that sprang from Jesse's root.*
*You are Aaron's rod that budded, though unplanted and unwatered.*
*You are the ladder seen by Jacob, which rose from earth to heaven,*
*on which God's angels ascended and descended.*
*You are the bush that Moses saw in the burning fire,*
*yet consumed not by the flame.*
*You are the field in which no seed was sown,*
*and yet living fruit came forth from you...*
*Where is the tongue that can utter what should be said about you,*
*O Virgin Mother of the Father-Word?*
*You have become the throne of the king borne by the cherubim.*
*Let us call you "Blessed" and proclaim your name to all generations.*

Excerpts from the Ethiopic manuscript *Weddase Maryam* ("Book of the Praise of Mary"), between 431 and 451

63

The *Epiphany of Protogenes*, the appearance of the firstborn of creation, comes from a 6th-century illuminated Syrian manuscript. The frontispiece of the so-called "Peshitto" (a vernacular Bible in the Syriac language and script) shows a Maria Platytera between Solomon, the king of wisdom, and "Ecclesia," the Church. In this way wisdom (Sophia) and the Church, important figures associated with Mary, are linked together (Bibliothèque Nationale, Paris).

word). A whole series of his sermons have been preserved. In one of them he says:

*Mary is greater than heaven, more solid than the earth, and vaster than the universe. She received in her womb the one whom the world cannot grasp. She held in her arms the one who holds the entire world. She became the mother of her Creator and nurtured the one who nurtures all living creatures.*

Another Latin poet, *Venantius Fortunatus,* wrote hymns that are still used in the liturgy today. The bishop of Poitiers, he must have died shortly before the year 600. He wrote an elegy on the downfall of the kingdom of Thuringia, seven lives of the saints, and over 200 poems, as well as theological treatises. In one hymn ascribed to him (*Mirentur ergo saecula,* "So let the ages wonder"), we read:

*So let the ages wonder*
*that the angel bore the seed*
*that the virgin received through her ear,*
*and, believing in her heart, bore fruit.*

The idea that Mary conceived by means of the Logos (the Word) through her ear goes back to *Origen* (d. ca. 254). Venantius's style already shows some peculiar features of late Latin that came into their own in the Middle Ages. It is marked, for example, by neologisms and echoes of Greek.

The 6th century saw the emergence of the motif of the *Mater Dolorosa,* the sorrowful Mother of God beneath the cross of her Son. The Syrian poet and hymnodist *Romanos the Melodious,* a baptized Jew, wrote for Justinian (emperor of Byzantium after 527) a Marian lament for the feast of Good Friday, in which he has Mary cry out:

*Overwhelmed am I, O my Son,*
*overwhelmed by love,*
*and I cannot bear it,*
*that I am in the chamber,*
*but you are there, in the wood of the cross.*
*I am in the house,*
*but you are there, in the grave.*

Romanos was the inventor of the *kontakion,* a hymn form in which the person leading the prayers in the pulpit dialogues back and forth with the congregation sitting below. This form was increasingly used in the West as well from the 9th or 10 century onward.

Romanos may also be the author of the passionate Greek song of praise, the *Akathist Hymn,* in which Mary is described as the only creature in whom opposites coincide. She is called the ladder to heaven on which God came down to earth, the bridge for humans to climb up to heaven, the sea that drowned Pharaoh and his army, the pillar of fire that leads those lost in darkness to the light, and the Promised Land, flowing with milk and honey. Then the hymn says:

*We greet you, the space of God, whom space cannot contain, access to the inaccessible mystery.*

*We greet you, a contradictory rumor to unbelievers, but to believers uncontradicted praise.*

*We greet you, who have reconciled the irreconcilable, you who have virginally borne a child....*

In the 7th century the culture of antiquity, mostly in decline by now, was still maintained by the kingdom of the Visigoths in Spain. There the orthodox Catholic Church had repressed the heretical Arianism of the Germanic tribes. The Visigothic bishops established a sort of state church and often exercised more power than the king. One of these bishops was *Ildefonso of Toledo.* We have the following prayer from him:

*I beg you, holy Virgin, that I too may conceive of the Spirit through whom you bore Jesus. Through this Spirit may Jesus come to me as well. In this Spirit, in whom you adore Jesus as the Lord and as the Son, may I too love Jesus.*

In the 8th century devotion to Mary in images and words suffered a severe blow from the *Iconoclast emperors* in Constantinople, who issued decrees banning the veneration of pictures and relics. This was aimed at sharply curtailing the position of Mary in the divine liturgy. Emperor Leo II, the Isaurian, his son Constantine V (nicknamed "Kopronymos," the dung-man, by his enemies), and later Emperor Leo V, tried by every means to end the cult of images, which had been promoted by the monks and which had sometimes practically degenerated into superstition. But they ran into equally stiff opposition, not just from the monks, but also

from the women of Constantinople, who around the year 727 staged a regular uprising in front of the imperial palace. Many adherents of the veneration of images left the Byzantine empire and went to Italy, because the pope and the Roman Church had condemned the Iconoclasts. Even back then the schism between the Roman and the Greek Catholic Church was heating up, although the definitive break would not come until 1054. It is worth noticing that the attack on images in Constantinople was twice interrupted—when a woman came to the throne, under Empresses Irene (780–815) and Theodora (842–856).

*Germanos,* a patriarch of Constantinople in the 8th century, has left us a number of writings. In his old age Germanos fought the iconoclasm of Emperor Leo III and lent his support to the liberation of the Church from imperial despotism. Here is his prayer to Mary:

*Mary, full of kindness and compassion,*
*who—apart from your Son—*
*cares so much about mankind as you?*
*Who unceasingly protects us in our*
*    distress?*
*Who sets us free from temptations?*
*Who intercedes for us sinners as you do?*
*Who decides in our favor as you do,*
*when we fall into despair?*
*As a Mother you have*
*freedom and influence with your Son;*
*you use your intercession to save us.*
*Whoever was cast down*
*and did not turn to you?*
*Who has not been heard*
*after having called for your assistance?*

Germanos died around 733. His successor submitted to the emperor's will. In this century Eastern Christianity suffered severe losses, not only from the Iconoclasts, but above all from the rapid advance of Islam. The sacred places of the Holy Land were no longer in the hands of the Church; Jerusalem had already fallen to the Muslims in 638. But under their protection *John Damascene,* in the monastery of St. Saba near Jerusalem, composed his attacks on the Iconoclasts. This poem of praise to Mary is likewise from his hand:

*Mary, you living ladder,*
*you stand on the earth and reach up to*

*Right:* The Pokrov Mother of God (Madonna of the Protecting Cloak) and Romanos the Melodious (Russian, 18th century, private collection). According to legend, the saintly hymnodist Romanos was urged in a dream by Mary to eat a piece of music. He did, and on Christmas day his ugly voice became tuneful.

*Above:* A detail from the Akathist icon, described below.

*Page 66: The Exaltation of Mary* in the Akathist Hymn icon by a 14th-century Balkan master is one of the most important depictions of the great Marian hymn by Romanos the Melodious (6th century). He was a deacon of the church of the Resurrection in Berytos (Beirut) and received his nickname Melodious because of his extensive *oeuvre* of hymns. The Akathist Hymn attributed to him is the artistic high point of early Greek church poetry. It consists of twenty-four strophes, one for each letter of the Greek alphabet. It is called Akathist because it is sung standing up (*Akathistos* = "not-seated") on the Saturday before the Fourth Sunday of Lent. The twenty-four pictures stand for the twenty-four strophes.

Hail, you who were initiated into God's ineffable decision,
Hail, you who were entrusted with things best shrouded in silence,
Hail, you prelude to the miracles of Christ,
Hail, you essence of all that is taught about Him,
Hail, you bridge for earthly beings to heaven,
Hail, you wonder, much discussed by the angels,
Hail, you agonizing wound to the demons,
Hail, you who bore the light in an ineffable way.

Romanos Melodos, from the Akathist Hymn

*heaven,*
*on you God comes down to human beings.*
*Mary, you door*
*through which God goes in and out;*
*you shell, hiding a precious pearl: Christ;*
*you mountain, higher than any peak—*
*from this rock comes Christ, the*
    *cornerstone,*
*who joins what is separated:*
*divinity and humanity,*
*angels and men,*
 *pagans and Jews.*
*You mountain, onto which God*
    *descended!*
*You book, written by the Lord*
*in the language of God!*
*You tree, nourished by the word of God*
*and bearing fruit from the Holy Spirit*
*in due time!*
*You temple of God,*
*adorned not with gold or precious stones,*

with the similarity in sound between *mare* (the sea) and Mary, as well as with the reversal of the name "Eva" (Eve, through whom sin came into the world) into "Ave," "hail," the first word (in Latin) of the archangel Gabriel's greeting to Mary.

*Ave, maris stella,*
*Dei mater alma,*
*Atque semper virgo,*
*Felix coeli porta.*
*Sumens illud Ave*
*Gabrielis ore,*
*Funda nos in pace,*
*Mutans Evae nomen.*

Another notable feature of this fine poem is that the characterization of Mary as "Stella maris" (the star of the sea) is evidently based on a copyist's error. In 420 St. Jerome had called Mary "stilla maris," a drop of the sea. This was

*Loose the bands of sin,*
*Give light unto the blind,*
*Ward evil off from us,*
*Grant us all good things.*

*Give us pure life,*
*Make straight our paths,*
*So that we may rejoice together,*
*When we catch sight of Jesus.*

From the anonymous antiphon *Stella maris*
(8th century)

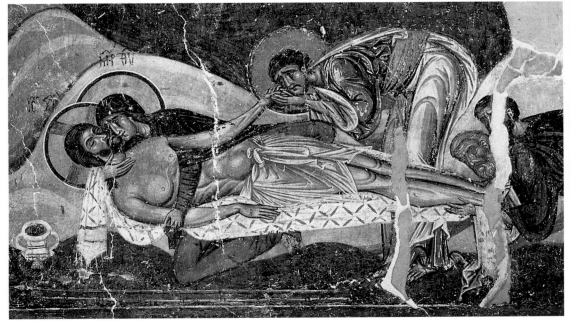

*but with the Holy Spirit*
*and the priceless pearl: Christ.*

When John died in 749, he had an unusual life behind him. Raised at the court of the Caliph of Damascus, he took over from his father the office of treasurer to the Caliph, but withdrew into a monastery around 726. His writings on religion and against the heretics still carry weight in Greek Orthodox dogmatic theology.

An anonymous Latin antiphon, probably from the 8th century as well, plays

changed into "stella," and in that form the hymn had many successors:

*Hail, Star of the Sea,*
*Exalted Mother of God,*
*Virgin now and always,*
*happy Gate of Heaven.*
    *You received the "Ave"*
*from the mouth of Gabriel,*
*Give us peace,*
    *by turning around the name "Eva." (*)*

The lament of Mary was a central motif not just in the fine arts, especially in the Gothic period, but in literature too. Widespread and popular Marian lyrics included such varieties as greetings to Mary and Mary's lament. The laments were dramatized by adding to them a dialogue between Mary and Jesus or John. These dramatic forms, performed in the churches before Easter, became the precursors to the Passion plays.

*Left:* Among the depictions of Mary's lament is the *Weeping over Christ* from the church of St. Pantaleimon in Nerezi, Macedonia (1164).

*Right:* The same theme is treated by Raphael Sadeler after J. Stradanus (ca. 1590) at the Coburg Fort.

*Do not lament to me, Mother, looking at your Son in the grave,*
*He whom you conceived in your womb as a virgin.*
*I shall rise and be glorified.*
*And in glory without end as God I shall exalt*
*those who praise you in faith and in love.*

From the Easter hymn of Cosmas

*Left: Mater Dolorosa*, the Sorrowful Mother, wooden sculpture from northern Germany (ca. 1230). The 13th century also saw the composition of the poem *Stabat mater* ("The Mother stood in pain"). Among the earliest writers of such works was Jacopone da Todi (1240–1306).

*Right: The Mourning.* Relief by Tilman Riemenschneider (ca. 1460–1531), linden wood, ca. 1510 (Mainfränkisches Museum, Würzburg). This scene from the Passion, with its animated gestures and lifelike drapery, expresses the inner movement of Mary's lament. With the finely nuanced lyricism of Riemenschneider's wood carving the Gothic carved altar reaches at once its high point and its end.

The wealth of Marian poetry and its narrative gusto in embellishing the legends of Mary can also be seen in the richly detailed, valuable book covers. Early book illumination provided the greatest scope to the artistic expression of the time.

*Page 70:* Ivory book cover with twelve scenes: above, the *Adoration of the Magi*, below, the *Presentation in the Temple*. The carving comes from the early 10th century and is found today in the Victoria and Albert Museum, London.

*Right: The Mother of God Enthroned* from a Pontifical (book containing rituals performed by a bishop) from St. Vaast in Arras. This northern French parchment manuscript, ca. 1050, contains richly ornamented images and two full-page miniatures.

*Left:* This Greek Psalter (1077) from Constantinople shows Mary as Theotokos (Austrian National Library, Vienna).

*Top:* This Greek manuscript from the 10th century (Lateran Library, Rome) shows in the medallions over the main figures the prophetess Anna and Simeon. The standing figures from right to left: the Virgin Mary, Christ, John the Baptist, Zechariah, and Elizabeth.

Beginning in the 10th century a new type of Marian literature begins to develop: the *Vita* (biography). It frequently falls back upon the accounts of the non-canonical gospels (Apocrypha) or on later summaries of these. It tells Mary's story anew, but in poetic form and often with all sorts of embellishments and reflections.

The oldest example of this genre is the *Historia nativitatis Dei genitricis* by *Roswitha of Gandersheim,* composed around the middle of the 10th century. Roswitha was a Benedictine nun from the monastery of Gandersheim, west of the Harz Mountains. She came from a family in Lower Saxony, was highly educated, and well acquainted with classical Latin literature. She wrote, among other things, six Latin legends in dialogue—in something like the style of Terence, but with a Christian moral—a historical work about the achievements of Otto I, and a history of the Gandersheim monastery. She had no successor and was forgotten after her death; but around 1500 she was rediscovered by the humanist Conrad Celtis. Her *Historia nativitatis* is written in Latin hexameters and is based on Pseudo-Matthew. Her main theme is Mary's intact virginity. The scene in which Mary resists the marriage plans of a priest with her desire for chastity is the high point of the story.

Another writer who drew upon Pseudo-Matthew was *Wernher,* a priest from Augsburg writing about two hundred years later, the author of *Driu liet von der maget* (Three Songs of the Maid). His style is elegant and attractive, mediating between Roswitha's poem and the later Lives of Mary. He avoids the latter's long, untidy descriptions of miracles. Here is his description of the Annunciation, as modernized by Hermann Degering:

*She strove to understand*
*how this miracle could happen,*
*and what the greeting might mean.*
*The virtuous one stood there anxiously.*
*The angel spoke comfortingly to her:*
*"Let all your cares be gone,*
*O praised above all other women,*
*God himself has chosen for himself*
*a chamber in your body.*

*You are to bear the Savior as your son*
*for men and women everywhere;*
*and he will grant them grace.*
*His name shall be Emmanuel,*
*the Savior of all Israel."*
*This word removed the maid's every fear,*
*so that she found new courage.*

*Thinking about her chastity,*
*she turned to the angel and said:*
*"In truth I cannot understand*
*how this could ever happen,*
*that I should have a child,*
*before my maidenhood is taken;*
*for to this hour I am still*
*ignorant of all those things*
*that have anything to do with the love of a*
*    man*
*I have never ventured into it*
*and I shall always resist it.*
*How could I bear a son?*
*I should find that a strange wonder."*
*Then said the noble angel:*
*"You must entertain no doubts,*
*for, behold, it will be heaven's blessing*
*and the power of the Holy Spirit*
*that create this child....*
*With the dew of his holy Spirit*
*he will sprinkle you, O woman...."*

*She raised her luminous eyes*
*to the high bower of heaven.*
*In the firm confidence of faith*
*she spoke with humility in her soul:*
*"God bless me with his kindness.*
*What I hear you say, Lord,*
*I shall gladly, joyfully, bear."...*

*Then spoke the angel's voice: "Amen."*
*And, behold, from the seed of faith*
*she was immediately with child.*
*God in heaven delayed not,*
*for he was in haste*
*to bring poor sinners salvation*
*by taking on human nature.*
*Then might he well bring himself*
*to stay at an inn so pure*
*as this maiden and mother.*

Later Wernher describes Mary's visit to Elizabeth:

*Elizabeth had already called to her from*
*    afar:*
*"O you crown of all women,*
*how do I deserve such an honor?*
*I must wonder greatly at this,*
*that I should be worthy*
*of your coming to my house*
*with that burden of yours.*
*You bear in your womb the gracious*

*Christ,*
*you virgin-mother of our Lord.*
*What could I now not do without,*
*since you have come to stay with me?*
*For behold, from you joy will spread*
*over all of Adam's race.*
*And so I rightly owe to you,*
*my striving to serve you,*
*and I will right away begin."*

The source for most of the Lives of Mary is the *Vita beatae virginis Mariae et salvatoris rhythmica,* composed in the first half of the 13th century by a German poet in Latin iambic fourteeners. The *Vita* is over 8,000 lines long and a sort of collecting tank for apocryphal sources. It has many repetitions and an abundance of interchangeable and inconsequential details, but it was repeatedly used by later authors for their own versions.

The *Vita* consists of four parts: Book I deals with Joachim and Anne and ends with Mary's betrothal; Book II describes the birth of Jesus, the Flight into Egypt, and Jesus' childhood; Book III carries the action up to Jesus' death and Mary's lament; finally Book IV tells of Jesus' resurrection and ends with Mary's death and assumption into heaven.

One of those inspired by the *Vita* was *Philip the Carthusian,* writing in the early 14th century from Seitz in Styria, who produced an even longer *Life of Mary.* At the end of his poem, on line 10,122, he introduces himself:

*I am called Brother Philip;*
*God, alas, I do not know.*
*In the order of the Carthusians,*
*in the house at Seitz,*
*I wrote this little book.*

His poem begins as follows:

*Mary, Mother, Queen,*
*as the world's Redemptrix,*
*grant me, Lady, such a mind*
*that I may begin this little book,*
*that I may praise you in it*
*and gain your grace,*
*and the love of Jesus, your child.*
*Help me to do this, wise Mistress.*

Philip's version is no doubt the most artistically free of all the known Marian lives. Somewhat older than Philip's is the *Graz Life of Mary* (ca. 1250), which has come down to us only in fragments.

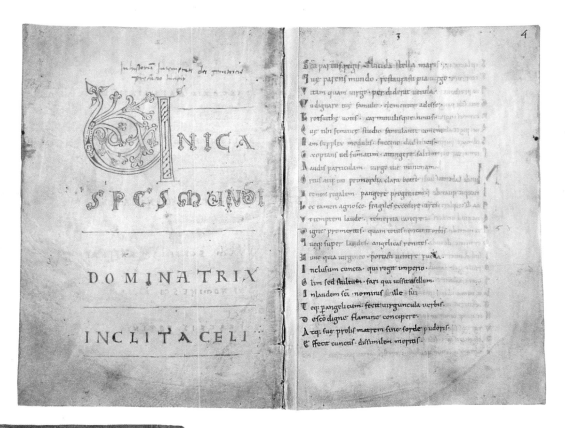

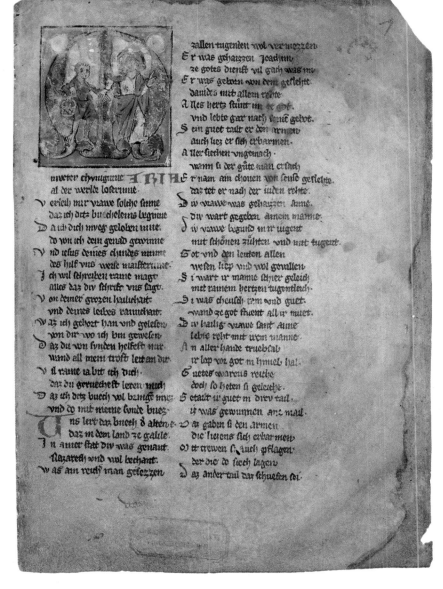

*Upper left:* Wernher the priest, *Driu liet von der maget* (Jagellonian Library, Cracow). This important example of the religious poetry at the close of the 12th century shows the state of the Marian lyric and epic of the day.

*Upper right:* Roswitha of Gandersheim, *Historia nativitatis Dei genitricis*, manuscript from the 11th century (Bavarian State Library, Munich). The great medieval poet and abbess Roswitha created unique works with her dramas and Christian spectacles. She also wrote many poems and legends of the saints.

*Below:* Gothic literature was attracted to the life of Mary and its many legends. Philip the Carthusian, the great poet of that eremitic order, is among the most important authors of Lives of Mary. The Codex shown here is in the Austrian National Library, Vienna. The same work is the source of the lines in the section reproduced at the top of the page.

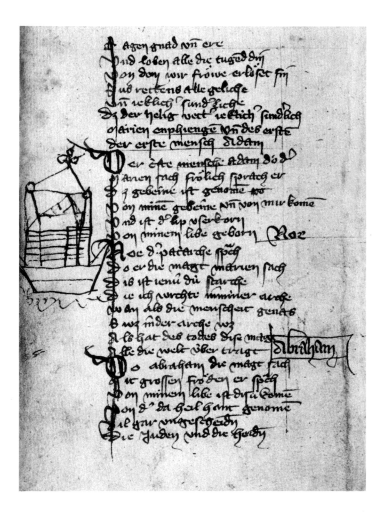

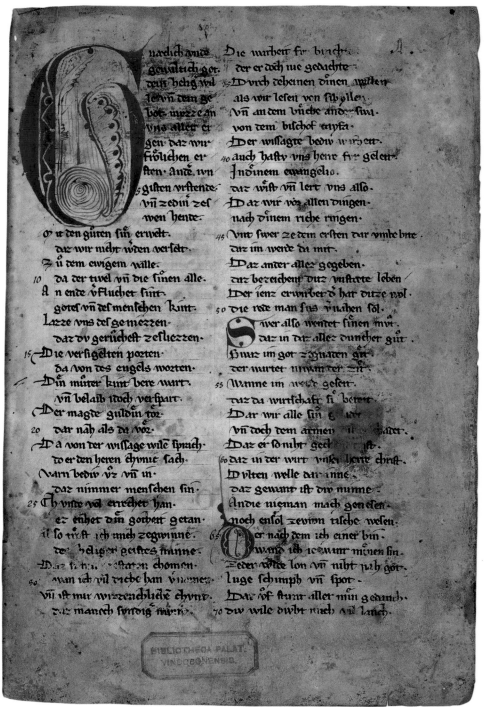

The first 400 lines are based on Pseudo-Matthew, the rest on the *Vita beatae virginis*. Still larger is the life of Mary by *Walther of Rheinau,* ca. 1278 or earlier, which sticks very closely to its Latin original. Its deviations from it consist mostly of theological reflections.

Now completely lost is the *Vita* of a certain Master *Heinrich,* invoked by the Lower Austrian *Konrad of Fussesbrunnen* in his poem about the childhood of Jesus. Konrad's poem, written around or shortly after 1200, strikes a legendary tone, yet one fundamentally different from the fairy-tale style of the contemporary courtly epic, of the sort used to adorn, say, the Arthurian legends. Konrad stays closer to reality.

The life of Mary by the Bavarian *Konrad of Heimesfurt, Von unserer Vrouwen*

*hinfart* (On Our Lady's Departure), shows the influence of Konrad von Fussesbrunnen, but basically relies on the old *Transitus* of Pseudo-Melito. This narrator displays a pronounced feeling for impressive scenes. It is followed by a *Rhenish Franconian* account of the Assumption (13th century), which has echoes of the medieval love motif of secular literature, then by a life of Mary from around Cologne, likewise from the 13th century, which would play a larger part in the creation of later poetic legends. The final life of Mary comes from the Swiss writer *Wernher,* and was probably composed shortly before 1380. As with Philip the Carthusian, Wernher treats the Assumption as a sort of counterweight to the Annunciation.—The most beloved Life remained

Philip's, which also later served as a model for a prose chapbook.

The further we proceed with these and many other lives of Mary into the High Middle Ages, the more powerfully obvious the tendency becomes to weave into the narrative new legends unknown to the Apocrypha and the older lives. These legends speak mostly of the miracles of Mary; they are often borrowed from other saints' legends, and are mostly Latin in origin. Many of them were probably first used as sermon material. As far back as Konrad von Fussesbrunnen we find a whole series of such new Marian legends.

The most beloved medieval Marian legend is about the priest *Theophilus,* who can be viewed, to some extent, as a precursor of Faust. Driven from his

*Left:* The manuscript of *Vita beatae virginis Mariae et salvatoris rhythmica* by an anonymous 15th-century author consists of 57 pages (Royal Library, Copenhagen).

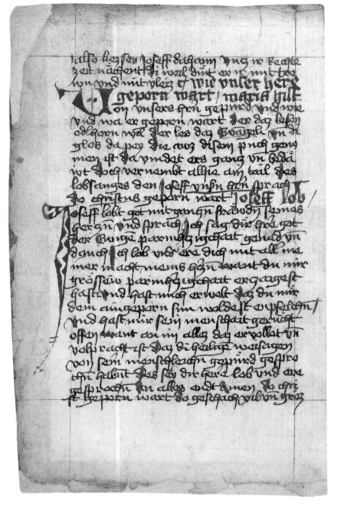

*Right: The Legend of Theophilus,* ca. 1200, by Gonzalo de Berceo, Royal Spanish Academy, Madrid. Mary sets Theophilus free from the devil and leads him back on the right path.

office, he makes a pact with the devil to get reinstated. He later repents and is helped by Mary's intercession. The older, Greek versions of the legend do not occur in manuscript until the 10th century; one of these is in the form of a report from Theophilus's servant. Older than this is the Latin prose version by *Paulus Diaconus* from Naples who spent some years at the court of Charlemagne, wrote an important history of the Lombards, and died in 795. Paulus stresses Theophilus's piety: the priest humbly turns down a chance to become a bishop and is slandered by the man appointed bishop in his place. After Theophilus is dismissed, a Jew arranges the bargain with the devil, in which Theophilus must deny Jesus and Mary. Thereafter he is reinstated in of-

fice, turns proud, but then is led by God to repentance. Mary sees to it that after three days of penance he is forgiven and even gets back his letter of renunciation. He confesses his guilt to the bishop, is pardoned, but dies three days later.

Subsequent Latin versions are no longer presented as eyewitness accounts, which allows for descriptions of heaven and hell. Roswitha too wrote an epic poem *Lapsus et conversio Theophili vicedomini,* which shows Theophilus as a pious and at the same time highly learned man. Around 1100 in France *Marbode* composed another Theophilus epic, less austere and more lyrical. Later French versions that followed the lead of Paulus were by *Adgar* (middle of the 12th century) and *Gautier de Coincy,* a

Benedictine monk from Soissons. Gautier's is the most voluminous treatment of the material and shows a certain anticlerical bias. Theophilus's denial of Jesus and Mary takes place here before a procession of devil worshippers; and after his reinstatement in office Theophilus receives regular instruction in demon worship from the Jew.

About the same time as Gautier, *Radewin of Freising* wrote a version of the legend that primarily discussed its philosophical-theological aspects.

Around the year 1200 the Spanish version of Gonzalo de Berceo was composed, which recounts the gradual transformation of the pious Theophilus into a sinner. His repentance involves touching the lance that pierced Christ's side.

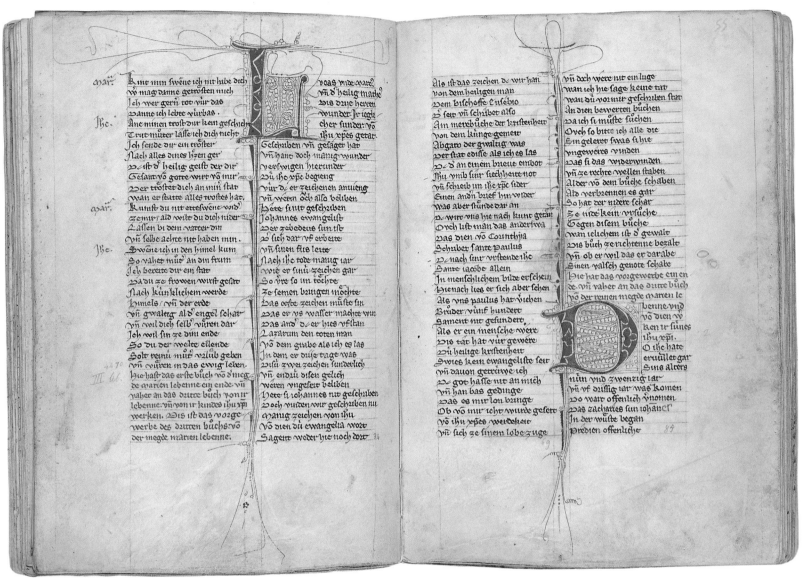

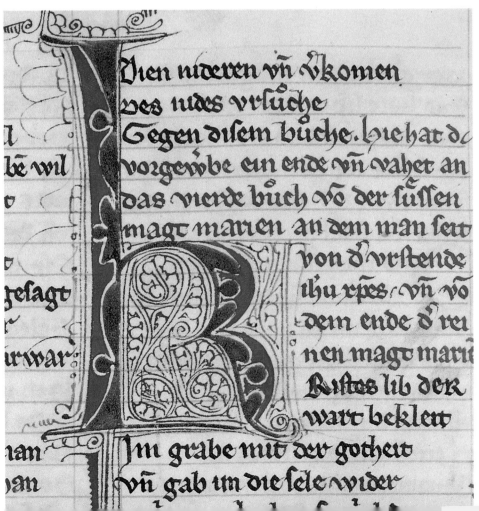

*Above:* This manuscript of Walther von Rheinau, composed in the second half of the 13th century, offers an extensive view of the Life of Mary (Baden Regional Library, Karlsruhe).

*Below:* An initial from the codex mentioned above.

*Page 77:* The legends according to which Mary leads repentant sinners back on the right road are also recounted in the work of Gautier de Coincy, ca. 1222 (Bibliothèque Nationale, Paris). Here the story concerns a nun who after many years of worldly living returns to the cloister and receives the veil back from Mary.

The German treatments of the legend from this period take a freer hand with the material. With *Poor Hartmann* (12th century) Theophilus is not a priest, but a nobleman. Mary plays only a minor role here. In *Brun of Schonebeck* (13th century) the letter of renunciation is signed in blood. But Mary's name is explicitly omitted from the pact, thereby preparing her later role as a mediator. Jesus denies Theophilus forgiveness, but Mary herself goes down into hell and appears with the devil before Jesus' throne.

Closer to the approach of Paulus Diaconus is the version of the Theophilus story in the so-called *Passional,* a very large collection of legends, composed around 1300. But here Mary's intervention is described as a dream sequence. In a 14th-century *Dutch* version the devil appears, as previously in the Spanish, on the way of the cross. Theophilus's repentance is psychologically motivated, but still directly caused by God. A 13th-century *English* version has yet another explanation for the repentance, namely, Theophilus's reaction to the execution of the Jew. In a later strophic version from late 15th-century England a voice from heaven makes Theophilus change his ways. Here too Mary descends into hell to reclaim the contract of renunciation.

In the drama *Le Miracle de Théophile* by the French poet *Rutebeuf* (1255–1285) the pact with the devil is arranged not by a Jew but by a Saracen. Theophilus feels no regret until seven years later, and once again Mary has to go down into hell. Here the poet uses rather stronger language as Mary cries out to the devil, "Et je te foulerai la pance" (And I will stomp on your gut).

In the later German retellings, such as the one by *Helmstedt,* the action begins, as in Rutebeuf, with a monologue by the dismissed priest, but there is no go-between. Instead there is a dialogue between Mary and Jesus. In a 15th-century *Swedish* version the story of the priest's removal from office is told; this time the go-between is a practitioner of black magic. A text from *Trier* brings still more characters onto the stage. After his honor has been impugned, Theo-

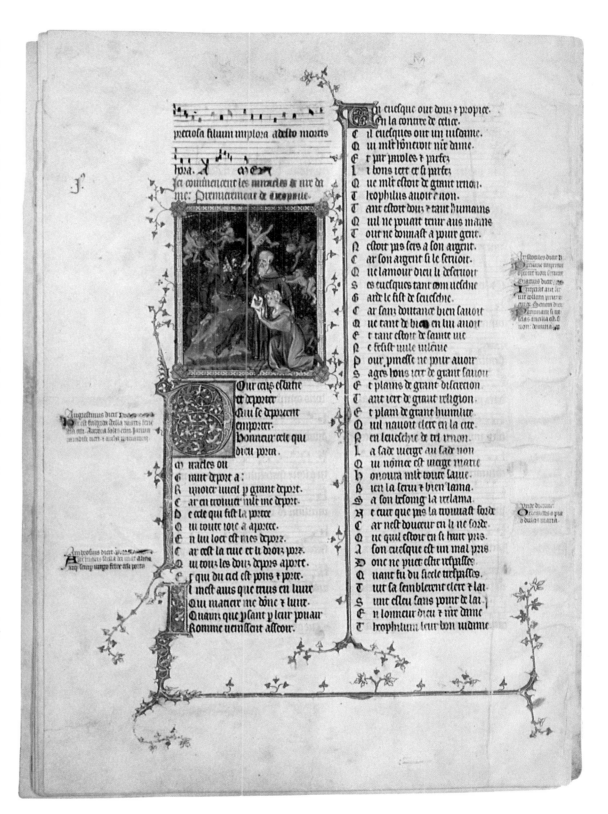

philus negotiates first with an evil magician, then with a Jew, and finally with the devil himself. The Italian Rappresentazione di Teofilo from the same century turns the slanderer of Theophilus into a henchman of the devil. In the end Theophilus renounces the world, is reconciled with his vicar, who blackened his name, and the Jew is whipped by the devil.

The Theophilus motif lost importance after the 16th century because Marian piety slackened as a result of Protestantism. Hence in the final English version of the legend by *Guilelmus Forestus* the veneration of Mary is defended in a long polemic. In 17th-century Jesuit drama the theme continues to be treated, but the focus is now on the allegorical meaning of the figures.—In the following centuries the Theophilus material was superseded by the Faustian motif of the pact with the devil.

Almost equally extensive is the legend of *Beatrix*. The two oldest and best-known versions of this tale come from *Caesarius of Heisterbach,* a Cistercian monk who later became the prior of his abbey in Heisterbach near Königswinter. He wrote homilies and sermons, a catalog of the archbishops of Cologne, but especially collections of anecdotes and novellas. He recounts the story of Beatrix twice, first in his *Dialogus magnus visionum atque miraculorum* (1219–1223), then in his *Libri VIII miraculorum* (of these "eight books of miracles" only two were completed). In the first version he tells of a nun, the portress of her convent, who runs away with a priest from the monastery after leaving the key in front of a picture of Mary. Her seducer soon abandons her; she becomes a harlot, but ten years later happens to return to the area of the monastery and hears that the nun Beatrix is still alive. Thereupon she prays before the image of Mary in the church. Mary appears to her in a dream and bids her take her place in the monastery once again (during her absence Mary herself had "spelled" her). In the second, more detailed version by Caesarius the seducer is a young man, and the nun returns in repentance to the monastery. Caesarius probably relied on his memory of an older source, which would explain the differences between the two versions. It is no longer possible to determine where the Beatrix legend originated.

Later tellings of it from northern France, the Netherlands, and the Lower Rhine follow Caesarius' *Dialogus.* One version in Latin hexameters and another from Darmstadt take over the repentance motif from his *Libri VIII.* But there is also a *British* version, in which Mary does not take the nun's place but has another nun do it. In still another British manuscript, from the early 14th century, an angel substitutes for Beatrix, and Mary goes forth to meet the calmly returning nun.

In *France* again as early as the 13th century an alternative form of the legend was making the rounds. Here the nun settles in an inn near the monastery and from there makes inquiries about what is happening. In the same century we have a variant from *Picardy,* in which after only two years Beatrix, already driven away by her seducer, feels regret, and on the advice of an abbot returns to the monastery. In a 14th-century *Norman* version she is actually seduced by the devil himself, comes back repentant, then hears from a washerwoman about someone's taking her place. She finds the key in front of the Mary altar and her nun's habit in her cell, and guesses that a miracle has occurred.

In the *Miracles de Notre Dame,* a prose account by *Jean Miélot* from the 15th century, Mary takes the nun's place, performing miracles and cures. In *Gautier de Coincy* (1222) the nun is married to her seducer for thirty years and has several children with him. Then Mary appears to him in a dream; she returns, and her husband becomes a monk. In this case there is no replacement of the nun. In another French tale from the same century about the "Trésorière Margerie," the nun feels regret after five years, begs her beloved for her freedom, and then, having returned to the monastery, pretends to be a foster-sister of the Trésorière. Mary gives her back her key and her veil.

The most extensive account of the legend is in a Dutch poem from the early 14th century, *Beatrijs,* where the nun flees the monastery because of a reawakened youthful love. She marries, but after seven years has a fight with her husband and leaves him and her children. After another seven years, in which she earns her living as a maidservant, she moves in with a widow who lives near the monastery, and then learns in a dream that Mary has taken her place. She hands over her children to the widow and returns to the monastery.

The Reformers, as everyone knows, took a critical view of the veneration of Mary and of all the saints. Nevertheless the Protestant court preacher in Amberg, *Hieronymus Rauscher,* could not

resist telling the story of Beatrix one more time. Now the seducer is a "young curate," who chases the nun away after a few days. For fifteen years she has to work as a prostitute, then returns to the monastery and asks the porter about Beatrix. "Yes," he says, "she has behaved devoutly and piously to this day." Beatrix is horrified and wants to leave, but then Mary appears to her and directs her to go into the monastery and do penance. Then, however, Rauscher adds:

*Ah, you pure, chaste Virgin Mary, / who knew no man, / How have you come to this/ that you have to replace / the nuns who go awhoring / and run about in the public brothels. / Couldn't the papists give you any other task in convents except this one? / They might have released you from this and thought you too good for it. / Fie on you, O devil, fie on you, devilish papistry, / can you not see the highly praised Virgin Mary in any other way but this? / If the Virgin Mary had such great authority in heaven, / and it was up to her to condemn and make blessed, / then she would plunge into the depths of hell / such lying papist writers.*

It is interesting that in the 17th-century *Spanish* version the motif of replacement by Mary is missing. In *Calderón* (1680–1681) a knight abducts the nun, wastes his fortune with her, and then wants to force her to prostitute herself. She refuses and returns to the convent. In *Lope de Vega's* (1562–1635) play *La encomnienda bien guardada* (1610) the superior of a monastery is seduced by her majordomo and abducted with the help of the sacristan. She repents and meets a shepherd looking for a lost lamb. Meanwhile both men have abandoned her, but all three can return to the monastery, because Mary had their place taken by three angels. Yet another treatment of the story can be seen in a writer known only by his pseudonym *Alonso Fernandez Avellaneda* (famous for his second part of *Don Quixote,* which was published before Cervantes'). Avellaneda links together motifs from different earlier versions—the motif of the youthful love from *Beatrijs,* Calderón's theme of impoverishment, and the role of the pimp—and, as in Lope de Vega, the seduced woman is the superior of the convent. Here the lover plays a greater role than in the earlier versions. Mary once again stands in for the nun, and even replaces the robbed church treasury and the rifled cashbox of the seducer's parents.

We shall return to modern variations of the Beatrix theme.

Another oft-told legend concerns the *little Jewish boy.* It is first mentioned by *Gregory of Tours,* a bishop and writer known for his history of the Franks. A 12th-century version by an unknown author provides more details. A Jewish boy in a great city where rich Jews live is sent to a Christian school. There he is attracted to a picture of Mary and brushes away the spider webs on it. Then he observes a communion service, sneaks in, and takes the consecrated bread. He is caught and supposed to be killed. He is thrown into an oven, but Mary keeps him unharmed because he cleaned her painting. She encourages him: "Get baptized and become a child of God. Even if your father is your enemy, I will be true to you as your mother." The boy calls for the bishop, who pulls him out of the oven, recites the creed to him, and baptizes him. The story concludes with a warning to serve Mary, who handsomely rewarded so slight a service.

Gregory of Tours also tells the legend of *Bishop Bonus* in his *Gloria Martyrum:* Bishop Bonus of Clermont serves Mary and on the night of the feast of the Assumption always says his prayers to her. On one such night he sees the heavens opened and watches as the saints, the apostles, and Mary come down to him. He wants to hide, but is brought out by Mary, who makes him say mass at the altar and gives him a rich, seamless chasuble. After Bonus's death his successor tries to see the same sort of miracle and goes to the church at night, but somehow or other finds himself back in his bed that morning, whereupon he acknowledges his arrogance.

In the Middle Ages there was a whole host of collections of legends, of which the most famous was no doubt that of *Jacobus de Voragine* (ca. 1230–1298), a

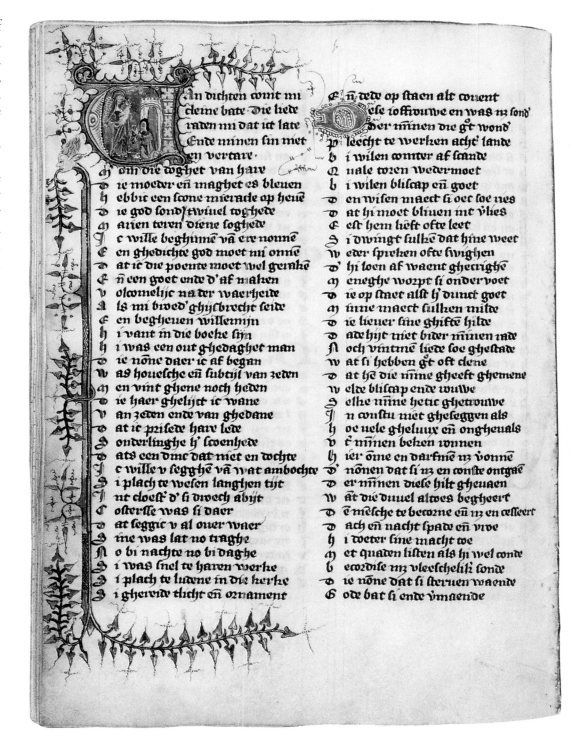

*Beatrijs-Legend*, the first page of a Dutch version around 1374 (Royal Library, the Hague). There are many legends in which Mary substitutes for wayward nuns in the convent and takes their place until they return. The legend of Beatrix is one of these. The nun Beatrix runs away from the monastery with her youthful love, but years later she leaves her husband and her children and returns.

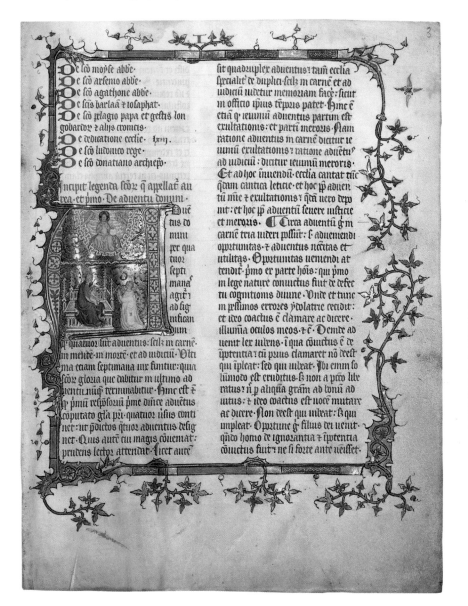

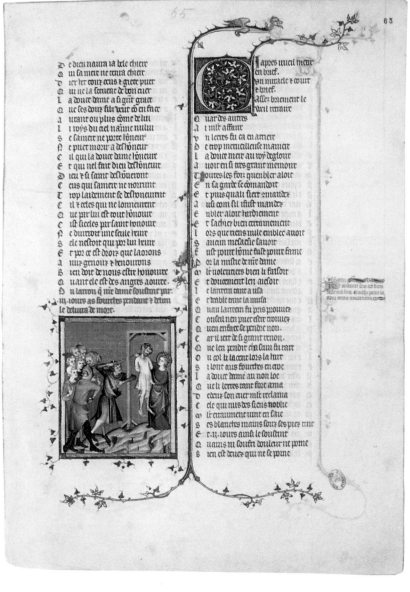

Dominican friar and archbishop of Genoa. After the invention of printing his *Legenda Aurea* ("Golden Legend") became one of the most widely disseminated books in the Western world. It also contains the story of the *hanged man saved:* a thief with great devotion to Mary hangs for three days on the gallows and feels no pain, sensing that Mary is holding him up. When he is found to be still alive, people think that the execution has been botched, and try to behead him. But Mary stays the hand of the executioner, and he is set free.

There were also collections of Marian legends such as the twenty-five by *Gonzalo de Berceo* (ca. 1200), the 360 legends of the *Cantigas de Santa Maria* (ca. 1250) by *Alphonse the Wise of Castille*, the *Miracles de Notre Dame* by Gautier de Co-

incy. In Germany there was the already-mentioned *Passional* and the collection of *Der maget crone* (the maid's crown) from the 14th century.

In these legends Mary appears in thousands of different situations and with ever new modifications, but always as the crowned Queen of Heaven, and always too as the kind, forgiving helper of the poor, the oppressed, and sinners. She always puts mercy before justice. Criticism of this concept had to wait until the rise of humanism and the Reformation, as the example of Hieronymus Rauscher shows.

*Right:* Among the legends in which Mary takes pity on sinners is the one about the rescue of the thief from the gallows. The depiction comes from an illustration of the miracles of Mary (*Miracles de la vierge*) by Gautier de Coincy (Bibliothèque Nationale, Paris).

*Page 81:* Cantiga 66 from the *360 Cantigas de Alfonso X* (Royal Spanish Academy, Madrid). Alfonso the Wise (1226–1284), king of Castille and León, was considered one of the most learned princes of the Middle Ages. He promoted poetry, jurisprudence, astronomy, and historiography. The legend pictured here tells how Mary rewards the faithful bishop for saying mass, as she had bidden, with rich vestments.

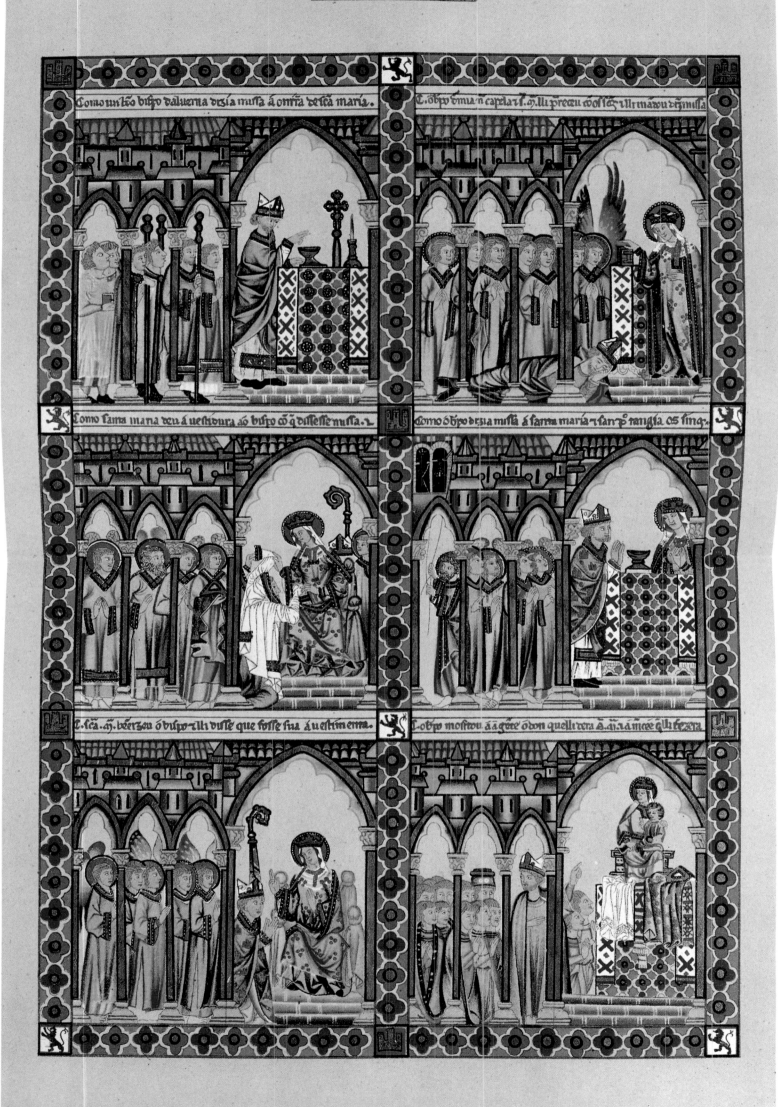

Como un bõo bispo dalueria drzia missa á onrra de sãta maria.

C. o bispo õ mia n capela i. m. lli precou õõ sõ ri llr maiou drzi missa

Como sãta maria deu á uestidura ao bispo cõ q dissesse missa.

como o bispo drzia missa á santa maria ri san p rangia os sing.

C. sãa. m. béerzou õ bispo ri lli disse que fosse sua áuestimenta.

C o bispo mostrou áa gẽte õdon quelli dera s. m. á mõõe q lli fezera.

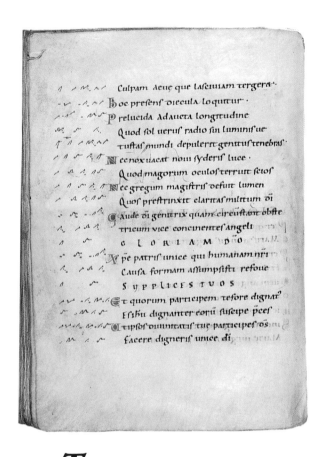

*Left:* The page reproduced here shows the Christmas sequence *Natus ante saecula* by Notker Balbulus (the stammerer), a monk of St. Gall, Switzerland.

*Right:* This picture of Notker from the end of the 11th century is in the State Archives, Zurich.

*Page 83, left:* From a manuscript in the State Library, St. Gall, written between 1516 and 1526 by the monk Hans Conrad, this is the first page of a *Salve, Regina* prayer.

*Page 83, center:* The "Arnstein Marian Prayer" or "Marienleich," ca. 1150, is part of the prayerbook of the Countess Guda, who was a cofoundress of the Premonstratensian double monastery of Arnstein. The manuscript is found today in the Main State Archives, Wiesbaden.

*Page 83, right:* The "Melk Song of Mary" from the Cathedral Chapter Library in the Monastery of Melk, Austria. The author is anonymous. One of the great centers of Baroque monastic life, Melk is famous for its splendid library, rich in tradition.

*T*he pure Marian lyric poetry of the High and Middle Ages is probably more important than the lives and legends. With its admiration and praise for the virginal Mother of God, its prayers to her and requests of her, it has links with the poetry of late antiquity. By way of novelty it contains a special form of the Marian lyric, the *lament of Mary:* Mary stands beneath the cross of her son and bemoans his death.

One Latin hymn invoking Mary (*) is ascribed to *Hrabanus Maurus,* who in the Carolingian period made the monastery school of Fulda the most famous in Germany. He then became archbishop of Mainz and the author of Bible commentaries, sermons, and theological writings. He was the teacher of Otfried of Weissenburg and of the anonymous author of the epic poem, the *Heiland* ("the Savior"). He died in 856.

About half a century after Hrabanus lived *Notker Balbulus* ("the stammerer"), a Benedictine monk in the monastery of St. Gall, who wrote about forty Latin sequences (hymnlike texts, sung in the mass after the Alleluia), some to his own melodies. He also wrote an anecdotal life of Charlemagne and many other hymns and sermons. He died in 912. Here is a passage from his famous Christmas sequence, *Natus ante saecula: Rejoice, you who have given birth to God—the angels who surround you take the place of a midwife; they sing the glory of God. Christ, the Father's only child, you who took on human shape on our behalf, give life to those who kneel before you ...*

In an anonymous 10th-century prayer we find this excerpt:
*You who have borne the source of immortality, grant me life, when I am dead through sin.... Make me worthy, O pure Virgin, to receive sanctity, that I may be saved in body and soul.*

*Give me repentance, let me acknowledge my guilt, that I may praise and laud you all the days of my life, for you are blessed and glorified to all eternity.*

As early as the lyric poetry of the 10th and 11th centuries we see the beginnings of a change in the understanding of Mary. She is no longer just the distant Queen of Heaven but the mild, gracious mother, for example in *Peter Damiani,* who died in 1072:
*Finally, let us turn to you in the name of love. We know your kindness and love. Your Son and your God has loved us in you and through you with boundless love. And we also turn to you because you have a special task to perform in God's plan of salvation: It does not please God that you should be inactive. He would have you use every opportunity to support the weak and show them mercy.*

Sometime in the 11th or 12th century the famous *Salve Regina* was composed, with a content similar to Peter Damiani's prayer. It remains the most beloved hymn in the Catholic world. In 1140 we find it for the first time in an antiphonal, a collection of responsorial hymns used in the liturgy. It is attributed by many to *Adhemar,* bishop of Le Puy, a leader in the First Crusade, who had died by 1098 (*). Others credit the hymn to Herman the Lame, a chronicler of Reichenau, who died in 1054.

At the beginning of the 12th century we meet *Lady Ava,* who died as a cloistered nun in 1127 at Melk on the Danube—the first poet in the German language whom we know by name. Her style is simple and free of rhetorical artifice, but is already marked by the mysticism of the later Middle Ages:
*She was the most glorious of all virgins; since, from the very beginning, she stayed*

*All the prophets greet you, O early proclaimed one,*
*Through the Spirit of the Father, poured out into you,*
*Mother of God, who brings the prophecy to fulfillment,*
*Virgin Mary.*

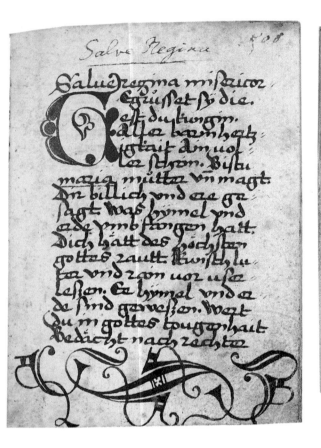

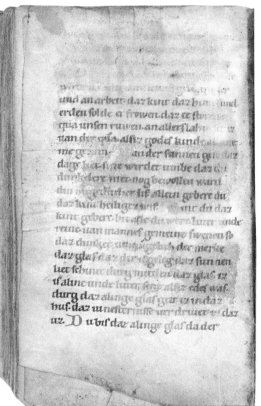

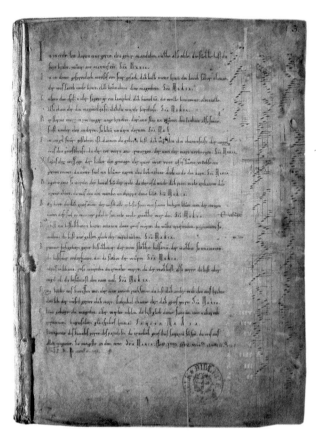

perfectly true to what she had promised: to be God's virgin and to avoid everything human; for the bliss of the world—she, the pure one, within and without....

Somewhat later, around 1150, the *Arnstein prayer to Mary* was composed:
*The light of day comes forth from the sun,*
*yet the sun is left no darker.*
*Nor was your virgin body stained.*
*Yet you have borne the child, holy Lady.*

From about the same time comes the *Marian song of Melk:*
*Then you bore the Son of God,*
*who washed eternal distress*
*from all our earthly sins*
*with his holy blood—*
*for this let him be praised forever –*
*so we wish to greet you, Holy Mary.*

Around this time *Peter Abelard* (1079–1140) was a famous teacher in France. Philosopher, theologian, and lover of Eloise, his bold theories and skeptical treatment of church authority kept causing scandal. He wrote a poem about the presentation of Jesus in the Temple of Jerusalem:
*The Lord comes to his Temple.*
*The parents present Christ,*
*Who is completely without sin,*
*but who submits to the law.*

*You, the truly virginal Mother of the Highest,*
*Bear, in reverent obedience, God,*
*Who became flesh.*
*Humbly you let yourself be purified*
*For your sinless Son.*
*In the high Temple Simeon receives you.*
*In his aged arms he takes, in holy ecstasy,*
*The Savior promised to us,*
*The image of redemption—Christ, the long-awaited.*

Hrabanus Maurus

## Salve Regina

*Salve regina, mater misericordiae, vita, dulcedo et spes nostra, salve!*
*Hail, holy Queen, Mother of Mercy,*
*Hail, our life, our sweetness, and our hope!*
*To you do we cry, poor banished children of Eve,*
*To you do we send up our sighs, mourning and weeping in this vale of tears.*
*Turn then, most gracious advocate,*
*Your eyes of mercy toward us,*
*And after this our exile show unto us*
*The blessed fruit of your womb, Jesus.*
*O clement, O loving, O sweet Virgin Mary!*

Adhemar, bishop of Le Puy

83

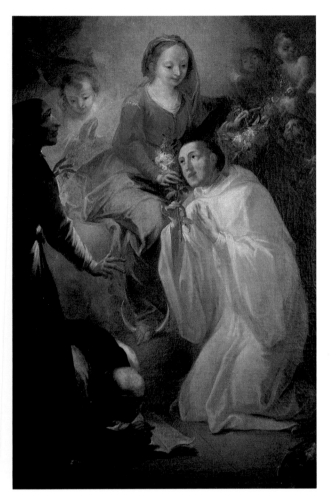

*Enter, queenly Virgin,*
*with the sacrifice present your child,*
*the eternal Father's true Son,*
*who has appeared for our salvation.*

The best-known German contemporary of Abelard is the abbot *Rupert of Deutz,* who lived until 1135. His many theological writings won him wide recognition in Germany. They were, of course, far more conservative than Abelard's. Here are two of his short poems to Mary:

*When you were born, Mary,*
*the true dawn appeared to us,*
*a harbinger of the everlasting day.*
*As the aurora announces the end of night*
*and greets the new day,*
*so your birth brought the end of pain*
*and the beginning of comfort,*
*the end of mourning and the source of joy.*
*Just as the moon shines not with its own*
*    light,*
*but receives it from the sun,*
*so you are shining, not from within,*
*but from the grace of God, you,*
*O "full of grace."*

when he writes, *Amor vincit timorem* (love conquers fear). This basic attitude corresponds to Marian mysticism, of which Bernard is the most important representative. In his poetry Mary is glorified as the advocate of sinful humanity.

Another figure from the 12th century is *Hildegard of Bingen*, who had visions even as a child and composed about seventy spiritual songs, which she set to music herself. Among her *Carmina* we find this prayer (originally in Latin):
*O bright Mother of sacred healing,*
*through your holy Son you have*
*poured oil of anointing on the wound and*
*    woe of death,*
*which Eve brought us to our misery.*
*You have annihilated death*
*and built up new life.*
*Pray for us to your Son,*
*Mary, Star of the Sea!*
*You mediator of life, you bliss full of*
*    splendor,*
*you sweetness of all joys, of which you*
*    lacked none.*

By contrast, the *Marian sequence from Muri,* a Benedictine monastery in the Aargau canton in northern Switzerland, was written in German interlarded with bits of Latin:
*Ave, vil liehtu maris stella,*
*ein lieht der cristinheit, Maria,*
*alri magede lucerna....*
*Hail, you brilliant star of the sea,*
*you light of Christendom, Mary,*
*lamp of all virgins.*
*Rejoice, God's chamber,*
*locked door.*
*Now see, what a pure vessel you were, O*
*    virgin, when you bore the one*
*who created you and all the world,*
*now see, what a pure vessel you were, O*
*    virgin.*
*Send to my mind,*
*O Queen of Heaven*
*true sweet speech,*
*that I may praise the Father and the Son*
*and the most Holy Spirit.*

Step by step with the political upswing of France in the 12th century, the French Church also took over the religious leadership in the West. Its chief spokesman was *Bernard of Clairvaux* (1090–1153), first a monk at Citeaux in Burgundy, later abbot of its daughter house in Clairvaux (Claravallis). His Cistercian order soon wrested supremacy from the monks of Cluny, who had become highly secularized, and through Bernard it became the great power of the 12th-century church. Bernard was a great preacher—for this he

The Benedictine nun Hildegard of Bingen (1098–1179) dictates her visions for the codex *Scivias* (Abbey of St. Hildegard, Eibingen). She is considered one of the most important women in the Middle Ages. Her wide knowledge of cosmology, medicine, and music marked her both as an influential mystic and as the author of Marian lyric poetry.

*Dearest Mother, please look*
*on your people, who confidently*
*honor you as their mother,*
*longing for your help and consolation.*
*Bless us in your heart,*
*comfort us in our pains,*
*stand by us in all distress,*
*show us Jesus after our death.*

Hildegard of Bingen

was called "Mellifluous Doctor"—and his writings had a decisive influence on the religiosity of the later Middle Ages. Moreover, he was an important poet. Here are a few examples of his Marian poetry:
*I greet you, Mary, full of grace,*
*the Lord is with you!*
*With you is the Father,*
*who makes his Son yours.*
*With you is the Son,*
*who in a wonderful mystery*
*hides in your motherly womb.*
*With you is the Holy Spirit,*
*who sanctifies you with the Father and*
*    the Son.*
*Truly, God is with you, Mary.*

*The Most Holy Trinity designated
 your name, Mary—
the name that, after your Son's name,
is above all other names.
Your name, Mary, was taken
from the treasure house of the deity....
All praise and blessing be to you,
invoked and honored in all humility.
Keep us from all danger ...
 Mary, you found grace with God.
He remains in you, and you in him.
You clothe him with a human body,
and he clothes you with his glory.
With a cloud you cover the sun,
and are yourself covered by the sun.
 Who was obedient to whom? God to
 humans!*

*God, to whom all power and might is
 subject,
obeys Mary, and not only her,
but Joseph too,
What to admire more?
The unique abasement of the Son,
or the wondrous dignity of the mother?...
That God obeys a human
is unmatched humility;
and that a woman gives orders to God
is unparalleled sublimity.
 Mary, you had the good fortune
to find grace with your Son,
to bring forth life and salvation;
grant that we too may come unto your
 Son,
he who was given to us through you;*

*may he also accept us through you....*

In other hymns Bernard compares the Virgin with an aqueduct that channels God's grace to believers, and with the aroma of a fruit, which lingers on the hand long after the fruit has been eaten. Writing about the name of Mary, Bernard says the following:
*It means, when interpreted, "Star of the Sea" .... Just as the star sends out rays without being damaged, so the Virgin gives birth unimpaired... . She sparkles through her good deeds, she shines through her good example... When the winds of temptation arise, when you run into the cliff of affliction, look up to the star, call on Mary....*

At the beginning of the 13th century

lived one of the great medieval saints, *Francis of Assisi.* His real name was Giovanni Bernardone, but his father always called him Francesco. Born in 1182 the son of a rich cloth merchant, he converted from his worldly way of life as a young man, and from 1208 onwards spent his life as a wandering preacher in total poverty. His free fellowship of like-minded individuals gradually grew into the Order of Franciscans (Friars Minor), the first of the two great mendicant orders. Some characteristic traits of Francis were his lyrical feeling for nature, his boundless humility, and his warm, simple piety. Just two years after his death (1226) he was canonized. Here is his *Salutatio Beatae Virginis Mariae,* his greeting of Mary:

Hail, Lady and Queen,
Holy Mother of God, Mary!
You are the Virgin, image of the Church,
chosen by the Father in heaven,
made holy by his beloved Son
and his Spirit, the Consoler.
In you was and remains the fullness of
    grace,
and all that is good.
Hail, you his palace,

hail, you his tent,
hail, you his dwelling,
hail, you his garment,
hail, you his handmaid,
hail, you his mother.

The spirit of Francis prompted the famous Latin sequence *Stabat Mater,* long attributed to the Italian poet *Jacopone da Todi* and often set to music:

Stabat mater dolorosa
Juxta crucem lacrimosa
Dum pendebat filius.
Cujus animam gementem
Contristatam et dolentem
Pertransivit gladius.

The familiar English translation is by Edward Caswall, first published in his *Lyra Catholica* (1849):

At the cross her station keeping
Stood the mournful mother weeping,
Close to Jesus to the last.
Through her heart, his sorrow sharing,
All his bitter anguish bearing,
Now at length the sword had passed.
Oh, how sad and sore distressed
Was that mother highly blessed
Of the sole-begotten One!
Christ above in torment hangs
She beneath beholds the pangs

Of her dying glorious Son.
Is there one who would not weep,
Whelmed in miseries so deep
Christ's dear mother to behold?
Can the human heart refrain
From partaking in her pain,
in that mother's pain untold?...
Virgin of all virgins blest!
Listen to my fond request:
Let me share thy grief divine.
Let me to my latest breath,
In my body bear the death,
Of that dying Son of thine.
Wounded with his every wound,
Steep my soul till it hath swooned
In his very blood away;
Be to me, O Virgin, nigh,
Lest in flames I burn and die,
In his awful Judgment day.
Christ, when thou shalt call me hence,
Be thy mother my defense,
Be thy Cross my victory;
While my body here decays,
May my soul thy goodness praise,
Safe in Paradise with thee.
Amen.

One work that unquestionably was written by Jacopone was the dramatic hymn, *Donna del Paradiso,* whose high

*Mamma, ove sei venuta?*    *Why have you come, mother?*
*Mortal mi dai feruta,*    *You have mortally wounded me,*
*Il tuo pianger mi stuta,*    *Your weeping cuts through me,*
*Che 'l veggio si afferrato.*    *as if it were the sharpest sword.*

The Virgin answers:

*Figlio, pur m'hai lassato?*    *Son, have you abandoned me too?*
*Figlio, bianco e biondo*    *Son, clear and bright,*
*Figlio, volto giocondo,*    *Son with the laughing face,*
*Figlio, perché t'ha el mondo,*    *Son, why has the world,*
*Figlio, cosi sprezzato?*    *Son, so despised you?*

Jacopone da Todi, from *Donna del paradiso*

Rutebeuf plays with the name Mary:

*Quar qui se marie*    *For whoever marries*
*En tele Marie*    *Such a Mary,*
*Bon mariage a:*    *Makes a good match.*
*Marions nos la.*    *So let her marry us.*

point is the dialogue between Mary and Jesus (*).

John Fidanza, known as *Bonaventure* (and the "Doctor Seraphicus") was a Franciscan and the antagonist of the great Dominican scholastics Albert the Great and Thomas Aquinas. He taught theology in Paris from 1245 onwards, then became cardinal bishop of Albano, and died in 1274 during the Council of Lyon. The *Meditations on the Life of Our Lord* that have been ascribed to him describe Jesus' birth as follows:
*The Virgin arose, stood up against a pillar there,*
*But Joseph remained sitting ... took hay*
*From the manger, laid it at the Lady's feet*
*And turned away.*
*Then came the Son of the eternal God*
*From the womb of his Mother,*
*Without a sound, without injury, in a moment....*

In France the poet and social critic *Rutebeuf*, whom we have already mentioned, wrote in a hymn:
*As the sun through a window pane*
*goes forward and backward*
*without harming it, so were you the intact Virgin*

*When God, coming from heaven, made you his mother and lady.*

In Germany around 1230 we run into a sequence known as the *Rhenish Praise of Mary*:
*Mary, how shall I begin to praise you, since when I do I look at the origins of the world?*
*For heaven and earth portray you in the picture,*
*Mother of God and Blessed Virgin!*
*Mary, you are the high heavens of which the Bible speaks,*
*calling it a perfect shining fire.*
*I recognize that fire in you,*
*when I contemplate your love,*
*most loving of all commanders!*
*You are the highest heavenly realm where God alone is dwelling.*

In the year 1230 *Walther von der Vogelweide* died, the most important lyric poet of Middle High German classicism. He once made the following request of Mary:
*Now we beg you, Mother,*
*and the Mother's Child as well,*
*Mary the Pure and Jesus the good— protect us.*
*Without your powerful help*

*no one can hope to prosper,*
*and whoever would dispute that must be a perfect fool.*

And in a further poem known as *Marienleich* ("Maid and Mother, look...") Walther prays:
*Maid and Mother, look upon the distress of Christendom, you blooming branch of Aaron, rising dawn, Ezekiel's gate that was never opened, through which the king in his splendor was let out and in....*
*A bush that burned, but none of it was scorched or burned; great and unharmed its splendor, untouched by the flame of fire.*
*That was the pure Virgin alone, who virginally became the mother of a child without the presence of any man, and contrary to all human wisdom bore the true Christ, who remembered us.*
*Blessed is she for bearing him who struck dead our death!*
*With his blood he washed away our shame, brought on us by Eve's false step.*

Somewhat younger than Walther was the minstrel and lyric poet *Reinmar von Zweter* (ca. 1200–1260), who, like Walther, was involved in the politics of his day. He writes about Mary:
*A great miracle has befallen us through a*

87

The great German medieval poet Walther von der Vogelweide (1170–1230) captures the religious mood of his age in his *Marienleich*. The text here comes from the beginning of the 14th century. In it Walther uses many Marian images, such as the staff of Aaron, the burning bush, or the throne of the wise Solomon. Courtly medieval poetry and minnesong are linked to the cult of Mary, which had already been in flower for two centuries. The service of *minne* (love) and the service of Mary developed from the same root. The elegant, smooth expressions of courtly speech match the soft charm of the Fair Madonna in painting and sculpture.

Virgin, as all Christians must grant me!

*He whom the endless breadth of heaven never enclosed, whom its height never encompassed, nor the wide, bottomless depths—him her little body enclosed; remember all this miracle!*

*She laid him lovingly in her lap; what miracle can compare with that?*

*He took the breast from her as a child; she nursed him as a mother, she turned her eyes toward him; we believe, she threw her arms about him and kissed him....*

Another lyric poet was the Alemannic *Meister Boppe,* who was active between 1275 and 1287 (*).

A contemporary of the minnesingers and lyric poets was the most important woman mystic of Germany, *Mechthild of Magdeburg* (*), who in 1270 entered the Cistercian convent of Helfta in Eisleben, where Mechthild of Hackeborn and Gertrude of Helfta were nuns at the very same time. Her work *The Flowing Light of the Deity* is intensely mystical and known to us only in Latin translation.

Her fellow nun *Mechthild of Hackeborn,* whose visions were written down by her sister, Gertrude of Helfta, greeted Mary in the *Liber specialis gratiae* with these words :

*Hail, Mary, with that reverence with which God the Father greeted you by his Ave and in his almighty power freed you from all guilt.*

*Hail, Mary, with that love with which the Son in his wisdom illuminated you and made you the brightest star of heaven and earth....*

*I remind you of the work that the Most Sacred Trinity did in you, when it united your flesh with the divine nature to a person, so that God became human and a human God.*

The third of the inspired nuns of Helfta, *Gertrude,* known as the Great, began her literary career in 1289 with notes about her mystical union with Jesus, *Legatus divinae pietatis,* and wrote a book of edification, *Exercitia spiritualia septem.* She died in 1302. She has Jesus say to his mother:

*Behold, Mother most rich in love,*
*I offer you my heart,*
*overflowing with all bliss,*
*and in it I offer you*

*all that divine love,*
*with which from all eternity*
*I freely predestined you, created, hallowed*
      *you*
*before all creatures,*
*and specially prepared you as my mother....*
*And I offer you that ineffable love,*
*in which on the day of your most holy*
      *Assumption,*
*I raised you above all angels and choirs of*
      *the saints*
*and appointed you Lady and Queen*
*of heaven and earth.*

The last of the courtly epic poets, *Konrad of Würzburg* (*), who died in Basel in 1287, was a very versatile, highly educated, and formally perfect writer. He was first a wandering bard, then settled down to work for his patrons in Basel. Along with a series of courtly epics and shorter narratives, he wrote the Marian hymn "The Golden Forge," one of the most beloved poems of the age. In it Konrad appears as a smith who wishes to make jewelry for "the empress of heaven" out of gold and precious stones:

*O if only I knew how,*
*within the forge of my heart,*
*to cast a work of art in gold,*
*and then rightly work in*
*gleaming wisdom of rubies*
*for you, O Empress of Heaven.*
*Then I would forge with the most joyous*
      *desire*
*praise for your high glory,*
*praise that would be brightly shining, full*
      *of splendor.*

The particular lyric form of the *Marian lament* goes back to Ephrem the Syrian. Ever since his day it had become a component part of Byzantine preaching and liturgy. But it did not reach the West until the late 12th century. With the sequence "Planctus antenescia" (She who had never known mourning before), attributed to *Gottfried of Breteuil,* it traveled from France to Germany. In it Mary's lament moves from the death of her Son to the degeneration of humankind and concludes with the hope of resurrection. The *Planctus* was much imitated, first in Latin but then in the vernacular tongues as well. The lyrical lament often turned into a kind of epic, in which depictions of the

*"When our Father's joy was disturbed by Adam's fall,*
      *and he was truly angry,*
*eternal wisdom counterbalanced that wrath with me.*
*Then the Father chose me for his bride, to have someone to love,*
      *for his dear bride, the noble soul, was dead;*
         *then the Son took me to be his Mother*
         *and the Spirit took me to be his Beloved.*
*Then I alone was the bride of the Holy Trinity..."*
*From Saint Mary's message the sweet sound of the timeless Trinity*
      *burst forth from the source of the eternal divinity*
            *into the womb of the chosen maid,*
         *and the fruit of that womb is an immortal God*
*and a mortal man, and a living consolation of endless joy,*
      *and our redemption has become a bridegroom,*
*the bride has become drunk from looking upon his noble countenance.*

Mechthild of Magdeburg, *The Flowing Light of the Deity*

*Ave Maria! Whatever creatures live,*
*whatever fly, swim, wade, walk, climb or hover,*
*to them the Virgin may loudly issue commands.*
*Mary, this is plainly the sign of salvation,*
*it proclaims that you are the Mistress of the broad sea,*
*a glorious road on which the steps of humanity*
      *move surely, safe from all danger.*
*Yet, I would say, one shall not tread*
      *this path so bright, so easy,*
      *with wet feet or unrestrainedly:*
*The foot shall be damp with repentance,*
      *the eyes shall weep for our sins,*
*Thus the Queen of the Angels will keep the heart free of lies.*

Meister Boppe

*Mary, Mother and Virgin, who, like the morning star,*
*guides the poor leaderless poor host, which swims in disarray*
*on the desolate, alien sea of life without foundation:*
      *You are the light that lives forever*
      *and has always shone as their salvation,*
*as soon as the magnet of sin swept them away with its power...*
      *Dominic and Francis*
      *proclaimed your praise to us.*
*The basilisk of hell suffered great damage at your hands.*

Konrad of Würzburg

descriue la forma d'sua pgh[i]era sicome
apparira nel seguente caplo. Et qusi
compie launtemptiou del penultimo caplo:
Cāto33 xxxiiij q ultimo d'laeza q ultima cā-
tica: de nella quale Sancto Bnardo Infi-
gura de lauctore fa vna oratione a lau-
gyne maria ch visibilmete Se gladiui-
na maestade lasci ve-
dere :-:

Ergine madre figlia d'l tuo figlio
Humile q alta piu ch creatua
termino fisso de etino q siglio
Tu se colei ch la humaa natia
  nobilitasti siche l suo factore
  no disdigno difarsi sua factua.
Nel ventre tuo si racese lamore
  p lo cui caldo nella etna pace
  cosi e germinato questo fiore.
Qui se q noi meridiana face
  di caritate q giuso intra i mortali
  se de speranza fontana viuace.
Donna se tanto grande q tāto vali
  ch qual vuol gratia q ate no ricorre
  sua desianza vuol volar senza ali.
La tua benignita no pur soccorre
  Achi domanda ma molte fiate
  liberamete al dimādar pcorre.
Inte misicordia inte pietate
  inte magnificetia inte saduna
  q uantunq in creatura ha di bontate.
Or questi ch dalinfima lacuna

delunuiso infin qui ha vedute
Le uite spiritali aduna aduna
supplica ate p gratia di virtute
tanto ch possa con gliochi leuarsi
piu alto uso lultima salute.
Et io ch mai p mio ueder no arsi
piu ch io fo p lo suo tucti miei pghi
ti porgo q priego ch no sieno scarsi
ch tu ogni nube li disleghi
Di sua mortalita coi pghi tuoi
si ch il sommo piacer lisi dispieghi
ancor ti prego regina ch poi
che tu ch ti uoli q co sui sani
Dipo tanto ueder gli affecti soi.
Vinca tua guardia i mouimenti humani
vedi beatrice con gli beati
p li miei prieghi ti chiuden le mani.
li occhi dadio dilecti q venerati
fissi nel oratore ne dimostraro
q uanto i deuoti pghi li so grati.
Indi alecto lume si adriczaro
nel qual no si dee creder ch s invii
p creatura lochio tanto chiaro.
Et io chal fine de tucti idesii
Apropinquaua sicome io deuea
Lardor del desiderio in me finii
ernardo maccennaua q soridea
p chio guardasse suso ma io mai era
Gia p me stesso tal qual ei uolea
Che la mia uista uendendo sincera
Et piu q piu intraua p lo raggio
De lalta luce ch da se e uera
Da quinci inanci el mio ueder fu magio
chel parlar mostra chal uista cede
Et cede la memoria a tanto oltragio.
Quale e colui ch sognando uede
Et doppo il sogno la pasion impssa
Rimane q laltro a la mete no rede
Cotal sono io ch quasi tucta cessa
mia uisione q anchor mi distilla
nel core il dolce ch nacque da essa
Cosi la neue al sol si disigilla
Cosi al uento nelle fogli leui
Si pdea la sibilla
O somma luce ch tanto ti leui
Da cōcepti mortali alla mia mente
Ripsta un pocho di quel ch paruei
Et fa la lingua mia tanto possente
ch una fauilla sol della tua gloria

*Page 90*: Dante Alighieri (1265–1321), the greatest of all Italian poets, managed to create in his *Divine Comedy* a comprehensive symbolic shaping of the Christian world picture in great philosophical depth and sensuous richness. On the descent into hell and the ascent to heaven Mary is always the protective companion of humanity. In Dante's work we see the liberation of the medieval person for the Renaissance. The page reproduced here is from the last canto of the *Paradiso*. It shows Mary enthroned as the Bride of Heaven and Queen, alongside Christ, who, clothed with the loincloth of the Crucified, stands in the foreground as a symbol of suffering humanity (Biblioteca Medicea Laurenziana, Florence).

descent from the cross, the weeping over Jesus, the entombment, and the return of the mourners were woven together. This in turn developed into the Passion and Good Friday plays, such as the *St. Gall Play* (ca. 1330) and the *Liechtenthal Lament* (13th century), from which the following derives:

*Alas for the pitiful lament*
*which I, a mother, bear in my loneliness,*
*in thinking of death!*
*Weeping was alien to me;*
*ever since I was called a mother,*
*and yet without a man.*
*Now I must weep, since I must see your*
*    death,*
*What pain, ever worse and worse!...*
*O for the pitiful distress;*
*that I am not dead from this pain, ever*
*    worse and worse;*
*It torments me so much*
*that I, poor woman, must live,*
*because of my great suffering.*
*I was completely free from grief*
*when, touched by no man,*
*O I became a mother and bore you:*
*that I must see you this way.*

Another 14th-century Passion play contains this Marian lament:

*Alas, death, you could*
*easily end my distress,*
*if you would send me*
*your messengers.*
*Alas, the sorrow,*
*death wants to part us:*
*Death, take us both,*
*lest he go off alone*
*and depart from me.*
*Alas, my dear son!*
*Alas for your great torment!*
*Alas, how pitifully you hang!*
*Alas, how you wrestle with death!*
*Alas, how your body trembles!*
*Alas, what am I, poor woman, to do,*
*since I saw this dear child of mine*
*suffer such great pain!...*
*Ah, dear child, say a word to me,*
*tell me whether I am your mother!*
*Ah, he cannot,*
*he is gone....*

In the later Passion plays Mary's monologue turned into dialogues with Christ and John, and the women and soldiers got to say their piece.

Another figure active in the early 14th century was *Heinrich of Meissen*, known as *Frauenlob* (= "praise of women"), who lived from 1250 to 1318, a poet and wandering bard at many courts who spent his last years in Mainz. He owes his nickname to his poem about Mary; he was also the author of many lyrics and minnesongs. Thus he sings in the *Marienleich*:

*And I saw on the throne*
*a lady, who was with child.*
*She wore a marvelous crown*
*before the meadow of my eyes.*
*She wished to be delivered –*
*that is how the most holy woman*
*    presented herself;*
*in that hour I recognized twelve precious*
*    stones*
*on the closed circle of that crown.*
*Now see, how she, the courteous one,*
*gave birth to satisfy nature the one who*
*    was given her to bear,*
*she saw sitting before her,*
*between seven candelabras,*
*understanding;*
*and yet she saw him*
*in the shape of a lamb*
*on Mount Zion,*
*    lovable,*
*and she had too what she was destined for;*
*indeed, the amiable one*
*bore the flower, like a crown of blossoms.*

Mary plays an important role, unsurprisingly, in the most famous of all medieval poets, *Dante Alighieri* (1265–1321). In *The Divine Comedy* he combines the highest Christian ideal of redemption through love with the love for an earthly creature, Beatrice. The Virgin Mary appears as the indispensable, crucial means to the attainment of heavenly grace that sinners, including Dante himself, long for. In the *Paradiso* Dante meets St. Bernard (of Clairvaux), who then prays to the Virgin Mary in the final canto:

*O virgin, mother, daughter of your Son,*
*more humble and sublime than any*
*    creature,*
*fixed goal decreed from all eternity!*
*You are the one who gave to human*
*    nature*
*so much nobility that its Creator*
*did not disdain His being made a simple*
*    creature!*
*That love whose warmth allowed this*
*    flower to bloom*

*within the everlasting peace—was love*
*rekindled in your womb; for us above,*
*you are the noonday torch of love,*
*and there below, on earth, among the*
*    mortals,*
*you are a living spring of hope.*

(trans. Allen Mandelbaum, *Paradiso* [New York: Bantam Books, 1984], p. 297)

Then Bernard prays for Dante, now that he has traveled through hell and purgatory:

*This man—who, from the deepest pit in*
*the universe to the heights, has seen*
*the lives of spirits, one by one—now pleads*
*with you, through grace, to grant him so*
*    much virtue*
*that he may lift his vision higher still—*
*may lift it toward the ultimate salvation.*
*This too, O Queen, who can do what you*
*    will,*
*I beseech you; that, after such a vision,*
*his senses may be preserved.*
*May your protection curb his mortal*
*    passions.*
*See Beatrice—how many saints with her!*
*They join my prayers! They clasp their*
*    hands to you!*

(trans. Allen Mandelbaum, pp. 297–299)

Dante's religious and philosophical attitude is based on Thomas Aquinas: God is love, and love is the source of all good ideas and deeds. In contrast to Petrarch, Dante was convinced that one could arrive at the beatific vision through earthly love. His love belongs to Beatrice; Mary remains a heightened heavenly vision that can only be gazed at from afar. Thus St. Bernard addresses to Dante:

*And he said, "Son of grace,*
*you will not come to know this joyous*
*    state*
*if your eyes only look down at the base;*
*but look upon the circles, look at those*
*who sit in a position more remote*
*until you see upon her seat the Queen*
*to whom this realm is subject and devoted.*

(trans. Allen Mandelbaum, p. 285)

Thirty years younger than Dante was the Swiss mystic *Heinrich Seuse* (Latinized to Suso), a disciple of Meister Eckhart, then a wandering preacher. He probably had the greatest poetic gifts of the great German mystics. In his

*Above right:* The Sienese painter Guidoccio Cozzarelli (1540–1615) shows the birth of Christ with Mary, Joseph, Dominic, and Catherine of Siena (Perkins Collection, Assisi). Of special importance for Marian lyric poetry is Catherine of Siena, the great poet on the far right of the picture. She wrote about her ecstatic states, in which she saw apparitions; but she was also a spiritual personality with enormous influence on events. Thus she brought about the return of the pope from Avignon to Rome in 1376.

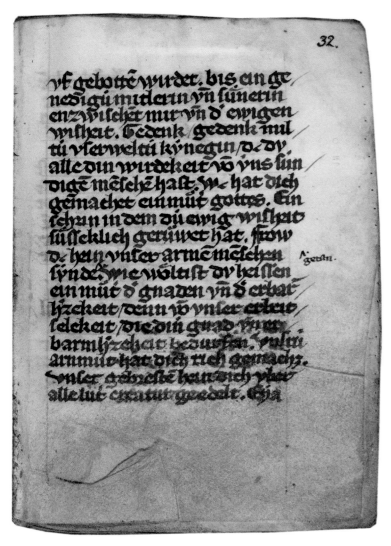

*Left:* Heinrich Suso (1295–1366), a Dominican friar and disciple of the great Meister Eckhart. Through the rich imagery of his writings, above all in his *Little Book of Wisdom*, shown here (Cathedral Chaper Archives, Engelberg, Switzerland), he had a profound influence on the writings of the German mystics.

*Lower right:* Francesco Petrarca (1304–1374), pioneer of humanism. Beginning in 1366 in his *canzonieri* (songbooks) he sang the life and death of the Madonna. His descriptions attest to a new, psychological interpretation of mental suffering.

*Horologium aeternae sapientiae,* he addresses Mary:
*But consider, wondrous Queen,*
*that you owe all your dignity to us,*
*us sinful men and women,*
*For who made you the mother of God,*
*a reliquary for the divine child?*
*It was the sins of us poor humans.*
*How could you be called mother of grace*
*    and mercy,*
*if not for our wretchedness?...*
*When I recollect myself in you,*
*tears of joy spring forth in me;*
*your name is in my mouth and in my*
*    heart,*
*bright as light and sweet as honey.*
*How often have you begged grace and*
*    mercy for us from God!*
*Turn to us and do not forget us!*

Another important mystic was the Dominican *Catherine of Siena,* who had visions even as a child. Although she never learned to write, she became a papal envoy in Florence and exerted such influence through her personality that she prompted the pope, Gregory XI, to return from Avignon to Rome. She dictated her letters and many of her mystical experiences. In the following three poems Catherine speaks with Mary:

*Mary, you prudently wished to know*
*    from the angel*
*how what he proclaimed to you could*
*    happen....*
*Not because you were lacking in faith,*
*but because of your deep humility,*
*since you considered your unworthiness,*
*you asked: how is this to be?...*
*If I rightly understand you,*
*you were not bewildered by fear,*
*although your behavior betrayed*
*amazement and a certain consternation.*
*Thus your clever question showed your*
*    deep humility.*
*In you, Mary, the strength*
*and freedom of humankind are*
*    articulated....*
*Until you had agreed,*
*the Son of God would not come down*
*    into your womb.*
*He waited at the door of your will*
*for you to open it,*
*since he wished to come to you.*
*He would never have entered there,*
*had you not opened with your words:*

*"I am the handmaid of the Lord,*
*let it be done unto me according to your*
*    word."*
*    Mary, I see how the word*
*that was given you, in order to be in you,*
*is nevertheless not separated from the*
*    Father.*
*It is like a word of language*
*that a man bears within him:*
*Even if it is spoken*
*it is not separated from the heart*
*  and remains bound to it.*

A contemporary of Catherine was Italy's second great poet, *Francesco Petrarca* (1304–1374). In contrast to Dante, who still lived entirely in a medieval intellectual climate, Petrarch became the pioneer of humanism and the Renaissance. He wrote many of his works in Latin, and thereby became the model for later Neo-Latin poetry and the literature of humanism. But his lyric poetry and above all his sonnets to Laura were composed in the Italian vernacular, which he decisively helped to unify. He was already very famous in his own lifetime. His 336th canzone (translated by James Wyatt Cook) is dedicated to the Virgin Mary:

*O Virgin fair, in sunshine all arrayed,*
*Who, crowned with stars, so pleased the*
*    Highest Sun,*
*That He concealed within you His own*
*    light,*
*To utter words of you Love presses me,*
*Yet I cannot begin without your aid*
*And His who, loving, set Himself in you....*
*O Virgin peerless, in the world unique,*
*Who with your beauties did enamour*
*    heaven,*
*Whose like there neither was before nor*
*    since,*
*Your sacred thoughts, deeds chaste,*
*    compassionate*
*Have formed a hallowed living temple for*
*True God within your fruitful maiden*
*    womb....*
*O Virgin bright, and fixed forevermore,*
*Above this ocean tempest-tossed the star—*
*For every trusty pilot, trusted guide,*
*Take heed in what a dreadful hurricane*
*I find myself alone and rudderless!...*
*The time's at hand, it cannot be far off,*
*For time so hastes and flies;*
*Virgin unique, alone,*
*Conscience now pricks and death now*

*stings my heart.*
*I pray that you commend me to your Son,*
*True man and truly God,*
*Who'll gather in my final breath in peace.*
(*Petrarch's Songbook* [Medieval Texts & Studies: Binghamton, 1995], pp. 411–17)

The 14th century also saw the songs of the *Flagellants:* these were penitents who whipped themselves. Especially after the havoc caused by the Black Death, which carried off millions of people, they wandered in droves all through Europe. Here is one example from France (*Ave Regina pure et gente*):

*Hail, pure and gentle queen,*
*noblest of all! Hail, you star of the sea,*
*dear Virgin, we greet you –*
*you moon where God hid himself.*
*Were it not for the Virgin Mary,*
*the age would be lost.*

In a Swabian chronicle by *Hugh of Reutlingen* from the same century (1349) we likewise find a Flagellant prayer to Mary:

*Mary, mother, pure maid,*
*have mercy on Christendom!*
*Have mercy on your children,*
*who are still in this wretched world!*

A completely different spirit breathes in a 14th-century French *miracle play,* which is linked to medieval legends in which Mary enters a marriage with a person consecrated to her. Here it is a young canon who has dedicated himself entirely to the Virgin. Then he hears from his uncle that he has inherited a great fortune and has to marry a girl whom his uncle has chosen for him. He refuses and swears that has dedicated his life to "Dieu et nostre dame." But then he discovers that the girl is an absolute gem, not just wealthy but beautiful and of high degree. So he consents, but on his wedding night the Virgin calls on John the Evangelist and several angels, and together they enter the young man's bedroom. She snaps at him:

*How can this be? I am who I am, and you*
*would leave me for another woman? It*
*seems to me that you greatly underestimate*
*my worth and my beauty.... You must be*
*drunk, if you give away all your heart and*
*all your love to an earthly woman. And you*
*abandon me, I who am the Queen of*

93

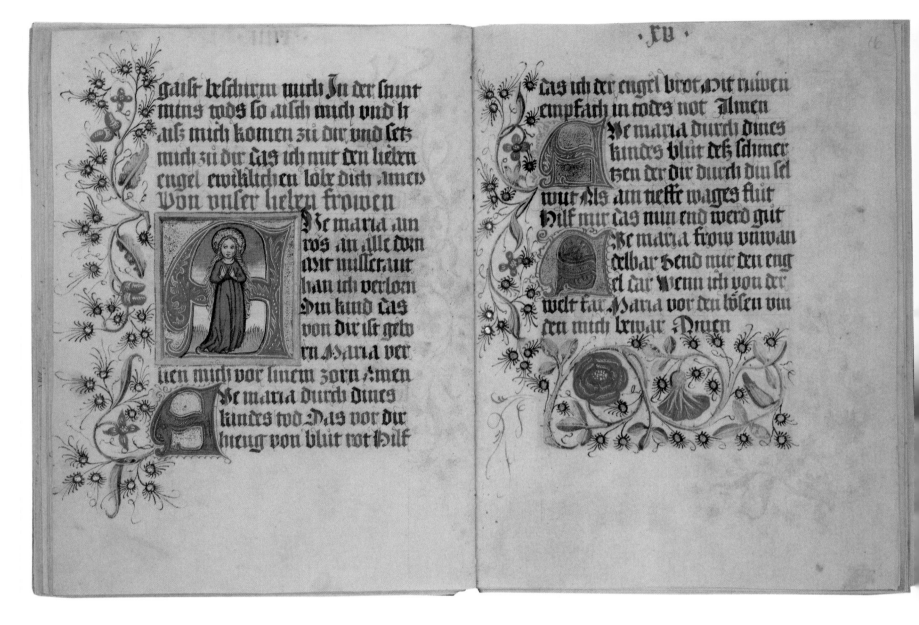

*A ship, laden, in*
*straight to the highest port,*
*bringing us the Father's Son,*
*the eternal true Word.*
*On a silent wave*
*the little ship comes in;*
*it brings to us rich gifts,*
*the lady queen.*
*Mary, you noble rose,*
*make us free from sin.*
*The little ship goes silently*
*and brings us rich freight,*
*Love is the sail,*
*the Holy Ghost the mast.*

Johannes Tauler

*Heaven? Tell me the truth: Where is the woman with more goodness and beauty than I?*

Then she announces to him that he must roast in hell, since he has been untrue to her. The bridegroom tears his hair—and asks his mother to spend the wedding night with him and his bride. She is astonished, and he runs away. The next morning the family finds not the young couple, but the girl all by herself. They assume that the groom has fallen asleep drunk somewhere else. But in the end they find a letter from him, in which he tells them that Mary became very jealous and made a bed for him in Paradise, which he had ruined through his great offense. The bride then decides to follow her husband's example and becomes a nun. The Virgin appears and takes the young man with her to her heavenly home.

One well-known poem may go back to the Strasbourg popular preacher and mystic *Johannes Tauler* (ca. 1300–1361), who is considered a disciple of Meister Eckhart (*).

In 15th-century Italy humanism and the Renaissance were in bloom. In the North, meanwhile, Marian poetry was sticking to the old patterns. The most important German religious poet of the century was *Heinrich of Laufenberg* (ca. 1390–1460), who ended his life as a monk in the monastery of St. John in Strasbourg. He composed about ninety mystical songs and sequences, along with a *Book of Figures,* i.e., the prefigurations of Mary. Here is his account of the Annunciation:

Then came a fine messenger from heaven,
down onto this earth,
he went in through closed doors
and greeted her:
"Hail, Mary,
crown of all women!
You shall bear a child
and yet remain a maid."
"How can I bear a little child
and still be a maid?
My heart desires no man;
you must prove this to me."
"I shall prove it to you,
you noble queen:
the Holy Ghost shall come,
to bring all this to fulfillment."
Gabriel went off again
and guarded her from all pain.
Mary, the very pure maid,
bore God in her heart.

The following simple, tender English Christmas carol likewise goes back to the 15th century:

I sing of a maiden
That is makeless.
King of all kings
To her sone she chees.
He cam also stille
Ther his moder was
As dew in Aprille
That falleth on the grass.
He cam also stille
To his modres bowe
As dew in Aprille
That falleth on the flowr.
He cam also stille
Ther his moder lay
As dew in Aprille
That falleth on the spray.
Moder and maiden
was nevere noon but she:
Well may swich a lady
Godes moder be.

In France at this time lived that country's greatest medieval poet, François de Montcourbier, alias des Loges, or François Courbeuil or Corbier. Ultimately he called himself François Villon. He studied at the University of Paris and apparently fell into bad company, because he was thrown into prison on one occasion for murder and on another for theft. After 1463 all trace of him is lost. He left behind a great ballad, in which he has a woman pray to Mary:

Lady of Heaven, Regent upon this Earth,
Empress over the infernal swamps,
I pray you to receive your humble Christian, That I may gain a place with your elect,
Although I never was of any worth.
Your merits are, my Lady and my Mistress, More great by far than I am a sinner,
Without which merits no soul can deserve
Nor possess heaven. In this I am no liar:
In this faith I desire to live and die....
A woman I am, a poor and ancient one
and ignorant; I never learned to read. At the
church I'm parishioner, I see Paradise
painted, where there are harps and lutes, and
also Hell, where the damned are boiled.
One gives me fear, the other joy and gladness. Make me to have the joy, exalted
[saint].

(*François Villon: Complete Poems,* trans. Barbara N. Sargent-Baur [Toronto: U. of Toronto Press, 1994], pp. 113–15.)

The following poem comes from a Stuttgart manuscript of 1476, the *Prayerbook of George II of Waldburg.* But it may go back to much older sources in the 12th century. In the interval, however, it was reworked many times:

Hail Mary, rose without a thorn,
with misdeeds I have lost
your child, who was born of you:
Mary, shield me from his wrath.
Ave Maria, through the death of your child
who hung before you red with blood,
help me to receive the bread of angels
in repentance when I lie in my death
agony....
Ave Maria, unchanging woman,
send me the angel,
when I leave this world,
Mary, guard me from evil enemies.

Likewise from the 15th century is the well-known and ever popular *Es ist ein Ros' entsprungen* (Lo, How a Rose E'er Blooming), which is still sung to the tune it was set to by *Michael Praetorius* (ca. 1571–1621).

We also have this period to thank for the *Litany of Loreto,* named for the pilgrimage site in Italy. Litanies are long petitionary hymns, alternating between a precentor and the community. Their prayer-clusters are bound together with invocations such as *Ora pro nobis* (pray for us) or *Kyrie eleison* (Lord, have mercy). The Litany of Loreto, which was set to music by Mozart, among

*Mystical Rose,*
*Tower of David,*
*Tower of Ivory,*
*House of Gold,*
*Ark of the Covenant,*
*Gate of Heaven,*

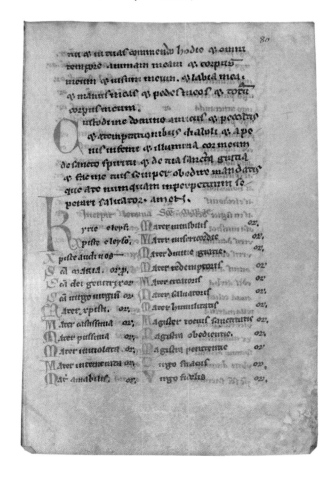

*Morning star,*
*Health of the sick,*
*Refuge of sinners,*
*Comforter of the afflicted,*
*Help of Christians,*
*Queen of angels,*
*Queen of patriarchs,*
*Queen of prophets,*
*Queen of martyrs,*
*Queen of confessors,*
*Queen of virgins,*
*Queen of all the saints.*

From the Litany of Loreto

others, is wholly focused on Mary. It contains an enumeration of her titles and qualities(*).

The 16th century is the age of the Reformation and of the flowering of humanism. Admittedly, in principle *Martin Luther* (1483–1546) swept away all "second order" religion, by which he meant the veneration of saints and relics, monastic life, pilgrimages, processions, etc. Nevertheless he clung to the belief in Mary's immaculate conception and virginity. At first he also professed his faith in Mary's assumption into heaven with body and soul. But later he struck the feast of the Assumption from his calendar. Here are some remarks and prayers from Luther's pen:

*The tender humanity of Christ on this earth came from Mary: without any doing of man or human beings, from the Holy Spirit alone, coming from on high. [1518]*

*All her honors have been summarized in one word, namely, when we call her God's mother. No one can say anything greater about her or to her, even if he had as many tongues as there are leaves and grass, stars in the sky or sand by the sea. But one must also reflect with one's heart what it means to be God's mother. [Magnificat]*

*We cannot conclude from the Gospel how Mary is in heaven, nor is it necessary that we should be able to say everything about how things are with the saints in heaven. It is enough to know that they live in Christ. [August 15, 1522]*

*[On the marriage feast at Cana:] Mary does not command, she does not ask, she only points out the lack.... That too is beautiful: She does not give the servants orders, but points to Christ: Listen to what he says! [Jan. 19, 1528]*

*[On the Annunciation:] It is a miracle that a woman could believe such a thing; for if it were said to one now, she would laugh at it. But Mary simply believed it; she did not grope after it with her reason. Then the Holy Spirit makes her in an instant into a mother. [March 25, 1534]*

*The incomparable thing, what the whole world cannot grasp, much less describe, is that from Mary's flesh and blood he takes his human nature. Then he lets himself be carried in her arms, nourished by the milk of the virgin, then she is a mother and a virgin. And she shall tower over all holy women, so that the angels are amazed. [July 2, 1536]*

*Erasmus of Rotterdam* (Desiderius Erasmus), the eminent Dutch theologian, philologist, and humanist (1469–1536), for a while Luther's ally, was a harsh critic of the externalized Catholic cult of his day. In his *Colloquia familiaria* (1518) he has Mary say:

*For my part, I am very grateful to you for following Luther's example and zealously preaching that it is superfluous to invoke the saints. Because hitherto the godless demands of mortals almost cost me my life. They demand everything from me alone—as if my Son were still a child....The godless soldier, led to the slaughter, calls out to me: Holy Virgin, grant me rich booty! The gambler cries: Be favorable to me, heavenly one, and part of my winnings will be yours!... When I deny something, they cry: Are you the mother of mercy?... The unmarried woman cries: Mary, give me a well-built, rich bridegroom! The married woman: Give me beautiful children! The pregnant one: Give me an easy birth! The philosopher: Let me untie inextricable knots. The priest: Give me a fat benefice!*

Meanwhile much of the material in the literature of the time remained untouched by the great Reformers and the new ideas: *Hans Folz* (1450–1515), a renewer of the tradition of master singing, who for a while had his own printing press, composed a great many religious lyrics, along with secular poetry, comic tales, and shrovetide plays. A Marian hymn from his *Passional* warns:

*O Christian, look and see*
*the ardent weeping*
*of Mary, the very pure one,*
*since she saw her child*
*hanging high on the cross....*
*Look and see her virginal heart,*
*as she implored with flaming desire:*
*"Ah, if only I were hanging with you,*
*all would be well with me.*
*O Son,*
*how am I to look upon the pain*
*of your saddened heart?"*

Another work from the beginning of this century is the following hymn, preserved in a manuscript from the monastery of *Neuburg*. It is a so-called contrafact, that is, the religious reworking of an older secular text.

*I know a pretty little house,*
*a little child runs in and out,*
*it may well be Jesus Christ.*

Marian song by Hans Folz, ca. 1496 from the Codex Germanicus Monacensis (Bavarian State Library, Munich; Cgm 6353).

*Mary is the little house.*
*Hail, you pure maid,*
*hail to your holiness,*
*hail to your clear brightness,*
*Lord Jesus Christ in Israel.*
*The noble little child cries,*
*who shines just like the sun:*
*Mary, the noble virgin fine,*
*wraps the pure, noble child.*
*She gives the babe her breast,*
*kisses his sweet little mouth,*
*"Quiet, tender little babe of mine,*
*then I will be your servant,"*

Also interesting is a *contrafact from Munich* (1505):

*The dearest lover that I have*
*is on the throne of heaven,*
*Her name indeed is Mary:*
*Win us peace and reconciliation...*

...Interesting because the model for this hymn was: "The dearest lover that I have lies in the innkeeper's cellar."

Another contrafact comes from *Nuremberg* (1551):
*A hunter went a-hunting*
*all 'round heaven's throne,*
*what met him on the moor?*
*Mary, the fair virgin.*
*The hunter I'm a-meaning,*
*is one we all know well,*
*he hunts with an angel*
*by the name of Gabriel.*
*The angel blew a little horn,*
*it rang out like this:*
*"Hail, Mary,*
*full of grace,*
*Hail, Mary,*
*you noble virgin fine,*
*Your body shall bear*
*a little tiny child."...*
*"Your will be done*
*without pain and suffering."*
*Then she conceived Jesus Christ*
*in her virginal heart.*

In the 16th century Catholic hym. displayed for a while a strongly anti-Lutheran tone, but toward the end of th century they went back to the old traditions. Here is a hymn by *Nikolaus Beuttner,* who wandered from Franconia to Austria, and whose songbook went through continuous new editions until 1718. Because of its refrains this song was called "the 'leisons":
*In God's name we make our pilgrimage*
*and we desire his grace.*
*Grant us Lord in your kindness,*
*O most Holy Trinity,*
*Kyrie eleison...*
*In God's name we make our pilgrimage,*
*Mary, we come to you as well.*
*Bestow your intercession on us*
*and help us attain your Son's grace,*
*Kyrie eleison...*

Whereas in the 17th century Marian literature played no role at all in Protestant countries or at most a very small one, in Catholic countries it developed further, especially in the legends and dramas of conversion by the *Jesuits. Jacob Bidermann,* born near Ulm in 1578, first a teacher of rhetoric and philosophy, then a censor and assistant to the General of the Jesuits in Rome, is an important representative of neo-Latin Jesuit theater in the Baroque period. In his *Jacobus usuarius* (1613) he brings Mary out on the stage. So does *G. Stengl*

*O you blessed Virgin and Mother of God,*
*how you were nothing at all and despised,*
*and yet God so profusely poured his grace on you*
*and looked richly on you and did great things for you.*
*You were indeed not worthy of any of this,*
*and far and high above all your merit*
*is the rich, abundant grace of God in you.*

Martin Luther, *The Magnificat interpreted,* 1521

*She is dear to me, the worthy maid, and I cannot forget her.*
*Praise, honor, chastity they say of her, she has possessed my heart.*
*I am fond of her, and should I have*
*great misfortune, that does not matter to me;*
*she will make me delight in it*
*with her love and loyalty to me, which she will show me*
*and do all I desire.*

Martin Luther (year of composition uncertain)

## THE BIRTH OF MARY

*...And so, you people, come hither, play your melody*
*to greet the little child.*
*Today her birthday joyously arrives,*
*Saint Anne brings her into the world, and lets you enjoy her.*
*...She greets everyone in humility,*
*for she is always the one who can comfort us*
*in all the pangs of grief.*

Friedrich Procopius, from *Festivale*

in his drama *Deiparae Virginis Triumphus* (1617).

By contrast, *Friedrich Procopius* came from a bourgeois Protestant family. Born around 1609 in Templin in the Mark Brandenburg, he soon converted to Catholicism and worked as a Capuchin in Prague, Vienna, Budweis, and other cities. He was an important preacher and a popular hymnodist. Here are some samples from his *Mariale festivale,* which dresses up old motifs in new forms:

### MARY ON HER JOURNEY

*Ah, why so lonely, why so fast?*
*Virgin Mary, do not hasten,*
*quick, bold, as the wind,*
*ah, why can you not tarry?*
*(Mary): "Why so lonely and so fast,*
*With all my heart I'll gladly tell...*
*It does not suit virgins*
*to go around a great deal among people....*
*Through the mountains, over hill and dale*
*my spirit takes wings in God,*
*like a heavenly nightingale,*
*I sing the Magnificat;*
*they who love to be alone and pray*
*spend their time so well."*
*Man, teach our women that art!*
*God grant you may succeed in that.*

Another poem by Procopius, which like the one above was brought to light by Arnim and Brentano's famous collection *Des Knaben Wunderhorn* (1805–1808), won especially high praise from Goethe in one version. Here is the second of three stanzas:

*I hear two nightingales singing,*
*an angel comes from heaven*
*to Nazareth, and not by chance,*
*into the virgin's room.*
*Oh, how lovely he sings*
*to the Virgin Mary;*
*no human tongue can describe*
*the sweet harmony.*

The following two poems are taken from the *Festivale:*

### BIRDS OF PASSAGE

*Ah, how beautiful, how pretty and fine*
*are your steps, pure Mary*
*in your little shoes, softly treading.*
*Ah, virgin, what have you in mind?*
*You know what you bear beneath your heart,*
*I am surprised that you can hasten.*
*"Listen to me, you pious woman,*
*I bear in my pure body,*
*I bear in me the eternal Word,*
*do not complain about me, help me*
*[help me] on my way...."*

### INSCRIPTION

*Listen to me, poor pilgrim woman,*
*as your mind is set on pilgrimage,*
*do not move on past this picture,*
*but stay, refresh your weary feet.*
*Mary, the sweet Mother,*
*stands quite peacefully here and waits,*
*to see whether you are well behaved.*
*If you have nothing more to give,*
*let her have just one pious tear....*

Procopius's contemporary *Jacob Balde* (1604-1668) was still more versatile. Raised in a completely Jesuit environment, he was ordained a priest, became a teacher of rhetoric, a court preacher and tutor to princes in Munich, and along with all that was a productive neo-Latin epic, dramatic, and lyric poet. His long *Song of Praise to Mary* is full of pathos but of genuine feeling as well:

*Ah, how long have I desired*
*to praise you, Mary!*
*Not indeed as you are honored*
*up in high heaven; that would be in vain!*
*My poor art would hang on the harp,*
*and this song, much as it glows,*
*would begin in a low tone....*
*When all my senses have weakened,*
*and those standing round say:*
*Now he is departing, he is gone,*

his pulse has ceased to beat,
glide your fair hand, your gentle hand,
O mother of my life,
glide it over me, revive me,
or else all is in vain.

Somewhat younger than Balde is the Baroque lyricist *Johann Klaj,* known as Clajus the younger. He was born in Meissen in 1616 and died as a parish priest in Kitzingen on Main in 1650. He wrote declamatory dramas, pastoral lyrics, and spiritual songs. In his very long poem *The Ascension of Jesus Christ* he recounts how:

*Prince Gabriel thrusts forward and leads
    with angelic splendor
a three-cornered silver banner unfurled
on which the morning star of women
    laughs and lives,
a woman and a virgin, and divine to look
    upon,
She presses to her mouth and lays on her
    breast
the loving salvation of humankind, the
    sweet joy of angels.
Thus the starry scripture here, O wonder,
    is read out.
It says: The Word was made flesh, which
    ever was with God.*

A Baroque poet of grand sweeping gestures was the much-celebrated *Siegmund von Birken* (1626–1681), the author of festival productions, meditations, spiritual songs, and pastoral poetry. In his long poem *Meditation on the Marriage of Heavenly Divinity with Our Earthly Humanity* we read:

*He whom no place has grasped
lies now in his mother's womb.
He whom no man's mind had entered
is borne by a woman.
The one who feeds and clothes all things
    on earth,
who gives them drink,
himself receives milk as food.
The God through whom we are human,
himself becomes a weak child of man.*

We feel moved in a totally different way by *Angelius Silesius,* whose real name was Johann Scheffler. Born in Breslau in 1624, he converted to Catholicism at the age of thirty, probably because he hoped to find in it a more favorable response to his mystical inclinations. He is in all likelihood the greatest poet of the German Baroque. A number of his hymns are still sung today. Strongly influenced by the great mystic Jakob Böhme, his poetry moves between pantheism and medieval mysticism, but often strikes us as altogether modern. We have no fewer than fifty-five works on religion from his pen, including anti-Protestant lampoons. He directs these verses "To the Virgin" from *The Cherubic Wanderer:*

*Mary is called a throne and God's tent,
an ark, a fortress, tower, house, a well,
    a tree and garden mirror,
a sea, a star, the moon, the dawn, a hill.
How can she be all that? She is another
    world.
Tell us, O dear woman, were you not
    chosen
for your humility,
That you should conceive and bear God?
Tell us, what else could it be? So that I too
    on earth
can become a virgin and bride and the
    mother of God.
I must be Mary and bear God,
if he is to grant me eternal bliss.
Mary is highly worthy; yet I can go higher
than she and all the hosts of saints ever
    climbed.*

No doubt equally important as a writer and historical figure was *Friedrich Spee von Langenfeld,* who was born in 1591 near Düsseldorf. This Jesuit priest became one of the forerunners of the Enlightenment. As the confessor of many women accused of witchcraft, he was convinced that the hysteria over witches was insane. Nevertheless he had to accompany about two hundred innocent victims to the stake. Apart from *Cautio criminalis,* his attack on the witchcraft trials, which led to their suppression in some regions, he composed religious songs and pastoral poetry, some of it in a highly Baroque style and on Spanish models. He died in Trier in 1635 while caring for plague-stricken soldiers in the Thirty Years War. The following *Sad Conversation, as Christ is Led to the Cross* sounds somewhat artificial (Jesus is speaking amicably to his mother):

*Ah, how could you give birth to me,*
*in such great pain and torment?*
*Would you, then, be (I would swear you*
*    were)*
*pure steel and marble?*
*Were your heart and courage and innards*
*made only*
*from the heart of the rock or metal?*
[His mother answers:]
*O desperate heart of hearts!*
*O you tender mother's child!*
*You were the model of my pains,*
*the blood rushes to my heart....*
*For I bore you*
*for sweet light and life,*
*but I never thought*
*of anything like your cross.*

Another poem by Spee is warmer and more natural, his *In stiller Nacht zur ersten Wacht* ("At the first watch of the silent night"), which was set to music by Johannes Brahms. The Savior speaks:

*Were you, Mary, tender virgin,*
*to know about my pain,*
*my hard suffering on this journey,*
*your heart would already be swept along.*
*Ah, my mother, I am no stone,*
*my heart would burst;*
*I must endure great pain,*
*must wrestle with death and torments.*
*Farewell, farewell, good night, Mary,*
*    mother mild....*

Another product of Jesuit education was the Tyrolean nobleman *Nicholas of Avancini* (1611–1686), probably the most successful author of Baroque festivals and Jesuit dramas. He wrote over thirty plays, in which splendid staging

and gorgeous scenery, as well as powerful lighting effects, played a major role. Avancini was a sincere admirer of the Habsburg imperial house, and it is thanks to him that after the Thirty Years War the center of gravity of Jesuit drama shifted from Bavaria to Austria. His odes glorify Mary in Baroque style.

Altogether different was the style of the popular religious songs of the time. Here is an example from the *Augsburg Songbook* of 1666 that derives from an older Dutch song:

*A dew fell down from heaven*
*into a virgin pure,*
*it was no evil woman*
*who had her little child.*
*Though she gave birth,*
*she remained a pure virgin.*
*O chosen virgin,*
*You must be ever praised.*
*Pray for us all*
*to Jesus, the sweet child,*
*that he will let us enter*
*the paradise of heaven,*
*there we shall sing forever*
*your unbounded honor and praise.*

This *pilgrims' song* from Fulda dates from around 1695:

*O queen, lovely lady,*
*look down on us from heaven.*
*Mary, O queen, pray for us,*
*O Mary!...*
*Pray for the fields and ploughland,*
*guard us from fire and blaze.*
*Mary, O queen, pray for us,*
*O Mary!...*
*Ah, stay by us at the very end,*
*O mother, turn not away from us!*
*Mary, O queen, pray for us,*
*O Mary.*

The following folk song most likely comes from the same time:

*Mary is to go to school,*
*what does she find on the way?*
*She found a sailor standing there:*
*"Ah, sailor, carry me over the sea!"*
*"I don't want to sail over the sea,*
*you must promise me your highest honor."*
*"I won't promise you my highest honor,*
*so long as heaven and earth still stand.*
*I shall never promise you my honor.*
*I would rather walk over the sea."*
*And when she got to the middle,*
*the bells all began to ring,*
*they all rang big and small,*

*they all rang together.*
*Mary knelt down on a stone,*
*and the sailor's heart broke in two.*

The poem of supplication *Mary, spread out your mantle,* taken from an Innsbruck print (1640), is intimate in expression and completely free of Baroque pomposity. In an edited form it is still a beloved hymn today (*).

*Robert Herrick* (1591–1674) was one of the most important of the "Cavalier poets" and a supporter of Charles I, whose unfortunate end caused him great difficulties. For a long time his sensitive lyrics were forgotten, but they came to light again in the 19th century. Here is an epigram from Herrick's *Noble Numbers,* n. 183 (1647):

*To work a wonder, God would have her*
*    shown*
*At once a Bud, and yet a Rose full-blown.*

It should be noted here that when it comes to the most famous poets of the 16th and 17th centuries, Mary plays only a minor role: Neither in the works of William Shakespeare (1564–1616) nor of the Italian epic poets Matteo Boiardo (1440–94), Lodovico Ariosto (1474–1533), or Torquato Tasso (1544–1594), nor of Spaniards Miguel de Cervantes (1547–1616), Lope de Vega (1562–1635), or Pedro Calderón de la Barca (1600–1681) does Mary have an important place. In John Milton's (1608–1674) long hymn "On the Morning of Christ's Nativity" she is barely mentioned.

Over the course of the 17th century a series of new religious orders was founded. One of the these (the "English Ladies") was founded in 1609 by Mary Ward, who had fled from England to France and adopted the Rules of Ignatius Loyola, so that her order was commonly thought of as a branch of the Jesuits. It was not, however, approved by the pope until 1703. It still exists today and runs schools for girls in many countries, including Germany and Austria. It is the order to which Mother Teresa belonged before she founded her own. Another order, the Christian Brothers (Frères Ignorantins), was founded in 1681 by *Jean Baptiste de la Salle* and proved influential in the 19th century. De la Salle (1651–1719) was a

Mary, spread out your mantle,
make of it a shield and screen,
let us all stand safely under it,
till all dangers are past.
Merciful patroness,
Come to our aid, Mary.

O mother of compassion,
your mantle is already spread out;
whoever diligently places himself under
it
will not be brought low in any danger.
Merciful patroness,
Mary, come to our aid.

Your mantle is so very broad and wide,
beneath it all of Christendom can hide.
It covers the whole wide world,
it is our refuge and shelter.
Merciful patroness,
Mary, come to our aid....

When war brings confusion to
everything,
when all is in flux and despair,
stay by us, don't leave our side,
then we shall not go astray.
Merciful patroness,
Mary, come to our aid.

Come hither, all you who are disturbed,
this mother loves you from the heart,
the mother of mercy
takes in all the pain of your hearts.
Merciful patroness,
Mary, come to our aid.

From an Innsbruck print (1640)

The Late Gothic woodcarver Friedrich Schramm, active ca. 1480–1515, was the creator of this Madonna with the protecting cloak, from Ravensburg (ca. 1480), State Museums, Berlin. The trust that echoes in the countless prayers for Mary's intercession took visual form in this Madonna.

canon in Rheims, and is considered a pioneer of public education. Here is an invocation to Mary from his pen:

*Virgin Mary, Mother of God and my Mother, advocate, refuge and protectress of my life, in deep humility I turn to you. I have great trust in you and in God. Accompany my prayer, accept my intentions and my inclination. Beg from your divine Son the graces I need, to be able to carry out my intentions....*

At around this same time the first official poet laureate of England, *John Dryden* (1631–1700), wrote a prayer to Mary in the face of the plague that was

ment did not quite know what to do with Mary. Marian poetry received no fresh impulses until the late 18th century, and that came especially from the Protestant side. Poets of the *Sturm und Drang*, and especially the Romantics, addressed themselves anew to Marian material and treated it in a deeper, more intimate way. This was the case in German literature, for example, with the very young *Johann Wolfgang von Goethe* (1749–1832), as we see in the famous prayer of Gretchen in *Faust*. Its later form is almost identical to that of the *Urfaust*, which was presumably written down before Goethe's time in Weimar

*Venerable mother,*
*Our chosen queen thou art,*
*Peer of gods, no other! (trans. Walter Kaufmann [New York: Doubleday, 1961], pp. 339–41)*

And then "One of the Penitents," otherwise known as Gretchen, prays as before:

*Incline, incline,*
*That art divine,*
*Thou that dost shine,*
*Thy face in grace to my sweet ecstasy! (trans. Walter Kaufmann, pp. 497, 501)*

At the end of the drama Mary, called the Mater Gloriosa, speaks only two

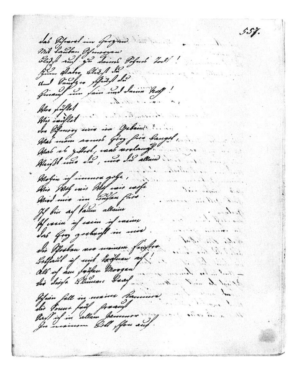

*Incline,*
*Mother of pain,*
*Your face in grace to my despair.*
*A sword in your heart,*
*With pain rent apart,*
*Up to your son's dread death you stare.*
*On the Father your eyes,*
*You send up sighs*
*For your and your son's despair.*
*Who knows*
*my woes—*
*Despair in every bone!*
*How my heart is full of anguish,*
*How I tremble, how I languish.*
*Know but you, and you alone!*

Goethe, Gretchen's prayer from *Faust* (trans. Walter Kaufmann (p. 338–40)

ravaging London: "Heaven's brightest Star, thy influence shed."

Dryden's younger contemporary *Alexander Pope* (1683–1744), born a Catholic, unlike Dryden, who converted to Catholicism in his maturity, was an important and much-celebrated critic, satirist, translator, moralist, and poet. In his "Messiah—A Sacred Eclogue," he wrote:

*A virgin shall conceive, a virgin bear a son!*
*From Jesse's root behold a branch arise,*
*Whose sacred flower with fragrance fills the skies.*

Otherwise the first decades of the 18th century brought little that was new in Marian literature. The Enlighten-

(from 1775 on). It is a poem that moves us even today (*).

In the final scene of *Faust* Part 2, which was not completed until 1830, Goethe makes a connection to this prayer: Mary appears fleetingly, like a vision. Only when she hovers near is she seen by the Doctor Marianus:

*Mistress of the firmament!*
*Let me in the bower*
*Of the heavens' outspread tent*
*See thy secret power!...*
*Courage invincible we feel*
*If thy glory wills it—*
*Swiftly tempered is our zeal*
*If thy glory stills it.*
*Virgin, beautifully pure,*

lines:
*Come, raise yourself to higher spheres!*
*When he feels you, he follows there. (Kaufmann, p. 503).*

And so Faust is taken up to heaven.

*Johann Gottfried Herder*, born in East Prussia in 1744 and long a friend of Goethe, was a pioneer of the movement called *Sturm und Drang*. Herder was an influential theologian, philosopher of culture and history, a literary critic, translator, and poet. In his *Letters on the Advancement of Humanity* (1795) he says the following about Mary:

*[The human mind's] concepts of religion were humanized, and thus the blessed Virgin, the Mother of the world's Savior, took*

*Left*: *The Madonna with a Rose Bush*, from Straubing, colored green sandstone. The blooming rose bush, which bears the Christ Child as its precious blossom, shows the mystical-symbolic fusion of *virga* (stem) and *virgo* (virgin), thus the root of Jesse with the Virgin Mary. The statue was carved around 1250 (Bavarian National Museum, Munich).

*Right*: Friedrich Schiller (1759–1805), *The Virgin of Orleans* (Regional and University Library, Hamburg). The struggle of Joan of Arc as the leader of the French army against the English is preceded by visions of Mary and a commission from her. Mary, who is often chosen as the patron-protector of armies and is depicted on their banners, is involved here with the fate of nations as well as the personal fate of Joan.

precedence over all others, in a unique idea for which the Greek Muses were of no assistance. The angel's greeting provided the help when he called her blessed and beloved of God; her own humility helped her to reach it when she called herself the handmaiden of the Lord. From these two features her lovable essence flowed together, which made itself familiar with the human heart ... [this is] Mary's character. Its decisive feature is ... that Christian naturalness in which the Mother seems to know about herself and her glory, hardly at all about her child.... (Here Herder is evidently thinking of Raphael.)

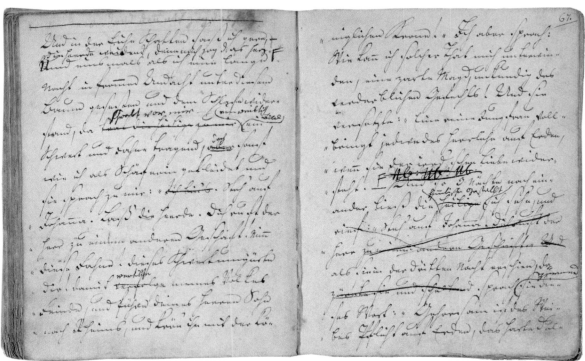

A maiden pure and chaste
Achieves whate'er on earth is glorious,
If she to earthly love ne'er yields her heart.
Look upon me! a virgin like thyself;
I to the Christ, the Lord divine, gave birth,
And am myself divine!"
(trans. T. Martin, A. Swanwick, and A. Lodge)

Likewise far removed from Goethe's tender lyricism and Schiller's dramatic flair is the simple prayer of *Matthias Claudius*. Nine years older than Goethe, he studied theology, law, and political science and eventually became a higher regional councilor in Darmstadt. But

With Goethe's great friend Friedrich Schiller (1759–1805) Mary appears in a completely different light. In his "Romantic tragedy" *The Maid of Orleans* Joan of Arc tells the French king and his court how she prayed before an old picture of the Madonna, who appeared to her:
... The Holy One appear'd,
Bearing a sword and banner, otherwise
Clad like a shepherdess, and thus she
    spoke:
"'Tis I; arise, Johanna! leave thy flock.
The Lord appoints thee to another task!
Receive this banner! Gird thee with this
    sword!
Therewith exterminate my people's foes...

then he eked out an existence as a writer and educator. The style of his prose and poetry is simple and popular, often naive, but always impressive. Many of his poems are still living today. Here is one, *Christmas Cantilena*:
*Mary was in Bethlehem,*
*Where she had come to be registered;*
*Then came the time when she was to bear.*
*And she bore him—*
*And when she had borne him*
*And saw the boy naked and bare,*
*She felt happy, she felt blessed.*
*And full of humility she took him on her*
    *lap,*
*And her heart rejoiced in him.*
*She touched the boy tender and fine*

*I see you in a thousand pictures,*
*Mary, lovingly expressed,*
*Yet none of them can portray you,*
*As my soul looks upon you.*
*I only know that the turmoil of the*
*world*
*Fades like a dream since then*
*And an ineffably sweet dream*
*Is ever in my mind.*

Novalis

*To you, Mary,*
*A thousand hearts rise up,*
*In this shadowy life*
*They wanted only you.*
*They hoped to get better*
*with presaging pleasure,*
*You pressed them, holy being,*
*To your true breast.*
*So many, consumed and burning*
*In bitter torment*
*And fleeing this world,*
*Turned to you alone,*
*Who came to us with help*
*In so much pain and need....*

Novalis, from *Hymns to the Night*

of the art of poetry was combined with the Romantic yearning for deliverance to create the characteristic Romantic sensibility, in which the modern experience of abandonment already played a role.

*With trembling and with blessing,*
*And wrapped him in swaddling clothes,*
*And laid him to bed softly in a manger,*
*For there was no room elsewhere.*

Two German poets of the early Romantic movement, Novalis and August Wilhelm Schlegel, were precursors of the new style in which Mary was now being celebrated.

Friedrich Leopold, Baron von Hardenberg, whose pen name was *Novalis,* was the son of a Saxon landowner and director of a saltworks. He studied philosophy and law, became an administrator, and in 1800 was appointed department head, but died the following year of consumption, not quite thirty. His poetic style, like his great fragmentary novel *Heinrich von Ofterdingen,* magically blends dream and reality. His poems express his rich imagination and his mystical longing for death, especially in his famous *Hymns to the Night* (*).

Still better known is his short hymn to Mary, which served as a model for many later Romantics (*).

Just as influential, though less original, was *August Wilhelm Schlegel* (1767–1845), a highly versatile and formally gifted lyric poet, balladeer, playwright, translator, and critic. He wrote this sonnet to *The Mother of God in Glory:*

*The angels bow to you in deep solemnity,*
*And saints pray where your footstep goes:*
*Glorious queen of heaven! Unto you*
*resounds*
*The lyre of the spheres, strung by God.*
*Your Spirit, clearly divine, looks through*
*the veil*
*of the unfolding, blooming form.*
*You bear a child full of sublime*
*omnipotence,*
*The conqueror of death and liberator of*
*the world.*
*O virgin, daughter of the one you*
*cherished!*
*Your womb is chosen to be the sanctuary,*
*where divinity stamps even her image.*
*Your life has reanimated life,*
*The eternal love that bears the universe*
*is unceasingly wedded to us through you.*

August Wilhelm's brother *Friedrich Schlegel* (1772–1829) was active as a literary theorist, a poet, and Orientalist. In

true Romantic fashion he envisaged a union of poetry, religion, and philosophy. In 1808 he converted to Catholicism. Here is an excerpt from his long poem, *Lament of the Mother of God:*

*I was founded from eternity,*
*The crown that wraps around my head*
*was placed there by the Father:*
*I carried the Son in my hands,*
*The Son's radiance cannot blind me.*
*My foot stands on the moon's orbit.*
*The Thrones call me queen,*
*They who dwell in everlasting light,*
*And God's sweet band of angels.*
*I rule in earnest over heaven's joys,*
*Yet in the blessed pains of love*
*God's glory is made manifest.*
*I kneel down at the Father's throne,*
*Turning my eye toward the Son;*
*My pleading heart flames out to God;*
*It begs for grace for the children of*
*repentance,*
*Redemption for the sinner,*
*In sympathy for every pang of love....*
*And so, dissolved in woe and pain,*
*Poured out in pleading intercession,*
*I look after my children;*
*The Father's heart beats out to me,*
*The Son's Word is fully present,*
*The Light of the Spirit is opened up.*
*Then burst in now, you holy pains,*
*Flood over my mother's heart,*
*Sweetly united with me in grace,*
*Come here, you sisters, children, brothers!*
*You creatures high and low,*
*Every creature weeping there....*

In his collection of songs, *The Defiant Nightingale,* Schlegel reworked a series of poems by Friedrich von Spee, such as *Christ in the Garden* (of Gethsemane):

*O tender Virgin, who gave me birth,*
*Should you know my hard suffering?*
*In truth, in truth,*
*Your heart would be torn apart.*
*Ah, mother mine, if you were to see the*
*pain,*
*My heart would break;*
*The bitter pangs overwhelm me,*
*Wrestling with death and torment.*
*Farewell, farewell, good night,*
*Mary, mother mild,*
*Is no one there to watch with me,*
*In this desert wild?...*

In England the Romantic movement began around the same time as in Germany. One of its leading figures was

"How am I? Bliss flashes from God's throne
And has wrapped me round with sweet bonds.
My longing has pierced heaven:
I see the Father with his dear Son.

Onward! Onward! that I may dwell with you,
Lightly lofted by the gust of love,
You saints, who have loyally struggled with me,
Believe, love, hope, and then receive the crown."

And as she thus vanishes on cloud and fragrance,
The youngest sons of heaven surround her smil-
ing,
The suns beneath her feet give way.

In the light a new light is kindled.
Thus the bride shines, transfigured in pure loveli-
ness,
And rests now, loving at the well of love.

August Wilhelm Schlegel, *The Assumption of the Virgin*

*Left*: *Mary's Assumption* from a ceiling fresco in the pilgrimage church of Schönenberg, painted in 1711–12 by Melchior Stiedl. In the tradition of Roman Baroque the exaltation of Mary is shown in her Assumption into heaven. Surrounded by angels, she is received by Christ, God the Father, and the Holy Spirit.

*William Wordsworth* (1770–1850). *Lyrical Ballads* (1798), which he published along with his friend Samuel Taylor Coleridge, is often taken to mark the beginning of the Romantic movement in England. About Mary Wordsworth wrote:
*A visible power, in which did blend*
*All that was mixed and reconciled in thee,*
*Of mother's love with maiden purity,*
*Of high with low, celestial with terrene.*

Born the same year as Wordsworth, the Swabian *Friedrich Hölderlin* had a restless early career as a tutor and failed as a writer, then pined away, mentally deranged, from 1808 till his death in 1843. His language, inspired by the spirit of ancient Greece that influenced Friedrich Nietzsche, among others, is entirely original and hovers between Classicism and Romanticism. For dec-

ades his work was all but forgotten and did not reach the public until shortly before the First World War. *To the Madonna* is the sketch of a hymn:
*I have suffered much for your and your son's sake, O Madonna, ever since I heard of him in my sweet youth....*

*Yet, heavenly one, yet I wish to celebrate you, and let no one chide me for the beautiful speech of my homeland, as I go off alone to battle....*

*And all-forgetting love has ruled over mankind. It all began when the divine boy was born from your womb and with him your friend's son, named John by his mute father—the bold one, to whom was given the power of the tongue....*

*So then they died, both of them; and you, divinely mourning, saw them die in the strength of your soul...*

*And if in the holy night of the future one*

*is concerned and worried about the carefree, sleeping, blossoming children, you come smiling and ask what he fears as long as you are Queen.*

*Clemens Brentano* (1778–1842) is one of the most important representatives of high Romanticism. Full of fantasy and creative power, he was a restless eccentric who succeeded equally well with melancholy songs, popular hymns, and satires. He too (* p. 107) greets Mary.

A classmate of Brentano's was *Johann Joseph Görres,* who started out as an enthusiastic supporter of the French Revolution and a spokesman for the Republic of the Rhine. But in disillusionment he changed his views and joined the German Romantics, becoming their spirited representative and publicist. His *Songs of Mary* appeared in

1843.

Though they cannot be fit into any strict chronological sequence, the *Fairy Tales* collected and edited by the *Brothers Grimm, Jacob* (1785–1863) and *Wilhelm* (1786–1859), were one of the most widely disseminated books of the entire 19th century. The brothers, who collaborated closely in this and other works, belonged to the famous "Göttingen Seven"—professors who protested a violation of the constitution by the King of Hanover and were removed from their posts. The tales date from 1812–1815, but they come from earlier times that cannot be specified exactly. Among them is "The Child of Mary," about the poor daughter of a woodcutter whom the Virgin Mary promises to care for and whom she takes with her to heaven. When Mary goes on a journey, the girl cannot resist the temptation to open a forbidden door.

Then she sees the Holy Trinity sitting in fiery splendor. Since she refuses to admit her guilt, Mary turns her out of heaven. She loses the ability to speak and ekes out a wretched existence in a dark forest. But one day the king goes hunting in this forest, takes her into her castle, and marries her. When she is about to bear a child, Mary appears to her and asks her to admit her guilt.

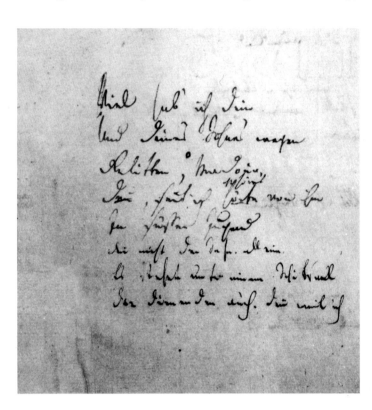

*Left*: Friedrich Hölderlin (1770–1843): *To the Madonna* (Württemberg Regional Library, Stuttgart). The unfinished poem is characteristic of a new subjectivity that expresses its own torn, broken condition. Hölderlin adopts the language of prayer to reflect on his personal situation. Mary for him is the symbol of a world epoch marked by the distance of God and at the same time by hope for a new nearness to God.

*Right*: Clemens von Brentano (1778–1842), *Romances of the Rosary*. The original is in the Frankfurt Goethe Museum. Brentano, who devoted himself to folk poetry in the spirit of the Romantic movement, returned to Catholicism in 1817. Thus in the spirit of the age he became another representative of a religious renewal, as expressed in the poem *Star of the Sea—Greetings to Mary*.

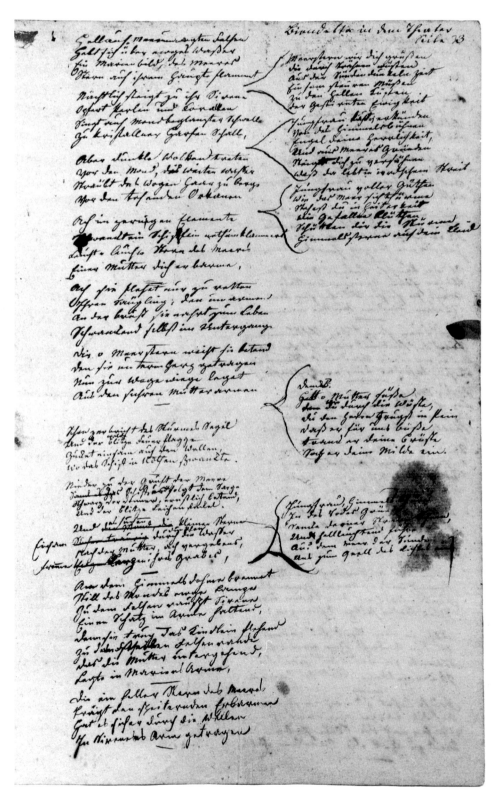

Since she refuses, Mary takes away the child, and the queen is suspected of having killed her child. This happens again the next year, but the king protects her. But when the third child comes and she still denies her guilt, the king can no longer shield her, and she is condemned to be burnt to death. On the stake she is moved by compunction and cries out, "Yes, Mary, I did it!" Then a cloudburst puts out the flames, Mary

appears, brings her three children back, and loosens her tongue.

Among the Grimms' "children's legends" is the story "The Little Glass of the Mother God," in which Mary asks a poor coachman for a glass of wine. The man doesn't have a glass, so Mary plucks a flower, which miraculously serves as a glass and thereafter is called the little glass of the Mother of God. In another legend Mary is looking for

*heaven in her womb,*
*Yet the little flower that she loves already*
*   senses it,*
*Looks sweetly disturbed;*
*It fades quickly away with blissful pains.*
*But soon the angel comes down on*
*   gleaming plumage.*
*O blissful hour!*
*He brings her the news,*
*And the woman dedicated to God sinks*
*   down in prayer,*

*Star of the sea, we greet you,*
*we who through the wilderness of tear.*
*from the time dark with sin must steer*
*   alone*
*   to the bright coasts*
*   of starry eternity!*

*Virgin, angels loudly proclaim*
*   your glory*
*from the stages of heaven;*
*and from the depths of the sea*
*all that lives there in earthly conflict*
*arises to make its peace with you.*

*Virgin full of kindness,*
*   as the sea swells up,*
*   you stand in brightness;*
*   like fallen blossoms*
*   the storms pour out*
*heavenly stars upon your dress.*

*Think, O sweet Mother,*
*   how you bore our Lord*
*through the wilderness in pain;*
*that he might expiate for us,*
*he drank from your breasts,*
*he sucked in your gentleness.*

*Virgin, gate of Heaven,*
*send down the gleam of your rays*
*   into the depths of death*
*and, brightly shining, lead*
*   us out of the sea of sin*
*   into the source of light!*

Clemens Brentano

strawberries for the child Jesus, is bitten by an adder, and hides behind a hazel shrub, which from then on is considered the surest protection against adders, snakes, and similar dangers.

*Justinus Kerner,* 1786–1862, studied medicine and was involved with occultism and spiritualism all his life. He developed into an emotionally powerful lyric poet and storyteller, and was considered the leader of the Swabian school of poetry. In *The Annunciation* he writes:
*There she sits, playing with other flowers,*
*Bud of the rose,*
*Still not feeling the ray of divinity within*
*   her,*
*Which will soon awaken the fullness of*

*A ray of heaven quivers through her limbs,*
*The bud ripens to paradisal fullness;*
*But she arises again in humility,*
*"I am your handmaid, Lord; may your*
*   will be done."*

The most important poet of the high Romantic period in Germany was *Joseph Baron von Eichendorff,* born in 1788 in Upper Silesia. His songs, with their great feeling for nature and their great musicality, are still popular today. His Catholicism is warm, simple, and full of *joie de vivre.* His poem *Mary's Longing* is typical:
*Mary went into the morning,*
*The earth gave a bright gleam of love,*
*And over the gay green hills,*
*she saw the blue heavens stand.*

Illustration for Heinrich Heine's *Pilgrimage to Kevlaar* from the first edition of 1822. The picture shows the Madonna of Kevlaar, surrounded by pilgrims. In the face of the Romantic enthusiasm for Mary, Heine wrote a ballad that combines skepticism and piety, irony and devotion.

## The Pilgrimage to Kevlaar
### Heinrich Heine

*The Mother of God in Kevlaar
Has the finest clothes to wear;
She is so very busy,
So many sick come there.*

*The sick and ailing come there
And bring, as offering,
Limbs molded out of waxwork,
Wax feet and hands they bring.*

*Whoever brings a wax hand,
His hand is healed that day;
And he who brings a wax foot
Walks well and sound away.*

*To Kevlaar came many on crutches
Who now go dancing again,
And many who now play the viol
Could not move a finger then.*

*The mother took wax tapers,
A wax heart she did make.
"Bring this to Jesus' Mother,
And she will heal the ache."*

*With sighs he took the wax heart,
And went to the shrine with sighs;
These words welled up from his bosom
As tears welled in his eyes:*

*"O blessèd in the highest,
O saint of purity,
O virgin queen of Heaven,
I wail my woe to thee!*

*We lived in Köllen city,
My mother and I, in town—
The city of hundreds of churches
And chapels of renown.*

*And near to us lived Gretchen,
But death took her away—
I bring thee a wax heart, Mary,
Heal my heart's wound, I pray.*

*Heal thou my heart of its sickness,
And early and late, I vow,
Thou wilt hear me fervently singing:
Hail Mary, praised be thou!"*

*The sickly son and the mother,
They slept in their little room;
And there the Mother of Jesus
Came softly through the gloom.*

*She bent low over the sick one,
And laid her hand upon
His heart with tender softness,
Smiled gently and was gone.*

*The mother saw all this dreaming,
And still more did she see;
She woke up from her slumber,
Dogs howled so noisily.*

*There lay outstretched before her,
Her son, and he was dead.
His pale cheeks in the dawn light
Were painted a sunrise-red.*

*She folded her hands in silence,
She felt—she knew not how.
She softly sang devoutly:
"Hail Mary, praised be thou!"*

(trans. Hal Draper,
*The Complete Poems of Heinrich Heine*
[Boston: Suhrkamp/Insel, 1982], pp. 121–22.)

*"Ah, if I only had a bridal dress of*
  *heaven's rays,*
*Two little golden wings—how I would fly*
  *within!"*
  *Mary went into the silent night,*
*The earth slept, heaven kept watch,*
*And through her heart, as she walked and*
  *pondered and thought,*
*Passed the stars with golden splendor.*
*"Ah, if I only had a bridal crown of*
  *heaven's rays*
*With golden stars woven in!"*
  *Mary went into the garden alone,*
*The brightly colored birds sang so*
  *enticingly,*
*And she saw roses on the green.*
*Many red and white so wonderfully*
  *beautiful.*
*"Ah, if I had a little boy so white and red,*
*How I would love him till death."*
  *Now the bridal dress has been woven,*
*And golden stars in her dark hair,*
*And in her arms the Virgin holds the little*
  *boy,*
*High over the darkly thundering world*
*And from the child a radiance goes forth,*
*That calls out eternally to us: Home,*
  *Home!*

*Heinrich Heine* (1797–1856) was completely different from these true Romantics. The son of a Jewish trader, he started out working at his uncle's bank in Hamburg, later studied law, attended lectures at the University of Göttingen by E.M. Arndt, the poet and historian, A.W. Schlegel, and G.W.F. Hegel. Sent down because of a duel, he converted to Protestantism in 1825 and lived in Paris after 1831. His lyricism (*The Book of Songs*) enjoyed a unique popularity, and his poems were set to music even more often than Eichendorff's. He was also the first important journalist in the German language. His romantic spirit, his *Weltschmerz*, and his sentimentality are often intermingled with mockery and skepticism. Alongside his very simple, almost folk lyrics and masterly ballads, we find a great deal of self-irony. With Heine, German Romanticism began to wane. Heine did not have much to say about Mary, except in the ballad *The Pilgrimage to Kevlaar,* from which we quote the second and third parts (Kevelaer, as it is spelled today, is a place of pilgrimage on the Lower Rhine) (*).

Heine's contemporary *Luise Hensel* (1798–1876) came from Brandenburg, became a Catholic in 1818, worked as a nurse and teacher, and ended her life in a convent. Her poems are late Romantic, simple and natural. This is *The Manger:*
*How fair a child is this*
*Whom we find in the manger.*
*Ah, such a sweet little child,*
*It must be from heaven.*
  *The woman who kneels by the manger,*
*And blissfully looks at the child,*
*That is Mary, pious and pure,*
*She may well be joyful in her heart.*
  *High praise to you, dark cell,*
*through which the whole world grows*
  *bright,*
*Little child in Mary's lap,*
*How infinitely great you are.*

*George Gordon, Lord Byron* (1788–1824), one of the greatest English Romantic poets, highly admired by Goethe, a perfect master of his language, was, like Heine, capable of moving lyricism as well as biting irony and social criticism. In his last great poem, generally acknowledged as his masterpiece, *Don Juan,* he devotes two beautiful stanzas to Mary. Here is one of them:
*Ave Maria! blessed be the hour!*
*The time, the clime, the spot, where I so oft*
*Have felt that moment in its fullest power*
*Sink o'er the earth so beautiful and soft,*
*While swung the deep bell in the distant*
  *tower,*
*Or the faint dying day-hymn stole aloft,*
*And not a breath crept through the rosy*
  *air,*
*And yet the forest leaves seem'd stirr'd*
  *with prayer.*

The great English theologian *John Henry Newman* (1801–1890) likewise sang Mary's praises. In 1845 he converted from Anglicanism to the Catholic Church and spent his life in theological debates. As a teacher, writer, and dramatist he had a considerable influence on the intellectual life of England. At his Oratory in Birmingham he wrote the poem *The Pilgrim Queen* (1849):
*There sat a Lady*
*all on the ground,*
*Rays of the morning,*
*circled her round.*
*"Save thee, and hail to thee*

*Gracious and Fair,*
*In the chill twilight*
*What wouldst thou there?"*
*"Here I sit desolate,"*
*Sweetly said she,*
*"Though I'm a queen,*
*And my name is Marie:*
*Robbers have rifled*
*my garden and store,*
*Foes they have stolen*
*my heir from my bower.*
*They said they could keep Him*
*far better than I,*
*In a palace all His,*
*planted deep and raised high.*
*'Twas a palace of ice,*
*hard and cold as were they,*
*And when summer came,*
*it all melted away.*
*Next they would barter Him,*
*Him the Supreme,*
*For the spice of the desert,*
*and gold of the stream;*
*And me they bid wander*
*in weeds and alone,*
*In this green merry land*
*which once was my own."*
*I look'd on that Lady*
*and out from her eyes*
*Came the deep glowing blue*
*of Italy's skies;*
*And she raised up her head*
*and she smiled, as a Queen*
*On the day of her crowning,*
*so bland and serene.*
*"A moment," she said,*
*"and the dead shall revive;*
*The giants are falling,*
*the Saints are alive;*
*I am coming to rescue*
*my home and my reign,*
*And Peter and Philip*
*are close in my train."*

With A.W. Schlegel and other Romantics, as with later poets such as Rilke and Schröder, the inspiration can often be traced back to paintings of Mary. But the Danish theologian and philosopher Soren Kierkegaard (1812–1855) expressly speaks out against this approach:
*Thus Mary has to be conceived of intellectually, and is in no way—it riles me already to say this word, but even more, that she has been thought of as mindless and coquettish—a Lady, who sits there as a feast for the*

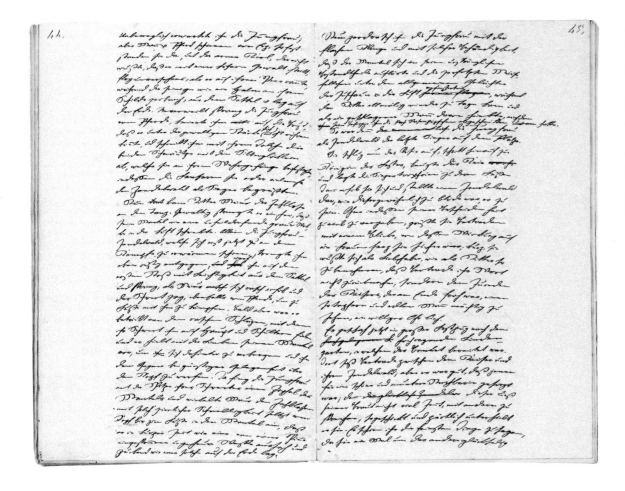

*eyes, playing with a divine child....*

The great Swiss writer *Gottfried Keller* (1819–1890) put Romanticism behind him. His fascinating art of storytelling seldom goes beyond his familiar Swiss environment, but in his *Seven Legends* he brings medieval sagas back to life. Four of these deal with old Marian legends, viewed in a new, more realistic light. Thus in the novella *The Virgin and the Nun* the Beatrix legend is given a fresh treatment. In *The Virgin as Knight* Mary steps down from an altar, takes on the form and armor of the young, lazy knight Zendelwald and, in this disguise, trounces his opponents "Mouse the Numberless" and "Swiftly Guhl" in a joust. This is how Mary's combat with "Mouse" goes:

*Then the Virgin caught with the point of her sword a tip of his cloak and wrapped up Mouse the Numberless in that cloak with such elegant speed from top to toe that he quickly looked like a wasp spun into a cocoon by a spider and lay quivering on the ground. Then the Virgin thrashed him with the flat of the blade and so deftly that his cloak dissolved into its original elements and a dust cloud of mouse-pelt fragments darkened the air, amid the general laughter of the spectators.... And thus the Virgin disguised as Zendelwald was the last conqueror in the square....*

In France too the Romantic period gave way to realism. *Alphonse Daudet* from Nîmes (1840–1897) described the world of the petite bourgeoisie and presented atmospheric pictures of provincial life in a popular, humorous style. But in 1858 he also published a volume of poetry, *Les Amoureuses,* which included *The Virgin at the Manger* (\*).

Realism in literature increasingly led to naturalism, which was buoyed up in France by Emile Zola, by the novelist George Gissing in England, and in Germany by Hermann Sudermann and, above all, Gerhard Hauptmann. The figure of Mary plays only a minor role in this literature, but a proportionately greater one in the following epoch, which reacted vehemently to naturalism.

One writer who stood between naturalism and regionalism was the Bavarian *Ludwig Thoma* (1867–1926), a storyteller, dramatist, and lyric poet. Thoma eagerly took up the cause against Bavarian clericalism, but nevertheless he wrote a cheerfully realistic *Ave Maria*:

*The workday is already over,*
*But St. Joseph is busy with his plane,*
*making a bed for a rich man in Nazareth.*
*The Virgin Mary is sewing away;*
*it was not too late for her to work.*
*Again she threaded the needle—*
*the job had to be done by the morning.*
*He goes on planing, she sews the dress,*
*The room soon lay in darkness.*
*Then an angel of the Lord opens the door,*
*And says: "Mary, the Lord is with you.*
*Yes, the fairest destiny awaits you,*
*You bear the Lord Jesus in your womb."*
*Now the angel has gone again.*
*Mary hears the cheering word*
*and laughs happily to herself.*
*Now she would soon be a mother.*
*But at once she pulled herself together*
*and busily went back to work.*
*Joseph planed away at his bed*

*The Virgin rocked the Christ child's cradle, where he lies in fresh*
*white swaddling clothes*
*And gaily twitters like a nest full of titmice.*
*She rocked him and sang the gentle words,*
*As we sing them to our little children....*
*The child would not sleep....*
*"My sweet Jesus," she said, faintly trembling,*
*"My lamb, sleep now, little white lamb,*
*It's late, it's late, the light has gone out.*
*Your forehead is red, your limbs are weary, sleep, darling,*
*sleep and don't worry."*
*But little Jesus would not fall asleep.*
*She sings in vain, keeps begging, in vain, Jesus would not sleep.*
*Then Mary, as if looking from behind veils, bent down her hopeless brow*
*to her son:*
*"Your mother is crying, and you're still not sleeping,*
*My friend, your mother must be in tears...."*
*At that moment little Jesus fell asleep.*

Alphonse Daudet, *The Virgin at the Manger*

*For a rich man in Nazareth.*

The new direction often characterized as neo-Romanticism came to full, brilliant expression in the work of *Stefan George* (1868–1933). Initially influenced by French symbolists such as Stéphane Mallarmé and Paul Verlaine, and closely linked to the English Pre-Raphaelites, as time went on he developed a highly personal, severe style. He gathered a group of devoted disciples around him, and became the head of a school of poets that renounced any widespread impact. He embraced an aristocratic, heroic sense of life and a feeling for beauty based on classical antiquity and the Renaissance. While his later poems express a sort of mystical religion of images, his early *Sagas and Songs* (1895) still move in the world of Christian ideas, as we can see in *Spur Watch* (1895):

*The youthful knight prays heatedly to the*
*One above*
*And breaks the narrow barriers of the*
*saying he has learned,*
*His hands piously thrust before his face.*
*Then unawares an earthly form is woven*
*into his thoughts:*
*She stood in the garden by the rosemary,*
*A child far more than a maid.*
*In her hair appeared golden flakes.*
*She wore a long, star-studded dress....*
*Into his cheeks shot a warm, red glow.*
*The candles strike him with straight*
*lightning bolts.*
*Then he sees sitting on the Virgin's lap*
*The world-Redeemer, his arms wide open.*
*I shall serve you in your army,*
*let no other striving awaken in me.*
*Let my life henceforth follow your*
*teaching,*
*Forgive when I am weak at the last....*

The poems of *Paul Claudel* (1868–1955), George's French contemporary, are marked by a mystical Catholicism. In his *Poèmes de Guerre* (1915) he invoked Mary (*p.112).

The work of the German *Ludwig Derleth* (1870–1948) likewise voices a mysterious, often effusive Catholicism. In his magnum opus, *The Franconian Koran,* over 15,000 lines long, the following verses (which, to be sure, betray a misunderstanding of Mary's position) appear:

*Mother of Christ,*
*I don't come here to pray.*
*I have nothing to give, and I don't know*
*What to beg for.*
*I've come just to see you, mother,*
*And to cry for happiness, because I am your child*
*and you are there.*
*My heart would like to sing in its language,*
*To say nothing, just sing, because it is full to overflou*
*For you are beautiful and immaculate,*
*The Woman full of grace, who appeared from God*
*In the morning radiance of his glory, unspeakably pur*
*Since you are the mother of Jesus Christ.*
*Because you are there, there for ever,*
*Quite simply, because you are Mary,*
*You mother of Jesus Christ,*
*We thank you.*

Paul Claudel, from *Poèmes de Guerre*

*But before Thomas the Apostle, come*
*too late, strode swiftly forth the angel who*
*was long prepared for this, and bade them do*
*whatever should be done about the tomb.*
*Roll the stone aside. Would you know where*
*she is now who has so moved your heart:*
*Behold: for a short while she was laid in there,*
*like a little pillow of lavender,*
*so that the earth may smell, in time to come,*
*of her among its folds, like a rich shawl.*
*All death (you feel this), all*
*sicknesses are overpowered by her perfume.*

*Behold the linen shroud! What bleacher's work*
*could, without shrinkage, yield such dazzling white?*
*This light streaming from the immaculate corpse*
*made it more perfect than could the full sunlight.*

*Do you not marvel how quietly she left?*
*You'd think that she were still in the smooth weft.*
*Yet the high heavens there are shuddering:*
*Man, kneel down, gaze after me and sing.*

Rilke, *On the Death of Mary*, trans. C.F. MacIntyre

This life-size stone sculpture of Mary from the cathedral of Bamberg, ca. 1235, unites Early Gothic treatment of folds with classical physicality. A severely classical face, the broad shoulders, and the solid standing position distinguish this figure from the tender, hovering Madonnas of the period.

*We adore you at the hearth of the universe,*
*the Mother of the gods,*
*We praise, envy, and greet you,*
*O goddess without beginning, preserved*
*    from every downfall,*
*Mistress of eternity, who moves through*
*    all the ranks of life,*
*Mover of the bright paths of the stars,*
*Who powerfully commands the rapid*
*    course of the hours*
*And comes along over the foaming waves*
*With the winged wheel of life and*
*    immortality.*
*In morning hymns and night vigils*
*May the smokeless flame of deep devotion*
*    arise to you.*
*O gracious image of heaven's mildness,*
*All blessed, holy, radiant comforter,*
*Virgin of the heavenly grove of roses,*
*Goddess of the firstborn world.*
*To make our adoration to you,*
*Our hearts plunge into the flames of*
*    prayer.*

At around this time in England *Laurence Housman* (1865–1959), brother of the much better-known A.E. Housman, was particularly successful as a dramatist (*Victoria Regina*). His poem *God's Mother* dates from 1898:

*A garden, bower by bower,*
*Grew waiting for God's hour:*
*Where no man ever trod,*
*This was the Gate of God.*
*The first bower was red—*
*Her lips, which "welcome" said.*
*The second bower was blue—*
*Her eyes, which let God through.*
*The third bower was white—*
*Her soul in God's sight.*
*Three bowers of love*
*Won Christ from heaven above.*

Housman's younger contemporary *Gilbert Keith Chesterton* (1874–1936) was a very prolific, very conservative writer and poet. He converted to Catholicism in 1922. This is his description of Mary and Jesus:

*The Christ-child stood at Mary's knee,*
*    His hair was like a crown,*
*And all the flowers looked up at him,*
*    And all the stars looked down.*

The outstanding and most influential lyrical poet of modern German literature, and at the same time the most sensitive singer of Mary, was *Rainer Maria Rilke,* born in Prague in 1875. He lived in Munich, Berlin, Worpswede, Paris, and finally in Switzerland. He traveled to Russia, where he met Tolstoy, and to Italy, Spain, Sweden, and Egypt. Many of his most beautiful poems—from his *Songs of Mary,* his *Book of Pictures,* his *Book of Hours,* and his *Life of Mary*—are dedicated to the Virgin. We can offer here only a very limited selection:

*Annunciation—the Words of the Angel* from the *Book of Pictures,* 1902:

*Thou art not nearer to God than we;*
*we are all far from him.*
*Wonderfully    nonetheless*
*are thy hands blessed.*
*No other woman's ripen so,*
*shimmering out so from the hem:*
*I am the day, I am the dew,*
*but thou art the tree....*

*    I spread my wings out and became*
*wonderfully    wide;*
*now thy small house overflows*
*with my great dress.*
*And still thou art alone as ever*
*and scarcely seest me;*
*because I am a breath in the grove,*
*but thou art the tree.*

*    ...Thou art a gateway great and high*
*and thou shalt open soon.*
*Thou, my song's dearest ear,*
*now I feel: my word was lost*
*in thee as in a wood.*

*    So I came and fulfilled for thee*
*a thousand and one dreams.*
*God looked at me: he dazzled...*
*But thou art the tree.*
*(trans. M.D. Herter Norton)*

From *The Life of Mary* (1913) come the following two poems. The second, *Mary's Visitation,* describes Mary's visit to Elizabeth:

*Not that an angel came in, understand,*
*was she alarmed. As little as others start*
*when a sunray or beam of moonlight darts*
*into a room and busies itself here and*
*    there,*
*would she have been made angry by the*
*    guise*
*in which an angel came. Could she surmise*
*how tedious angels find such tarrying*
*    here?*
*(O, if we knew how pure she was! A hind,*
*once when resting, saw her in the wood,*
*and gazing lost itself until it could—*
*all without any coupling with its kind—*
*conceive the unicorn, pure animal,*
*the beast of light.) Not that he entered, but*
*that he bowed down so close to her the*
*    face*
*of a young man, this angel, that her gaze*
*as she glanced up joined with his, as if all*
*outside there suddenly seemed void and*
*    what*
*the millions saw, were doing, suffering,*
*seemed forced into them: only she and he—*
*the seeing and seen, the eye and eye's*
*    delight*
*nowhere else but in this one place. See!*
*this is frightening. And they were both*
*    afraid.*
*Then the angel sang his melody.*
*(trans. C.F. MacIntyre)*

VISITATION OF THE VIRGIN
*At first it all went easily with her,*
*but oftentimes in climbing she already*
*felt the wonder stirring in her body—*
*and panting then she stood upon the lofty*
*Judean hills. Not by the land below,*
*she was encompassed by her plenitude;*
*walking, she felt that no one ever could*
*surpass the bigness she was feeling now.*
*She had to lay her hand upon the other*
*woman's body, still more ripe than hers.*
*And they both tottered toward one another*
*and touched each other's garments and*
*    hair.*
*Each, with a sanctuary in her keeping,*
*sought refuge with her closest woman kin.*
*Ah, the Savior in her was just in bloom,*
*but joy already in her cousin's womb*
*had quickened the little Baptist into*
*    leaping.*
*(trans. C.F. MacIntyre)*

*Hermann Hesse* (1877–1962) from Württemberg, only two years younger than Rilke, became famous principally for his confessional psychological novels and stories. His lyric poetry is musical, simple, and impressive. Here are two of his *Songs of Mary:*

*Don't chide me! I cannot pray,*
*I only wish, as I pass by,*
*to walk up to your steps*
*and see your eyes.*

*    It is a pure radiance*
*around your forehead that makes me glad;*
*I have so often as a child*
*adorned it with garlands.*

*    Without jewels or the glow of pearls,*
*let me lay on your steps,*
*the withered garland of my youth,*

*Little child from eternity, now I wish to sing to your mother!*
*My song is to be beautiful, like the morning-colored snow!*
*Rejoice, Virgin Mary, daughter of my earth, sister of my soul!*
*Rejoice, you joy of my joy!*
*I am a wandering through the nights, but you are a house beneath the stars,*
*I am a thirsty glass, but you are an open sea of the Lord!*
*Rejoice, Virgin Mary, I bless those who bless you.*
*Never again should a human child become disheartened!*
*I am nothing but love, I wish to speak forever to everyone:*
*The Lord has exalted one of you!*
*Rejoice, Virgin Mary, wings of my earth, crown of my soul!*
*Rejoice, you joy of my joy: I bless those who bless you!*

Gertrud Freiin von LeFort, *Christmas*

*silently pleading for your blessing.*
*Many battles, journeys, wounds,*
*the untasted bitter victories of*
*battles fought through without glory*
*now find their weary goal.*
*Bright and colorful lusts*
*Lay down hands which have grown*
*weary.*
*Their laughter now is at an end,*
*their red flame has died....*

Gertrud Freiin von Le Fort, born in Westphalia in 1876, came from a Huguenot family and studied Protestant theology. But at the age of fifty she converted to Catholicism. Her many free verse poems and hymns are expressive and bolstered by a strict Catholic faith (*).

*VIGIL OF MARY'S ASSUMPTION*
*The angel of the Lord greeted Mary,*
*and she received the call home of eternal*
*love.*
*Set out, Mary's soul: the heavenly*
*messengers have come!*
*They fetch the cradle in which your divine*
*child lay!*
*Now lay yourself to rest on your heart,*
*under which his life slumbers.*
*Now nestle deeply into your shell*
*That so tenderly shelters it.*
*Set out, Mary's soul, set forth in the cradle*
*of the Most High!*
*How will it be with you, pure as snow!*
*You shall journey to heaven.*

The following lines were composed under the impression of the Second World War:
*You who were greeted by the spirit of*
*peace,*
*beg peace for us.*
*You who received the Word of peace*
*within you,*
*beg peace for us!*
*You who bore the holy child of peace to*
*the world,*
*beg peace for us—*
*You helper of the All-Reconciler,*
*you willing partner of the All-Forgiver,*
*devoted to his eternal compassion,*
*beg peace for us!*
*For the sake of creaturely fear,*
*we beg you for peace—*
*For the sake of the little children, who*
*sleep in their cradles,*
*we beg you for peace—*
*For the sake of the old people,*

*who would be so glad to die in their beds,*
*we beg you for peace—...*
  *Let us pray for the peace of our earth,*
*for the peace of the earth is deathly ill.*
*Help it, Virgin Mary,*
*and help us speak:*
*Peace be to the peace of our poor world. . .*
*You bright star in all clouds of confusion,*
*we beg you for peace.*
*You who were with the dying,*
*when their blood soaked the battlefield,*
*have pity on peace...*
*Mother, mother,*
*our peace has already died,*
*there is peace only in the heavens...*
*You who remain powerful—even if your*
    *tender throne on earth breaks,*
*pray for the resurrection of our peace.*

*Rudolf Alexander Schröder,* born in Bremen in 1878, was a lyric poet, storyteller, translator, and essayist. His poetry developed from Art Nouveau into a severe, formal, religious lyricism. He always was a guardian of old educational tradition. As with Rilke, his *Sonnets to the Sistine Madonna* are strongly pictorial:

*Should despair come forth from the gates*
*of the old, obsolete world, and were it to*
    *find*
*the gray snowy landscape of pure clouds,*
*that you chose as the field to tread on,*
  *if in eyes wept blind from horror,*
*a flash should strike, as if at your feet*
*the distance shone, they would greet you*
*and suck themselves back to health from*
    *the coolness.*
  *You dwell in a light that looks gently,*
*not all too brightly, not all too warmly:*
    *for hearts*
*withered by the whirling fires of this time*
*gladly plunge, refreshed for the last time*
*from all conflict between lust and pain,*
*into the ever-mild bath of eternity.*

Another orthodox Catholic in his basic attitude was *Konrad Weiss* (1880–1940), Munich-born, the son of peasants. His darkly mystical but richly pictorial poetry is not aimed at the masses, as his poem *The Conception shows* (*).

The Catholicism of the Salzburg poet *Georg Trakl* (1887–1914) is fundamentally different from that of Weiss. Trakl became addicted to drugs as a pharmacology student; at twenty-two he en-

tered into an incestuous relationship with his sister, and at the age of twenty-seven—driven mad by the horrible massacres of the First World War—he died of an overdose of cocaine. In his poem *Blood Guilt* he begs Mary for forgiveness; but he cannot show any repentance, since passion keeps overpowering him:

*That a passion which preserves*
*meaning must suddenly be sacrificed,*
    *Mary listen,*
  *Mary was spared this,*
*then came the angel's greeting to her.*

*That the lust of discovery torments*
    *our heart*
  *from the way to God's guidance,*
    *Mary listen,*
*and this heart went unawares through*
*animal and plant as if hardened.*

*Till one picks the other to pieces,*
*then the song breaks like a pommel,*
    *Mary listen,*
*and comes stifled like a marble tone,*
  *so that it flows up the source.*

*She sank down, sank onto her bed,*
*well-informed, O no, like foliage,*
    *Mary listen,*
*my book fills up, my poor equipment,*
*a limp and dry theft of the senses.*

*And that she cannot fill it,*
  *and so she kept her face,*
    *Mary listen,*
*now the lust for sacrifice catches fire,*
*Mary sings and does not know it.*

Konrad Weiss, *The Conception*

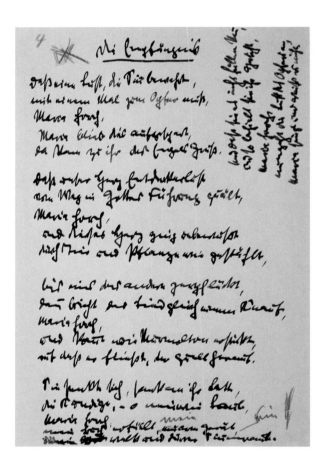

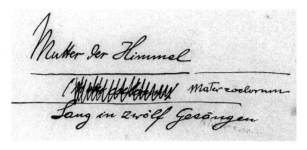

*God needed you for the purest
self-epiphany,
Through you he had to see himself
purely as human before us,
us, turned away from God,
us the beguiled,
Through you he had to
make a pure appearance in his creation,
Thus justifying overstrong essence,
Through you purely redeem
the earth-creation,
You unspotted body,
pure God-willed,
mediating womb,
that God himself honored—
In you God will not be lacking to me,
nor will grace....*

Reinhard Johannes Sorge
*Mother of the Heavens*

116

*The night turns on the camp of our kisses.
Somewhere someone whispers: Who'll
take away your guilt?
Still nimble with the sweetness of
loathsome lust
We pray: Forgive us, Mary, in your grace!
Greedy scents arise from flower husks,
Caress our foreheads pale with guilt.
Wearying beneath the breath of the sultry
scents
We dream: Forgive us, Mary, in your
grace!
But louder roars the well of the Sirens
And darkly towers the Sphinx before our
guilt,
That our hearts more sinfully ring out
again,
We sob: Forgive us, Mary, in your grace!*

*Heinrich Lersch* (1889–1936) was the
son of a boilermaker and at first he too
worked at this trade. In his poems he
described his life and proclaimed the
unity of all working men. In the First
World War he was buried alive for a
time, but managed to survive. Later he
went over to National Socialism.
Lersch's following poem is bitter:

*O Mother of God, of course you can't
go into the splendid houses of the rich.
Just come to us,
we can understand the great love of God,
you only want to have around you
the poor, pure, and pious,
only loving humanity:
O mother of God, then come to us,
to us in the frontline trenches.*

Like Rilke, *Franz Werfel* (1890–1945)
was born in Prague and, like Lersch,
served as a soldier in the First World
War. He began with Expressionist lyricism and then became a productive and
successful playwright and novelist. He
kept returning to the theme of the
search for God and world brotherhood.
In his novel *The Song of Bernadette* (1941)
he describes the miraculous apparitions
of Mary at Lourdes, and then launches
into a mystical Catholic piety. The work
was composed to keep a vow Werfel
made during his flight from the German
troops invading France, and within a
year no fewer than 400,000 copies were
sold in the USA alone. Actually Bernadette is not the heart of the book, nor
is Mary, but the incomprehensibility of
miracles and—as so often with Wer-

fel—the problematic relationship between knowledge and faith. Reason has
to capitulate here; the ignorant girl stays
loyal to her "lady" despite all the chal-
lenges. But the book was often criticized, for example by Thomas Mann,
who thought it a "flirtation with Rome."

Among the materials Werfel left un-
published at his death is the highly interesting poem *Mary and the Women* (*).

*Edith Stein* (1891–1942), a student of
philosopher Edmund Husserl, was, like
Werfel, born a Jew, but converted to
Catholicism in 1922 and became a Carmelite. She died in Auschwitz. Her
poem "Iuxta crucem tecum stare"
("Standing with you next to the cross")
was written after her flight to Holland
from the pogroms of 1938 (*).

*Reinhard Johannes Sorge*, born near
Berlin in 1892, likewise converted to
Catholicism and became an Expres-
sionist lyric poet and dramatist who
rebelled against the reigning naturalism.
At the age of twenty-four he fell in the
Battle of the Somme. One of his poems
sends a greeting to the *Mother of the
Heavens* (*).

*Ruth Schaumann* (1899–1975), born in
Hamburg, likewise converted to Catholicism. She was not only a versatile
writer, but also a sculptor and graphic
artist. In her stories she shows a deep
sense of connection to nature and a
strong, genuinely Catholic sensibility.
She illustrated many of her own books.

MARY IN THE EVENING

*With her lips she plucked
the child's smile from his
and held him in front of the garden stones
on her knees weary from travel.
She asked the pale star of evening
to stand by her in such joy
and tried to strew thanks like blooming,
a white cherry tree of the Lord.
She raised her son to her breast
but held him there like an alien possession.
And in the garden's evening branches
the nightingale of grief began to sing.*

PIETÀ

*Raise your eyes and look
without defense or confused horror
to the dark women on the hill's edge
and the One man on the One woman's
knee.
No forehead and no lip cried out,*

*Above*: *The Royal Good Night* by German writer, sculptor, and graphic artist Ruth Schaumann (1899–1975).

*Page 116*: Reinhard Sorge (1892–1916): *Mother of the Heavens*, early 1913 (Literary Archives, Marburg). Sorge approaches the subject of Mary with Expressionistic, highly individual language.

*Yes, we are bashful, we who venerate Mary.*
*For us her sex seems almost not human.*
*We wonder, when women rebel*
*and are lowly, and unjustly quarrelsome.*
*And yet no defect will make it harder for us,*
*To shudder at beauty, deeply and authentically,*
*Never hoping that it may condescend to look at us—*
*Virgin, why? That is YOU in them!*

*The Spirit's Spirit entered you,*
*The deity came forth from you into the house of*
*time.*
*From them only is mindlessness received*
*And comes to the light of lostness in death.*
*And from their eyes, body, and cheeks*
*Gleams a reflection of transfigured materiality.*
*When we shyly turn to their shining,*
*Virgin Mary, that is YOU in them!*

Franz Werfel, *Mary and Women*
(the men are speaking here)

*Today I have stood under the cross with you*
*And felt it more clearly than ever before,*
*That under the cross you became our mother.*
*How much care people take to be true to an earthly*
*mother,*
*To do the son's last will!*
*But you were the handmaid of the Lord,*
*Your life and being completely inscribed*
*In the life and being of the God made man.*
*So you have taken His own into your heart,*
*And with the heart's blood of your bitter pains*
*You have bought new life for every soul.*
*You know us all: our wounds and weaknesses,*
*You know too the radiance of heaven which your*
*Son's love*
*Would pour over us in the brightness of eternity.*
*Thus you carefully guide our steps,*
*No price is too high to lead us to the goal.*
*Yet those whom you have chosen for an escort,*
*To stand around you one day at the heavenly*
*throne,*
*They must stand here with you at the cross,*
*And must with the heart's blood of bitter pain*
*Purchase the heavenly splendor of dear souls,*
*That God's son entrusted to them as a heritage.*

Edith Stein, *Iuxta crucem tecum stare*

117

*...In eternity God will say to you:
my Mother.
The One who instituted the Fourth
Commandment
honors you forever.
I adore you, Our Father in heaven,
for you gave your only-begotten Son
to the pure womb of Mary.*

*I adore you, Son of God, for you
were born of the Immaculate,
You really became her Son.
I adore you, Holy Spirit, for
in the womb of Mary you shaped
the body of your divine Son.
I adore you, most holy Trinity,
one and threefold God, since you
honored the Immaculate one
so divinely.*

Maximilian Kolbe

*only the mantles rustle on the stones,
but in the skies there is a weeping
and a flutter of wings as never before.
    Raise your eyes and speak:
My guilt has caused his death.
Your voice hesitates,
and his mother's hands tremble bitterly.*

The fate of the Polish Franciscan *Maximilian Kolbe* was a tragic one. Born near Lodz in 1894, he was imprisoned in Auschwitz; he volunteered to take the place of a man with a large family and was starved to death. He was beatified in 1982. Here are some excerpts from his poems about Mary:

*Mary, Queen of heaven and earth,
I know I am not worthy
To approach you,
But as I love you so much
I dare to beg you:
Be so kind to explain who you are.
I would like to get to know you better and
    better,
So that I can love and honor you more
    and more.
With a zeal that knows no bounds,
I would like to tell others, who you are,
So that more and more people
may know and love you ever more
    warmly,
So that you can be the Queen of all people,
of all hearts that beat here on earth.
Some dò not even know your name.
Others do not dare to look on you,
And again others believe that they can
reach the goal of their life without you.
There are many people who love you,
But few prepared to do anything
out of love for you: for labor, for suffering
or even for sacrificing their lives.
When will you be Queen in all hearts?
If the dwellers on this earth
acknowledge you as Mother,
If the Father in heaven really can be a
    Father,
And all people feel that they are brothers
    and sisters?*

Another modern Polish martyr was the priest *Jerzy Popieluszko,* who fought for Solidarity and was murdered in 1984. He invokes Mary:

*Mother of those who hope in Solidarnosc,
    pray for us!
Mother of the deceived, Mother of the
    betrayed,
Mother of those arrested in the night,*

*Mother of the terrified,
Mother of the shot miners,
Mother of the shipyard workers,
Mother of the interrogated,
Mother of the unjustly condemned...
Mother of those despised because they
    carry the sign with
your holy face,
Mother of those whose jobs have been
    taken away...
Mother of the crying mothers,
Mother of the careworn fathers,
pray for us.*

In his poem *Mary,* Bertolt Brecht (1898–1956), the socialist playwright and lyrical poet, looks behind the scene of a supposed idyll:

*The night of her first birth
had been cold. But in later years
she completely forgot
the frost in the crossbeams of sorrow and
    the smoking stove,
And the choking of the afterbirth toward
    morning.
But above all she forgot the bitter
shame of not being alone—
a shame peculiar to the poor.
Mainly because of this
in later years it became a festival
where everyone gathered.
The rough talk of the shepherds fell silent,
Later in the story they turned into kings.
The wind, which was very cold,
turned into the song of angels.
And of the hole that let in the frost only
the star that looked in was left....*

A moving poem from the Second World War comes to us from *Arno Pötzsch.* Once again he understands Mary as the great bringer of consolation in the most desperate situations, in this case the tragedy of Stalingrad in 1942 (*).

The idea that Mary as the all-caring mother takes the suffering in her lap corresponds to the Russian folk belief in which "little Mother Russia" and "Mother Earth" are closely linked with the concept of the Mother of God. A Russian hymn puts it this way:

*O mother earth, moist earth,
we are all born from you,
O graves, O oak coffins,
you will be our dwelling!
You never-resting worms,
then you will be our hosts!*

W–1942 LICHT

WEIHNACHTEN IM KESSEL

LEBEN LIEBE

FESTUNG STALINGRAD

*Page 118*: Maximilian Kolbe (1894–1941). Painting by an unknown artist shows Kolbe in the uniform of a concentration camp prisoner. The Polish Franciscan, who was beatified in 1982, died in a starvation bunker in Auschwitz when he took the place of the father of a family.

*Above*: *The Madonna of Stalingrad* sketched by a German private in the encircled area of Stalingrad (1942–43). The caption reads: "Christmas," 1942 in the pocket, Fortress Stalingrad, Light, Life, Love."

*The Madonna of Stalingrad*
*spends today with the German soldiers.*
*In the icy winter night*
*of the Russian steppe*
*she has set forth,*
*the Lady and Mother full of grace.*

*The Madonna of Stalingrad*
*visits today the poorest of the poor.*
*They crouch in the ruins in bitter distress,*
*only one thing is close, and that is death;*
*so the Mother will have mercy.*

*The Madonna of Stalingrad,*
*she comes through the icy winds*
*into huts and caves she comes*
*and sits down in the meager light,*
*the woman with the heavenly child.*

*The Madonna of Stalingrad,*
*O listen, now she sings so softly!*
*It sounds to the men like home and light,*
*The rigid face secretly relaxes.*
*O wonder of the divine tune!*

*The Madonna of Stalingrad,*
*wrapped in her broad garment—*
*what do I see? Now she spreads her mantle out!*
*Now she speaks:*
*Come one and all, I'll bring you home,*
*I, your mother, will take care of you!*

*The Madonna of Stalingrad,*
*now she lays her hands on everyone,*
*she silences the grief, the pain and suffering,*
*the loneliest heart fills with peace,*
*now joyful and silent till the end.*

*The Madonna of Stalingrad,*
*knows about the unspeakable pains;*
*she knows all the misery, knows all the want*
*nd a thousand times, a thousand times she suffers death,*
*after all she once bore a child at her heart!*

*The Madonna of Stalingrad,*
*she came, the mother of graces,*
*to the poorest of the poor in the holy night,*
*because the mother was still thinking of the poorest,*
*she came to the German soldiers.*

*The Madonna of Stalingrad*
*sent by love from heaven,*
*she blessed them in a frightful world,*
*in trenches and graves, in the gruesome field,*
*the living and the dead.*

Arno Pötzsch

*My neighbors—the stones,*
*the worms—my friends,*
*the sand—my camp,*
*O you moist mother earth,*
*take back your poor child!*
*Think of us, O Lord—of the times,*
*when your eternal kingdom begins!*
*O wonderful queen, mother of God,*
*moist mother earth!*

The critical viewpoint of modern feminism vis-à-vis Mary has also entered literature. A passionate poem by the feminist and pacifist *Elisabeth Burmeister* from 1983 charges that by exalting Mary the Church has reduced all other woman to a second-class, dependent status:

*MARY*
*you're not my mother*
*it's time*
*that the people know it.*
*My mother's form, my mother's face—*
*God's judgment and sentence*
*have ravaged, broken, and torn them,*
*bitten with burning pincers;*
*my mother's face, my mother's form*
*is violated, blinded, disfigured with*
   *violence,*
*become like the earth—*
*so wretched, so old,*
*so bitter, so evil,*
*so hard,*
*so cold*
*—and YOU have her on your conscience!*
*Mary,*
*keep your smooth face,*
*the false humility,*
*the false renunciation,*
*the false obedience, the false duty,*
*the false patience till the Last Judgment.*
*I don't WANT them, do you hear?*
*I don't WANT them!*
*keep them,*
*let God repay you for them,*
*the God who rewards and punishes,*
*I want to dwell in the darkness*
*where my mother dwells.*

Yet another vision of Mary—as caring for the poorest of the poor—is recurrent in the work of Mother Teresa (1910–1997). Born Agnes Gonxha Bojaxhio in Skopje, Macedonia, she first joined the Loreto Sisters in Ireland, then worked for twenty years as a teacher in India. In 1950 she founded the Congregation of the Missionaries of

Charity, which spread through Europe and the Third World. In 1979 she received the Nobel Peace Prize. Here is one of her prayers to Mary:

*Mary, Mother of Jesus,*
*give us a heart,*
*as beautiful, as pure, as immaculate,*
*as loving and as humble as yours,*
*so that we can receive Jesus and love him*
*as you loved him,*
*so that, as you did, we can serve him,*
*hidden as he is, in the poorest of the poor.*

Elsewhere she maintains that Marian piety can help people to follow Christ better:

*Because the same Jesus who entered Mary's body also comes to us, we should hurry up and climb the hills of our difficulties and joyfully serve others, so as to be able to give them Jesus. So we should always ask: Mary, give us your heart—so lovely, pure and immaculate.... You are for us the cause of joy, for you have given us Jesus. Help us to become a cause of joy for others by giving them Jesus.*

In his poem *Cologne I*, *Heinrich Böll* (1917–1985) comes to grips one more time with the city of his birth and its Catholicism. To him Cologne is the "dark mother," whose attempt to reconcile paganism with Christianity ends up linking the Madonna and Dionysus, the god of wine and fertility:

*Anyone who listens*
*by the sewers*
*can hear them*
*in the labyrinths*
*beneath the city*
*stumbling over debris, potsherds, bones*
*the Madonna follows Venus to convert her*
*—in vain*
*in vain her Son goes after Dionysus*
*in vain Gereon follows Caesar*
*scornful laughter*
*whoever listens by the sewers*
*can hear it*
   *The dark mother,*
*not improved*
*throughout history,*
*looks good*
*with filth on her face*
*in the labyrinths*
*beneath the city*
*she procures the Madonna*
*for Dionysus*
*reconciles the Son with Venus*

*forces Gereon and Caesar*
*into the Great Coalition*
*she prostitutes herself*
*to whomever has the cash.*

In the poem *And Mary* by the Swiss pastor and poet *Kurt Marti* (born 1921), the crucial point is the opposition between idealization and reality. Mary sets herself free from this and so becomes the liberator of other women:

*(2)*
*and mary could barely read*
*and mary could barely write*
*and mary was not allowed to sing*
*nor talk in the jewish house of prayer*
*where the men serve the man-god*
*but instead she sang*
*to her eldest son*
*instead she sang*
*to the daughters the other sons*
*about the great grace and her*
*holy coup.*
*(5)*
*later much later mary looked*
*helplessly down from the altars*
*on which she had been placed*
*and she thought there must have been a*
   *mix-up*
*when she—a mother many times over—*
*was glorified as a virgin*
*and she feared she was losing her mind*
*as more and more people*
*kept kneeling down before her*
*(6)*
*and mary came out of her pictures*
*and climbed down from her altars*
*and she became the maiden courage*
*the holy cheeky jeanne d'arc...*
*and she was burned a million times over*
   *as a witch*
*to honor god the idol*
*and she was little therese*
*but rosa luxemburg too*
*and she was simone weil, "la vierge rouge"*
*and witness to the absolute*
*and she became madonna leone who rides*
   *naked*
*on the lion's back for her indios....*

We have been able here to cite or barely allude to only a very small selection of the immense, abundant literature on Mary. Hence it may be appropriate to offer a brief, summary review.

The earliest Marian literature that we know of—that is, composed before the Council of Ephesus—consists of poems, most of which are prayers to Mary. Mary is always viewed in connection with her Son. Either she is called upon ("rejoice...," "hail ...") or the scene of the annunciation of the birth of Jesus is recalled.

After the Council of Ephesus, which gave the decisive impulse to the veneration of Mary, we find poems in which Mary is linked allegorically with various images: a candlestick, the field of God, Jacob's ladder. The miracle of the little body, from which, along with Jesus, the whole world is born, is observed with amazement. In the 6th century we meet for the first time the motif of the Mater Dolorosa, the mother of Jesus beneath the cross. From the 8th century on we increasingly hear invocations of Mary begging her to intercede with her Son for human beings.

But in the same 8th century there are also considerable setbacks: for one by the iconoclasts, for another by the rapid advance of Islam. In reaction to iconoclasm we see the emergence of new, imaginative modes of praising Mary.

With the 10th century the Marian legends come to the fore—first by Roswitha, then in long descriptions by Wernher, later too in various Lives of Mary, composed in a number of Christian countries from the 12th to the 14th centuries. Mary's life is embellished with increasing richness, and some of the countless legends are retold again and again in ever new variants. In all these legends, often later gathered into extensive collections, Mary always appears as the crowned Queen of Heaven. At the same time, along with such stories a new form of lyric developed, in which Mary is praised and invoked as a helpful mother.

Starting in the 12th century a new, more mystical tone gradually enters these lyrics; and various forms and motifs blend together. The high points of the medieval veneration of Mary are reached in France with Bernard of Clairvaux, in Italy with Francis of Assisi (later too with Dante and Petrarch, the latter, of course, linking up with the Renaissance), in Germany with Walther von der Vogelweide, the mystics Johannes Tauler and Henrich of Laufenberg,

and the mystical poets Mechthild of Magdeburg, Mechthild of Hackeborn, and Gertrude of Helfta. Among the mystical singers of Mary in the 14th century we also have to add Catherine of Siena.

In the late Middle Ages we witness the crude contrast between, on the one hand, the Flagellants and their fervent prayers to Mary and, on the other, the almost frivolous Miracle plays, in which Mary gets married to her admirer. Alongside all this we see quite simple songs, some of which have been preserved to our day.

The Renaissance and humanism brought a fresh setback to Marian piety. Nevertheless even Martin Luther kept tackling the problem of Mary. François Villon's ballad-like prayers to Mary are still impressive today. Then there were the imaginative 16th-century "contrafacts." Religious orders, above all the Jesuits, dedicated themselves to Catholic Reform and the Counter Reformation, over the course of which old Marian strains were taken up again.

In the 17th century new paths opened up; with Angelius Silesius Marian piety took on almost pantheistic overtones. With Friedrich Spee we see the beginnings of the Enlightenment. Then too this century also produced simple folk poetry and the Marian works of the English poets Dryden and Pope.

In the 18th century the subject of Mary underwent an increasing variety of transformations, partly no doubt in reaction to the anti-Marian current of the Enlightenment: the difference between the Mary of the young Goethe and the Mary in Schiller's *Maid of Orleans* is enormous.

The work of the Romantics again relied completely on medieval atmosphere. Herder looked at Mary analytically, with Hölderlin the spirit of Greece was resonant, while with Matthias Claudius and in Grimms' *Fairy Tales* once again the simple, folk Mary reemerged. In England the Romantic view of Mary was represented by Wordsworth and Byron as well as Bridges, in France by Daudet, and in Germany by Heine, even as Romanticism was coming to a conclusion with

him. With Gottfried Keller we hear other tones, and Ludwig Thoma strikes us as almost naturalistic. In reaction to naturalism, we see in Germany the work of George and Derleth, in France of Claudel, and in England of Housman and Chesterton.

Rilke has to be acknowledged as the outstanding representative of 20th-century German poetry. After him in the age of the World Wars conceptions of Mary split up even more markedly: Hermann Hesse in his lyrical intensity speaks of Mary more simply than Rilke. The work of Gertrud von Le Fort and Konrad Weiss is highly Catholic in the traditional sense. The First World War influenced the Marian poetry of Le Fort, Trakl, and Lersch—though differently for each of them. By contrast, Rudolf Alexander Schröder was more conscious of form and more tied to tradition. Some opponents and victims of Nazism, including Edith Stein and Maximilian Kolbe, were close to Mary. Arno Pötzsch invoked her from the hell of Stalingrad.

In the postwar period the Marian poetry of Brecht and Marti was marked by a crude realism, while Elisabeth Burmeister's work had a feminist orientation. The spectrum spanned the distance from Böll, whose realism simultaneously conjured up images from antiquity, all the way to Mother Teresa, who found in Mary a point of identification for her service to the poor.

The poets of our century, male and female, can hardly be reduced to a common denominator. Their approaches to Mary mirror the inner conflict of our time. While we note that in the last few centuries, especially in our own, Mary has played a lesser role than in earlier times, in the Middle Ages for example, one can always add that never before was she so illumined, observed, interpreted, and claimed by so many different sides as in the 19th and 20th centuries.

*I see you, Mary, lovingly expressed*
*in a thousand pictures,*
*But none of them can portray you,*
*as my soul looks upon you.*

Novalis

# My Soul Seeks the Land of Freedom

Dorothee Sölle

Page 123: Edvard Munch (1863–1944), *Madonna*, 1895, colored lithograph, Kunsthalle, Hamburg. In the spirit of symbolism Munch takes a purely subjective approach to the topic. He distances himself from the traditional attributes of the religious theme and transforms Mary into the Feminine *tout court*. In this way he creates a new icon, in which the secular and the sacred achieve a new linkage.

The adjacent verse by the Romantic poet Novalis came to mind à propos of the "thousand pictures" of a fascinatingly rich and confusingly varied religious tradition. Who was Mary, actually, what kinds of access can we find to her—in the New Testament, in the dogmatic interpretation of who she was, in the history of piety, so full of poetry and creative imagination? From the Queen of Heaven to the "secret goddess" of Christianity, from the "Madonna of the rogues" in Polish folk legend to the teacher of the teachers (*magistra magistrorum*) and patron of universities, between "Our Lady of the good delivery" and "Our Lady of the happy death"—who was Mary really?

There is no one picture that can claim to be "right" and "complete." *De Maria numquam satis* is an old principle of Christian tradition: about Mary there is never enough. The abundance of the various names and forms of praise, pictures and legends, places of pilgrimage, rituals, prayers said and prayers answered—all this points to another question that is even harder to answer: Who is Mary *today,* at the end of the second millennium? Who is she for us? Can I dare to articulate how "my soul looks upon you"? Do I have a right to say for whom she is a real person, whom she blesses and protects, for whom she is a comfort and challenge, a figure of life without whom we would be the poorer? Here is Novalis once again:
*I only know that the world of turmoil*
*since then drifts away from me*
*And an ineffably sweet heaven*
*Is forever in my mind.*

In fact Mary is somehow tied in with the "ineffably sweet heaven" that many among us, women and men, think they can do without. In self-destructive hyperrationality they have robbed themselves of the right to something that might be "forever in our minds." But against this process of self-impoverishment, which we inflict on ourselves by repressing our deepest wishes, the "thousand pictures" have something powerful to say. Here is how I understand the point of this book about the Mother of God: The pictures remind us of things—perhaps of our childhood Christmases, but still more of our own longings for a different life. Their beauty draws us to their truth. They can teach us to see something about this "ineffably sweet heaven" with our own eyes. They remind us how within religious traditions the fears and wishes of simple people could be named and therefore healed. That way the world was not just an incomprehensibly muddled "turmoil," but became a pointer to the land of freedom that we call heaven.

I would like to learn how to hold together the two questions, "Who was Mary really?" and "Who is she for us?" The historical view all by itself is not enough. It wanders back and forth between the New Testament and the concrete history of Marian devotion. It clings to dogmas or the critical unmasking of dogma, clarifies and enriches our understanding of the past. We come to know Mary as a woman who could be at once a virgin and a mother, a suffering woman full of pain and a crowned queen, learned and a simple maidser-

123

vant, a healer and benefactress. But the root of the actual fascination here can at best be hinted at by the perspective of history and its know-it-all interpretations, which find everything in tradition suspect.

Another question, an existential question, is needed here. The Enlightenment effort to distinguish between miracle stories and actual events from the standpoint of what is in principle superior (the facts) does not get us very far. In the postmodern period this degenerates into an estheticizing disconnectedness. Our relationship with the great traditions to which Mary belongs turns sterile when we casually scan the thousand pictures while ignoring the religious soil from which they grew. A real understanding may require the power of hope for healing in our world too; but at the very least it calls for a sense of the "ineffably sweet" that has repeatedly opened up in her paintings and legends.

In the thousand pictures I look for an understanding of Mary stamped by the biblical perspective and the history of piety—and not much damaged by dogmatic theology. The Protestant, Scripture-based tradition in which I have my

own roots accepted and passed on belief in the virginity of Mary, but not in the sense of the "semper virgo" dogma (553 A.D.). That doctrine from Constantinople unalterably declares that Mary was a virgin "before, during, and after the birth of Christ" (*ante partum, in partu et post partum Christi*). On the other hand, the oldest Gospel speaks without embarrassment of Jesus' brothers and sisters (Mark 6.3). Did Jesus have siblings? Can the word "brother," as used in the New Testament, also be used to describe cousins or does it have to be taken literally? This exegetical disagreement between Catholics and Protestants points to another, deeper problem that has been broached only by the women's movement: Is it true that Mary is radically different from all other women? Does she have to be viewed as a sexless and *therefore* sinless being? Is she alone "pure," while the rest of us women, following the example of the *other* mother, Eve, are impure? Do we have to go along with the problematic polarization, both anti-Judaic and hostile to sexuality, of Western tradition? Do we have to choose between Eve, the mother of all the living, and Mary, the mother of God? Or is there in fact some

common ground where these two archetypes can meet, as expressed in the lovely reconciling name "Eva Marie"?

In the old German Christmas hymn (Trier, 1587) there is an allusion to Isaiah 11.1 ("There shall come forth a shoot from the stump of Jesse, and a branch shall grow out of his roots"), as applied to Christ:

*Isaiah 'twas foretold it,*
*The Rose I have in mind.*
*With Mary we behold it,*
*The Virgin Mother kind.*
*To show God's love aright*
*She bore to men a Savior,*
*When half spent was the night.*
(trans. Theodore Baker)

This hymn too contains the doctrine of the perpetual virginity of Mary, but it is articulated and praised so as not to exclude other women. It can reopen and deepen our understanding of virginity. It is as if we were seeing the young woman Mary in her great, continuous admiration for God's dealing with her. Virginity, perhaps, has more to do with the ability to marvel than with the technical patriarchal concept of the "virgo intacta." In that case "pure" simply means open to God and empty, like a page on which God can write his

message. In many passages of Marian tradition the concept of purity has a mystical rather than a technical sense.

I am trying to get around the problems caused by a legalistic and property-based notion, by turning to popular piety rather than to dogmatic theology. In venerating the Mother of God this piety took different, twisted, and more realistic paths. These are the ones I wish to follow. Their imaginative freedom in handling tradition has encouraged me to tell Mary's story in the language of the present.

A Mariology "from below" is today ecumenically possible and necessary, as opposed to one that relies on playing off Eve, the door to sin, against Mary, the Gate of Heaven. This other relationship with Mary has come about in the last quarter century within feminist theology. It tries, with many voices, of black and white, poor and rich women, to question and name in a new way what is special about Mary, her being-in-God, her holiness, her "ineffable sweetness."

At the end of the 20th century a Carmelite and teacher of the poor from Brazil reports about places of pilgrimage dedicated to Mary, where people

flock by the tens of thousands. Long lines of trucks and buses bring the pilgrims together from all directions. The people pray and sing uninterruptedly, one rosary is recited after another, one hymn to Mary intoned after another.

A simple woman, a widow and mother of seventeen children, of whom ten are dead, was asked: "Why are you making this pilgrimage?" The answer from Dona Raimunda was not so far removed from what Novalis looked for. She expressed in a simple way what the mystery of Mary is for all those who love her. She said, "You feel heaven very close."

*Left*: Martin Schongauer (1450–1491), *Madonna in the Rose Bower*, around 1473, church of St. Martin, Colmar. The motif of Mary in the rose bower, also called the *hortus conclusus* (garden enclosed), is a symbol of the Immaculate Conception.

*Center*: Carlo Crivelli (1430–1492), a Venetian painter, *Madonna of the Passion* (Museum of Castelvecchio, Verona). On the left is the rooster, a symbol of Judas' betrayal.

*Right*: The Mother of God as the *Queen of Heaven*, by Simon Zugravu, ca. 1820 (Dancu Collection, Laz). Mary appears as the Theotokos, Christ as the Pantocrator.

*Page 124, left*: Luca Signorelli (1445/50–1523): *The Holy Family*, 1498–1500, tempera on wood (Uffizi, Florence). On a tondo the Holy Family is depicted in deep tranquillity by themselves. In keeping with tradition Mary is seen as reading and learned.

*Page 124, center*: The Master of Flemalle (Dutch, 1350–1444), *Maria lactans*, (Städelsches Kunstinstitut, Frankfurt am Main). The young Mary is depicted in warm intimacy with her child. Her serious facial expression shows her knowledge of future suffering.

*Page 124, right*: Limestone Pietà, Bohemian, ca. 1400 (formerly Seeon Monastery, today the Bavarian National Museum, Munich).

126

## THE YOUNG GIRL

**M**ary grew up in Nazareth, not in Tiberias, where the rich have their lake-shore villas, but in Nazareth, a wretched little hamlet in the interior of the country, half forgotten in the Galilean hills, somewhat higher than Lake Gennesaret. The village was considered a den of thieves. "Can anything good come out of Nazareth?" people wondered (John 1.46). There were only a few huts, some of them built into the mountainside. Everyone knew everyone else; and, as things go in villages, anyone who was the least bit different got gossiped about. When Mary's grown son Jesus returned to his hometown one day, the word was immediately: "Who? Where does he claim to get all that, this wisdom and these miracles that supposedly happen through him? Isn't that the son of Mary, the carpenter?" (freely adapted from Mark 6.20). There was no mention of Joseph.

Nazareth had a single well, which had to suffice for everybody. It was the meeting point for women, who drew their water there to fill the large storage jugs they had at home. And there was the synagogue, where the community gathered on the Sabbath. Right next to it was the little school where the children learned to read the Bible in Hebrew. Among themselves they spoke Aramaic.

Perhaps Mary learned to read with her mother. In northeastern Brazil the girl Mary is depicted being taught "the Scriptures" by St. Anne. People have a feminist tradition of passing on the faith from woman to woman. Today it has been reactivated by the base communities of the Church in which women are often the group leaders. Throughout the history of piety there is a tradition of Mary's knowing how to read, of being well-read and teaching others. Some accounts even say that on the Flight into Egypt Mary sat quietly reading on the donkey, while Joseph held little Jesus. In the late Middle Ages the learned mother of God gives poor maids a psalter—thereby promoting the education of women.

Was she also reading when the angel Gabriel entered the room to announce the great joy to her? On this question too there are varying traditions: In the Orthodox Churches Mary is likely to be depicted as a young woman weaving the curtain of the Temple, spinning silk and purple. The West prefers the meditative Mary, reading the Psalms—or perhaps also a young girl dreaming away.

In any case the painters and storytellers did not reduce the girl Mary to the role of busy housewife. There seems to be evidence against that view in the New Testament story of Mary listening devotedly to Jesus' words while the practical-minded Martha is concerned with his bodily well-being (Luke 10.38–42). Granted, this little story is not about the mother of God, but about a sister of Martha named Mary; still, in the history of piety that was often forgotten. The Western tradition has viewed these two women as archetypes for the contemplative and active lives. Meditation and action, quietly hearing the Word (*vita contemplativa*) and restless concern for the daily needs of the body (*vita activa*), were not merely contrasted, but classified in the rank order of Aristotelian rather than Jewish thought. The contemplative life was considered higher, because it was more intellectual and more essential. Active or practical life was necessary, but subordinate. This Mary had "chosen the better part" (Luke 10.42) by listening and keeping silent.

### Mary's Roots in Jewish Tradition

Mary cannot be understood apart from Jewish tradition. She was called "Miriam" by her mother. The Hebrew word "maryam" means "to bear the bitterness of the time." Mary takes the bitter things upon herself that the time, which is hostile to love, will bring. She is a poor country girl who is ready to bear the bitterness. Later as an asylum-seeker, the wife of a refugee, and the mother of a subversive criminal, she will be exposed to bitter times, a mother of sorrows. The *Mater Dolorosa* is already built into her name, which does not conceal the bitterness.

But, above all, the name recalls the time when the chosen people were en-slaved in Egypt. After the Exodus through the Red Sea, Miriam, Moses' sister—some interpret the name to mean "the exalted"—seized the initiative: God has saved us from the hand of the slavedrivers, she sang out loud, took a timbrel in her hand, and began to dance with all the women of Israel (cf. Exodus 15.20):

*"Sing to the Lord, for he has triumphed gloriously; the horse and his rider he has thrown into the sea."*

This song of the prophetess Miriam is one that as a child Mary would have sung in the synagogue with all the women and girls. It is not very gentle and not exactly modest. It points back to the exodus of God's people from Israel, and it points ahead to other op-

*Above: Mary taught by Anne*, southeast German pen drawing from the end of the 14th century (Germanic National Museum, Nuremberg).

*Page 126*: A variant of the *Immaculate Conception* is seen in this colored collotype after a 1910 painting by C. Bosseron Chambers (b. 1883). The depiction of Mary Immaculate blends here with the images of the Sacred Heart, which were very popular at the time.

pressed peoples who thought of Miriam and Mary as fitting together and who did not separate redemption from liberation. Black women in America, enslaved to field work and exploited for the pleasure of their masters, continued to sing a song from this same tradition: Miriam and Mary belong together, they cannot be sundered. The drowned army of the Pharaoh points to Miriam's old song, and thus the grief of mother

Mary over her tortured son will also come to an end. The black woman who bears the name of Mary knows that the name of the liberator is indelibly written on the three links of the slave chain that she, like her people, wears:

*Oh Mary, don't you weep anymore,*
*Pharaoh's army got drownded.*
*Oh Mary, don't you weep anymore, don't*
*    you mourn,*
*Pharaoh's army got drownded.*

*Mary wore three links of chain,*
*every link was Jesus' name.*
*Mary wore three links of chain,*
*every link was freedom's name.*

*Left*: *St. Anne and St. Joachim*, verre églomisé from the area of Alba Iulia, 1804, Ciobanu Collection, Bucharest.

*Right*: *Joachim and Anne carry offerings to the high priest*, wall painting (Mistra, Peloponnesus). The picture unites two episodes: Owing to their childlessness, Anne and Joachim were excluded from the community, and Joachim's offering was rejected by the high priest. After the announcement to Anne that she would conceive a daughter, Joachim's offering is accepted by the priest.

*Page 129*: From Sveti Kliment in Ohrid, Macedonia (1310/11), comes this fresco showing scenes from the life of Mary's mother Anne. On the left we see the *Meeting at the Golden Gate* and on the right the *Birth of Mary*.

### "What Good Can Come out of Nazareth?"

The people in Nazareth lived from physical labor, some in the fields, some as simple manual workers, carpenters, or smiths. But the field hands were not the owners of the land they farmed; they worked for big landowners who lived on the lake near the harbor. The women lived in the house. Their work, like that of the old women and little girls like Mary, remained invisible. They washed, baked, raised the children. Girls were married very young, often at the age of twelve. There were many diseases in Galilee, and the people were familiar with hunger. It was not from high spirits but from hunger that they plucked ears of grain and chewed them, even on the sabbath.

The country was occupied by the Romans, who extorted taxes from the Jews. The tax collectors who collaborated with the Romans generally enriched themselves at the expense of the population. The big landowners too were on the side of Rome and got along well with the occupiers. In Galilee there was also a guerrilla movement; its members were known as Zealots, people given to violence. Whenever they could, they killed Roman soldiers, especially under cover of night. Then the civilian population in the villages would be set upon and punished. No one was sure of his or her life. When the women met at the well, they would hold their hands to their mouths as they talked about what was happening. The topic was liberation. Farther to the south the word "Galilean" practically meant "insurgent against the Romans." The region that Mary grew up in was explosive. The song of praise (pieced together from biblical texts) that she later sang, the Magnificat, deals with power and oppression, of going hungry and being filled, of God's intervention on behalf of the wretched. It is not just the personal song of praise of the individual woman who has been blessed, whose "low estate" God has regarded. It is the song of her people—and the good fortune of the people is seen, as always in the Bible, in those at the bottom of the pile. God has again and again shown himself to be mighty.

### Joachim and Anne, Mary's Parents

This great context of the exaltation of the lowly and the uplifting of the downtrodden is where the (postbiblical) tradition of Mary's birth belongs. This tale links up with the many stories of barren, childless women, who against all expec-

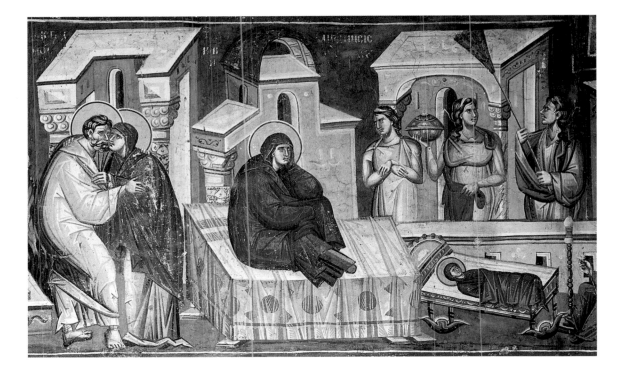

tation become pregnant thanks to God's intervention: women like Sarah, Abraham's wife, like Rachel, Jacob's wife, who bombards her husband with the desperate cry, "Give me children, or I shall die!" (Genesis 30.1). In biblical tradition God is the one who opens the womb and gives life. When Rachel later becomes pregnant and bears her son Joseph, she says, "God has taken away my reproach" (Gen. 30.23).

In this tradition fruitfulness meant blessings and care in one's old age, while sterility was experienced as being forgotten by God. Joachim and Anne too, Mary's parents, shared in this tradition. They had been married for twenty years without having children. That was for both of them a misfortune felt and tasted every day. It was not just heartbreak, it was a public shame. Women were mocked and despised, like the childless Hannah, later the mother of Samuel. And Joachim, Mary's future father, was excluded from the Temple—indeed he was cast out and cursed—when he tried to present a burnt offering. In his grief he went out into the wilderness. Anne ran with tears in her eyes into the garden. One legend says that there she saw a nest full of baby birds that had just hatched. She is said to have called out to God: "Ruler of heaven and earth, why do you deny me what you grant even to the birds of the air (heaven)?" Suddenly an angel appeared to her and promised her a child, a daughter, whose name countless women would one day bear.

An old, infertile woman became a mother: an insignificant, useless creature in the eyes of the world around her was inscribed in the great history of God with his people. The whole story is full of those crazy things that biology cannot explain. Sarah was old and postmenopausal when she had Isaac. Hannah was an old woman when she had Samuel. Anne conceived Mary. And so Mary too became pregnant, without any man's assistance.

# THE MOTHER OF GOD

## The Annunciation to Mary

How did it happen? The New Testament story of the Annunciation to Mary by the angel Gabriel is augmented in one of the apocryphal gospels. This *Protevangelium of James* comes from around the middle of the 2nd century and was widely disseminated early on, no doubt in part because it collected the legends about Mary.

The priests of the Temple in Jerusalem have conferred and decided to have a curtain made for the Lord's Temple. According to the Jewish historian Flavius Josephus, it was supposed to be an image of the universe. Philosophers of nature in antiquity looked on nature, indeed on the whole world, as "a beautiful fabric made by God." Spinning and weaving was the art of connecting what was loose and bringing together disparate elements. The raw material, silk and wool, is woven into thread by the turning of a spindle. What is shapeless is given a shape; it is a creative process with a lofty symbolic content.

Greek philosophers too are said to have turned their spindles when tying together the strands of their thoughts. In an old hymn about Mary it says that she will "reconcile the irreconcilable" because "in her a garment [was] woven for the deity." The apocryphal account of the Protevangelium links Mary with the philosophy of nature of the ancient world. A simple country girl is brought into the Temple environment and into the culture of spinning and weaving.

Still more amazing is another change that James makes in the sparse New Testament material. In his story the priests seek out seven immaculate virgins from the House of David, one of whom is Mary. In the Temple lots are drawn to see which girls get which colors and materials. "And the genuine purple and the scarlet were assigned by lot to Mary." Both were rare luxuries, entrusted only to kings and gods.

*Mary, taking the scarlet, spun it. She took her pitcher and went out to fill it full of water; and, behold, there came a voice saying, "Hail, highly favored one! The Lord is with you, you are blessed among women."*
*Mary looked about, to the right and to the left, to see whence this voice might be coming to her. Filled with trembling she went into her house; and putting down the pitcher, she took the purple and sat down on a chair and drew out the purple thread.*
*Behold, an angel of the Lord stood before her saying, "Do not fear, Mary, for you have found favor before the Lord of all, and you will conceive by his Word." Mary, having heard this, considered to herself, saying, "Shall I conceive by the Lord, the living God? As all women do, shall I give birth?"* (The Other Bible, p. 388).

Then the story goes back to following the account from Luke 1. The novelty in this apocryphal version is that the angel's greeting and his message are separated. The flow of the narrative is slowed down, as at first only the voice of the Invisible One is heard. Mary's amazement and terror expand; and as her doubt is first suggested by the way she looks around questioningly, it is then explicitly mentioned, and she becomes more human. She is not just a mute vessel that willingly receives what is presented to it. In some pictures she defends herself with a gesture of protest and a body that recoils. Only after some hesitation does Mary agree and say her yes:
*Then Mary said, "Behold the servant-girl of the Lord is before him. Let it be to me according to your word."*
*She worked the purples and the scarlet and brought them to the priest; and the priest blessed her* (The Other Bible, p. 388).

In the Protevangelium Mary oddly forgets about the annunciation of the archangel when she visits Elizabeth. The text says: "But Mary forgot the mysteries of which the angel Gabriel spoke; and she looked up toward Heaven, and said, 'Who am I that, behold, all the families of the earth bless me?'" She is amazed, astonished, and seems not to know what has happened to her.

## As Told Today

Thus far the ancient story. But might it not also have been entirely different? Might the angel, though he could be heard within her, have remained invisible? Might not his words, once heard, recede and then be forgotten? And would the miracle then not remain just as much God's action?

At the time Mary was already engaged to Joseph, who came from Bethlehem. But, as was the custom, she was still living in her parents' house. It happened with her as it does with many women to this day. She waited, she calculated the days; but she couldn't be quite sure. Perhaps she thought, it

*would* have to come; she waited. And then she went off to Elizabeth, her older friend, perhaps because one cannot always talk to one's own mother about the most important things. And so she simply ran away from Nazareth, she cleared out of the house. Perhaps someone gave her a lift on a donkey. She asked her way to her old relative's place.

We do not know what she thought, but thoughts and questions from other women, including those living today, accompany her on this long way.
*Mary, who were you worried about?*
*Mary, how come you were expecting?*
*Mary, why didn't you get an abortion?*
*We're worried about how it's getting on*
*We have no expectations even though*
  *we're expecting*
*We abort joy with pain*
*Mary, who were you worried about?*
*Mary, why didn't you get an abortion?*
*Mary, how could you be expecting*
*in a world with nothing to look forward*
  *to?*

*Page 133*: The Madonna Platytera from the portal of the Abbazia della Misericordia, Venice (now in the Victoria and Albert Museum, London). The stone relief was made by the sculptor Bartolomeo Buon. Mary stands as the Madonna of the Protecting Cloak with her royal family tree, the root of Jesse, in the background.

*Above*: The 20th century approaches traditional Christian themes in art from a highly personal and even provocative angle. The picture *The Virgin Spanks the Son of Man before Three Witnesses* (André Breton, Paul Éluard, Max Ernst) by Max Ernst, oil painting, private collection, Belgium, has caused not a few scandals. With drastic realism the artist shows us the humanity of the Son of God and Mary too, in her impatience.

*Page 130*: The *Annunciation* by El Greco (1541–1614), end of the 16th century, Szép-müvészeti Museum, Budapest, is one of the most impressive works on this subject. While in earlier centuries Mary was depicted with a distaff by a well, from the early Middle Ages on she is shown with a book. The point is that she is reading Isaiah 7.14, "Behold, a young woman shall conceive and bear a son, and shall call his name Immanuel (God with us)." The book in Mary's hand points to the Book of Life, and popular belief claims that no one was more learned in the Law of God and in wisdom than the Virgin Mary.

*Page 131*: In his Annunciation from 1931 the French painter Maurice Denis (1870–1943) has depicted the scene in the spirit of Art Nouveau as part of the here and now. Mary appears as a modern woman, with the angel kneeling before her (National Museum of Modern Art, Paris).

## A Mariology from Below

Articulated as it was by men, Christian theology has often turned virginity into a central concern, as if it was the only condition for Mary's being-in-God. By so doing, theology separated Mary from other women, including her foremothers in the Bible, and tried to exclude everything earthly and realistic from her life. Thus the doctrine arose that she felt no labor pains, because she was free from original sin and hence from the curse that has been hanging over women in childbirth ever since. But even such simple, natural touches as Max Ernst's painting of gentle Mary walloping Jesus, who is howling unbearably), are a shock to theological correctness. Such theology has at the same time constructed a picture of women (and an anthropology) that polarizes and prescribes the roles of the sexes: action versus passivity, power versus kindness, justice versus mercy, autonomy versus putting up with things, self-consciousness versus humility.

But, thank God, theology in the West was not done only by theologians. The history of piety and its expressive forms in art, literature, and music speak an entirely different language. They look for a Mariology from below. In their love of Mary the people have not stuck by the rules, which posited the masculine-hierarchical will-to-power. They continually broke these rules, got around them, and changed them. Their goal was not, as the mistrustful hierarchy often feared, to drag Mary down, but to bring her closer to real men and women.

There is a famous legend telling how Mary stood by a nun who had gotten pregnant. She took her place singing in the choir and stood in for her until after the very pregnant sister, having given birth to and nursed the baby, could return. And Mary's intervention occurred without the mother superior's noticing anything.... In the later Middle Ages a beekeeper dedicated a pound of wax to the all-pure Virgin so that she would restore his virility.... In Poland a story is told about a robber who was to be hanged and who prayed to Mary. For three days the Mother of God stayed beneath the gallows and supported the criminal's feet (while remaining invisible, of course). He pretended to be dead, and when he was cut down, he jumped up and ran away, an Ave Maria on his lips.

In popular piety Mary's most important roles are those of providing energetic help, interceding, recommending, and even objecting on people's behalf. Because she herself is a mother, she has a motherly understanding; and it is much easier to approach her than God, who is often feared as too rigorous. In many paintings and sculptures Mary spreads a gigantic mantle over a great crowd of people. Her body is larger than that of all the others. She appears as the "Great Mother," who cares for and defends all her descendants, old and young, adults and children. God hurls the lightning bolts of his wrath down from heaven, but the Virgin spreads out her great mantle of protection and hides the little humans from the wrathful judgment of God. People liked to believe that Jesus—the judge at the Last Judgment—could refuse his mother nothing.

Thus popular piety has continually undermined the theologically correct view of the humble virgin and her "Be it done unto me according to thy word." The Mary of the Bible has not just said, "Fiat," but also, "Magnificat anima mea Dominum," "My soul glorifies the Lord." She was not just the little girl nodding her head that she is often made out to be. Humbly saying yes to everything that comes from above is a patriarchal, not a biblical, ideal. Mary asked Gabriel, the angel of the Annunciation, how he saw the message happening; and she listen attentively and reflectively. She had, after all, been asked to cooperate in the liberation that the people of God had been waiting for so long, But the fiat of consent is only half the story. Mary then set off; she didn't want to be alone, she needed her friend: another woman who was also caught up in this puzzling business, who was also expecting a baby.

## As Told Today

It was the last days before the birth, and Mary went from office to office, to Building X, Number XYZ, and then there was a long wait for the bureaucrat who turned out to be the wrong one, then filling out forms, on which the husband or father always comes first and a signature is always required. But Mary, unmarried, looking for a place to stay, pregnant, unemployed, couldn't manage it.... Somehow the pains began and she dragged herself into an empty house ready for demolition. It was dark, a stray dog had wandered in and stayed with her. As it happens with women having their first child, it took a long time. Mary had to throw up on the swollen, stinking mattress that lay there.

The whole night the noise never stopped from the gas station nearby. Joseph padded about, sullen and sympathetic at the same time. He had scrounged a blanket and even a bucket of lukewarm water to wash the baby with. He took care of both of them, the whole time. He felt fear, as the shepherds did in the old Christmas story—but the angels took their time. Joseph was restless; with one ear he listened in case the owner of the abandoned building might be coming-—or a policeman to evict the squatters.

But then, instead, something very beautiful happened. Somehow word of the young girl's pregnancy had gotten around; and a few people came by. They knew all about the business with the work permit and residence rights and

the fear of getting thrown out. They looked around, and everybody had brought something. All at once there were so many of them there that they couldn't all just be run off. Suddenly the tumble-down room was full of people and much warmer. It got bright; the stove was lit, and rock music blared from the portable radio that one of the young people had brought. Passersby asked: Is that another demonstration? Yes, for a baby, shouted the demonstrators. And the single mother laughed and was glad about the mutt, and the many friends and the music and the warmth and above all the baby, the illegitimate baby, but who cared about that, about the healthy, crowing child.

## Children's Happiness and Child Murder

Later Mary and Joseph brought their son to the Temple, where a wise old man was already waiting for them. Simeon took the child into his arms and praised God. Then he turned to Mary and murmured something that she did not quite understand at the time, something about the child's "being set for the fall" of some people and the "rising" of others. "And a sword will pierce through your own soul also" (Luke 2:34–35).

fact the idyll of a nonviolent, happy life is something that Mary never had. Perhaps that is why she is so much the protecting or at least consoling mother of all those who have to suffer from violence—in wars, the economy, diseases, and rape.

And the situation with the child Jesus was not exactly simple either. He is said to have been a cheerful boy, at least until he had to go to school. He could not deal with the teachers, who kept repeating, "You have heard what was said to the men of old." When he countered with his, "But I say," he was

Many swords, that was how tradition read it. Shortly after the birth Mary and Joseph had to flee with their baby from the murderous soldiers of King Herod and seek asylum in Egypt. Herod, a Roman collaborator, feared for his dominion, for his power; and so as a precaution he had all the babies and small children under two years eliminated. The slaughter of the children in Bethlehem presaged what would later happen in Jerusalem. The murder of the innocent, one of whom was suspected of being the Messiah, who was to bring the kingdom of justice, is part and parcel of the sacred history of the couple. All the Christmas romanticism cannot charm away the real, political threat to life. In

chided for being a troublemaker, rebellious, or stubborn. A painting from the Lady Church in Nuremberg shows Mary looking morose as she, with a bundle of flax thrown over her shoulder, grabs her son under the arm to bring him to school. The boy, at once bearded and mature, yet no bigger than a child, lets himself be dragged along, perhaps because he already knows all that can be learned in the classroom.

## Neighborhood and Family

At twelve years of age Jesus ran away from his parents, hung around in the Temple for three days, and was still surprised when his relatives, full of con-

cern and anxiety, ordered him, "Get going, back home!" Jesus was not exactly born for obedience to rules and regulations. "O woman, what have you to do with me?" (John 2.4) he barked at his mother the first chance he got—and out in public at a wedding feast. He no longer fit into the village community of Nazareth. When he returned from the wilderness, he read out in the synagogue the scroll of scripture that deals with the mistreated who make their way to freedom. But the people in Nazareth flew into a rage, because Jesus had cured the sick only in the neighboring village, not in his hometown. They wanted to lynch him and throw him off a cliff. Things worked out all right that time—he walked through their midst and left his home. But what must that have meant to Mary!

The Jesus of the Gospels did not give much thought to the family. "Who is my mother, and who are my brothers?" he asked rather ironically (cf. Matthew 12.47–50). That must have hurt Mary, because at the time she did not understand this criticism of blood ties and, still less, the way all those who went around with her son stuck together.

The band was later called "familia Dei," God's family, people who belonged together because of their faith and their unusual way of life. Homeless, unmarried women, fishermen with no nets or boats, old beggars—those were the kind of people who hung around with the Nazarene. Not a sensible person among them: no job, no money, no family, no fixed place to stay. It took a long time for Mary to become like the disciples of the Jesus movement—before she knew where she belonged.

139

*Mary, what do you know about the disturbed?*
*Mary, how is it with the ones who are finished?*
*Tell us, what can be done against death?*

*We have forgotten how one gets to the land of freedom*
*We break into little pieces when we crash,*
*so little that nothing hits us anymore*
*and we die long before death*

*Mary, what do you know about the disturbed?*
*Mary, how is it with the ones who are finished?*
*Mary, what can be done about death in a world of concrete?*

Dorothee Sölle

*Left*: Johan Thorn Prikker (1868–1932), *Christ on the Cross with Mary* (1891–92). The theme of grieving, in the style of the fin de siècle, shows Mary turned to the viewer, but wrapped up in herself.

*Right*: *Grieving Mother of God* (Byzantine, last quarter of the 13th century). The Sorrowful Mother crosses her arms on her breast in a gesture of grief.

*Page 141*: *Crucifixion* (Greek icon from the first half of the 17th century, Amberg Icon Museum, Kölliken, Switzerland). The subject of Mary's pain is given an especially impressive rendition in the crucifixion groups of Byzantine art.

## The Mother beneath the Cross

The sword that pierces through the soul—Mary thought back to that thirty years later, when she stood on the Hill of Shame outside the city where the criminals were executed. All around her there were gaping spectators and Roman soldiers cracking jokes. All night Mary had stood in front of the government palace to find out what they were going to do with him. She could hear the raucous shouts and the crack of whips. Ah, she thought, like so many mothers of the disappeared and of the camps, why didn't they spit on *me* and humiliate *me*? If only they had taken my life, so that I didn't have to stand by, while he whom I brought into this life is being tortured to death. On this night in Jerusalem Mary was very alone. The men, his friends, had all fled, and the women only met under the cross.

Mary did not cry like Mary Magdalene; she had turned to stone. Like her son, she could only ask: "My God, why? Why have you abandoned us?" She never shook off this question for the rest of her life. This story was later called "the Passion," a term that fuses desire and pain. Perhaps Mary's love was never greater than in these hours under the torturing gallows.

Painters have sometimes portrayed her as a quiet young woman with the child on her arm, but already seeing everything that will happen: blood, thorns, the cross. Perhaps she really did know already as a girl that love becomes complete only in God's fearful darkness.

141

"Mary has helped." The notion of Mary as the mediator between heaven and earth—between God and humans—found its most popular expression in the miraculous images.

*Left*: Madonna Platytera from Sveti Sofije in Ohrid, Macedonia; apse of Bogorodica Agidria.

*Above right*: Lovingly and richly embroidered garments of Our Lady of Guadalupe in Spain. She is considered the oldest of the Black Madonnas.

*Below right*: The Madonna is also the protectress of sailors, as the statue shows. This small

# THE OLD WOMAN AND THE MANY NAMES

*A*nother part of the picture is the old woman who after Christ's resurrection lived in the circle of the disciples. Acts of the Apostles 1.14 tells how after Jesus' ascension Mary stayed with the disciples. They prayed together for nine days. Finally the spirit of fear disappeared from among them—and as the fruit of the common prayer with Mary the Holy Spirit came down upon them. The Spirit made them into new men and women. They lost all their fear. Massive threats could not touch them (Acts 14.18–21), no more than what befell them later: imprisonment and torture (Acts 5.40). Until the end of her life Mary stayed with the first Christian community, praying and teaching.

She was still on the path to the land of freedom, where the hungry are satisfied. She was still a worker for liberation, still the young girl who sang about the end of oppression, still the Mother of Sorrows for whom no misfortune was too small or insignificant for her not to feel pity for it.

She kept on working to reconcile the irreconcilable. This can be seen in the history of piety from the many holy places of older cultures, once dedicated to other gods and goddesses and taken over by Christianity. On the foundation of ancient sanctuaries, there arose, under more favorable circumstances, a syncretism, for example, of the sort between the great deities of old Mexico and the saints of Christianity. In these assimilations Mary played the role of the reconciler. The Virgin of Guadalupe is one of the loveliest examples of this kind of cultural mix, where Mary links the old and the new. She became the ally of the Indians. She took sides against the oppressors; and she spoke Nahuatl, the language of the Aztecs and others despised by their colonial masters. The vision of the simple Indian Juan Diego, and the conversation that took place between him and the Virgin Mary on December 8, 1531 not far from Mexico City, are a moving testimony to such reconciliation. At the site where Tonantzin, the Mother Goddess, used to be worshipped, people today pray to Our Lady of Guadalupe, who has made the cause of the Indians her own. Later

Mary was sometimes tenderly called *indianita,* little Indian girl, or *morenita,* little dark-skinned woman.

It is strange how the three phases in Mary's life fit together and kept fusing more and more: the young girl, the sorrowful mother, and the old woman, crowned and bodily assumed into heaven. They cannot be separated. The young woman sees before her what will happen to her son. The mother under the cross remembers what the angel promised her; and perhaps she also sees how her later life in the Christian community has a share in God's becoming visible. She became a teacher and a consoler. She listened with wisdom, she reconciled those who had quarreled, and slowly all the names given by the people who "sense heaven" in her began to accumulate.

One of these names refers to the fact that, like all poor mothers, she nursed her son for a long time. She was called the "Mother of God-Milkgiver." In feudal times that meant something to the women from the lower classes. Rich women did not nurse their babies, they handed them over to wet nurses. Mary was also called the "wet nurse of true life."

Thus she remained poor and rich, small and great, terrified and consoled. Sometimes one rediscovers on the faces of old women the amazement, the curiosity, the wonder of a young girl. And sometimes—perhaps less often—a ripe old wisdom shines forth in children. In the same way the beauty of the many depictions of Mary rests on this strange coexistence, which transcends time and its exclusivity, of the phases of a woman's life. There can be an eternity in a moment.

Slowly Mary, who was still a young girl with the wonderment of the beginning, still the *Mater Dolorosa* with the seven swords piercing her heart, still open to God, became the Mother of God, Our Lady of Refuge, without whom we would all be the poorer. No one within the Christian tradition has so clearly and unmistakably expressed as she did what it means to be at every time, in every situation, and for all men and women, the one to whom everyone

In his *Pouring out of the Holy Spirit*, El Greco (1541–1614) thrusts Mary into the center of the sacred event. Surrounded by the apostles and the disciples, she receives the Holy Spirit in the miracle of Pentecost (Prado, Madrid).

143

The high point of Marian veneration around 1400 also marked the artistic mode of the "Loving Mother of God," which had already been a vital presence in the hearts of believers for many centuries. A beautiful example of this is the *Nursing Madonna*, a sculpture from Styria around 1380, now in the Germanic National Museum, Nuremberg.

can turn—and turn regardless of whether they are too stupid or too fat, too nasty or too irreligious. In the learned language of theologians this has been called "ontological openness," complete openness to God's radiance and light. God's spirit can settle in a woman; he finds a dwelling, a definitive human reception in her.

It is no accident that the Church Fathers applied to Mary a long series of images from the Hebrew Bible. They speak of her as the ark of Noah and Jacob's ladder, as the impregnable tower and the closed garden from the Song of Solomon. They see Mary in the splendid city of God, Jerusalem, with its foundations on the Holy Mountain (Psalm 87.1,3). They identify Mary with the Ark of the Covenant (Exodus 25.10), and the house that eternal Wisdom built herself (Proverbs 9.1), with the Wisdom of God that (according to Ben Sirach 24.3) came forth from the mouth of God, perfect, beautiful, beloved by God above all things and forever protected from the shadow of guilt. In all these interpretations Mary appears as "the dwelling of God," as a pure and receptive "place" where God can enter, where he wants to stay, without his presence meeting contradiction or resistance. This is a matter of God's presence in the earthly world, and that means: in his people. And here theology, which makes use of Scripture in a way that often strikes us as strange, jibes with the people's Mariology from below. There are never enough names and images for what we love.

Over the centuries the number of Mary's names has grown, and wherever she is loved new names are discovered for her; that is how love is. And so poetic love calls Mary by a thousand names. She is "Our Lady of Seafarers" as well as "Our Lady of Joy." She can be the Madonna of Loneliness or of Exile, as well as of Escape and Relief.

Some say Mary is the Queen of Heaven or a sacred goddess in Christianity. But Mary's Son only managed to get a torturing crown of thorns and electrodes. Recently a group of young people who work in a London slum dedicated their house to "Our Lady of

Justice." In Brazil as the millennium draws to an end people like to invoke her as "Mary of the Oppressed." She is called the Madonna of the Street Children, and she is also the mother of the many girls who bear her name, still half children, who are abducted and taken to brothels for tourists. They die early from sniffing drugs, from infections, from untreated diseases; but their mother is Mary too, the one who listens to them and sometimes consoles them.

The little subversive Madonna who once sang the song of liberation is not made of plaster and plastic. In Latin America the Madonna Leona rides naked on a lion, more witch than Madonna, at least to our tamed and corrupted understanding of religion. Perhaps in this way we can get a little closer to a new, better image of the girl Mary who is also a woman; the woman who does not have to stifle the girl that she once was, and who combines militancy and mercy as an image of hope.

Where does her mystery lie? She tells us that the world is not just the disastrous stage of an absurd tragedy, in which conqueror and conquered are always the same. It is a place for the hope that protects life and makes the improbable thing that we call compassion come true. In Russia there is a "Mary Bringing Home Adam." And what could be more necessary these days than to bring home Adam—who in a world of machines has gone astray, obsessed with death—to bring him home to this limited and unique creation? Holy Mother of God, pray for us!

*Page 145*: Another instance of the "soft" style is the especially valuable Bohemian *Madonna Enthroned* (ca. 1430), a wooden figure from the monastery of Seeon, now in the Bavarian National Museum, Munich. The crown, the throne, and the dignitary's cushion mark her as a ruler. But the gentle curve of her body, the loving expression, and the gestures stress her tender maternity. The Christ Child as boy Logos with the book smiles as his mother does. Mary, the new Eve, holds in her hand the apple, which is also a symbol of the world.

The glorification of Mary finds eloquent expression in the works of many great composers.

1. Giuseppe Verdi (1813–1901)
   Pastel by Giovanni Boldini, 1886
2. Richard Wagner (1813–1883)
   Photographed in Lucerne by J. Bonnet
3. Franz Liszt (1811–1886)
   Photo
4. Antonio Vivaldi (1678–1741)
   Painting by F. Morellon La Cave, 1723

# Mary in Music

Joe H. Kirchberger

5. Camille Saint-Saëns (1835–1921)
   Portrait around 1895
6. Arthur Honegger (1892–1955)
   Charcoal drawing by Ferdinand Ochsé
7. Felix Mendelssohn-Bartholdy
   (1809–1847)
   Drawing by Joseph Schmeller, 1830
8. Franz Joseph Haydn (1732–1809)
   Oil painting by Guttenbrun
9. Giacomo Puccini (1858–1924)
   Pastel by Arturo Rietti, 1906
10. Johannes Brahms (1833–1897)
    Painting by Olga Miller von Aichenholz,
    around 1890
11. Gioacchino Rossini (1792–1868)
    Chalk lithograph by A. Lemoine, 1861
12. Johann Sebastian Bach (1685–1750)
    Painting by E.G. Haussmann, 1746
13. Francis Poulenc (1899–1963)
    Photo
14. Wolfgang Amadeus Mozart (1756–1791)
    "Mozart as a Knight of the Golden Spur ";
    Copy of the portrait made for the Academy
    in Bologna in 1777
15. Georg Friedrich Händel (1685–1759)
    Painting by T. Hudson, 1749
16. Jules Massenet (1842–1912)
    Portrait by Nadar, around 1890
17. Franz Schubert (1797–1828)
    Aquarelle with landscape around Vienna,
    detail

The role that Mary has played in music from the Middle Ages to modern times is surely just as varied as in the visual arts or in literature. But in this framework it can be dealt with only in brief excerpts and a few examples.

We can be certain that in many Christian countries of Europe and the Near East songs about Mary were composed as early as the 5th or 6th century. Unfortunately they were not written down and so they have been lost to us. The actual bearer of culture in the early Christian era was the Church. The only music of the early Middle Ages that has been preserved and has survived the passage of time is church music.

In the tradition of early Christianity a kind of speech-song developed, for which Pope Gregory I (d. 604) prescribed a definite order. This *Gregorian chant* was at first a substructure of melody for the word. What gradually took shape from it and became the foundation of Western music is an artful solo chant of the priest to which the community responds in a simple fashion. Two styles evolved: the word-stressed, recitative "syllabic" chant, which, following ancient tradition, assigns a note to every syllable, and the freer "melismatic" style, which goes back to the synagogal chants and in which many notes can be sung on one syllable. This style flowered chiefly in hymns and antiphons. In public worship, however, these two methods of composition were not sharply contrasted but often combined. The contrast between solo singing by the priest and the community choir (responsorial chant) led to the development of *antiphonal chant,* in which two choirs sing alternately.

Along with Gregorian chant there was, as early as the first Christian centuries, *hymn singing.* This can be traced back to Bishop Ambrose of Milan, who died in 397. Hymnody was more closely bound up with popular songs: spiritual texts were set to familiar popular tunes. Hymnody later fused with the Gregorian style, when the latter had taken on more permanent forms.

In the cultural centers of this time, the monasteries, the life of the monks was liturgically regulated throughout the day. The Rule of St. Benedict of Nursia, the founder of Western monasticism, divided the day into seven times of prayer (matins and lauds, prime, tierce, sext, nones, vespers, and compline) at which the monks gathered in the church. According to the canonical "hours" they had to be present for a stipulated number of psalms, antiphons, hymns, prayers, etc. One essential part of these services were the antiphons, short prose texts sung before and after a psalm. But there were also the special *Marian antiphons,* dedicated to the Virgin, in which not a psalm but a canticulum (song of praise) formed the center. Some of these antiphons go back to the dawn of the Middle Ages, such as the *Sub tuum presidium* ("Under your protection") mentioned in the preceding chapter.

Four of the antiphons became perma-

1

2

3

4

5

6

7

8

9

10

11

13

15

16

2

14

17

147

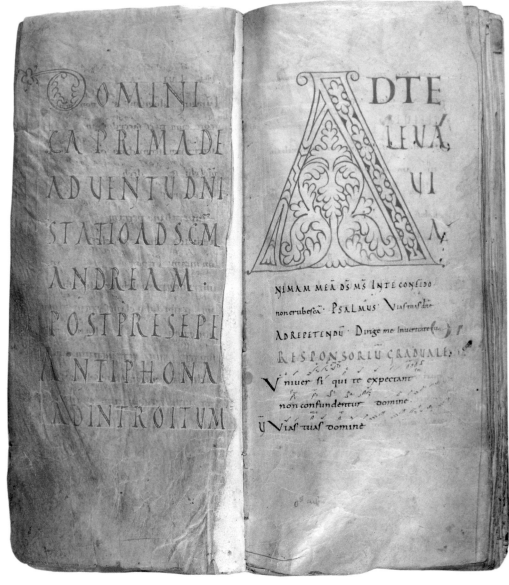

*Left:* The first page of a Gregorian choral. This page is kept in the Biblioteca Laurenziana in Florence.

*Above right:* The *Cantatorium* is the oldest manuscript with Gregorian chants in the Cathedral Chapter Library of St. Gall (no. 359). It was written down around 920–930 by the monks of St. Gall. The medieval notation is made up of "neumes." These unison chants still have their place in the Catholic liturgy. The most important feature of these chants is the text that the music supports.

*Below right:* The Codex Vaticanus (Reg. 11), before the 10th century, is the oldest textual source for the Ambrosian hymns.

*Above left:* The *Colmar Compline Salve*, the earliest extant print in the musical library of Einsiedeln, dates from 1715 and comes from a *Manuale chori* by the Colmar canon Thomas Franciscus Haupt.

*Upper right:* The oratory of St. Bernardine in Siena, upper portion with elaborate coffered ceiling from the year 1496. Between the pillars a splendid series of frescoes unfolds with works by Sodoma, Pacchia, and Beccafumi, all devoted to the subject of Mary. The main painting behind the altar shows Mary as Queen of Heaven.

*Below:* This *Alma Redemptoris Mater* is on page 2 of the St. Gall manuscript no. 375. It is an *antiphonarium missae* (mass songbook), likely written around 1135 by the monk Luitherus in the monastery of St. Gall. Early on, the liturgy that was laid down by the pope and Doctor of the Church Gregory the Great around 600 (and with that liturgy the musical interpretation of the texts) stressed the theme of Mary. Her veneration was from the outset firmly anchored in the chants.

The flowering of Marian veneration in the Middle Ages also created new antiphons which, no doubt because of their length, became detached from the Psalms and were sung as processional antiphons or separate pieces. Out of the great many antiphons that were written, four, doubtless the most important ones, have stayed in use. Here are examples of them:

*Right: Ave Regina Caelorum* from the Codex Germanicus Monacensis 716, fol. 89r (last third of the 15th century, Bavarian State Library, Munich). The antiphon itself dates from the 10th century and has been set to music many times.

*Far right: Regina coeli laetare* from the Codex Latinus Monacensis 5539, fol. 66r (14th-15th century, Bavarian State Library, Munich). It is ascribed to Pope Gregory IV (10th century). The hymn was repeatedly set to music through the centuries by, among others, Palestrina, Mozart, and Pietro Mascagni.

*Above:* The sequence *Ave praeclaris maris stella* from Codex 631 (915), before 1314, the Cathedral Chapter Library, Einsiedeln.

*Below right: Salve Regina* from Codex 598 (1692, Cathedral Chapter Library, Einsiedeln).

nent parts of the official liturgy, and they were later set to music again and again by various composers.

The most famous of these texts was surely the *Salve Regina:* Cistercian monks have been singing it regularly since 1218, the Dominicans in Bologna since 1230, and after 1250 it was sung in all monasteries. We know settings of the text by the Burgundian Guillaume Dufay (ca. 1400–1474) and the Spaniard Tomas Luis de Victoria (1548–1611). Giovanni Pierluigi da Palestrina (1525–1594), the leading composer of the Italian Renaissance and the Counter-Reformation (introduced by the Council of Trent), also set it to music. The "Belgian Orpheus," Orlando di Lasso, along with Palestrina the most important composers of the period, did so four times. Roughly as old as that is the musical setting by Gregor Aichinger (1564–1628), who went to Italy and became acquainted with the new methods of composition. Antonio Vivaldi (1678–1741) likewise wrote four musical settings of *Salve Regina,* and we know two by Giovanni Battista Pergolesi (1710–1736) and three by Franz Joseph Haydn (1731–1809). The Köchel Verzeichnis also lists one by Mozart (KV 92), but its authenticity has been doubted. There is, in addition, a series of settings from the pen of Franz Schubert (1797–1828) to German and Latin texts. In 1844 Anton Bruckner set it to music at the age of twenty, but the manuscript has been lost. Finally Franz Liszt (1811–1886) composed a *Salve Regina,* and Arrigo Boito (1842–1918) used it in the Prologue of his opera *Mefistofele* (1868).

The texts of two of the other Marian antiphons come from the 10th century. *Regina Coeli* is attributed to Pope Gregory V, who died in 999. To this day it is sung at certain times of the liturgical year at the end of compline, the Church's night prayer. Palestrina and Aichinger set it to music. Mozart dealt with the text on several occasions, once (KV 108) in C major in 1771—aged fourteen; the next year in B major (KV 127), and finally in C major again (KV 276) in 1779 or 1780. Pietro Mascagni (1863–1945) worked it into his opera

*Cavalleria Rusticana* (1890).

The other antiphon from the same century, *Ave Regina Coelorum,* was set by Dufay for four voices. The composer is supposed to have wanted his work sung as he lay dying. Palestrina set it four times, Orlando di Lasso five times. Victoria set it for eight voices; Carlo Gesualdo (1560–1613) for five.

From the 11th century comes the text of the fourth official Marian antiphon, *Alma Redemptoris Mater,* which, like the *Salve Regina,* begs the Mother of God for help at the Last Judgment. Dufay composed a setting for three voices, as did the Flemish master Johannes de Ockeghem (1430–1495) and the Dutchman Jacob Obrecht (1452–1505). From Ockeghem's famous pupil Josquin Des Prés (1450–1521) we have two settings, and one each from the Fleming Nicolas Gombert (1490–1560), Victoria, and Aichinger. Palestrina used the text in his famous mass for six voices *Missa Papae Marcelli* (1567). In 1777 Mozart set it for four voices, two violins, bass, and organ (KV 277).

An interesting contribution to medieval music was made by King Alfonso X of Castille and León, a grandson of the German king Philip of Swabia. His great ambition was to become German emperor—but his plans were blocked by the resistance of the pope. He did a great deal for the culture of his country and composed over 400 Marian songs (*Cantigas*) to texts of the already mentioned Gautier de Coincy.

From time immemorial the most important part of the service of vespers had been the *Magnificat,* Mary's song of praise from Luke 1.46–55. This text, already quoted in the first part of the book, has no close links with Mary; it is largely based on Hannah's similar song of praise in the Old Testament. And there is no mention here of either Mary's pregnancy or of the expected Christ Child. There are even some noncanonical manuscripts that place the song of praise not in Mary's mouth but in Elizabeth's, which, as far as its contents go, would be altogether possible. Nevertheless this splendid hymn of praise to God was undoubtedly understood at all times as a politically explosive piece. Lines such as "He [God] has put down the mighty from their thrones and exalted those of low degree" did

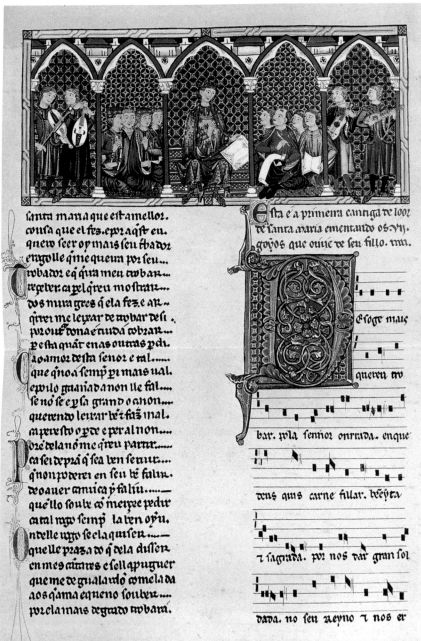

Medieval music, of which liturgical chants formed the most important part, is bound up with a great body of musical theory based on ancient Pythagorean and Platonic doctrines about harmony and numerology. The teaching about measures and numbers, which God used to make the world, was carried over by the medieval artist into music, painting, and architecture. Knowledge of the harmonic sound effects of octaves, fifths, and fourths influenced the height of arches, the size of windows, and the division of façades in the cathedrals.

*Left:* The *Ave sanctissima Maria* comes from the famous songbook of Margaret of Austria.

*Above right:* Title page of the *Magnificat* of Palestrina, 1602 (State Library, Augsburg).

*Right:* The *360 cantigas of Alfonso X* for Alfonso the Wise (1180–1230) are to be found in the Royal Spanish Academy in Madrid.

not fail to make an impression. The Magnificat was regularly recited from the days of St. Benedict (ca. 480–547) and from around the 11th century was elaborated into a monophonic chant. But then came what was probably the greatest revolution in the history of music, the introduction of polyphony, with several independent voices singing at the same time being woven together harmonically. The beginnings of this kind of music go back as far as the 9th century. But its first important flowering occurred during the Renaissance under the great masters Palestrina and Orlando di Lasso. Palestrina, who was declared by the pope and the Council of Trent to be the standard for polyphonic church music, composed more than thirty settings of the Magnificat.

Altogether we have about one thousand settings of the Magnificat. Guillaume Dufay set it to music five times, as did the Fleming Antoine Brumel (ca. 1460–1520) and the German Thomas Stoltzer (ca. 1465–1526). The Frenchman Jean Mouton (ca. 1475–1522) wrote seven settings; Johann Walther (1496–1570), the friend and musical adviser of Martin Luther, wrote six. The Spaniard Cristobal Morales (ca. 1500–1553), very popular in his day, wrote twenty, the Fleming Benedictus Appenzeller (16th century) thirteen. But the record belongs to Orlando di Lasso, from whose hand we have about one hundred settings of the Magnificat. Victoria, Palestrina's colleague in Rome, left eighteen. As court composer in Mantua, Claudio Monteverdi (1567–1643), whose influence on European music was felt all the way into the early 18th century, composed a splendid Magnificat for his *Marian Vespers* of 1610. Later, as director of music at San Marco in Venice, he composed yet another in his old age. There are also well-known Magnificats by Heinrich Schütz (1585–1672) and Antonio Vivaldi, and what is probably the most famous, the Magnificat by Johann Sebastian Bach (1685–1750).

There are two versions of Bach's work. The first dates from 1723; it was meant for Christmas and contains interludes in the form of German Christmas texts. Later Bach thoroughly revised the work, transposing it from E major to D major, a key better suited for trumpets. He removed the interludes and added flute accompaniments. In this form the work could be performed not just at Christmas but on Easter and Pentecost. It maintains a bright cheerfulness throughout and represents one of Bach's densest compositions. It consists of twelve unusually brief sections and is framed by a powerful entrance chorale, whose melody is picked up again in the final chorale ("Sicut erat in principio"). No listener will forget the impact of these pieces, whether the "Quia fecit" or the aria "Deposuit." In the setting and orchestration of the work we find an almost incredible variety. There are chorales with or without trumpets and timpani, two soprano arias, one alto, one tenor, and one bass aria, and a duet, a trio, and a quartet for voices.

Other 18th-century composers after Bach wrote Magnificats, including Giovanni Battista Pergolesi, Bach's son Carl Philipp Emmanuel (1714–1788), and finally Mozart. Mozart used the Magnificat as the last movement for his *Vesperae de Dominica* for four voices, trumpets, timpani, bass, and organ. In the 19th century Franz Schubert, Felix Mendelssohn-Bartholdy, and Anton Bruckner wrote Magnificats. In the 20th century too it has been set to music many times, for example by the Englishmen Ralph Vaughan Williams (1872–1958) and Lennox Berkeley (1903–1989), the American Alan Hovhaness (born 1911), and the Pole Krzystof Penderecki (b. 1933). In this, as in many of his religiously motivated works, Penderecki achieves massive choral effects, which alternate with almost bizarre solos. Quite in contrast to Bach's Magnificat, the tone of Penderecki's is almost continuously gloomy and oppressive. With his seven Magnificat antiphons and a Magnificat (1988–89) the Lithuanian Arvo Pärt (b. 1935) created a new meditative sonority.

The famed *Stabat Mater,* which was regularly being sung by the Franciscans as far back as the 13th century, has been

*Stabat Mater Dolorosa* by Josquin Des Prés (ca. 1440–1521); Bruxellensis manuscript 215-216; Royal Albert the First Library, Brussels. Of all Josquin's Marian works the *Ave Maria* has been the most frequently used as the basis of many compositions relating to Mary.

set to music almost as often as the Magnificat. At the end of the Council of Trent in the 16th century it was removed from the liturgy, but reinstated by Pope Benedict XIII in the year 1727. Josquin Des Prés set it to music even before the Council. Later composers to write a *Stabat Mater* were Palestrina, Orlando di Lasso, Aichinger, both Alessandro Scarlatti (1660–1725) and his son Domenico (1685–1757). So did Händel's rivals at the London Opera Giovanni Bonincini (1670–1748) and his contemporary Antonio Caldara (1670–1736).

Between 1700 and 1883 over a hundred known settings of the *Stabat Mater* were composed. This included important 18th-century composers such as Antonio Vivaldi, Giuseppe Tartini (1692–1770, famous for his *Devil's Trill Sonata),* and Pergolesi, who died at the age of 26 of tuberculosis. His opera *La Serva padrona* and above all his *Stabat Mater* made him famous. It was his last work and is considered a high point of Neapolitan church music. Finally mention should be made of Luigi Boccherini, who died poverty-stricken in Spain in 1805. He is considered the father of the string quartet, of which he left behind no fewer than 125.—Outside Italy there was Franz Joseph Haydn, as well as Mozart, whose brief *Stabat Mater* (KV 33) is thought to have been written in 1766 by the barely ten-year-old composer on a trip from Paris to Salzburg; unfortunately it has not been preserved.

In the 19th and 20th centuries a whole series of notable composers treated the *Stabat Mater:* Gioacchino Rossini (1792–1868); Franz Liszt (1811–1886) in his oratorio *Christus,* extremely successful in its day; Franz Schubert, who set it to music twice; and Giuseppe Verdi (1813–1901) in his *Quattro Pezzi Sacri,* which he wrote toward the end of his life. Others include Charles Gounod (1818–1893), Gustave Charpentier (1860–1956), best known for his folk opera *Louise,* and Antonin Dvořák (1841–1904), who composed his *Stabat Mater* after losing three of his children within a few months. Although written in a time of pain, this composition expresses a life-affirming, powerful

faith. It also won Dvořák fame abroad and has remained his most famous choral work. In our century the Poles Karol Szymanowksi and Krysztof Penderecki, the Hungarians Ernst von Dohnanyi and Zoltán Kodály, the Czech Rudolf Karel, the Frenchman Francis Poulenc (a member of the famous "Six," who composed in a neo-classical style), the American Virgil Thomson, and the Englishman Lennox Berkeley have all composed a *Stabat Mater.*

The last of the great Marian poems, the *Ave Maria,* was already known in the early Middle Ages and appears in manuscript as far back as the Codex Sangallensis. It has been set to music innumerable times. The first part of the text was initially sung on the feast of the Annunciation (March 25) to a melody from the 10th century. Among the later musical versions, some of the more familiar ones are by Guillaume Dufay and Josquin Des Prés, the Flemings Jacob Arcadelt (ca. 1514–1575) and Adriaan Willaert (1490–1562), Tomas Luis de Victoria, and Cristobal Morales, Palestrina, and Orlando di Lasso. Then there is Mozart, who set the text to a canon for four voices; and, above all, Franz Schubert, who borrowed his text from Walter Scott's *The Lady of the Lake* (1810). His appealing composition is often compared to the likewise very well-known composition by Charles Gounod—not quite fairly, since Gounod's somewhat sugary tune was originally published under the title *Meditation* and not until later combined with Bach's First Prelude from *The Well-Tempered Clavier.* Still later we find settings of the hymn by Franz Liszt, Giuseppe Verdi, Peter Cornelius (1824–1874, known for his *Barber of Baghdad)* and his contemporary Anton Bruckner. Felix Mendelssohn-Bartholdy also used the text in his *Lorelei,* opus 98; and as a young man Johannes Brahms composed an *Ave Maria* for choir. Camille Saint-Saëns actually composed five settings of the prayer.

*Page 154:* The *Magnificat* by Johann Sebastian Bach was sung at vespers. Bach combines the choral music with Baroque orchestration to reach one of the high points of church music. His deep piety shines through even his secular compositions. The page shown here is from the Prussian Cultural Legacy, in the State Library, Berlin.

*Above:* An *Ave Maria* from a manuscript of hymns and sequences from the early 16th century (Cathedral Chapter Library of St. Gall).

$A$s we turn now from the liturgy to Mary's place in secular music, once again, even though the history involved is significantly shorter, we can cite only a few examples.

In the history of *opera* Mary does not play a role until the 19th century. Friedrich von Flotow (1812–1883), still known today for his opera *Martha*, wrote another opera, equally successful at the time, called Alessandro Stradella. First performed in 1844, it ends with a hymn to the Virgin ("Virgin Mary, Heavenly Transfigured One"). Richard Wagner's (1813–1883) opera *Tannhäuser* was premiered in Dresden the following year. Here Mary plays a key part in the struggle between earthly love (Venus) and heavenly love, embodied by Elizabeth, for the soul of Tannhäuser. When Tannhäuser invokes Mary's name, Venus has to give way. And when in the last act Tannhäuser apparently fails to return from his journey of repentance to Rome, Elizabeth prays to Mary and begs for death.

For Giuseppe Verdi (1813–1901) the Virgin plays a primary role in the opera *La Forza del Destino,* which had its premiere in 1862 in St. Petersburg. In the second act the tragic heroine Leonora seeks refuge at a monastery in the mountains of Spain, Our Lady of the Angels. She prays to the Virgin, after a repetition of the theme first announced in the overture. In the following scene she finds lodging in a nearby cave, and she and all the monks join in a prayer to Mary. In the final scene of Verdi's next to last opera *Otello* (1887) Desdemona in deep distress prays an *Ave Maria.* An *Ave Maria* is also sung in Pietro Mascagni's one-act opera *Cavalleria Rusticana,* the work that made him famous overnight.

The French composer Jules Massenet (1842–1912) wrote an entire opera on the old legend about *Le jongleur de Notre Dame.* That work is scarcely performed nowadays, just as Giacomo Puccini's (1858–1924) *Suor Angelica* has practically disappeared from the stage. In this one-acter Puccini shows us a nun who years before had led a very different kind of life and borne an illegitimate child. When she finally learns that her child, whom she longs to see, has died, she tries to poison herself, but then has second thoughts, and prays to the Virgin Mary for a sign that she has been forgiven. The Madonna appears at the entrance to the church holding the boy Jesus by the hand. Her conscience eased, Sister Angelica dies praying.

Eugen d'Albert, born in Scotland of German, French, and Italian extraction, won worldwide fame as a piano virtuoso. He then devoted himself to composition and wrote twenty-one operas, of which only *Tiefland* (Lowlands, 1903) and *Die toten Augen* (The Dead Eyes, 1916) were successful. In the prelude to *Tiefland* the poor shepherd prays for a wife, and the Madonna promises him one. He finally wins the beautiful Martha, despite the intrigues of her rich sweetheart Sebastiano.

The Swiss composer Arthur Honegger (1892–1955), another member of "les Six," based his dramatic oratorio *Jeanne d'Arc au bûcher* (Joan of Arc at the Stake, 1938) on a poem by Paul Claudel. Joan stands at the stake and looks back

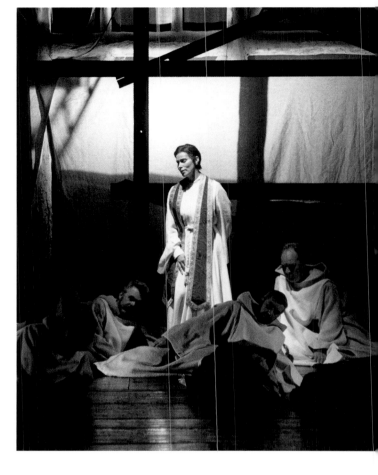

Page 156: Photograph of a production of *Cavalleria Rusticana* (1890) by Pietro Mascagni (1863–1945) in La Scala, Milan. During the Easter procession, here gathered around a Pietà, the aria "Regina Caeli, laetare, alleluia" is sung.

*Left:* Scene from *La Forza del Destino* by Giuseppe Verdi. Wearing men's clothes, Leonora seeks refuge in a Franciscan monastery. Behind her the Madonna is visible (production at the Deutsche Oper, Berlin, 1982).

*Right:* The scene from the same opera where Leonora prays with the monks.

*Below left:* Desdemona's night prayer to Mary from Verdi's opera *Otello.* Fearful premonitions and prayerful devotion unite in this dramatic aria (from the 1991 premiere at the Deustche Oper, Berlin).

on her life, her triumphs, and the betrayal to which she has fallen victim. In a vision several saints appear to her, while the Virgin too encourages her and urges her to accept her fate as liberation. The earthly world fades away, the heavenly world remains. The end of the opera recalls Schiller's *Maid of Orleans* ("The pain is short and the joy eternal").

But the most resounding musical echo of Mary's life has surely come in the *song,* first of all in folk songs and popular melodies. Granted, these did not spontaneously write themselves. They must at some point or another have had "composers," although in most cases their names have been forgotten. In all Christian countries the *Christmas carol* plays a major role in this regard. Among German carols *Es ist ein' Ros' entsprungen* (Lo, How a Rose E'er Blooming) has already been mentioned. Of the many others, some of which go as far back as the Middle Ages, the following might be mentioned:

*Vom Himmel hoch, da komm' ich her* (From heaven's height I come to you), *Ihr Kinderlein, kommet* (Come, you little children), *Schlaf wohl, du Himmelsknabe du* (Sleep well, heavenly boy), *Maria durch ein' Dornwald ging* (Mary was going through a thorn wood). This last can be found in an early version in the Andernach Songbook from 1608. It was obviously very popular in the 19th century, and in 1850 it emerged from Thuringia into a wider audience through the Harthausen collection of spiritual folk songs:

*Mary was going through a thorn wood,*
*Kyrie eleison!*
*Mary was going through a thorn wood,*
*that for seven years had never been green!*
*Jesus and Mary.*
  *What was Mary bearing under her*
    *heart?*
*Kyrie eleison!*
*A little tiny child without any pain,*
*Mary bore him beneath her heart!*
*Jesus and Mary.*
  *Then the thorns bore roses,*
*Kyrie eleison!*
*When the child was carried through the*
    *woods,*
*then the thorns bore roses!*
*Jesus and Mary.*

Scene from the opera *Suor Angelica* (1919) by Giacomo Puccini (1858–1924). Sister Angelica, forced to enter a convent because of her illegitimate child, learns that the child has died. In her despair she takes poison. Then, realizing her sin, she begs forgiveness from Mary (seen here). In the dramatic final tableau Mary hears her plea, and the soul of her child comes forward to meet her.

*What is the child's name to be?*
*Kyrie eleison!*
*His name is to be Christ,*
*that was his name from the first!*
*Jesus and Mary.*
  *Who will baptize the child?*
*Kyrie eleison!*
*That will be Saint John,*
*He will baptize him!*
*Jesus and Mary.*
  *What will be the child's baptismal gift?*
*Kyrie eleison!*
*Heaven and the entire world,*
*that will be his baptismal gift!*
*Jesus and Mary.*
  *Who alone has redeemed the world?*
*Kyrie eleison!*
*The Christ child, he redeemed the world!*
*Jesus and Mary.*

One may notice that in the German carols Mary is indeed mentioned, but she definitely plays a secondary role. The focus instead is on snow-covered fir trees, on gifts, happy children, the Christmas tree, the shepherds, and of course the Christ Child—much less is said about Mary and Joseph.

This is even more true of the English Christmas carols. Mary is mentioned, but almost always as a supporting figure. An old 15th-century carol of a cheerful wassailing sort goes as follows:
*Bring us in good ale, and bring us in good*
    *ale,*
*For our blessed Lady's sake, bring us in*
    *good ale....*

Among many other English carols here is an excerpt from *The Holly and the Ivy:*
*The holly bears a blossom*
*as white as any flower,*
*and Mary bore sweet Jesus Christ*
*to be our sweet Saviour....*
*The holly bears a bark*
*as bitter as any gall,*
*and Mary bore sweet Jesus Christ*
*for to redeem us all....*

Things developed quite differently in France, perhaps because the country always remained Catholic. In the French Christmas carol, simply called *Noël,* Mary plays a quite central role. A lullaby for the Christ Child describes an idyll:
*Entre les deux bras de Marie*
*Dort, dort, dort le fruit de vie....*

*Above:* Prayers and songs to Mary often appear at crucial moments of plays and operas, for example, Leonora's aria, *La vergine degli angeli* from the second act of Verdi's *La Forza del Destino* (1862). Shown here is Verdi's original score, from the Casa Ricordi, Milan.

*Top:* The same is true of Desdemona's aria *Ave Maria* from Verdi's opera *Otello* (1887).

In the arms of Mary
sleeps, sleeps, sleeps the fruit of life....
Another carol says:
*Ce n'est pas que grace, amour et courtoysie.*
*Elle est bien jolie, Marie,*
*elle est bien jolie!*
It's pure grace, love, and courtesy.
She is really pretty, Mary,
She is really pretty!
And yet another bids the listeners:
*Chantons a ce Noël joly,*
*—Ne vivons plus piteusement,*
*Une pucelle,*
*De Dieu ancelle,*
*A enfanté, comme était dict,*
*Un beau mignon a plein minuit.*
Let us sing on this lovely Christmas,
We no longer live in misery,
A virgin,
God's handmaiden,
has, as prophesied,
borne a beautiful little darling
in the middle of the night.

One especially pretty carol is a very long one, structured as a dialogue, partly in a deliberately antique French, where Mary is addressed and replies:
*Chantons, je vous emprie,*

*Par exultation,*
*En honneur de Marie,*
*Pleine de grand renom,*
*"Or vous dictes, Marie*
*Qui fut le messagier,*
*Qui porte la nouvelle*
*Pour le monde sauver?"*
*"Ce fut Gabriel l'Ange*
*Que sans dilation*
*Dieu envoya sur terre*
*Par grand compassion."*
*"Or vous dictes, Marie*
*Que vous dist Gabriel,*
*Quand vous porta nouvelle*
*Du vrai Dieu éternel?"*
*"Dieu soit o toy Marie,*
*Dit-il sans fiction,*
*Tu es de grace emplye*
*Et bénédiction."*
Let us sing, I beg you,
in exultation,
in honor of Mary,
full of great renown.
"But tell us, Mary,
Who was the messenger
who brought the news
of the world's salvation?"
"That was the Angel Gabriel

*Left:* Excerpt from the original manuscript of Arthur Honegger's (1892–1955) opera *Jeanne d 'Arc au bûcher* (1942). Honegger gives his music a severe coloring. In a simple harmonic folk song and responsive Gregorian chant, he captures the tone of medieval music. As she hears the voice of the holy Virgin, Joan remains firm, even in the hour of her death (Bibliothèque Nationale, Paris).

*Center: Nun wandre Maria* (Now go, Mary) by Hugo Wolf (1860–1903) from the *Spanish Songbook,* Austrian National Library, Vienna.

*Right:* Likewise by Hugo Wolf is the *Schlafende Jesuskind* (Sleeping Child Jesus) from his setting of poems by Mörike (1888). (Austrian National Library.)

*whom God sent at once*
*To earth in his great compassion."*
*"But, tell us, Mary,*
*What did Gabriel tell you,*
*When he brought the news*
*From the true eternal God?"*
*"God be with you, Mary,"*
*he said truly,*
*"You are full of grace*
*And blessing."*

(There follow another eighteen verses, in which Mary is similarly questioned and responds.)

The *art song* in Germany goes back to the 17th century. Heinrich Albert (1604–1651), a student of Heinrich Schütz, published several volumes of his *arias,* as he called them. After Albert, "lieder" in the modern sense were composed by, among others, Adam Krieger, Carl Philipp Emmanuel Bach, Christoph Willibald Gluck, and—toward the end of the 18th century—Johann Friedrich Reichardt, Carl Friedrich Zelter, Goethe's friend. Much more important songs were composed by Haydn, Mozart, and Beethoven, but they seldom deal with Mary; that was left to church music and the folk song, as always.

The actual founder of the "lied" in the modern sense, not just in Germany but everywhere, was Franz Schubert (1797–1828), who in the 19th century was acknowledged almost exclusively as a composer of songs. We have already spoken of his *Ave Maria.* He also wrote settings for Goethe's *Ach neige, du Schmerzensreiche* and Novalis' *Ich sehe dich in tausend Bildern,* as well as (with a great deal of counterpoint) Friedrich Schlegel's *Vom Leiden Mariae.*

The next important lieder composer who dealt with Mary is Johannes Brahms (1833–1897). Brahms dedicated a whole song-cycle to the Virgin under the name of *Marienleben* (The Life of Mary). It is interesting, by the way, that the two more modern composers who gave us Marian song-cycles, Johannes Brahms and Paul Hindemith, had no Catholic roots. Brahms, born in Hamburg, was a Protestant, and Hindemith, who was born in Hanau, was far removed, at least at the beginning of his career, from any serious involve-

ment with religion.

Brahms, who consciously opposed the innovations of his contemporaries Berlioz, Liszt, and Wagner, revived archaic motifs in his *Marienleben,* which was written for a cappella mixed choir. But at the same time he also reached back to the folk song. In *Mariae Kirchgang* (Mary's Going to Church), in the authentic medieval fashion he assigned the melody not to the soprano, but to the mezzo; and his *Magdalena* chorus seems to be coming from the lips of medieval pilgrims. He himself recommended his *Marienleben* as "written in the style of German church music and folksongs."

An entirely different kind of composer was Hugo Wolf (1860–1903), whose harmonies were strongly influenced by Wagner. But instead of Wagner's "endless melody," Wolf worked with short, expressive motifs. With gifts that were more lyric than dramatic, he realized his greatest achievements in the domain of the song, where he can be compared with Schubert and Schumann. In his great successes (for example, the Mörike, Eichendorff, or Goethe songs), he shows himself to be a master of the most subtle description of character and situation. His setting of *Nun wandre, Maria* (Now go, Mary) and *Sohn der Jungfrau, Himmelskind* (Son of the Virgin, Child of Heaven) bear witness to his powerful poetic sensibility.

Max Reger (1873–1916), longtime director of the famed Meininger orchestra, is less known as a composer of songs than for his piano and organ compositions; but he composed about 290 songs. Reger's strong connection to Bach and his polyphony can be seen in most of his compositions. His version of the *Mariae Wiegenlied* (Mary's Lullaby, "Mary sits in the rose bower and cradles the child Jesus") is interesting, because Brahms had already made use of this melody in *his* lullaby ("Joseph, dear Joseph mine/, help me rock my babe so fine"). The melody, in fact, goes back to an old folk tune that can be found as early as the work of Erhard Bodenschatz (1576–1636) and was probably composed in the 14th century.

Like Reger, the Austrian Joseph Marx

(1882–1964) showed romantic inclinations and avoided the radically modern style. He is influenced rather by French Impressionism and Slavic music. And he too wrote a setting for Novalis' *Ich sehe dich in tausend Bildern.*

Finally, Paul Hindemith (1895–1963) began as a wildly rebellious anti-Romantic who dared to make fun of Richard Wagner, and who with his revolutionary radicalism was determined to snub the public, which was still biased in favor of the '20s Art Nouveau. He was considered the *enfant terrible* of German music and was violently rejected by the great majority of his listeners and critics—even when he had become more self-reflective and presented the public with one of his most important works, his *Marienleben,* based on poems by Rainer Maria Rilke. In this work Hindemith also found his way back to Johann Sebastian Bach and polyphony. But his compositions were not programmatic. He did not try to give a musical illustration of every word, but developed a grand vocal line worked into the polyphony. The total picture that emerges from this expresses the subtlety of Rilke's words with great precision.

In 1948 Hindemith reissued his Mary cycle and wrote an extensive foreword to it. There he says that the older version, which he labels a "loose potpourri," followed no overall compositional plan. In the newer version he alters the more random harmonies of the earlier version and subjects them to a severely regular pattern. Hindemith also mentions that he rewrote some of the songs as many as five times and changed some passages as often as twenty times. He acknowledges that the composition of the Mary cycle brought about a drastic reversal in him, a complete turning away from his youthful works.

The beginnings of music about Mary are obscure. We can only guess how the Marian songs of the first centuries may have been sung—they were not preserved. For the early period we can only rely on church music, which at first was scarcely more than a background for the spoken text. A strictly regulated cult

was coming into existence then in the monasteries. Four of the Marian antiphons, brief texts set to music, became an essential part of church tradition and so were continually attracting the attention of composers: the *Salve Regina,* the *Regina Coeli,* the *Ave Regina Coelorum,* and the *Alma Redemptoris Mater.* All of these were taken up in the liturgy and as late as the 19th century some of them were being given new settings. The style of these compositions underwent a radical change with the introduction of polyphony, which reached its zenith in the 16th century.

Even more often than these antiphons the *Magnificat* was continuously set to music from the 11th century until our own day. The most famous of all Magnificats is the one by Bach, but from the 15th to the 17th centuries there was scarcely a single composer who did not write a Magnificat. The same is more or less true for the *Stabat Mater.* Likewise the *Ave Maria* has been set to music again and again since the 9th or 10th century.

Leaving behind Mary's role in church music, we see Mary's great role in opera, from Friedrich von Flotow's *Antonio Stradella* to Wagner's *Tannhäuser,* from Verdi's *Forza del Destino* to Mascagni's *Cavalleria Rusticana,* Massenet's *Jongleur,* d'Albert's *Tiefland,* Puccini's *Suor Angelica,* and Honegger's *Jeanne d'Arc au bûcher.* In none of these works, however, does Mary occupy center stage.

In modern times Mary celebrates her actual triumph in the song. In German and English Christmas carols—unlike their French counterparts—she is admittedly not the focus; and the early German art song does not have a great deal to say about Mary. But this changes with the founder of the art song in the

*Above:* Franz Xaver Gruber (1787–1863), *Silent Night, Holy Night.* One of the world's best-known Christmas carols, it has been translated into countless languages. The original score shown here is in the music collection of the Austrian National Library in Vienna.

narrow sense, Franz Schubert. He is followed by Johannes Brahms, who partly engages in archaisms, partly goes back to the folk song, and by the more modern Hugo Wolf and Max Reger, who again returned to older polyphonic music. Paul Hindemith took an interesting stance toward the Rilke poems about Mary, turning away from his earlier radicalism and producing some highly sensitive settings.

There can be no doubt: Mary lives, even in the music of the 20th century.

161

# Mary: Dogmas, Cult, Customs

Joe H. Kirchberger

*Page 163:* Wall-hanging from Alexandria, 6th–7th century (Museum of Art, Cleveland). This early work shows Mary enthroned and surrounded by angels. In the early Church's disputes over the simultaneous divinity and humanity of Christ, the title "Mother of God" (Theotokos) prevailed in popular belief immediately after the First Council of Nicaea (near Byzantium). At the Council of Ephesus in 431 it was declared official church teaching. For the first millennium of Christianity the Byzantine Church shaped the images of Mary.

We have already seen that the veneration of Mary began to play an essential role with the Council of Ephesus. In part this was because Mary was not a martyr; in addition, there were no relics of her, and hence no veneration of them.

The Fathers of the Church who continued the tradition of the Apostles and the authors of the Apocrypha no more thought of a female component in the deity than did the leaders of Judaism before them or of Islam, the other great monotheistic religion after them. In the polytheistic religions, by contrast—in Egypt, Babylon, India, Greece, and Rome—there have always been female divinities. And there is no doubt that the cult of Mary as it finally developed received its impetus from the chief pagan deities of the Near East, whence it spread to the West. This can be seen, for instance, with the Arab Christian sect of the *Collyridians* in the late 4th century, priestesses who offered breadcakes (*collyrides*) to Mary, just as had been done with Demeter. Epiphanius, the patriarch of Constantinople, inveighed against this superstition.

In the great controversies and struggles that marked the first centuries of the history of Christianity, the position of the patriarchs solidified. For example, in the deep, long-lasting conflict between Arius and Athanasius that broke out openly in 325, the personalities involved played a decisive role. These individuals were: the church leaders Eusebius of Nicomedia (who defended Arius' teaching that Jesus was not the Son of God, equal to him in essence, but only the noblest creature and the transmitter of salvation), Athanasius (metropolitan of Alexandria from 326, proponent of the orthodox, anti-Arian doctrine), and Eusebius of Caesarea (a spokesman for the middle position, following Origen), along with the Emperor Constantine. The same is true of the *Nestorian controversy* in the next century, which saw the actual emergence of the cult of Mary.

Around the year 400 the goal of the patriarchs of Alexandria was to make Egypt into a sort of autonomous ecclesiastical state. They were relying on the numerous Egyptian monks, the Coptic minority in the country that resisted Hellenistic influences, and also—at least for a time—the bishop of Rome. (The pope needed an ally against his rivals in Constantinople.) This political situation intensified the clashes between the metropolises, above all in the dispute now breaking out.

Around 430 Patriarch *Nestorius* of Constaninople, born in Antioch, objected in three sermons to the characterization of Mary as "Theotokos" ("God-bearer"), a term that had been used in Alexandria for around fifty years. Instead he advocated the title "Christotokos" ("Bearer of Christ"). This led to an enormous stir in the capital of

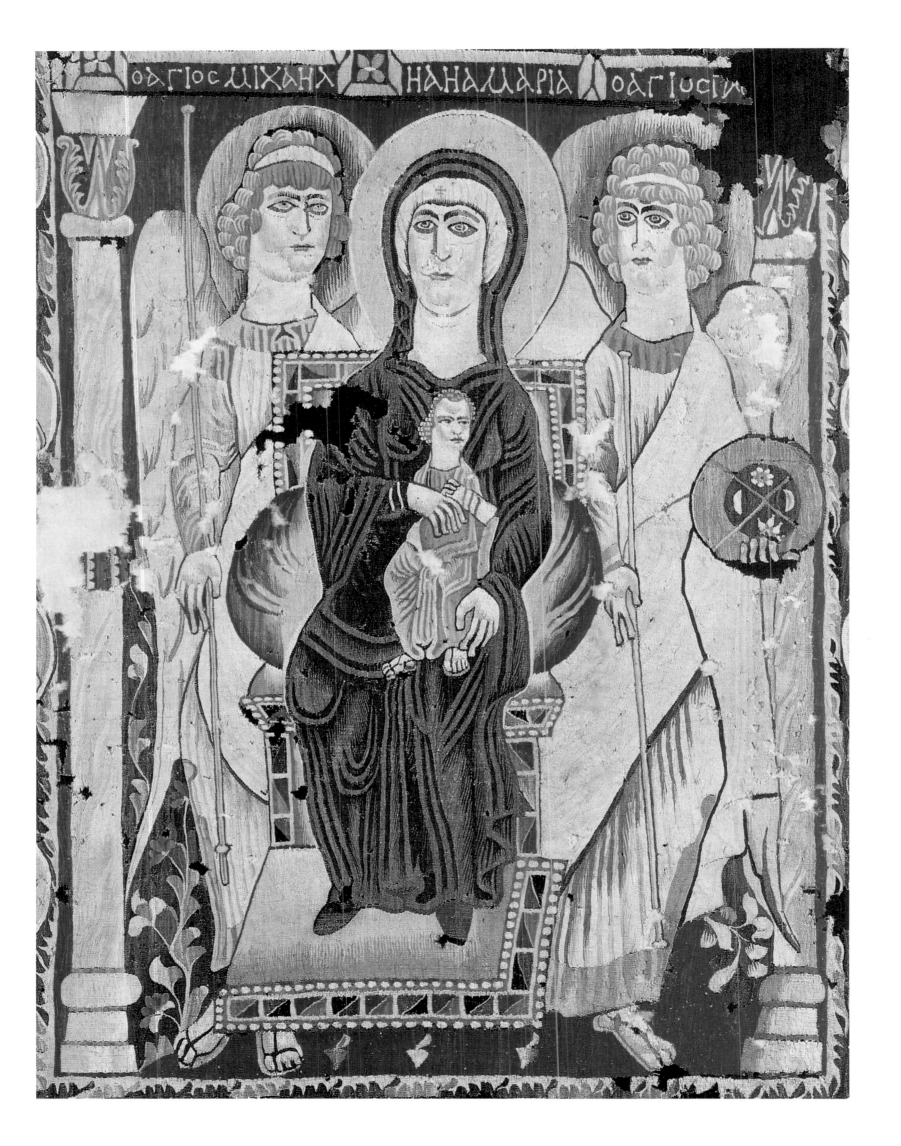

163

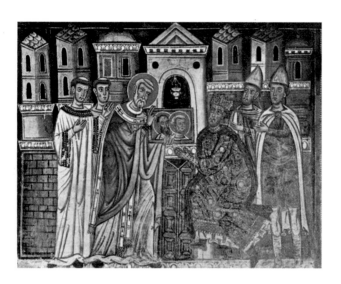

*Left:* Pope Silvester and Emperor Constantine on a fresco from the 13th century (oratory of Sylvester in the church of the Quattro Coronati in Rome).

*Right:* Madonna Enthroned, wood sculpture from the time of the Council of Constance (1414–18).

the empire, Constantinople. Patriarch *Cyril* of Alexandria, who was very ill-disposed to the choice of someone from Antioch for the patriarchate of Alexandria, took the opportunity to become involved, and in his Easter letter for 429 spoke in favor of the term "Theotokos." There followed an agitated correspondence between Nestorius and the domineering Cyril, whereupon the pair turned to the bishop of Rome. Unlike Nestorius, Cyril supplied his petition with a Latin translation of the Greek texts. This gave him a decisive head start, and at the Roman synod of 430, Pope Celestine backed Cyril. Cyril then launched twelve "Anathemas" against Nestorius, who fired back twelve "Counter-Anathemas".

At this point Emperor Theodosius II called a general Council for Pentecost, 431, at Ephesus. This was the Third Ecumenical Council. Cyril, a power-loving man who gave no quarter and who knew a thing or two about intrigue, arrived with his retinue before the papal legates and the Nestorians. Despite the protests of the imperial commissioners he inaugurated the Council and

issued a condemnation of Nestorius. A few days later John of Antioch appeared, and with the help of thirty Syrian bishops he had Cyril condemned. At first the emperor confirmed the removal from office of both men, but court conspiracies and popular feeling gradually brought him over to Cyril's side. Cyril returned to his diocese, but the condemnation of Nestorius remained.

The dispute raged on as letters flew back and forth. Under the leadership of Theodoret of Kyros, the Antiochenes-Nestorians fought back and won many adherents. Then in 433 the emperor imposed a compromise: Cyril had to sign an imperial agreement that was essentially framed along Antiochene lines. He could do so only by denying his convictions. But in exchange John of Antioch dropped Nestorius, who was exiled, first to Petra in Arabia, then to an oasis in Egypt, before he finally died in misery. Meanwhile John, who had forced his bishops to recognize the imperial document, thereby caused the strict Antiochenes to emigrate. The latter founded in Persia, in the Sassanid empire, a *Nestorian Church*, which broke once and for all with the imperial Church in 483. This Church flourished from the 7th to the 10th centuries, spreading to India and China. It still exists today and despite persecution from the Kurds and Turks numbers around 100,000 members.

Of course, this dispute was over more than just a title. That title was designed to make a statement not so much about Mary as about Christ (the preexisting incarnate Son of God). No one denied, and no pope or council needed to confirm, that Mary had borne Jesus, since it was univocally clear from the Gospels.

But this was not the case with the second Marian doctrine, namely, the *virginity of Mary*. That had been proclaimed twenty years after the appeasing of the Nestorian conflict. At the Fourth Ecumenical Council of *Chalcedon* in 451, the Fathers went far beyond Ephesus: Mary was awarded the official title *aei parthenos*, ever virgin. (This, in turn, would not receive papal confirma-

tion until 200 years later—by Martin I, who was later taken captive by the Byzantines, jailed, and brutally mistreated, dying in exile shortly thereafter in 655.)

The goal aimed at and achieved in Chalcedon was a compromise in the dispute over the nature of Christ. This was designed to counter the eastern Monophysites, who wanted to make it an article of faith that Christ had only *one* nature. (The theological position that ultimately prevailed speaks of Jesus Christ as "true God and true man.") But the declaration issued simultaneously about Mary was very bold and new. It did not assert the virgin birth of the boy Jesus (which was already stated in the New Testament and not seriously challenged by anyone), but the fact that Mary always remained a virgin. This corresponded to folk belief, but it was hard to prove, mainly because of Jesus' brothers and sisters who are mentioned in the Gospels. Some Church Fathers, above all Origen (d. 254) and Gregory of Nyssa (d. 394), found the solution in claiming that Jesus' siblings must have come from an earlier marriage of

164

## Overview of Mariological Dogmas *(after W. Beinert)*

| Statement | Confirmed by the Magisterium | Content |
|---|---|---|
| Mother of God | Council of Ephesus (431) | Christ is the Son of God; God really became human. |
| Virgin | Baptismal Professions (from 3rd century on) | Christ is the Son of God; God alone took the initiative. |
| Ever Virgin | Baptismal Professions (from 4th century on) | The birth of the Redeemer is the beginning of the new creation. |
| Immaculate Conception | Pope Pius IX (1854) | Mary is preserved from original sin. |
| Bodily Assumption into Heaven | Pope Pius XII (1950) | The human Mary is wholly and completely, with her history and identity, taken up to God. |

Early Christianity faced the need for a feminine deity, especially in cult sites dedicated to ancient goddesses. Notions of the feminine principle as a cosmic entity were kept all the way into the Baroque period. One important example from iconography is the page shown here from the Krumau Codex of Pictures (Bohemia, ca. 1355–1360). It depicts the Madonna as an apocalyptic sun-woman and queen of heaven.

Joseph's. This led to Joseph's being depicted as an old man alongside the young Mary. Jacobus de Voragine, the author of the *Golden Legend*, explained much later that James was called Jesus' "brother" only because he bore such a strong resemblance to him.

The idea of the virgin birth was by no means strange to the ancient world; it plays a part, for example, in the Buddha legend. It probably goes back to the matriarchal age, when the male's share in reproduction was not yet recognized, and the woman alone incorporated the creative principle. (Thus "Mother Earth" was thought of as feminine.) When the involvement of the male in the birth of a child was discovered and society turned into a patriarchy, controlled by men, many women evidently wished to withdraw from this masculine regime and founded a polity for women, the so-called Amazon states, which play a large role in legends. The city of Ephesus is said to have been founded by Amazons. At all events the figure of the virginal goddess Artemis (Diana) was always especially popular there. This is something, according to

Acts, that even Paul was forced to acknowledge when he tried to preach in Ephesus and incurred the vehement rage of the silversmiths, who made and sold devotional objects. So it is perhaps no accident that the cult of Mary took its start in Ephesus four hundred years later. Incidentally, the feast day of Artemis in Ephesus was August 15—the date on which Mary's Assumption into heaven is now celebrated.

The question of how to represent the virginal pregnancy of Mary and therefore the manner in which she had conceived had never been given a univocal answer. Some of the earlier theologians said that she received the generative word of God through her ear; others proposed her mouth or nose.

After Pope Martin I it was not until Sergius I (687–701) that a pope dealt officially with Mary's status. Admittedly, he did not proclaim a dogma, but he did organize feasts and processions for the major Marian holy days: the Annunciation (March 25), the Purification of Mary in the Temple (Candlemas, February 2), Mary's Birthday (September 8), and her "Dormition" (Falling

Asleep, August 15), which later became the feast of the Assumption. On that day Sergius himself went barefoot as he led a group of believers in Rome from the Lateran to the church of Santa Maria Maggiore—a custom that was not discarded until Pope Pius V did so in 1566.

Thereafter the popes refrained for many centuries from doctrinal definitions concerning Mary, although—or perhaps precisely because—the struggle of opinions within the Church continued through the entire Middle Ages. There was more at stake here than just

*Left:* In early Byzantine art depictions of imperial dignity and Christian symbolism often coincide, as in this example of Mary as empress (fresco from the church of St. Clement in Rome, 847–855).

*Right:* Cosime Turas (1430–1495), *Madonna Enthroned with Child*, from 1480 (National Gal-

lery, London) borrows the dignified portrayal of Mary as ruler from Byzantine tradition. For centuries Italian art remained indebted to this type.

*Page 167: Mary Enthroned as Ruler* appears likewise in this 10th-century Romanesque manuscript from the School of Reichenau. The Psalter Codex was commissioned by Archbishop Egbert of Trier (in office 977–993) and executed by the painter Ruodpecht. It was destined for the Cathedral of Trier. Now in the Archeological Museum of Cividale (Friuli).

the teaching about Mary's "Immaculate Conception." (The New Testament says nothing at all about her conception and birth, and the accounts of the Apocrypha are not without ambiguity.) The issue, then, was not simply whether Mary had been conceived immaculately (i.e., free from original sin) by her mother Anne, but also whether she had gone to heaven with her earthly body.

Most medieval theologians had taken a stand on these questions, but no unity was achieved for many centuries. Not until long afterwards, when a part of Christendom, namely, the Protestants, had lost interest in Mary and, thanks to the Enlightenment in the 18th century, many intellectuals had been lost to the Church, did two popes attempt to settle these issues permanently through dogmatic decisions.

*Pius IX*, whose pontificate was the longest in church history (1846–1878), became head of the Church at a stormy time. Even before the revolutionary year of 1848 he was driven from Rome by Italian nationalists, who wanted to seize the Papal States. After his return he was able to stay in power only with the help of the troops of Napoleon III. He had taken office as a progressive-liberal, but after his expulsion from Rome he became a bitter enemy of liberalism. When Napoleon was dethroned after his defeat in the Franco-Prussian War in 1870–1871, the French troops withdrew from Rome. Pius no longer left the Vatican and refused to recognize the new regime. That was the end of the Papal States. The situation did not change until Mussolini's Lateran treaties of 1919, in which the Papal States—in a greatly reduced, in fact purely symbolic form—were revived.

With his bull *Ineffabilis Deus*, proclaimed in 1854, Pius decided the question of the Immaculate Conception that even the Council of Trent (1545–1563) had left open. As it happened, his choice turned against the Dominicans and in favor of the Franciscan and Jesuit position.

*To the honor of the holy and indivisible Trinity, to the adornment and distinction of the Virgin and Mother of God ... we declare, proclaim, and define that the doctrine which maintains that the most Blessed Virgin, from the first moment of her conception, through the unique grace and preference of almighty God in view of the merits of Jesus Christ ... was preserved from every stain of original sin, was revealed by God and hence is to be believed firmly and constantly by all believers....*

By promoting the Jesuits, who were disliked by the people and who preached obedience to Rome as necessary for salvation, Pius IX sharpened the conflict between the Catholic Church and liberal currents of the period. He thereby drove his Church back into a rigid faith in authority and a rejection of liberal culture, which in turn provided the liberals with more ammunition for their anticlerical campaigns. Along with the Immaculate Conception, Pius also defined the likewise controversial dogma of the pope's infallibility (when he speaks *ex cathedra* on matters of faith) at the First Vatican Council.

The final dogma about Mary is that of the *bodily Assumption of Mary into heaven*, defined by Pope Pius XII in 1950. This pope (Eugenio Pacelli) had been for years papal nuncio of the Vatican in Berlin and a spokesman of its diplomatic corps. Later he became Vatican Secretary of State, and as such led the negotiations that arranged the Concordat with the Third Reich. As pope (from 1939) he did oppose totalitarianism, but during the Second World War he avoided criticizing Hitler, in particular about the Nazi genocide of the Jews and other minorities, for which he was later often attacked.

With this latest dogma Mary was officially recognized as the only person, along with Christ, to have been assumed into heaven *body and soul*. In the Old Testament some personages appear about whom the same is said (Moses, Enoch, Elijah). The Reformed Churches have reservations about the physical assumption of Mary into heaven, because this puts Mother and Son on the same level.

Basically the doctrine of the bodily Assumption of Mary into heaven was just the logical consequence of the teaching of the Immaculate Concep-

tion. According to an old idea, every sinful being had to fall victim after death to corruption. Through Adam and Eve all of humanity—in keeping with the doctrine of original sin, developed especially by Augustine—was exposed to this fate, except for the two

human beings who from their birth had not suffered from this flaw: Christ and Mary.

Thus it was only consistent that the same pope, in his encyclical *Ad caeli Reginam* of October 11, 1954, four years after the proclamation of the bodily Assumption of Mary into heaven, should also declare her the *Queen of Heaven*. In doing so he was following an old tradition going back to the Salve Regina of the 11th century and beyond. It is worth noting that Pius XII did not resolve by dogmatic definition the issue of whether Mary was the Co-Redemptrix, but chose to leave that for the theologians to discuss.

The Marian feast days are among the most important in the yearly Catholic liturgical cycle.

*Left: Annunciation of the Archangel Gabriel* (Lectionary of Pantaleimon 2, ca. 1100, Monastery of Pantaleimon, Mount Athos). The feast of the Annunciation is celebrated on March 25. In many old calendars this marked the beginning of the new year.

*Right:* Vittorio Carpaccio (1450–1522), *The Birth of Mary* from 1495 lets us look into a patrician house in Venice. The hares in the

*E*ver since the 5th century there have been celebrations and special feast days in honor of Mary in all Christian countries. Many of them were limited to certain regions or parts of the country; many have disappeared over the course of the centuries. A whole series of them have been preserved over time and have played an important role in the history of the Christian religion.

From the 8th to the 13th centuries

there were only four officially recognized feasts of Mary, and even today, except in the Reformed Churches, they are considered liturgical feasts:

*February 2: Mary's Purification*
*March 25: Annunciation*
*August 15: Mary's Assumption*
*September 8: Mary's Birthday.*

While the presentation of Jesus in the Temple, which is mentioned in the New Testament, was already being ob-

background are symbols of divinity and immortality. On Mary's birthday, September 8, medicinal herbs are picked and dedicated in a special service as a source of blessings for house and home.

*Below right:* The feast day of the Presentation in the Temple (Candlemas, February 2), seen here in the Book of Hours of Catherine of Cleves, is dedicated to Mary's purification. Popular belief claims that the candles blessed on this day protect against evil spirits.

The day of Mary's death and resurrection is August 15, "the Assumption." The page shown here is from the feast-day Gospel with tablets of the canon from the School of Reichenau (ca. 1030). The period from Mary's assumption—including her birth (Sept. 8)—to the memorial of the "Seven Dolors" (Sept. 16), popularly known as "Our Lady's Thirty (Days)," was considered particularly rich in blessings.

served festively as far back as 360, the "Purification" of Mary was not generally recognized by the Church until around 650. This feast was brought to the West by Eastern monks who had fled there after the conquest of Jerusalem by Islam. Originally it was celebrated on November 21, then the feast was shifted to February 2, to connect it with a pagan feast of light and thus solidify its position in popular belief. The pagan feast had processions at which torches and candles were carried at night to drive away evil spirits, famine, earthquake, and other catastrophes. In the year 701 Pope Sergius I made February 2 an official Christian feast day, and down to our time on this evening young girls with white veils and burning candles march through the night. Martin Luther kept the feast and preached on this day the year he died, 1546.

The feast of the *Annunciation*, which goes back to Luke 1.26–38, was known in Constantinople as early as the 5th century and was brought to the West by the monks who had fled Islam. It was originally celebrated on Ash Wednesday, but then it was shifted to the time of the vernal equinox, nine months before Christmas. Sergius I organized a candlelight procession for this feast too. But it did not become a tradition in the West until the 11th century, particularly because of the efforts of the Italian Scholastic Peter Damiani. At the same time the feast also became popular in England and the Netherlands. The Protestants preserved it as the day of Jesus' conception in Mary's womb.

In contrast to the feast of the Annunciation, the Assumption has no basis in the New Testament. We have already seen that the primary source for accounts of Mary's death and the Assumption are the Apocrypha. The oldest witness to her bodily ascension comes from a Syrian fragment known as the *Obsequies* of the Holy Virgin, dated by some scholars to the middle of the 4th century. In this piece the Apostles Peter, John, and Andrew dispute with Paul "before the entrance to Mary's tomb", with the first three arguing for complete continence, while Paul suggests a milder approach—and wins Jesus' support. Jesus then bids the Archangel Michael lift Mary's corpse up to heaven, and has the Apostles follow on clouds. In this and other variants of the motif the sleeping Mary is carried off into heaven. That is why the feast was originally called the *Dormitio* (falling asleep, in Greek *koimesis*). It was proclaimed in the East by the Emperor Mauritius as early as the year 600, and again was brought to the West by fleeing monks. On the other hand, the well-known Benedictine monk Bede ("the Venerable Bede"), author of the first history of England, who was active around the year 700, evidently never heard about Mary's assumption and he never mentions it. But we know for certain that around this time Pope Sergius I was leading the crowd of believers barefoot through Rome. While most 8th- and 9th-century writers voiced res-

ervations about Mary's assumption into heaven, the feast was expressly promoted by Popes Paschal I and Leo IV in the 9th century.

The feast of *Mary's birth* was also brought to the West around 650 and celebrated by Sergius I with a candle-lit procession. Martin Luther initially kept the feast, but his last sermon on this day dates from the year 1522; obviously he changed his mind about it.

Of all the Marian festivals that emerged in the High Middle Ages, that of the *Immaculate Conception* on December 8 is no doubt the most important.

when the pregnant Mary came to visit Elizabeth. Perhaps he was showing that he felt liberated from his sinfulness through the mere presence of the Virgin Mary. In any event the feast was introduced into England some time after 1140, and from there it spread to France, then to Italy. At the Council of Basel, Pope Felix V declared (1439) that belief in the Immaculate Conception was part of the Church's official teaching. But he was deposed soon afterwards and replaced by an antipope. Thus it was not until 1854 that the doctrine was defined for the Catholic

*Left: Mary of the Seven Dolors*. This miniature, ca. 1340–1350, from the Lake Constance circle (now Kreimünster, Austria) shows Mary carrying instruments of torture and slaying the dragon. The memorial is celebrated on Sept. 16 and marks the conclusion of "Our Lady's Thirty."

*Center:* Domenico Ghirlandaio paints the *Visitation of Mary* (1491) against the background of an arch that provides a view of a broad landscape. Tempera on wood (Louvre, Paris).

*Right:* The *Annunciation to Anne and Joachim* by Bernhard Strigel (1460–1528), Thyssen-Bornemisza Collection, Lugano.

This feast did not become established until relatively late, and even then with some hesitation; because the tenet upon which it is based is not mentioned in the New Testament or explicitly related in the Apocrypha. The only point to be added here is that two great Doctors of the Church, Anselm of Canterbury (d. 1109) and Bernard of Clairvaux (d. 1153), energetically opposed it. So did the Dominicans later on, while Anselm's nephew and biographer Eadmer zealously campaigned for the feast, along with the Franciscans and the Jesuits. Not until 1220 was there a "Mass of the Immaculate Conception." Its proponents clearly made a great effort to find New Testament passages to claim as support for their case. According to Luke 1.41 little John the Baptist had leaped for joy in his mother's womb

Church by Pius IX. In Wittenberg the feast had not been celebrated since 1520.

By contrast, until the end of his life Luther acknowledged the feast of the *Visitation of Mary* on July 2, commemorating Mary's visit to Elizabeth. The central liturgical text for this day is the Magnificat with its thesis that "The Lord has worked redemption for his people." Luther called upon Mary for concrete help against the Turks, who were besieging Vienna in 1529. The feast was mentioned for the first time in Le Mans, France in 1247; the Franciscans celebrated it from 1263 onwards. It was elevated to a feast of the entire Church in 1389 by Pope Urban VI.

In connection with the danger from the Turks in the great sea battle of Lepanto in 1571, Mary is said to have

*Page 171:* Albrecht Dürer (1471–1528), *The Feast of the Rosary* (National Gallery, Prague). The name "rosary" for a chain of beads as a traditional memory-aid for prayer goes back to the 13th-century Marian legends. Such legends are also the basis for this picture, painted by Dürer in 1506 on a commission from German merchants in Venice. Beginning in the late Middle Ages the motif of the rosary was often evoked in portrayals of Mary.

helped the admiral of the Christian fleet, Don Juan of Austria, the half-brother of Philip II of Spain, win the victory. Beginning in 1573 the *victory festival* was celebrated on October 7; in 1716 it was replaced by the feast of the Rosary.

One very old feast was that of *Mary's Virginity*, though celebrated on different days (on the Sunday before Christmas in Byzantium, on December 18 in Spain, on January 18 in France, and on January 1 in Rome).

In Cologne the feast of the *Seven Dolors of Mary* was introduced in 1423. But in 1506 when Pope Julius II was asked to extend it to the whole Church, he refused. Nevertheless in 1814, at a time when Napoleon was harassing the Church, Pius VII instituted a feast of the *Virgin of the Seven Dolors* on Septem-

ber 15. The old feast had been held on Good Friday, the day of the greatest solemnity honoring Christ, when it naturally could not be celebrated. For similar political motives Pope Pius XII established the feast day of the *Immaculate Heart of Mary*, primarily as a response to the atheistic ideology of the Soviet Union.

There were other Marian feasts: Mary's wedding (January 23), Mary's Transfiguration (August 6), Mary's Motherhood (October 11), Mary Help of Christians (May 31), and Mary of Good Counsel. Mary also plays a considerable role in the feast in honor of Joseph, which was introduced at the Council of Constance (1414–1418) by Jean Gerson, Chancellor of the University of Paris, and ultimately fixed on March 19. In Catholic parts of the

world May and October are considered Mary's months and are often marked by special devotional exercises.

In his Apostolic Brief *Marialis cultus* of 1974 Pope Paul VI gave the renewed support of the magisterium to the veneration of Mary along lines proposed by the Second Vatican Council.

### Virgin

In the mythology of classical antiquity a virgin birth as such was nothing unusual. Even historical figures such as Pythagoras, Plato, or Alexander the Great were said to have been born of virgins. This could not have been pleasant to early interpreters of the New Testament, because it meant that the virgin birth of Jesus Christ was no longer the unique event that believing Christians had thought it to be. Hence Origen argued that God had used such precedents to prepare the world for the great event of the virgin birth.

Meanwhile Justin Martyr, who died in Rome in 165, had already pointed out that there was a crucial difference between the classical myths and the New Testament story. Unlike the Greek women, Mary was not wooed or seduced, much less raped by a god. There had been no sinful feelings of pleasure, and so it was a new, unique phenomenon. By contrast, Origen viewed all forms of "parthenogenesis" in nature as equal. Just as (according to popular belief back then) beetles could come forth from donkeys, wasps from horses, and snakes from corpses, so Mary could bear a child without the help of a man. The Church Father Lactantius (d. ca. 320) even compared Mary's conception to the Greek myth of the impregnation of the twelve mares of Ericthonius by Boreas, the north wind. The Antiochene scholar Dio-

dorus of Tarsus and Nestorius, familiar to us from the Council of Ephesus, tried a tamer explanation. The spiritual and the material worlds, he maintained, were not mutually exclusive, so that Jesus could have been both the Son of God and the son of his parents—but this opinion did not prevail.

Origen's thesis was understood to mean that Mary had conceived from the Holy Spirit through her ear. The Spirit was often imagined and depicted as a dove; and, like the Hebrew Shekinah, the Spirit of God was thought of as feminine. (In ancient Egypt the hieroglyph of a dove also stood for the soul of a dead person.) In an apocryphal "Gospel of the Hebrews" Jesus calls the Holy Spirit his mother. And this was cited in the 3rd century by Origen and St. Jerome without a breath of criticism. Furthermore the ancient Jewish notion that with God nothing was impossible conflicted with the Greek idea that in nature certain things just could not happen.

Thomas Aquinas (1225–1274) borrowed Aristotle's thesis that the man provided the actual life force for the child, while the woman merely "incubated" it. Only the case of Jesus was different: his body and soul came down into Mary's womb as a sanctified whole. Dante Alighieri said much the same thing.

Not until the appearance of the natural sciences, and specifically with Karl Baer's discovery (1826) of the function of the ovum in mammals, was the collaborative role played by the woman in the generation of human beings fully recognized. But this raised new problems for belief in the virgin birth. In the 16th century the Council of Trent had specifically confirmed the virginity of Mary. By contrast, the Second Vatican Council (1962–1965) refused to "decide any questions that have not yet been fully explained by the work of theologians" (*Lumen gentium* 54).

Page 172: Piero di Cosimo (1461–1521): The Immaculate Conception, painted around 1500 for the church of Santa Annunziata as an altar piece (Uffizi, Florence). As a virgin conceived without original sin, Mary stands on a pedestal; over her is the Holy Spirit. Because of the severe, symmetrical composition of the picture Mary stands uplifted in the center as in a space specially created for her.

## Immaculate Conception

This doctrinal issue, as we have seen, was not decided for the Catholic world by papal authority until the 19th century. It has nothing to do with the problem of virginity, although that was and is a common misunderstanding. The "Immaculate Conception" does not mean that Jesus was born of a virgin, but that, when she was conceived by her parents, Mary herself was exempted from original sin.

Since even the Apocrypha are not clear on this point, many Church Fa-

Beginning in the 14th century, as the cult of the Immaculate Conception spread, St. Anne, Mary's mother, also became the object of increased veneration. The theme of "Anne's immaculate conception" became a frequent motif in the fine arts.

Left: Bernardino Luini (ca. 1485–1532), An angel announces to Anne the birth of a daughter. In the background, following a similar pattern, Joseph's prayer is heard (Pinacoteca di Brera, Milan).

Right: In the Arena Chapel in Padua around 1305 Giotto frames the subject of the Annunciation to Anne in an interior room; the angel enters through the window.

thers felt a need to insist that the Redeemer of the world could be brought into the world only by a sinless being. But this was all the harder to demonstrate since Augustine, who died as the bishop of Hippo Regius in North Africa, and whose influence on Western theology was decisive, had successfully promoted the teaching of original sin. According to Augustine every human being is fundamentally corrupted by Adam's fall. From his translation of the Letter to the Romans (5.12: "in *him* [Adam] *all* have sinned") he concluded that men and women inherit sin from birth. But then how could Mary, who without a doubt was only human, be untouched by it? Like Ambrose (d. 397) before him, Augustine insisted that Mary had never actually committed a sin. But Augustine failed to answer the question of whether this sinlessness came from her having been conceived and born without sin. On the other hand, some of the Eastern Fathers of the Church pointed to sins that Mary *might* have committed. For example, at the marriage feast of Cana she arrogantly interfered with Jesus' affairs. Still, it was Eastern monks who in the 8th century fled from the Iconoclasts in Constantinople and brought the cult of the Immaculate Conception to the West, beginning with Italy and Sicily. In the 10th and 11th centuries it made its way to England. Bernard of Clairvaux had objected that Mary could not have been free from original sin, because then Christ would not have been the redeemer of *all* human beings. To this the English Franciscan Duns Scotus replied that Mary was conceived immaculately, and that her sinlessness did not lower but heightened Christ's sacrifice and redemption of the human race, since prevention is better than a cure. Mary, Scotus argued, was preserved from sin at her conception *in anticipation* of the time when she, like all men and women, would be redeemed by Jesus' death on the cross. The Reformed Churches, it should be noted, could make nothing of such interpretations.

The struggle between these contrary opinions, which went on throughout the entire Middle Ages, was not ended

by the Council of Trent, since it merely followed Augustine and affirmed that Mary was free of original sin. Trent adopted the dubious interpretation by Jerome of Genesis 3.15 ("I will put enmity between you and the woman, and between your seed and her seed; he shall bruise your head, and you shall bruise his heel"). Jerome saw in this passage a prophecy of the Virgin's victory over Satan, while the text actually says nothing about a *victory* by the woman, much less by a particular woman.

We can judge how heated this dispute (especially between the Jesuits and the Dominicans) became from the fact that in 1616 Pope Paul V forbade all further discussion of the topic.

When Pius IX finally raised the Immaculate Conception to the status of dogma, some thought this step was confirmed by the events in Lourdes four years earlier. There a simple, uneducated country girl had seen eighteen visions of Mary, and the Virgin had ultimately explained to her, "Que soy era Immaculata Conceptio." This is a topic to which we shall return.

## New Eve

In the Middle Ages new, contradictory theories about Mary's role and importance kept being proposed. There are a number of reasons for this, of which ignorance of the Bible was only one. Another factor was the basic thinking about the relations of men and women, which had changed several times over the centuries. Against the background of primordial matriarchal notions, the tales of classical mythology were not so hard to accept—not even when it was a question of historical figures. Classical antiquity did not distinguish as sharply between myth and history as we are accustomed to doing today. As we have seen, both the idea that males were the

*Left: Mary and Eve under the tree of the Fall.* Book illustration by B. Furthmeyr, 1481 (Munich, Bavarian State Library).

*Above right*: From the prayer book of Catherine of Cleve (ca. 1440): Eve and the Mother of God, the "New Eve", by the Tree of Knowledge.

exclusive agents in procreation and the dogma of original sin rendered the ideas of the Immaculate Conception and the virgin birth particularly problematic. In addition, sexuality and sin were viewed as practically identical, which made it all the more necessary to clarify the role of Mary.

The notion that *Adam's* fall was atoned for by Jesus' sacrificial death was simple enough. But then one needed, as it were, a second figure as an answer to Eve's sin; and that could only be Mary. First Corinthians (15.22) said: "For as in Adam all die, so also in Christ shall all be made alive." St. Jerome went further: "Now, since a virgin has conceived in her womb and borne us a child, the curse of the ages is lifted. Death came through Eve, but life came through Mary...." But had she not been born in sin? Anselm of Canterbury (1033–1109) speaks of Mary as a "peccatrix virgo" (virgin sinner) and assumes that Mary must have been freed from original sin by Jesus only by anticipating his sacrificial death.

While Thomas Aquinas saw the role of woman in fertilization as purely passive, Duns Scotus followed the Greco-Roman physician Galen (129–199), who assumed that the woman played an active role in procreation. Scotus argued that the lack of maternal potency in Mary's womb would have cancelled her maternity. The Franciscan Bonaventure (1221–1274) even claimed that Mary had more motherly power than other women, since she was in league with supernatural powers. The Italian Scholastic Peter Lombard (12th century) tried to reach a compromise: Mary's flesh, though sinful in itself, was purified by the Holy Spirit. According to Thomas Aquinas, Mary kept increasing in sanctifying grace her whole life long and with her death she reached the highest level of grace. According to Bonaventure, on the other hand, this degree was already reached with the birth of Jesus. Theologians today are as puzzled over the meaning of grace as they were back then.

To measure the significance of the opposition between Eve and Mary for the medieval person, one has to recall

that especially since Tertullian (ca. 160–ca. 220) and Augustine, woman was looked upon as guilty for the Fall of the human race and the incarnation of all evil. Tertullian says, in fact: "Don't you know, Eve, that this is what you are? The curse that God laid on you still lies heavy on the world. You are the devil's gateway—you betrayed God's law. You shattered Adam, God's image, as if he were a toy. You deserved to die, and it was God's Son who had to die." Along these lines Ephrem the Syrian wrote in the 4th century: "Eve wrapped Adam in a shameful robe of skins, but Mary has woven a new garment of redemption.... The wine that Eve pressed for humanity poisoned it; the wine that grew in Mary nurtures and saves the world."

But there were also other voices. Some Church Fathers went so far as to welcome the Fall. For instance, Ambrose, bishop of Milan, spoke in the 4th century of the *felix culpa* (happy fault), because sin had prompted the incarnation of God in Mary. And in a quite similar vein an anonymous English poet of the 15th century sang:

*Ne hadde the apple taken been, the apple taken been,*
*Ne hadde never our Lady aye been Heaven's queen.*
*Blessed be the time that apple taken was,*
*Therefore we may singen: "Deo Gracias"!*

## Enraptured Beloved

The fact that in the Middle Ages Mary was idolized as a beloved may seem disconcerting to us. One of the reasons for this was that the Song of Solomon in the Old Testament, a passionate and unabashed love poem, had already been interpreted by the rabbis as a symbolic expression of Yahweh's love for his people. Thus the God of the Jews (and later Christ) became the bridegroom and the people of Israel (later the Church) became the bride. Subsequent interpreters replaced the Church with the Virgin Mary. This identification was made in the East by Origen and Gregory of Nyssa, in the West by Ambrose.

The notion that certain women could enter into a mystical marriage with Christ continued throughout the Middle Ages. We find it in the martyr Catherine of Alexandria, said to have been put to death in 307, as well as in St. Catherine of Siena, who died in 1380. This notion came into full bloom thanks to Bernard of Clairvaux, who between 1135 and 1153 gave no fewer than 86 sermons on the Song of Solomon. For Bernard God is the same as love. Christ is the bridegroom, and his bride is sometimes the Church, sometimes Bernard's audience, and sometimes the Virgin Mary. This love of the soul, he says, is quite spontaneous and exists only for its own sake. The lust of the flesh disfigures the pure soul, and only by turning again to God can it regain its original purity. Nevertheless in Bernard both kinds of love are described, as in the Song of Solomon, with the same erotically colored images and expressions.

This highly personal love for the Virgin that Bernard keeps describing gradually brought about a fundamental change in the cult of the Virgin. Until Bernard's time Mary was rather a majestic, distant figure who embodied the authority of the Church. At least in the West there was no passionate individual devotion to her. It was always the collective, the community, that had sung songs of praise in her honor.

True, there *are* poems by individual persons to the Virgin that suggest a more personal devotion as early as the

The idea of the mystical marriage of holy women with Christ became a theme in the fine arts and literature from the Middle Ages to the Baroque.

*Left:* This Bohemian illumination (1313–1321) shows Christ and Mary in a "mystical embrace" (University Library, Prague). Mary, identified with the bride of the Song of Solomon, becomes, as the Bride of Christ, his companion on the throne. Medieval symbolism sees in Mary the symbol of the Church, the Ecclesia. In this function she is the Bride of Christ. The scene is at the same time an image of union of the pious soul with Christ after death.

*Right:* Lorenzo Lotto (1480–1565), *The Mystical Marriage of St. Catherine* 1506–7 (Pinakothek, Munich).

late 10th and 11th centuries, but only in the middle of the 12th century did a complete turnabout take place, primarily because of Bernard. Still, other factors were at work, notably the experiences of pilgrims, crusaders, and merchants in Constantinople, where the veneration of Mary had long been warmer and more intimate. Bernard's monastic order, the Cistercians, was spreading all over Europe. Mary's image appeared on the seal of his abbeys, and people began to add special Mary chapels to the churches.

In the 14th century Mary is sometimes depicted as a young bride sitting next to Jesus, who holds her hand, as a bridegroom holds his bride's. Gottfried von Admont claimed that all three divine persons of the Trinity had Mary as their beloved.—The Reformed Churches could not warm to such notions, and their criticism did not fail to make an impression on the Catholic Church. From the 16th century on Joseph was again shown at Mary's entrance into heaven. Or else God the Father appeared far off in the farthest heights, while farther below the Holy Spirit spread his wings over the Virgin.

There was one area in which passionate love for the Virgin enjoyed special triumphs, namely, in the songs of the troubadours and minnesingers. From around the end of the 11th until the beginning of the 13th century a new kind of love poetry blossomed in southern France. It did not view passion and reason as opposites, but combined them and put them at the service of a higher refinement. Body and soul were not at war; both had the capacity to lift the person above himself and to separate him or her from the animal. A loving man or woman was neither the victim of bestial lust nor the plaything of diabolical spirits. It is often assumed that the love described by the troubadours had to be chaste, especially since they so often talk about suffering and separation of the lovers. But the early troubadours did not celebrate chastity for its own sake; and their suffering often derived from the fear of losing the beloved. Needless to say, this sort of unbridled love was quite alien to the Church.

But that changed in the early 13th century. Now the minnesingers began silently to assume that the beloved was worthy of love only if she was too pure to return it. The old struggle between body and soul revived. Heaven and earth, passion and reason were once again set off against one another, and in this kind of love lyric Mary could again take the place she had long been used to.

This turnabout was surely connected with the new religion of the Cathars that spread throughout Provence and Languedoc around the end of the 12th century. Their beliefs, which went back to Oriental sects, particularly to the Manichaeans, were based on a strict dualism: an evil spirit had created the material world, and the pure human soul was held captive in the sinful flesh. The Cathars were strict ascetics, but they thought occasional sexual intercourse less blameworthy than organized sex (i.e., marriage). After violently suppressing the Cathars (their name, which means "pure," is the root of the German word *Ketzer* or heretic) as well as the other great heretics of the day, the Albigensians and the Waldensians, the Church used the figure of Mary as a way of restoring the old order. Mary as a pure virgin took away the justification of free love, and as a woman who had acquired her importance only through her Son, she put in the shade historical figures such as Eleanor of Aquitaine who, thanks to her great power and independent behavior, had caused the Church a great deal of grief. Now Mary could once again be sung as the troubadour ideal, freed from earthly passions. And while the Church contrasted the perfect purity of Mary with earthly women, a harsh light was shone on earthly love. Men were not supposed to look up to women, but to heaven. The heroes of the great medieval epics had by no means been sexually abstinent; now that changed. While the old troubadours complained that their fidelity was not rewarded, they now wailed that earthly love as such was a sad illusion. The free, unbound Lancelot was followed by Parsifal, the "pure fool."

In the 12th century for the first time Mary began to be called *Notre Dame, Madonna, Our Lady, Unsere Liebe Frau.* One of the first singers to celebrate her was the already cited Gautier de Coincy. In the following centuries Mary once again turned into an altogether earthly woman who became engaged to pious devotees and even showed signs of jealousy. This particular role of a passionate, very concrete woman is something that Mary never took back, not even in the heat of the Counter-Reformation. By then she was a distant figure. And no unsuitable word ever passed her lips. Love for her became the polar opposite of earthly love, and the gulf between Mary and all other women became still wider.

## Mater Dolorosa

The harshest conceivable contrast to Mary the beloved would be her image as the sorrowful mother under the cross of her Son, as the *Mater Dolorosa.*

The idea of the mother grieving for her son is primordial and can be traced back to Sumerian culture in the third millennium B.C. There Inanna, the queen of heaven, mourns for Dumuzi, her son, who has been sacrificed to the demons of the underworld. The grieving Inanna is characterized as Dumuzi's mother, but also as his bride. In Babylonian culture Inanna becomes Ishtar, and Dumuzi—which means "true son"—becomes Tammuz. The ritual mourning of women for Tammuz is mentioned several times in the Old Testament. It evidently continued in some Arab countries till at least the 10th century A.D.

A similar rite was known from time immemorial in Egypt. There the goddess mourns for her husband—and son—Osiris. The recurrent image of Isis with Osiris in her lap survived in Egypt until the 6th century A.D., when the Emperor Justinian closed her last temple in Philae. Isis may well have inspired the medieval representations of the grieving Mary with the dead Christ on her lap.

In the Christian East there was a Good Friday ritual mourning centered around Mary as early as the 6th century; and a similar liturgy was created in the West in the 9th or 10th century. This was in the form of the "kontakion," in which two deacons hide behind the great crucifix and in the character of Jesus chide the human race for having betrayed him. But not until the Crusades, i.e., from the early 12th century onwards, was a regular cult of the Mater Dolorosa brought from the East to the West, first to Italy, then to France, England, Holland, and Spain. It reached its high point in the 14th century, as pilgrims streamed to the Holy Land.

Bernard of Clairvaux preached that Mary was a martyr, not indeed with her body, but with her soul. The Franciscans raised this concept to its peak. Pilgrims returning from the Holy Land

*Page 176:* In his poem *Frauenlob* (the praise of women) Heinrich of Meissen (1250–1318) linked courtly love and the Song of Solomon with veneration of Mary.

*Above:* The "Mater Dolorosa," spread through many devotional images, became the "model" of sympathy. The picture of the sorrowful mother with the pitiful corpse of her son (1889) is placed by Vincent van Gogh (1853–1890) in the loneliness of a wild landscape.

described the Via Dolorosa, that is, the path that Jesus had taken to Golgotha. And, although in this context Mary is mentioned only by John, images emerged in which Jesus meets her on his path of suffering. She stanches his bleeding wounds, and after he is taken down from the cross she enfolds his corpse in her arms, anoints it, and prepares it for burial. The sufferings of the mother for her Son brought the sufferings of Christ home to the viewer. We have already seen that the *Stabat Mater* was rooted in this spirit. The frightful epidemic of the black plague in Europe, which reached its zenith around 1348–1350 and wiped out at least a fifth of Europe's population, was looked upon by most people as a pun-

Search for the Child Jesus in the Temple, the Meeting with Jesus on the road to Calvary, the Crucifixion, the Taking Down from the Cross, and the Burial of Jesus. This tradition, which was sanctioned by Paul V (1605–1621), inspired the picture of the Mother of God whose breast has been pierced by seven swords. The Servites celebrated the feast day of the Sorrowful Mother during Lent, but the Church shifted it to September 16.

Still, there were different concepts of the sufferings of Mary. Francis de Sales (1567–1622) thought that Mary had always had a strong heart and showed no weaknesses. Besides, she had known about the resurrection in advance and hence suffered less. On the other hand,

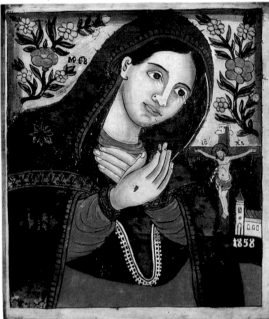

ishment for the corruption of human beings. It drove crowds of self-flagellating penitents out into the streets. They sang the *Stabat Mater* and other hymns and begged Mary for help in their misery. The "Black Death" relented after a few years, but the image of Mary as the sympathetic helper in the depths of distress remained.

The mendicant order of the Servites, which had begun in the 13th century, explained that the Virgin had revealed to the founders of the Order her *Seven Dolors*: These were the Prophecy of Simeon, the Flight into Egypt, the

the Spanish nun Maria de Agreda, who lived in the 17th century, reports in her book on *The State of God* that Mary prayed to be able to feel all the tortures and pains of her Son in her own body. Taking yet another position, Counter-Reformation theologian Francisco Suárez interpreted Mary's role at the Crucifixion quite differently. Mary, he said, "was not only a witness of the cruel spectacle; no, she heartily rejoiced that her only Son was sacrificed for the salvation of the human race."

How deep a mark the image of the Mater Dolorosa left on the Catholic

*Page 178, left:* The *Pietà* of Jean Malouel (d. 1415), painted around 1400, unites the motif of the Mercy Seat (depiction of the Trinity along with the suffering of Christ) in an unusual fashion with the Pietà and the mourning apostle John.

*Page 178, center:* The *Grieving Mother of God* (1858) by Ilie Poienaru I is an example of peasant *verre églomisé* painting (Ethnographic Museum of Transylvania, Cluj-Napoca).

world can be seen by the miracle of the *weeping Madonna*, which keeps recurring even in our day. One modern example of this is the Madonna delle Lagrime (Our Lady of the Tears) in Syracuse, Sicily. This is a plaster relief that hung over the bed of a communist worker and his wife. It wept tears from August 29 till September 1, 1953, and later performed many miraculous cures. In view of this the bishop of Syracuse said, "Crying is fruitful. There have never been sterile tears. Just as the falling rain waters the land and prepares it to bear fruit, so it happens in the realm of the spirit. A weeping woman becomes a mother that way. And when Mary wept by the cross, I tell you, her weeping was fruitful, and made her a mother."

*Page 178, right:* The so-called *Acholshäuser Madonna* shows Mary as an old woman (1505, limewood colored sculpture by Tilman Riemenschneider). The sideways turn of her head expresses her agitation (Mainfränkisches Museum, Würzburg).

*Left:* Giovanni Bellini (1430?–1516), *Pietà* (Pinacoteca, Pesaro). The artist positions Mary Magdalene in the center of the action of taking Jesus down from the cross.

*Right: Pietà* from Steig, near Blitzenreute, Germany, Ravensburg district, mid-14th century.

*Right:* This French ivory sculpture from the 13th century links the theme of the coronation of Mary by Christ with the motif of Mary as the bride of Christ (Louvre, Paris).

## Queen of Heaven

When we imagine Mary in our minds, we mostly see her as *Regina Caeli*, the Queen of Heaven. A large number of the best-known depictions of Mary show her either at her coronation or as a majestic ruling figure, often enough with the child Jesus in her arms—which, of course, is an anachronism: Since Mary outlived her Son by many years, he cannot have been a

Roman Forum, Sancta Maria Antiqua, she appears in the early 6th century as a royal majesty on the throne, richly adorned with pearls, jewels, and other regalia. She represents Rome and the power of the pope, ruling now where the almighty Roman emperors had ruled before. This legacy no doubt also had a wide-ranging political importance; but it transferred the imperial Roman hierarchy to the princes of the Church. Jesus' words at the beginning

small child when she was assumed into heaven and crowned there.

Meanwhile, the crown—even though at times, especially in the early representations, it may be barely visible—is of crucial importance. That is because Mary was often identified with the Church, and as a crowned ruler she also symbolized the power of the Church vis-à-vis secular powers. Typically, in the periods when the Church found itself on the defensive it gave special stress to Mary's position as Queen of Heaven, while this role lost importance when the Church's power was on the rise.

In the oldest Christian church on the

of the Sermon on the Mount, "Blessed are the poor in spirit, for theirs is the kingdom of heaven" (Matthew 5.3), had obviously been forgotten.

On the sarcophagi and church walls of the 3rd and 4th centuries Mary had played only a supporting role. But in the ancient Roman basilica of Santa Maria Maggiore, built by Pope Sixtus III at the time of the Council of Ephesus, she is already represented in a very prominent and majestic style. In the somewhat later church of Sant' Apollinare Nuovo, endowed by the Ostrogoth King Theodoric in Ravenna around 500, Maria acts as a symbol for the Church when she receives the gifts of

the Three Kings. Mary's political role in the Church became even clearer after the invasion of the Germanic tribes, when the Western Roman empire went under (476) and the papacy took over the administration of the city of Rome. This led to conflicts with the nominal head of Rome, the Eastern Roman emperor in Constantinople. Pope Sergius I organized Mary's official solemnities, and on a marble tablet in Sancta Maria Antiqua his successor John VII (705–707) called himself "Servant of the Mother of God." He was the first pope to have himself portrayed prostrate before the Madonna (at Santa Maria in Trastevere).

The conflict between the popes of Rome and the Byzantine emperors intensified in the 8th century when the emperors, with Leo II, the "Isaurian," at their head, fomented the controversy over image-worship. Over the centuries the veneration of pictures and reliquaries had spread and continued to be popular with the common people and the monks, while the army sided with the iconoclastic emperor. The West never accepted the ban on images, and this paved the way for the definitive break between the Eastern and Western Churches. The venerators of images who fled to the West strengthened the cult of Mary there; and the popes, who had previously viewed Constantinople as their natural ally, now looked to Western patrons. When Pope Stephen III (752–757) journeyed over the Alps and asked the Frankish King Pippin the Short for help, the latter conquered the Lombards and founded the Papal States in 756.

ceremonial stateliness of the gestures blend into a balanced play of forms.

Thus the image of the Virgin as a triumphant queen, which increasingly moved into the foreground, stressed not only the legitimacy of sacred images, but the pope's authority both as spiritual head of Christendom and as a secular power. The popes who followed Stephen did their best to promote this development with further grand depictions of Mary. This was especially true of Hadrian I (772–796), Paschal I (817–824), and later Calixtus II (1119–1124), who embellished the old basilica of Santa Maria in Trastevere with newly decorated floors and walls. Calixtus achieved one of the great triumphs of the medieval Church, the Concordat of Worms (1122), in which the Emperor Henry V conceded the right to appoint bishops. Calixtus celebrated this victory over the emperors in the Nicholas chapel of the church of St. John Lateran, where Mary is shown enthroned with two popes.

Things worked out differently in the East. After the controversy over Iconoclasm was finally settled, around 840, many new images of the Madonna were created. But the blending of the secular and spiritual spheres, as it had developed in the West, was totally alien to the Byzantines. They never allowed the Virgin to be depicted as a richly adorned worldly ruler. Mary could hold a crown in her hands, in order to place it on the heads of others, but she herself never wore one. And even though the Eastern Roman emperor was understood to be Christ's representative on earth, he never sought to be portrayed like the divine Redeemer, as the successors of Pippin and Charlemagne in the West had done. Pictures of Otto III (983–1002) sometimes show him enthroned on a cloud, surrounded by symbols of the evangelists. Roger II of Sicily (d. 1154) is shown being crowned by Christ, and his face resembles the Redeemer's.

Mary was viewed by both Otto II and Roger II as a special patroness, which may have something to do with the fact that their fathers died when they were still under age, and that both were raised by women. In the following centuries we also find women on the

thrones of Europe, especially Blanche of Castille, the mother of St. Louis IX of France (d. 1270). She richly furnished the cathedrals of Chartres and Paris with images of Mary.

From around the time of Louis IX a new motif began to appear in Western portrayals of Mary: her coronation. This was obviously related to the Byzantine pictures of the crowning of the emperors by Christ or Mary. In the West it was Christ who crowned his mother,

*Above:* Luca della Robbia (1399–1482), *Madonna with Child and Saints*, terracotta relief in the church of Santa Croce in Florence. Mary is depicted as the Queen of Heaven, surrounded by John and Fathers of the Church. Her crown is carried by angels.

and in these images heaven was more or less like the royal court, seen through the eyes of a French churchgoer. The idea of Mary as a crowned queen lasted for centuries. As late as the apparitions of the 1800s, such as those in Knock and Pontmain, Mary wore a medieval crown. We have already seen that the Queen of Heaven played an even greater role in the hymns and songs of the Middle Ages than in the pictures from that epoch. And in 1954 Pius XII raised this development to its highest point when he officially declared Mary *Regina Caeli.* One particular quality of Mary may have heightened this process: her function as comforter and helper, the advocate of sinners to whom Christ himself can deny nothing.

## Helper and Advocate

It used to be said, and not entirely without reason, that in some Catholic countries, such as Italy, people prayed more often to Mary than to Jesus or God the Father. This is probably because she was thought of as a mediator between God and humankind; hence she would behave with more humanity and understanding than the severe judges. We have already seen that in certain legends, such as the one about Theophilus and Beatrix, Mary plays a crucial role precisely because of this quality, which does not seem to have a great deal in common with that of Queen of Heaven. But above and beyond that, there are countless tales, anecdotes, and accounts of Mary's protecting and supporting men and women in sin or trouble. Most of these stories are recorded in the famous *Golden Legend* of Jacobus de Voragine. A few of these can be mentioned here:

Mary as *helper in childbirth:* Lucia, a noble Spanish woman, had fallen captive among the Moors and lay in a stall on Christmas Eve when she went into labor. Mary appeared and comforted her. The Savior himself baptized her baby boy. Then Mary helped her to escape slavery, and she became a Poor Clare.

Mary as *healer:* It is reported of Pope Leo that when he was distributing communion a woman kissed his hand, which led him into such temptation that he hacked his hand off. But the people grumbled because he could no longer celebrate the sacrifice of the mass. So the pope prayed to Mary and abandoned himself to her care. With her own hands Mary restored his severed hand.

Still stranger is the story of a farmer who was struck by lightning, which tore off one of his legs. He hid it away in the church dedicated to Mary and begged for a cure. Then Mary appeared to him at night and replaced his leg, "like a shoot on a tree"—but he suffered such pain when she did so that he woke up the whole house with his screams. The people who came to his aid saw that he was completely healthy and scolded him for making so much noise. He explained things to them, but the new leg was weaker than the old one and could not bear the weight of his body evenly; so he had to spend a whole year limping.

Mary as *giver of grace:* Once she handed a staff to a Jewish girl named Rachel so that she could leave her father's house in Louvain. Rachel then became a nun in Brabant.—Lidwigis of Schiedam (15th century) had a vision in which Mary gave her a floral wreath, which she sent through her confessor to her church back home.—Hyacinth of Poland was praying before the Blessed

*Left:* Votive painting from Italy. *Accident with a horse carriage,* the inscription of thanks dates from 1888 (private collection, Italy).

*Right:* Votive painting from Upper Bavaria, dated 1797 (German National Museum, Nuremberg).

*Below: Mary's Advocacy with Christ,* painted around 1400 for the Cathedral of Florence, shows Mary with the words, "Dear Son, think of the milk that I gave you, and have mercy on them," as she points to the kneeling petitioners. Thereupon Christ speaks to his Father, "My Father, save those for whom you made me suffer the passion."

VIRGO CLEMENS. O. P. N.
*Visitur hic gemini custos Clementia regni;*
*Vna ubi Virgo Polum sustinet, una Solum.*
28

*Left:* Votive pictures and gifts had their own symbolism. Following a vision to St. Dominic the so-called plague images were created. They show Christ hovering in the air, hurling down arrows with catastrophic diseases on the corrupted world. These threatening missiles are helpfully turned away through the protective "shield of Mary."

*Right:* This wall in the pilgrimage church of Heiligwasser (Holy Water) in Tyrolia is decorated with numerous votive tablets.

Sacrament and saw a great light come down upon the altar. Despite its brilliance it did not hurt his eyes. The light divided and Mary said to him: "Rejoice, my son, your prayer has found favor with my Son. From now on you will receive everything for which you ask in His name."—To avoid her overzealous suitor St. Lucy is said to have plucked out her eyes and sent them to him. In exchange she received from the Virgin Mary a new and more beautiful pair.—A child named Veronica of Mercatello (18th century) threw a shoe at a beggar woman that caught on the doorframe. All of a sudden the beggar woman became so tall that she could pull the shoe down: it was none other than Mary.

Mary as *protector:* At the Anger convent in Munich in the year 1742 a Poor Clare named Marianne saw the Mother of God spread her mantle between the towers of the Lady church and over the city.—Around 600 when Rome was ravaged by the plague, Pope Gregory the Great had a picture of Mary, supposedly painted by St. Luke, carried through the streets, and the disease disappeared. Angels' voices were heard from heaven singing *Regina caeli, laetare* (Queen of Heaven, rejoice).—Aemilia Bicheria of Vercelli (d. 1314) received from Mary a prayer to drive away storms.—In Constantinople a Jewish boy went into a church with his Christian friends and took communion with them. When his father learned this, he threw him into a burning oven. His mother went looking for him and three days later passed by the stove. Then the boy called out to her and told her that a woman in a purple dress had fanned him with cool air and fed him; so he remained unhurt.—In the 15th century the Dominican Alanus de Rupe was so terribly battered by the devil that after seven years he would have died, had not Mary helped him. In his distress he wanted to kill himself, but Mary poured her milk over his wounds.

Mary as *saver of souls:* A monk who venerated Mary once went down forbidden paths, but before that he had honored the Virgin. He drowned, and demons seized his soul. But angels came to help him. Then Mary obtained a merciful decision from the supreme Judge; the sinner returned to life and changed for the better.—The head steward Ebroin (7th century) had run away from his monastery. Some monks stood on the bank of a river and saw a ship rapidly approaching. They asked where she was headed and were told: "We are demons taking the soul of Ebroin to hell." The monks called out to Mary for help, leading the demons to remark: "If you hadn't done that, we would have ducked you under, since you were wasting your time chatting."

Mary as the *helper* pure and simple: She helped the twelve-year-old Birgida complete some sewing when the girl feared she would be rebuked by her foster-mother.—Rainald, a disciple of Bernard of Clairvaux, was tireless in doing manual labor, and one day Mary wiped his sweating brow.—The pregnant Mirireldis lost her mind after

*Right:* Both pictures show how Mary saves from the grasp of the devil those entrusted to her care. *Left,* a painting by Niccolò Alunno from the Galleria Colonna in Rome; *right,* a painting from the end of the 15th century from the Pinacoteca in Montefalco.

*Lower left:* The holy Virgin on the "banner of Christ." As a protectress Mary is depicted on many army flags, guild coats of arms, and city insignia.

*Lower right: Mary, Star of the Sea* appears as a protective mother goddess on a Javanese work now in the Missions Museum in Aachen.

184

Page 186, left: *Filippo Lippi,* The Madonna of the Girdle *(Museo Andrea del Castagno, Florence). In the life of the Savior and the legends that grew up around it the Apostle Thomas always appears as the doubter—and* so too in the case of Mary's Assumption into Heaven. Three days after her death he incredulously demands to see the empty tomb. Thereupon Mary appears to him and gives him her girdle as proof of her resurrection.

According to tales of the Crusaders the girdle reached Italy. From 1365 on it was venerated in the Cathedral of Prato as a Marian relic. Since the 15th century the "giving of the girdle" has been a favorite theme in Italian art.

*Left:* The Madonna as protectress of Brazil, surrounded by the coats of arms of the federal states.

*Right:* Neroccio di Bartolomeo di Benedetto de Landi (1447–1500), miniature of the cover of the Siena City Customs and Tax Book of 1480. Mary, Siena's patroness, hands the city over to her Son with the words, "This is my city".

dreaming that the devil had persuaded her that she was carrying the Christian faith between her breasts and was in danger of losing it. On the feast of Mary's Purification she stayed overnight in a church and was cured.—The Abbot Helsinus of Ramsay faced extreme danger on the high seas while in the service of William the Conqueror. He called upon Mary; a worthy bishop appeared to him and announced to him that Mary would help him if he swore to introduce the feast of her Immaculate Conception into England.

Mary has also been declared the *patroness* of cities, countries, indeed whole parts of the earth—although more frequently in the regions discovered since 1492 than in the old Christian countries. The Virgin of Guadalupe was long considered the patron saint of Mexico; she is now the patroness of all the Americas. Mary the "help of Christians" is the patroness of Australia and New Zealand and, as the "Queen of the Angels," of Costa Rica. The Immaculate Conception is the patroness of the USA. Since around 1850 Mary has been the patroness of eighteen dioceses in England and Wales; and since 1922 she is patroness of France. And again in the 20th century Mary was declared the patroness of the pilots and taxi drivers of Rome.

### Relics and Icons

The oldest known invocation of Mary is the prayer *Beneath your protection* (ca. 300). Prayers to Mary were not really a direct request for help; the mother of God was not authorized to do that. It was always just a request for mediation with Christ or God the Father, with whom alone the decision lay. Hence the usual formula in prayer was: "Ora pro

nobis—pray for us." On the other hand, it was taken for granted that the Son could not refuse his mother any request, so that a prayer to Mary was practically equivalent to a prayer to God. From the 12th century on, the Hail Mary was prayed as often as the Our Father. While the Church clung strictly to the difference between *prayer to* the saints and *adoration* (which applied only to God), these fine distinctions remained alien to popular piety. The result was that at times the cult of the saints was reminiscent of ancient polytheism.

The Catholic Church has always promoted the use of external stimuli, not just through paintings, sculpture, religious dramas, and musical backgrounds for ritual, incense, and processions, but also through the recognition of holy places and relics. This sensuous, palpable expression was quite consistent with a religion whose God and founder had made himself perceptible and involved in the life of the senses.

We have already seen that in the first centuries the lack of relics had put a brake on the cult of Mary. That changed

in the 5th century. Eudocia, the wife of the Emperor Theodosius II (d. 450), showed great zeal in the finding of relics, and in some mysterious way she got hold of Mary's veil. In the chapel of the Blachernae Palace in Constantinople around this time there was also a long blue veil that Mary had worn. In Thessaloniki around 470 a basilica was built for a miraculous picture of Maria Hodegetria (Mary who shows the way), supposedly painted by angels. Many old pictures and statues were credited to Saint Luke, for example, the wonder-working Black Madonna at Montserrat in Catalonia, which as a matter of fact was probably Byzantine and dated from the 12th century.

In a sermon ascribed to Bishop Theophilus of Alexandria, the story is told of a Jew who ordered Christian workmen to destroy an icon of Mary. When they refused, he smashed it himself and bade his men throw the pieces into the river. But the picture began to bleed. The workers collected the fragments in a basket, while the blood kept dripping out of it. The Jew was horror-stricken, converted to Christianity, and built a church for the icon, where countless healings and exorcisms took place.

In medieval accounts paintings and statues of Mary often come to life. They also often cry, as in the already-mentioned episode from Syracuse in 1953. In a widespread legend a mother begs the Virgin to save her dying child, and takes the Christ Child from Mary's arms as a sort of hostage. After Mary has restored her child to health, the woman returns the Christ Child.

We find examples as far back as the Acts of the Apostles that not just Christ but saints also can perform miracles. Paul healed the sick by the laying on of hands—the mere touch of his handkerchiefs could do the same (Acts 19.12). Similar qualities were attributed to relics of Mary. In the reliquaries of the Blachernae Palace and the Chalkoprateia in Constantinople many miracles were attested to, supposedly brought about by Marian relics. There was a tradition according to which the dress that Mary wore on the day of the Annunciation had been brought to Constantinople by Charles the Bald, grandson of Charlemagne. After his death (876) it was transferred to Chartres. When a fire destroyed the cathedral there in 1194 the holy dress remained miraculously preserved.

The rulers of the period were likewise interested in Marian relics. On the way to the First Crusade Robert of Flanders and his nephew, Robert of Normandy, enjoyed the hospitality of Robert Rorsa, Duke of Apulia. The latter turned down all the expensive presents that the first two offered him in gratitude; but he was glad to get bones of Sts. Matthew and Nicholas and some hair of Mary's. In the 12th century relics began to appear in significantly greater numbers. The

*Page 186, right:* Rueland Frueauf the Younger (1465/70–1545) shows in his painting *The Finding of Mary's Veil* from 1505 the miracle that happened to the Empress Eudocia, wife of the Emperor Theodosius II (Cathedral Chapter Museum, Klosterneuburg).

*Left:* Our Lady of Montserrat, Catalonia, is a Black Madonna. She is also called "the Little Bride." The story of the pilgrimages to this wonderworking image begins in the early 12th century with reports of miraculous cures. Right

canons of Coutances in France were surprised when their bishop, Geoffrey de Montbray (d. 1110), discovered some hair of Mary, precisely labeled; because, as they said, "no relics of the Virgin are known here on earth." In general the Byzantines laid claim to Mary's clothes, while in the West believers venerated her hair, her milk, and even her fingernail parings, which were kept in a red silk case in Poitou. Hairs of the Madonna were preserved in various Roman churches, as well as in Padua, Venice, Assisi, Bologna, Paris, and many other places. Bits of her clothing were stored in Marseilles, Toulon, Novgorod, Assisi, Brussels, and elsewhere. Her slippers were kept in Soissons and were the cause of many miracles. Her wedding ring was on display at Chiusi in Tuscany. Emperor Charles IV (1346–1378) had a large collection of Marian relics.

A special form of veneration took place at sites dedicated to Mary. In *Walsingham*, England, since 1130 there had been a replica of the Holy House of Nazareth, to which pilgrims flocked from all over Europe for more than 300 years. In the reign of Edward the Confessor (d. 1066) Maria is said to have appeared to Richeldis de Faverches, a widow in Walsingham, and to have told her every detail about her home in Nazareth so that she could set up a copy of it in Walsingham. Many miracles took

from the start countless numbers of people came to the site. Over the centuries it remained a religious center of the West. Ignatius Loyola, later the founder of the Jesuits, kept vigil here for several days in 1522, during which time he decided to give up his life as an officer and imitate the great saints. He handed over his weapons to the Madonna.

*Right:* Sveti Kliment in Ohrid, Macedonia. Icon of Bogorodica Hodegetria, Mary the Pathfinder, 13th century.

place in this shrine, but it fell victim to the Reformation zeal of Henry VIII, who destroyed it in 1538 when he had the whole pilgrimage site leveled.

But Walsingham had already found a counterpart in *Loreto*, in the Italian province of Ancona. Local tradition claimed to have not just a copy, but Mary's house itself. It had been carried through the air by angels after the capture of Jerusalem by the infidels in 1291 and set down in various places in Europe. But it had not been received with the necessary degree of reverence until it reached Loreto in 1296. This legend was written down in 1472, whereupon a deputation went to visit the Holy Land and found that the house in Nazareth had in fact mysteriously disappeared and that its dimensions matched those in Loreto. And so in 1507 Pope Julius II officially elevated the Holy House to a place of pilgrimage, although he carefully noted, "ut pie creditur et fama est" (as is piously believed and report claims). Loreto became more and more popular as a destination for pilgrims, and in 1920 Our Lady of Loreto, whose house had been transported through the air, was de-

clared the patron saint of flyers.

The Reformation took a hostile view of this sort of veneration of Mary. Under Henry VIII not only Walsingham, but the Mary chapel in the cathedral of Ely, was destroyed. In Luther's Germany, as a rule, the Protestants were more tolerant. Nevertheless from the 16th century onward the cult of Mary underwent serious reverses.

The Catholic Church met the criticism of the Reformers not with any basic reorientation, but by cleaning house. Under the leadership of the Cardinal Archbishop of Milan, Charles Borromeo (d. 1584), all remaining doubtful relics and icons were removed; but the authentic ones were thrust into all the greater prominence. Borromeo's passionate defense of the cult of Mary at the Council of Trent was successful; and many old Marian shrines were revived and restored. In the Borghese chapel of Santa Maria Maggiore in Rome an ancient icon of Mary was brilliantly adorned. This icon, called the "Salus Populi Romani" (Salvation of the Roman People), was long considered a Byzantine work, but is now thought to be much older. The

icon was henceforth supposed to honor not just Mary herself, but also the successes of the pope, who belonged to the Borghese family. At the same time Mary's crown in the old church of Santa Maria in Trastevere was newly decorated, again with the help of Borromeo. In both churches the new, overcharged Baroque style showed itself in full splendor, along with the determination of the Catholic Church to maintain the old traditions despite all the criticism.

Page 188, left and center: These two panel paintings show angels holding Mary's garments and the swaddling clothes of Christ (Cologne, second half of the 15th century).

Page 188, right: Giovanni Battista Tiepolo, sketch for the Transferral of the Casa Santa to Loreto (ca. 1743, oil on canvas). The legend claims that angels carried Mary's house from Nazareth through the air to Loreto. The waves of pilgrims, by now in the millions, who have come to Loreto began in the 14th century.

Left: Interior view of the Loreto chapel in Italy. The Casa Santa (Holy House) is overarched by a mighty basilica. The Black Madonna in Loreto is one of the most frequently visited of all the miraculous images of Mary.

Right: The Madonna of the Rosary from the 18th century, wooden sculpture (Erlingshofen, Eichstätt district).

*Right and below:* The house at Meryem Ana in Ephesus (modern Efes, Turkey) was venerated early on as Mary's house. Taken in by John, Mary was thought to have spent her last years here. At Ephesus in 431 the dogma of Mary's divine motherhood (Theotokos) was proclaimed. In 1833 the German visionary Katharina Emmerich had a vision, written down by Clemens Brentano, the well-known Romantic poet, in which she gave a precise description of the house. In 1891 excavators discovered foundations from the 1st century that exactly matched her description.

As early as the 4th century relics were kept and displayed on the altar. The forms varied between shrines, boxes, busts, and head reliquaries. The reliquary became the true marvel of the goldsmith's and enameler's art, in which small-scale medieval sculpture displayed its finest achievements. The following works provide examples of the richness and splendor of old reliquaries.

*Above right:* Reliquary built between 1220 and 1238 on commission from Frederick Barbarossa (Cathedral treasury, Aachen).

*Middle left:* Mary's veil was kept in the reliquary from the Basilica of St. Francis in Assisi. It was donated in fulfillment of a vow by Tommaso Orsini in 1320.

*Lower left:* Reliquary with Mary's veil from the cathedral of Chartres.

*Center:* Reliquary (Parisian school) with Marian relics and the seamless garment of Jesus, said to have been made by his mother.

*Above left and lower right:* Mary's tomb and sarcophagus in Jerusalem.

*Above:* The 12th-century apse mosaic shows on the left Pope Innocent II (1130–1132), the donator of the church of Santa Maria in Trastevere. It depicts *Christ Enthroned with Mary*, in imitation of the Byzantine mode of representing the imperial couple. The cornerstone for the church had already been laid in the first half of the 3rd century by St. Calixtus. The Church, dedicated to Mary, was probably the first one in Rome that believers could visit openly.

*Page 193:* Mary altar and stained-glass window from the Cathedral of Notre Dame, Paris.

## Churches Dedicated to Mary

Over the centuries countless churches and cathedrals have been dedicated to Mary. We can list only a few of the best-known ones here:

In *Rome* among the oldest Marian churches are the already-mentioned Santa Maria Maggiore and Santa Maria in Trastevere. Then there is Santa Maria Antiqua, which was built in a temple of Augustus behind the Forum, and which shelters many Roman-Byzantine frescoes; Santa Maria in Aracoeli on the Capitoline Hill—according to legend, the place where the Sibyl announced the birth of Jesus to the Emperor Augustus—with frescoes by Pintorrichio; Santa Maria sopra Minerva, the only Gothic church in Rome; Santa Maria degli Angeli on the Piazza della Repubblica, originally designed by Michelangelo, but then radically changed. Santa Maria del Popolo is located over what is said to be the tomb of Nero; and on the Piazza Bocca della Verità is the ancient Santa Maria in Cosemeddin, with the famous "Mouth of Truth" (a large stone mask that supposedly bites off the hand of any liar who dares to put a hand in the opening).

Elsewhere in *Italy* we have the imposing Santa Maria della Salute in Venice, built in the 17th century by Longhena; and Santa Maria dei Frari, from the 15th century, with two famous Titians and the tomb of Tintoretto. On the neighboring island of Torcello is the Cathedral of Santa Maria Assunta, the oldest building in the whole lagoon still standing, with a splendid ceiling mosaic of Mary from the 13th century. In Naples there is Santa Maria Donna Regina, in Florence the famous Cathedral of Santa Maria del Fiore, whose grand cupola was designed by Brunelleschi, as well as Santa Maria Novella, begun in 1278, with frescoes by Masaccio, Orcagna, and others. In Pisa we have Santa Maria della Spina, begun in 1323, and in Siena the 13th-century Santa Maria dei Servi; in Arezzo Santa Maria delle Grazie, in the Gothic style from the 15th century. Practically evey sizable city in Italy has at least one church dedicated to Mary.

Many old Marian churches are also to be found in *France*, most notably, of course, the Cathedral of Notre Dame in Paris, begun in 1163. It was decorated by Suger, the abbot of St. Denis and a French statesman, with a window whose stained-glass paintings show the triumph of the Virgin. The window survived the destruction of the church and in the 13th century was integrated into the structure that even today dominates the cityscape. Unfortunately the stained-glass window is gone, because an 18th-century art historian judged it to be too primitive and had it smashed.

In Suger's own church of St. Denis stained-glass windows depicting the coronation of Mary were defaced by a mob during the French Revolution. Considerably older than these churches is that of Soissons, which was dedicated to Mary in a former temple of Isis in the 5th century. Then there are the churches of Notre Dame in Laon (begun in 1160), Noyons (begun in 1164), Rouen (12th to 15th centuries), Mantes-la-Jolie and Amiens (both ca. 1220), and many others.

Of the numerous *German* churches to Mary we may mention here only the Lady church of Nuremberg (built 1352–1361), the Munich Lady church (1468–1488), the church of St. Mary in the Capitol in Cologne, the church of the Assumption and the Lady church in Dresden (built in the 1720s, and thought of as a sister church of Santa Maria della Salute in Venice; it was destroyed in the fire-bombing of February 1945). In northern Germany we have the Mary churches of Rostock, Lübeck, Neubrandenburg, and Berlin. The Berlin Mary church, built around the end of the 13th century and rebuilt in Gothic brick after a fire in 1380, is the only old church in the former East Berlin to survive the Second World War.

Other renowned Marian churches of Europe are Sankt Maria am Gestad in Vienna, the Mary church in Gdansk, one of the greatest churches in Poland; in Bulgaria the Lady church in Plovdiv, the former Philippopolis, and the church of Veilko Tirnovo. In Athens the Parthenon was dedicated to Mary in the 6th century, and so was a basilica built around 470 in Thessaloniki. In Spain we have Santa Maria del Mar in Barcelona, in Toledo the church of Santa Maria la Bianca from the 12th and 13th centuries, originally a synagogue, and in Saragossa the famous pilgrimage church of Nuestra Señora del Pilar, overshadowed by its eleven domes (17th and 18th centuries).

*Page 194:* The west façade of the Cathedral of Chartres (1145–50) contains the first stepped portal. In the central portal Christ appears as the Judge of the world, with the symbols of the evangelists, in the left portal the Ascension of Christ, and in the right the enthroned Mother of God, as shown here, flanked by angels.

*Above left:* Detail from the sculpted altar of the Marian church in Gdansk. Shown here is *Mary enthroned.*

*Left:* View of the choir of the Gdansk Marian church, with the crucifixion group of Mary and John.

*Right:* Chartres, which is considered one of the early Gothic Marian cathedrals, displays subjects from Mary's life, above all in the gleaming church windows. Along with the symbolism of the architecture and the figurative representations of the sculptures, the light is thought of as one of the most important expressive ingredients of Gothic mysticism. The picture shown here is of the stained-glass window on the south side of the choir of the cathedral (Notre Dame de la Belle Verrière) comes from the middle of the 12th century, and depicts the enthroned Mother of God as the Queen of Heaven. She wears a crown with a halo, which is framed by a wide wreath of stars.

*Right and outside right:* An example of Catalonian Gothic, the church of Santa Maria del Mar, Barcelona, begun in 1328. The builder was Berenguer de Montagut. The stained-glass window show the Madonna and child.

*Center left:* The Dresden Lady church, built in 1726–1738 by Georg Bähr, captured here in a copperplate etching by Gottfried Friedrich Riedel.

Page 196, below left: Late Gothic Mary chapel in Würzburg, a 19th-century oil painting by Peter Geist.

Page 196, lower right: Painting by Max Emanuel Einmiller (1854) of the nave of the Munich Lady church (1468–1488), built of Gothic brick. Human figures by Moritz von Schwind.

Left: "Sankt Maria in Kapitol" in Cologne, formerly a collegiate church for noble ladies, built around 1060, contains the first three-concha choir of German Romanesque and a beautiful crypt from the 11th century. Among the rich decoration is the "Beautiful Madonna" in the French-Rhenish style, ca. 1400.

Below left: Transept of the Cathedral of Strasbourg (ca. 1200). The stained-glass window of Mary Praying with Child was done by Max Ingrand (1956). The apse paintings are by Eduard Steinle (1877).

Above: View of the main altar of the Gothic hall church of Maria am Gestad in Vienna.

## Marian Orders and Religious Communities

Brotherhoods and sisterhoods that placed themselves under Mary's special protection and sometimes expressed this in their name have been in existence ever since the early Middle Ages. Even today official statistics of the Catholic Church show no fewer than 435 papally approved religious organizations with a name related to Mary. There are also groups with no standing in canon law, as well as those that are dedicated to Mary but whose title does not explicitly mention this. The grand total of such groups is estimated to be around 900. They call themselves the sisters, daughters, handmaids, or sons of Mary in many different shapes and guises.

The earliest of these Marian institutes were based on the rules of St. Augustine or St. Benedict. The first Marian brotherhood seems to have been that of Naupaktos, which was founded in Greece around 1048. Its members honored Mary with an icon that they carried in procession on certain days. In Cologne a similar brotherhood is said to have been founded around 1065. Orders specially dedicated to Mary were the *Johannites* (11th century), the *Carthusians* (1084), the *Cistercians*, *Premonstratensians*, and *Carmelites* (around 1180). The *German Order*, founded around 1190 during the siege of Acre during the Third Crusade, had well-defined Marian features; its members were popularly known as Mary's Knights. By the beginning of the same century Peter de Honestis had already founded the *Sons and Daughters of Mary*.

The great new orders of the 13th century—the *Dominicans*, *Franciscans*, *Servites*, and others—likewise had a strongly Marian tinge. Also famous were the *Brigittines*, founded by Brigit of Sweden (1300–1373). Considered one of the greatest Scandinavian saints, she had many visions of Jesus and Mary that were often shown in paintings. She fought for the return of the popes from Avignon to Rome.

The 16th century saw the *Theatines* (1525), *Barnabites* (1530), *Jesuits* (1540), *Camillians* (1582), *Piarists* (1597), and others. The Jesuits soon founded the *Congregations of Mary*, movements with a large membership, some of which still exist under that name, while others have been succeeded by the Communities of Christian Life.

Around 1600 a community for girls was founded in Mattaincourt, France, by Peter Fourier, later reorganized in 1864 by Abbot Orestes Passeri in Rome. It was dedicated to the Immaculate Conception. In the 17th century the Cistercian monastery of Port Royal displayed strongly Marian features. This period also saw the founding of the *Order of Mary's Visitation* by Francis de Sales and Jeanne Frémyot de Chantal as well as three new groups by Cardinal Pierre de Bérulle. In the 18th century the *Passionists* and the *Redemptorists* date from 1720, and the *Congregation of the Holy Spirit* from 1734. Even after the French Revolution more new Marian institutes kept developing, three of them in 1822 alone. At the same time the *Brothers of the Presentation* were founded in Ireland, the *Sisters of Our Lady* in Holland, in Italy the *Oblates of the Blessed Virgin Mary*, and two Marian congregations created by Guillaume-Joseph de Chaminade. The order of priests known as Marists were founded in 1816; they are dedicated to pastoral and mission work. A Marist father later founded the *Marist Brothers, a community of lay brothers dedicated to teaching in the schools. In 1824 the Sisters of Mary's Compassion* were founded in Germany. We should also mention the *Brotherhood of the Immaculate Conception*, confirmed by Pius IX in 1853, shortly before the definition of the dogma.

From the 1860s to the 1890s new congregations were founded in all parts of the Christian world, such as the *Servi della Carità* in Italy, the *Steyler Missionaries* and the *Steyler Missionary Sisters* in Germany, and the *Nursing Brothers* of Constantinople and many others. The sect of the Maravites was created in 1893. From 1909 to 1924 they belonged to the Old Catholic Church; then they became autonomous and dedicated themselves to the special veneration of Mary.

Giovanni Battista Tiepolo (1696–1770) painted this picture in the Venetian church of Santa Maria del Rosario of the Madonna and Child with three Dominican women saints, Catherine of Siena, Rose of Lima, and Agnes of Montepulciano (1740); the Order of Preachers or Dominicans was founded by Dominic (Domingo de Guzmán) in Toulouse in 1216.

Our century has seen the formation of a series of Marian organizations, not orders in the classical sense, but larger movements. Their center of gravity lies in everyday spirituality and the lay apostolate; they have many members with varying but strong degrees of connection to the parent organization. One might mention, for instance, the *Schön-statt Movement*, which includes among others the *Sisters of Mary* (1926) and the *Brothers of Mary* (1942) and the *Women of Schönstatt*. The movement venerates Mary under the title of "Thrice Wondrous Mother and Queen of Schönstatt." The Polish Franciscan Maximilian Kolbe, who died a martyr in Auschwitz, founded the *Militia Immaculatae* in 1917, and Irishman Frank Duff created the *Legion of Mary* in 1921. The Italian movement *Focolare* started around 1943; its spirituality likewise has distinctive Marian features.

Even after the Second World War we find new Marian foundations; in Germany alone there was the *Rosary-Action*, the *White-Blue Army*, the *Patrona Bavariae*, as well as the *Women's Association of All Nations*, and others. The *Brotherhood of the Holy Virgin Mary*, which was founded by the Jesuit Johann Leunis in 1563, was confirmed again in 1950 by Pope Pius XII. In Darmstadt toward the end of World War II the *Protestant Marian Sisterhood* came into being.

Among the countless associations oriented (with varying degrees of intensity, of course) toward Mary, only a small selection has been named here. They are completely different from one another, but they all express in their own way the "Marian spirit." And the fact that they can all ultimately be viewed as having common ground is no doubt due to Mary's special meaning as the embodiment of the three "evangelical counsels," poverty, chastity, and obedience, for which she at all times served as a shining example.

## Cult Sites and Places of Pilgrimage

In all Catholic countries there are places of special Marian veneration and pilgrimages, some of them local, others of broader importance. In *Germany* alone there are between 400 and 700 such places. Once again only the best-known ones can be cited. The ones in which apparitions of Mary play a role will be dealt with separately in a later chapter.

One well-known place of Marian pilgrimage is Altötting in Upper Bavaria. There in the chapel of Grace is a black Mother of God. There are also Black Madonnas in other shrines, such as Chartres, Rocamadour, Le Puy, Orleans, Czestochowa, Loreto, Santa Maria Maggiore, and on Montserrat. Why Mary is depicted as black here has not been fully explained. Some trace it back to the Song of Solomon 1.5 ("I am very dark, but comely, O daughters of Jerusalem"); others have connected the blackness with the smoke of countless votive candles; and others again believe that the color black is supposed to express the magic of Mary's healing powers.

Likewise in Bavaria there is the pilgrimage site of Andechs on the Am-mersee and the pilgrimage church of Birnau with a miraculous image of Mary in an old Cistercian church. On the Lower Rhine there is the world-famous pilgrimage place of Kevelaer with a Marian sanctuary from the 17th century. More than 600,000 pilgrims visit this little place every year. In the district of Soest lies Werl with a pilgrimage basilica; in Würzburg, above the fortress of Marienberg and its Mary chapel, is the "Käppele," a pilgrimage church from the 18th century.

*Austria* too is full of Marian pilgrimage sites. There is Mariazell in Upper Styria with a Gothic pilgrimage church and a

*Left:* The miraculous image of Birnau on the Lake Constance, from the year 1400. The Birnau pilgrimage site is documented as far back as 1222.

*Right:* The "Black Madonna" from Altötting (Burgundian, 13th century) is rendered here on a knit carpet from 1720. Since around 1300 there has been a "mercy chapel" in Altötting, with miracles attested to since 1489.

statue from the 12th century. A Pietà in the pilgrimage church of Maria Taferl is the regional sanctuary of Lower Austria. Not far from there is another pilgrimage site, Sonntagsberg. The pilgrimages to Maria Roggendorf have experienced a certain revival in past years. In Carinthia there is Maria Saal, a Gothic pilgrimage site with Roman reliefs. Near Salzburg is the Basilica of Maria Plain with a crowned miraculous statue. In 1779 Mozart wrote his *Coronation Mass* for the yearly "Coronation feast."

The most famous Marian pilgrimage site in *Switzerland* is Maria Einsiedeln in the canton of Schwyz, with a Benedictine cathedral chapter that was founded in the year 937 and then rebuilt in the Baroque style. The "chapel of grace," which is cut from the rock, from the Benedictine abbey of Mariastein in the canton of Solothurn, looks back over a 600-year history of pilgrimages.

Czestochowa on the upper reaches of the Warthe has been, since the founding of the Pauline monastery of Jasna Góra, the most important pilgrimage site in *Poland*, visited every year by more than a million pilgrims. The Black Madonna is said to have been painted by the evangelist Luke, but it dates from

*Far left:* The miraculous image from the Franciscan church of Werl, archdiocese of Paderborn. The Madonna is one of the oldest such images in Germany. It was presumably made in Sweden in 1170. Werl is the leading place of Marian pilgrimage in Westphalia.

*Above:* View of the interior of the pilgrimage church in Andechs, decorated by Johann Baptist Zimmermann.

*Left:* The center of the monastery church of Andechs is the miraculous image of a *Madonna Enthroned with Child* from the school of Erasmus Grasser (ca. 1500).

*Above:* Madonna Vladimirskaya from the early 15th-century Moscow school, depicted in the manner of the "tender Mother of God" (Eleousa).

*Right:* This miraculous image is venerated in the pilgrimage church of Mariazell, Styria. It is a late Roman work, today covered with a brocade mantle and a veil. The pilgrimage began with a visit of the Margrave Henry of Moravia (1198–1222), whose wife experienced a cure there.

*Page 203, left:* The Gothic image of a Pietà in the Pilgrimage Church of Maria Taferl in Austria is surrounded by a Baroque aureole.

*Page 203, right:* An Andalusian Madonna with tears (from a Holy Week procession in Seville).

the 14th century. In the year 1655, when Charles X of Sweden invaded Poland, the monastery was defended only by the monks and a handful of soldiers. When the Swedes lifted the siege after forty days, the population saw this as a miracle by the Virgin. In 1702 the monastery was defended yet one more time. Since then Our Lady of Czestochowa has been venerated as the "Queen of Poland" and a sort of national symbol.

In *France* we have the pilgrimage place and episcopal see of Le Puy, in the picturesque surroundings of the department of the Haute-Loire. The most famous *Italian* place of pilgrimage is Loreto, which we have already seen. And again we have already mentioned the old *English* shrine of Walsingham, destroyed by Henry VIII.

One of the most famous religious sites of *Spain* is Montserrat, northwest of Barcelona. The old Benedictine abbey from the 11th century lies in ruins. A new monastery from the 18th century was torn down by French troops in 1812. Meanwhile the Renaissance church from the 16th century has been restored several times. It contains the well-known Black Madonna, likewise supposedly created by Luke and brought to Spain by Peter. During the centuries of Arab occupation of Spain, it was hidden away in a cave. Montserrat has often been identified with legendary Monsalvat, the castle of the Holy Grail.

In *Russia* before the Revolution of 1917 there were over 200 icons venerated in shrines, about half of these dedicated to the Mother of God. This form of devotion was brought from the Byzantine empire after the capture of Constantinople by the Turks in 1453. (In Byzantium itself, after the end of the Iconoclasm controversy in 843, the cult of icons had enjoyed a long flowering until the Turks took over.) Most Russian icons are painted in accordance with strict rules and show the Madonna as the majestic Queen of Heaven.

1                    2                    3

4

5

6

7

8

The "Black Madonna" is a widespread feature of medieval art, especially in the miraculous images. It was held in especially high honor. The Black Madonnas were viewed in the tradition of Black Artemis of Ephesus, but other origin legends grew up about them as well. Of particular importance were the Black Madonna of Breznichar in Bohemia (1), which was made on commission from King Wenceslaus in 1396. It is found today in the national Gallery in Prague. In her aureole is inscribed the line from the Song of Solomon that is so crucial for understanding the Black Madonnas, "I am very dark, but comely, O daughters of Jerusalem." Like this one, most of these Madonnas were painted black to begin with.

Further examples of "Black Madonnas":
2. *La Vierge Noire* of Le Puy.
3. *La Vierge Noire* of Clermont Ferrand.
4. *Notre Dame du Pilier* (at the pillar) from Chartres, a Gothic stone figure from the 15th century.
5. *Madonna Enthroned with Child*, from Rocamadour. It is one of the earliest sculptures of Mary (12th century).
6. San Sebastian, León.
7. Miraculous image from Einsiedeln in Switzerland, ca. 1440. The chapel, which was originally dedicated to the Redeemer was transformed into a Marian chapel in the 12th century.
8. Miraculous image from Altötting, Burgundian, probably late 13th century.
9. Black Madonna of Czestochowa. The miracle-working Mother of God is the Patroness of Poland.

9

## Apparitions

As we have already seen, there were many accounts from the Middle Ages of miracles performed by Mary. Since the Reformation important cult sites have grown up at some of the scenes of these miracles. Even today they are visited by hundreds of thousands of believers, with countless miraculous cures being reported. Obviously many modern people find it hard to believe in these miracles and would never take part in that sort of Marian veneration. At any rate, one must concede that the Catholic Church has been very cautious in recognizing such apparitions and has subjected all claims of miracles to extremely strict scrutiny, often lasting years. Let us deal briefly here with a few

of these phenomena.

The oldest apparition still celebrated today occurred in the year 1531 in *Guadalupe*, then the capital of Mexico. An Indian convert to Christianity named Juan Diego, who was traveling through the mountains near Tepeyac, suddenly heard a "song, as though many rare birds were singing together; their voices sounded like an echo through the hills...." Then he saw "on the crest of the hill ... a lady," whose great shining beauty enchanted him. Her clothing gleamed like the sun, and the stones of

the hills and the caves reflecting her splendor were like precious gold. He also saw a rainbow spanning the countryside, so that the cactus and other plants growing there seemed to be heavenly flowers.... Then the apparition charged him to build a church in her honor. Juan went to his bishop, but he would hear nothing of it. Thereupon the lady appeared to him and promised him a sign: He was to climb up to a certain place in the mountains and bring her the roses he would find there. This was in December, when nothing grew on the mountains except thorns; but Juan believed the apparition, found the roses, and when he brought them to his Lady, she put them in his cloak. Juan returned to his bishop, opened his cloak, and spilled out the roses; suddenly the picture of the Virgin appeared, imprinted on his cloak. Now the bishop believed, and had a shrine built in his church. The "Virgin of Guadalupe" is today the most frequently visited pilgrimage site in the world. In 1754 she was declared the patroness of Mexico by Pope Benedict XIV; since 1910 she has been the patroness of all of North and South America. In 1976 a great circular basilica was built and consecrated in the Distrito Federal, to which Pope John Paul II made a visit in 1979.

At a little place in southeastern France, *Laus*, Mary appeared several times to a seventeen-year-old shepherdess, beginning in May 1664. Pope Pius IX recognized the appearance and in 1872 named the girl a "venerable servant of God."

In the early 19th century there were the already-mentioned visions of Sister *Anna Katharina Emmerich*, who saw the house and tomb of Mary in Ephesus, although she had never been there. Her visions were taken down by Clemens Brentano; and after they had been published in 1876, archaeologists visited the site she described, where they actually uncovered the foundation walls of a house that matched her account. In 1896 the Vatican authorized pilgrimages to this site.

In the year 1830 Mary appeared three times to a 23-year-old cloistered nun

*Left:* The revolutionary movement against Spanish rule in Mexico began in 1810 with the hoisting of the flag of the Virgin of Guadalupe. After the achievement of national independence the flag remained a national symbol.

*Above:* Maria appears in 1864 to the shepherd children Melanie and Maximin in La Salette, France. The painting of the scene is by Luigi Peregrini. Not long afterwards a spring gushed forth on the site of the Marian apparition. The Madonna of La Salette is venerated today as a reconciler of sinners.

*Top:* "Miraculous medal," silver. In the monastic church on the Rue du Bac in Paris Mary appeared to a nun, whom she commanded: "Have a medal stamped. All those who wear it will receive grace." The first medals were distributed in 1832.

named *Catherine Labouré* in the Rue du Bac in Paris and told her to have a medal struck. The apparition was not officially recognized by the Church, but Catherine herself was canonized by Pope Pius XII in July 1947.—In 1842 the Virgin appeared to the Jewish banker *Alphonse Ratisbone*, who was an enemy of the Catholics, but who was later baptized and became a priest.

In 1846 the Virgin appeared to the eleven-year-old Maximin Giraud and the fourteen-year-old Melanie Calvat, two shepherds who could neither read nor write, at *La Salette* near Grenoble in a vision of light and roses. In 1851 their bishop acknowledged the vision as believable, but the two children grew up in ways that the Church found disappointing: Maximin founded a liquor business, which he called Salettine; Melanie was sent from one convent to another and published a book, *The Mystery of La Salette*, that won the local bishop's approval but was put on the Roman Index.

The apparitions enjoyed a boom starting in 1849, i.e., after the so-called *Age of Mary* was proclaimed by Pius IX, who at the time was preparing to define the dogma of the Immaculate Conception. From this point many popes devoted special attention to Mary: since 1849 there have been over 500 documents on Mary issued by the Vatican. Leo XIII (1878–1903) promoted the feast of the Rosary in honor of Mary that was supposed to have averted heresy in the 16th century and the Turks in the 17th. In 1904 Pius X (1903–1914) celebrated the fiftieth anniversary of the dogma of the Immaculate Conception. Pius XII (1939–1958) in particular is characterized as the "Marian pope." Apart from the dogmas already discussed, Pius called the Marian Year from December 1953 to December 1954 on the centenary of the definition of the Immaculate Conception and of the apparitions at Lourdes. In his brief *Marialis Cultus* (1974) Paul VI (1963–1978) issued detailed instructions for promoting Marian piety.

No doubt the most famous of all the apparitions of Mary took place shortly after the start of the Marian Age in *Lourdes* at the foot of the French Pyrenees. The Virgin appeared there no fewer than eighteen times from February 11 to July 16, 1858 to Bernadette Soubirous, a poor fourteen-year-old girl, who suffered all her life from asthma. Mary took the form of a very young girl wearing a veil and a sky blue sash, with eyes "blue as forget-me-nots." Bernadette called her "aquero" (*vous* ["you"] in the dialect of the region); Bernadette was told to ask her name, and at her sixteenth appearance she finally said that she was the "Immaculate Conception," an expression Bernadette did not understand. She did not know how to write, had a weak memory, and took three years to put her report of the apparitions down on paper. She was shown pictures of the Ma-

donna by Raphael and Botticelli, but she thought they did not do justice to her visions. Eight years later, after she had become a nun in the convent of Nevers, she wrote to Pius IX: "I would like to believe that you are especially beloved of the Mother of God, because

after four years (from the declaration of the dogma of the Immaculate Conception) she personally appeared on earth to say, 'I am the Immaculate Conception.' I did not know what these words meant." The shrine of Lourdes is now visited by over 3,000,000 people every year, including about 400,000 of the sick, who arrive in hospital trains. Many pilgrims are convinced that they have been cured by the water from the grotto where the apparitions occurred and take a bottle of Lourdes water home with them.

Under the pontificate of Pius IX there occurred yet another sensational appearance of Mary in *Pontmain* in the *département* of Mayenne, France. Here Mary appeared to a twelve-year-old cowherd, his ten-year-old brother, and two other children, one of whom, the nine-year-old Jeanne-Marie, who later became a nun—and denied that she had seen Mary. In any event the Virgin had appeared to the other children in a long dress with a sash, veil, and crown. After Jeanne-Marie's denial the case of

The story of Lourdes as the greatest place of pilgrimage in Europe today began in 1858. Bernadette, a girl from a poor family, had a vision of Mary near the Massabielle grotto. Mary asked her to uncover a spring in the grotto, which she did. The water that poured out soon brought cures to many sick people. A few days later Mary revealed to her that a chapel was to be built to her on this spot, so that pilgrims could go there in procession. The statue of Mary was carved by sculptor Joseph Fabish of Lyon according to information supplied by Bernadette.

*Left:* A procession at night.

*Right:* The grotto with the statue.

Pontmain was investigated again by the Church, but it was confirmed in 1920.

Mary also wore a crown in her apparition at *Knock Muir*, Ireland, in 1879. A group of villagers saw her on the façade of their parish church, surrounded by a group of saints. Knock Muir became a national pilgrimage site, and the apparition was recognized as authentic by the local hierarchy in 1939.

A particularly interesting case was *Fátima*, Portugal, where Mary appeared every 13th of the month from May to October 1917 for a total of six times, to ten-year-old Lucia dos Santos, her nine-year-old cousin Francisco, and their seven-year-old cousin Jacinta. The latter two died very shortly after the event and have been since beatified. Lucia's

account was recorded in 1924; she became a nun and wrote the story of her experiences. Fátima is visited by more than 1,000,000 visitors a year; Popes Paul VI and John Paul II have likewise traveled there. Nevertheless serious misgivings exist about the authenticity of the statements that Lucia claimed the Virgin had made. Among other things, Mary supposedly announced that the First World War would end on October 13, 1917, and that a second war would break out under Pius XI, neither of which came true.

In *Beauraing* in the Belgian diocese of Naumur Mary again called herself the "Immaculate Conception." She is said to have appeared there thirty-three times between November 1932 and

January 1933 to six girl students at a convent boarding school. After long negotiations the bishop of Naumur declared the apparitions credible.

At almost the same time other apparitions of Mary were reported in Belgium, in *Banneux*, the diocese of Liege. She appeared to the twelve-year-old Mariette Béco, the daughter of a poor worker. In the first vision Mary remained mute, in the second she plunged Mariette's arms into the water and said: "This spring is reserved for me." The third time she announced, "I am the Virgin of the poor; the spring is meant for all nations to give relief to the sick." At her last apparition she said, "I am the mother of the Redeemer, the Mother of God. Adieu." In 1949 the

visions were recognized as authentic.

In 1936 Antonie Rädler was visiting the "Lourdes grotto" of *Wigratzbad* in the diocese of Augsburg. She heard a "rustling that grew louder and louder.... Then singing began,... which finally became loud and powerful as if countless heavenly hosts ... were chiming together in wonderful harmony.... They all sang, 'Immaculately conceived Mother of victory, pray for us!' I heard the words about fifty times ... then it seemed to me as though Mary were smiling...." Antonie's experience lasted for two to three hours. The little grotto she built was completed by a chapel in 1938; the first mass was celebrated in 1940. The number of visitors increased so rapidly that by 1972 the building of a larger church was planned. The Catholic Church has not yet officially recognized this place of pilgrimage, but in June 1982 the bishop of Augsburg confirmed the veneration of the "Immaculate Conception of victory".

There have been numerous Marian apparitions in recent years, such as those in *Finca Betania*, Venezuela. There Mary appeared first to a woman, then on seven occasions to a group of children, all told to about 150 persons, as they were leaving their church after Sunday mass. This was repeated on many Saturdays and Sundays in the years 1984 to 1987. The bishop there recognized the apparitions in November 1987.

Recognition has not yet been ex-tended to the apparitions that occurred at around the same time in *Kibeho*, Rwanda. These are said to have begun around November 1981 and have evidently not ended. The recipients of the visions were six girls aged sixteen to twenty-one and a fourteen-year-old shepherd boy, who was not yet a Christian, but who then had himself baptized. The bishop of Butare supported the prayers of the faithful, but did not officially speak out on the supernatural character of the apparitions.

Much more widely publicized than these were the apparitions in *Medjugorje*, Bosnia, which have occurred almost every day since June 24, 1981. They came to five young people between ten and sixteen years of age, who

were later examined by doctors and psychologists. The Church got into a difficult situation when the bishop of Mostar condemned the apparitions as false, but the Franciscan parish priests pronounced them genuine. At any rate since that time many pilgrimages to Medjugorje have taken place, and the Church has at least tolerated them. Mary is said to have introduced herself with the words, "I am the Blessed Virgin Mary," and "I am the Mother of God and the Queen of Peace."

In summary, one can say that the astonishing increase in reports of apparitions by Mary within the Catholic Church in the last few decades has prompted a considerable amount of controversy. It should not be forgotten that the Church has *not* recognized the

majority of the visions reported. This is also true of a remarkable phenomenon that was played out in *Ezkioga*, a little Basque town on the southern edge of the Pyrenees in 1931 when two children claimed to have seen the Virgin Mary. In the same year about a million pilgrims went to Ezkioga, and hundreds of children and women then reported seeing similar apparitions. This happened at a time of conflict between Church and state in Spain, and the flare-up of the cult of Mary may be seen as a reaction of religious groups against the anticlerical measures taken by the government. At any rate the movement collapsed after the Church officially distanced itself from this cult.

Many passionate defenders of these apparitions have come forward, people

who continually go on pilgrimage from place to place where such phenomena are said to have occurred. But many skeptics and opponents have also been heard from, along with some neutral observers. They keep stressing that most of the witnesses to the apparitions have been children and adolescents, at an age when fantasy can often go unchecked. On the other hand, many thousands of pilgrims are undeniably convinced that they have been cured of their diseases at these sites, and the many hundreds of crutches and canes gratefully left behind by cured patients at places like Lourdes bear impressive witness to their conviction.

The Marian apparitions in the second half of the 19th century and in the 20th have been many and powerful. Despite the spiritual uncertainties, doubts, and radical changes in society, the Marian form of popular piety is unshaken. Among the most recent apparition sites is Medjugorje in Herzegovina. Mary appeared almost every day to three young people, Ivan, Jakov, and Marija, beginning on June 24, 1981.

*Below:* Young people during an apparition on July 25, 1987.

*Above left:* The miraculous chapel of the Sacred Hearts of Jesus and Mary and Atonement church in Wigratzbad.

*Above right:* The Madonna at Medjugorje.

*Center:* The church at Wigratzbad.

*Center left:* Fátima, forecourt of the pilgrimage church and the tree beneath which the apparitions occurred.

*Page 210:* Fátima in Portugal is considered one of the great pilgrimage sites in the world. As in Lourdes and La Salette the apparitions in Fátima are traced to visionary experiences of children. In 1917 two girls and a boy saw the Virgin on the 13th of the month from May to October. Fátima is famous for the "three mysteries," dark prophecies, the third of which has not yet been made known. Thousands of people were present at the visions of the children. In 1919 a chapel was built on the site. In 1930 the events at Fátima were declared credible.

## A Far-flung Name

People seldom realize how deep an impression the name Mary has made on every language touched by Christianity.

Mary—with all its combinations and variants—is no doubt the most widespread feminine *forename* in the Christian—and not just the Catholic—world. This was not always the case. In the Middle Ages out of reverence the name was seldom used. Not until the Reformation did it enter upon a veritable triumphal march. We have already seen that the meaning of the name has not been explained, except for the fact that it derives from the Hebrew Miriam.

Some familiar combination forms of the name are Annemarie and Marianne—the latter is often jocularly used as a symbol for the France of the Revolution of 1789. Then there are Marlene (Mary and Magdalene), Marlies (Mary and Elizabeth), and the common Swiss name Maryvonne (Mary and Yvonne).

In Germany short and variant forms of Mary include Marie, Mia, Mieze, Mizzi, Mimi, Marei, Mareile, Maja, Mieke, Mirl, Mari, Marieke, Ris, etc. France has Marion, Marian, and Manon; England and the USA have Mary or Marilyn, Mary Jane, Mary Jo, etc.; Ireland has Maire, Maura, or Maureen; Holland has Marijke, Maaike, Marieke, Maryse; Denmark Maren or Mie; Sweden Marika; Hungary Mari, Maris, Marika, Mariska, Marka. Italian variants include Mariella, Marietta, and Marita, Maris, Marisa, and Madrisa; some Spanish variants are Marita, Marica, and Marihuela. The name Mercedes comes from "Maria de las Mercedes," or Mother of Graces. There is a special abundance of nicknames in Russia: Mariya, Marya, Marika, Mara or Masha, and many others. In Slavic countries such names as Maya, Marula, Marushka, or Marienka are widespread. On the other hand the name Marina does not come from Mary but is a feminine form of the Latin *marinus* (sailor); it may also go back to Mars, the god of war.

The name Mary is also found in many *surnames*, as, for example, the 19th-century French Egyptologist Auguste

Mariette, the Italian sculptor and painter Marino Marini, the French philosopher Jacques Maritain, the Italian writer Marinetti, and many others.

Mary has also been used for centuries as a *masculine* forename—one of the relatively rare epicene names. One thinks of the composer Carl Maria von Weber, the poet Rainer (actually René) Maria Rilke, and the French philosopher Voltaire, whose original name was François Marie Arouet. The Latin masculine name Marius (with its more recent Italian form Mario) does not come from Mary but from the Roman family of the Marii.

We cannot even try to cite all the famous personalities who have borne the name Mary in one form or another. Some of the *rulers* named Mary include, in France, Mary of Burgundy, consort of the later emperor Maximilian I (15th century), Marie de Médici (d. 1612), regent for Louis XIII, Marie Antoinette, the unfortunate queen of Louis XVI, Marie Louise, the second wife of Napoleon I. In Austria, Maria Theresia (1717–1780). In England, Mary Tudor, known as "Bloody Mary" (1516–1558); Mary II, queen of William III; Mary, queen of King George V, and finally Mary Stuart, famous for her tragic end (16th century). In Spain, Maria Christina of Bourbon (19th century), Maria de Molina, Queen of Castille and León (13th–14th centuries), Queen Maria Luisa (often painted by Goya). In Hungary, Mary of Austria, queen in the 16th century. In Poland Maria Leszynska, queen of Louis XV; Maria Kazimierz, queen of Poland (17th–18th centuries). In Russia, Maria Fedorovna, wife of Tsar Paul I (early 19th century). In Italy, Maria Carolina, queen of Naples in the time of Napoleon.

We find the name Mary still more frequently in *place names*, especially in Austria: In Carinthia there is Maria Gall, Maria Rojach, Maria Elend, Maria Saal, Maria Wörth, Maria Feicht, Maria Rain, Maria Höfl, Maria Luggau, and Maria am See. The last three are places of pilgrimage. In Styria the famous pilgrimage site of Mariazell, then Maria Buch and Maria Lankowitz; in Lower Austria Maria Dreichen, Maria Enzers-

dorf, Maria am Jauerling, Maria Lanzensdorf, Maria Taferl, Maria Anzbach, and Maria Schutz, likewise a place of pilgrimage. Maria Plain near Salzburg is another, nearby is Mariapfarr. In Upper Austria we find Maria Neustift; two districts of Graz are named Maria Grün (from *greinern*, to lament) and Mariatrost; a section of Innsbruck is called Mariahilf; in the Burgenland we have Mariasdorf, in the Tyrol Mariastein and Marienberg.

*Germany* too is full of geographical names with Mary in them, and not just Catholic southern Germany: in Bavaria we have Maria Beinberg, Maria Birnbaum and Maria Limbach, all places of pilgrimage, then Mariaeck, Maria Thann, Maria Vesperbild, Maria Steinbach, Mariaburghausen, and Maria Gern near Berchtesgaden. North of Würzburg is fortress Marienburg. The city center of Munich is formed by the Marienplatz. In the Rhineland are the famous Benedictine church of Maria Laach on the Laacher See, with a beautiful Romanesque church, Maria Rosenberg, the monastery of Marienstatt and Bad Marienberg in the Westerwald. In Saxony Marienberg near Chemnitz and Marienthal near Dresden; in Lower Saxony Hildesheim-Marienburg, Maria Glück and Marienried; in North Rhineland-Westphalia Marialinden, Maria Veen, Marienfeld (now Harsewinkel), Marienmünster, Marienthal, Marienheid, Marienhausen and Marienborn, Marienweiler, Mariagrube, and Marienwald. A section of Cologne is likewise called Marienburg. In Schleswig-Holstein we run into the Marienleuchte (on Fehmarn); a section of Rostock in Mecklenburg is called Marienehe. Even a name like St. Märgen in the Black Forest conceals St. Mary.

But in other European countries as well many names recall Mary: in England, for example, we find Maryport (Cumberland) and Marylebone, part of London. In Oxford there has been a St. Mary College since 1379, and Eton College is dedicated to Mary. In France there are a great many smaller places bearing the name of Mary. To name but a few, Sainte Marie de Campan (Hautes

Mary is the patroness of the "German Order," which was founded in Palestine in 1190 as a group of Hospitalers, but shortly thereafter was turned into a religious order of knights. Under Grand Master Hermann of Salza it became the basis of the Teutonic Order of Knights in Prussia and the Baltic region. In 1309 the headquarters of the Grand Master was transferred to Nogat in West Prussia. Shown here is the great statue of Mary from the Marienburg.

Pyrenées), Sainte Marie du Lac (Marne), Sainte Marie du Mont (Manche), Sainte Marie-La-Blanche (Côte d'Or), and Saint Marie-sur-Mer (Loire-Atlantique). In Sweden we find Mariannelund, Mariefried, Marieholm, Mariehamn and Mariestad; in Poland Marienhöfchen, a section of Breslau (Wroclaw), Marienburg in former West Prussia, and Marienwerder (Kwidzyn) in former East Prussia. In the Czech Republic there is Maria Kulm (Chulm) and the well-known Marienbad (Marianske Lazne); in West Bohemia, Mariaschein near Teplitz (Teplice) in North Bohemia, and Marienberg (Marianske Hory) near Mährisch Ostrau (Ostrava); in Slovakia there is Mariatoelgyes; in the former Yugoslavia Maria Neustift (Pujska Gora), in Banat the former Maria Theresienpol (Subotica) and Marienfeld (Teremia Mare); in Lithuania Marijampole, in Hungary Maria Kalnok (Gahling) and Marienburg (Feldiora), in Italy Mariano Commense in Lombardy, Maria di Pietrasanta near Pisa, Maria di Ravenna and Mariano on Lake Albano.

This roster could be extended outside Europe as well. In the USA we find Marion (Ohio) and Marion (Indiana), Maryknoll (New York), Santa Maria (California), and no fewer than eight Marysvilles. The state of Maryland is named after Mary, the consort of Charles I of England. Close to the American border in Ontario lies Sault-Sainte-Marie. Santa Maria is the name of a rather large city in Brazil and a provincial capital in Colombia. There is a Maryborough in Queensland, Australia, and a Maria Luisa region in Argentina, as well as Marianhill in Natal, South Africa, and Marijinsk in western Siberia.

Santa Maria is the name of a volcano in Guatemala, and the Marienkanal links the Volga with the Baltic. One of the Azores is named Santa Maria, and finally we have the Marianas Islands in the Pacific, named after Mary of Austria, the consort of Philip IV of Spain (17th century). Magellan, who discovered them, originally called them the "Ladrones" (robbers).

Beyond the world of geography the name Mary plays an important role in other areas. In *botany*, for example there is Our Lady's thistle (*Silybum marianum*), a composite flower of the Mediterranean basin; Mary grass; a daisy known as Mary leaf; the Mary bell-flower (a Mediterranean ornamental plant, also called mariette); Mary's tears, the pericarp of a species of grass; Mary's balsam, a greenish resin once used for waterproofing ship's planks, and the Mary rose, a popular name for various kinds of flowers. In *zoology* there is the lady bug (*Marienkäfer* in German), of which there are several thousand species all over the world.

Mary glass is a term for sheets of transparent plaster, and there used to be coins called Mary's groschen and Mary's guilden. A jointed puppet moved by springs—that is, a marionette—takes its name from the French Marion and actually means "little Mary".

\* \* \*

This chapter was meant to show, if only in excerpts and allusions, the positively inexhaustible abundance of Marian images and traces in the cultures of all countries that have been reached by Christianity. We have seen how the phenomenon of Mary was defined and consolidated through dogmas, how it was continuously made part of people's consciousness through official and unofficial celebrations. We could follow the process by which Mary was understood as the Virgin, herself immaculately conceived; as the new Eve, who through her obedience compensated for the disobedience of the first Eve; as the Beloved; as the crowned Queen of Heaven; as the symbol and archetype of the Church; as the Sorrowful Mother; as the Helper, Protector, and Comforter. She has been depicted countless times in paintings and sculptures, has been and is venerated in relics, icons, chapels, churches, and places of pilgrimage. We have seen how since 1531 she has appeared to believers all over the world. We attempted to get an overview of how many churches were named after her and, finally, how her name is reflected in hundreds of forenames and surnames, place names, animal and plant names. Mary has deep roots in all Christian cultures. The old saying about Mary still holds: *De Maria numquam satis*—one can never say enough about Mary.

When we look at the transformation of art down through the ages, we realize that the relationship of humans to the sacred has been subject to constant transformation too. This can be shown to an extraordinary degree in the representation of Mary. In her role as mediator and advocate between believers and God she has established herself in the realm of both the divine and the human. In her image we see reflected the

private and ecclesial places she enters into dialogue with the individual. Votive tablets in the great pilgrimage sites express gratitude to the wonder-working images of Mary. The protective image of God's Mother adorns rooms and houses. The powerful statues of Mary one sees in European marketplaces are centers of urban and rural life. As the patroness of guilds, arts, and sciences, of cities, fraternities, and orders Mary

*Left: The Crowning of Mary by the Trinity* (ca. 1457, Art Museum of Basel) clearly shows Mary's preeminence in the center of Christian cosmology.

*Page 215: The Virgin and the Child Jesus,* 1941, by Vaclav Bostik (b. 1913) interprets Mary in the severe form of the Theotokos. The oversized proportions of Mary indicate her protective function. Her monumentality is a symbol of her strength.

# Mary in Art

Caroline H. Ebertshäuser

earthly—which means historically changing—ideas of human beings about their relations to the divine.

The stations of Mary's life and suffering and the numerous aspects of her being are emblematic of human life in a great wealth of symbolically rendered motifs. The Great Helper in birth and death protectively spreads her mantle against fear and distress as well.

Yet before we consider the individual themes and motifs of the representation of Mary in art, we have to shed some light on the most important aspect of the portrayals of Mary, namely, their sacral function and, consequently, believers' various attitudes toward the images. In this domain we can see the development of forms of prayer and devotion as an expression of changing images of the world and humanity at their most palpable.

The Madonna appears as a holy, honored cult image of the early Church. Later, as a towering figure on the great altars, she comes close to the center of worship services. Enthroned at the entrance way of the cathedrals, she receives the community as its advocate and symbol. As a devotional image in

becomes an identifying figure of human community and togetherness.

Her image in art lies at the intersection of the divine and human spheres. The question of artistic freedom within the framework of religious art has in all centuries given rise to confrontations between iconoclasts and their opponents, but so have the changing concepts of the effect of word and image on the human soul. In an effort to describe the connection between images and forms of devotion, we can take the example of cultic images and devotional images as possible ways in which humans turn to the realm of the divine—through pictures.

**Cultic Image and Devotional Image**

Cultic images do not primarily derive from individual human situations but from the attempt to make the "heavenly" spheres shine through in the work. We are accustomed to equating religiousness with inwardness, but so long as we do that, we misinterpret the cultic image, because religion has no inwardness in the human-psychological

*Above:* Italian panel painting from the beginning of the 8th century, *Madonna with Child and Angels* (Santa Maria in Trastevere, Rome). The church is one of the oldest in the Christian world and was accessible to the faithful as early as the first half of the 3rd century. Mary is enthroned as ruler with a Byzantine crown, holding Christ as the boy Logos in front of her, in a strict frontal pose. Far removed from human beings, she is the symbol of a higher order, to which men and women submit in cultic events.

*Page 217, above left:* Jan van Eyck (ca. 1390–1441): winged altar from 1437 (Gemäldegalerie, Dresden). Center section: *Mary with the Child, Enthroned in a Church;* left wing, *Archangel Michael with Donor;* right wing, *St. Catherine.* Van Eyck's altar, which incorporates new studies of perspective into its artistic composition, shows Mary on the "throne of Solomon." The latter—as the "sedes sapientiae"—a symbol of the wisdom that is in the figure of "Sophia" (or, as Hildegard of Bingen writes, "Mother Wisdom"), is linked with Mary.

sense. It points beyond the temporal, the momentary, our passing moods.

To clarify this point, we can refer to icon painting. Making icons was the domain of the monastery and was thought of as a devotional form, not as an expression of free artistry. The monk who used painting to depict what was holiest was purifying himself through this exercise, in order to open himself up to the divine power working in him.

Thus, according to legend, the first icons and images of Mary came into existence by supernatural means. They were, it was said, painted by the evangelist Luke, or by the Madonna herself, or at least they were completed by her. To alter this image, the *vera icona*, in the name of artistic freedom would be to deny its divine origin. For the icon as a copy of a divine archetypal image opens up for humans—in and through the veneration of the earthly image—direct access to the space of these images: to the sacred. Thus cultic images lift the person out of his or her earthly world into a higher order.

Hence the appropriate place for the cultic image could only be the sanctuary. The believer approaches the cultic image in ritual and religious practices. These lift the individual out of the everyday world, leading him or her beyond the limitations of time and space into a more objective order. Hence the cultic image belongs in a public, not a private, sphere. One goes on pilgrimage to a place where the cultic image is kept, in churches or sanctuaries built especially for it. The cultic image is not personal. The ritual in the community "generates" the presence of the divine, in which the believers are bound up at the moment. The cultic image, as the gateway to the sacred, is part of this event.

The periods and epochs—such as Byzantine art or, in the Western Church, the early phase of Romanesque—in which the pictures of saints and the Madonna are experienced as cultic images display a religious attitude that merges with the believers' self-forgetful piety and devotion. Thus the works of Byzantium and the early period in Western Christian art reveal the compelling loftiness and majestic sever-

ity of expression that mark an image as cultic.

"History seems to show," writes Romano Guardini, "that the cultic image is related in a peculiar fashion to early periods—think of the concept of the archaic…. Cultic images dominate in early Christian, Romanesque, and even in the first stages of Gothic art. But then the devotional image comes to the fore."

Within the framework of the cultic image the miracle-working image has a special place: Most of the Christian miraculous images are images of Mary, because her role as advocate and mediator is expressed most vividly in the miraculous image.

In that miraculous image aspects of the cultic and devotional image meet. The characteristic feature of the devotional image—direct personal reference and dialogue of the person with the divine—is bound up with the elevated and sacred qualities of the cultic image and the holy place associated with it. The idea of Mary as the great reconciling, helping, and protecting mediator between God and human beings thus receives its deepest expression in the miraculous image.

Hence the history of a place of pilgrimage is very closely tied in with the history of the miraculous image there and gives the Madonna her name—such as the Madonna of Montserrat or Maria of Altötting. The goal of the great pilgrimages is, along with the hope of a cure, the pilgrim's path itself. Imposed penances and the very dangers and difficulties of the journey are exercises in overcoming and purifying oneself that constitute the essence of the pilgrimage. And so the pilgrim's path counts as part of the ritual and belongs to the holy place with the miraculous images.

There are many different types of miraculous images, with most of the Byzantine ones tracing their roots back to the paintings by Luke. Among the early Byzantine images are, for example, "Mary of the Snow" in Rome and Our Lady of Czestochowa, the patroness of Poland. But medieval miraculous images, especially pietàs, enthroned Madonnas or Madonnas with a protecting cloak, may be cited as examples of the

Right: Geertgen tot Sint Jans (1460/65–1495), Mary in Glory (Museum Boymans van Beuningen, Rotterdam). The picture presents Mary as victorious over evil in a blaze of light, with a black devil at her feet. In the spirit of the Gothic mystique of light the artist symbolically

shows the identity of light and divinity. The angelic creatures, who are part of the world of light, are likewise provided with symbols. The angels on the edge of the circle and already in contact with earthly reality, the dark part, are playing musical instruments. Music was seen as mediating between the heavenly and earthly spheres.

Below left: Lucas Cranach the Elder (1472–1553) painted this picture in Wittenberg. In 1611 a copy arrived at Mariahilf, the pilgrimage church in Passau, where for many years it became the center of a great Marian pilgrimage.

*Right: Beautiful Madonna from Kruzlowa*, ca. 1410–20, painted wood (Naradowe Museum, Cracow). In keeping with the "soft style" of the time, the fullness and elegance of the folds of the garments are emphasized through the S-shaped flow of the posture, underlining the softness, sweetness, and elegance of the figure.

*Left:* The so-called *Roettgen Pietà* (Middle Rhenish wooden sculpture ca. 1300, Regional Museum, Bonn) is an early example of the expressive devotional image which, by over-emphasizing pain, is supposed to awaken the believer's *compassio*. Here for the first time the lamentation over Christ is separated from the taking down of his body from the cross and treated as an independent scene.

various types. With miraculous images the artistic value of the representation is not what matters. The popularity and dissemination of the image are determined by its charisma, the legend of how it originated, and the miracles ascribed to it.

Unlike the cultic image, the devotional image thrusts the personal experience of the believer, his or her human emotions and sympathy, into the foreground. Beginning with the early Gothic period the devotional image expresses a new self-understanding by believers in their striving after God. It is a sign of the individual's personal dialogue with God. And in this context of the devotional image Mary plays the most important role.

With the form of the Gothic devotional image the work of art moves out of cultic space, i.e., the church, into private living space. Above all in Italy, but also in other countries, we see small-format images of the Madonna developing that become the center of personal devotion in each person's house. Images of the Madonna on houses, depictions of the patroness of cities and guilds, have now become part of ordinary life. With their nearness and familiarity they move men and women to devotion and meditation.

In the cultic image people become aware, as they look upon the divine majesty, of their own creaturely limitations. "Cult prohibits any loss of self-control and directs the individual toward the creaturely-sacral attitude. By contrast, the devotional image is based on the relationship of similarity and transition. It builds bridges. In it the divine comes down, and the human ascends" (Guardini). The devotional image touches the individual in his or her spontaneous feelings. In the images, especially in the depictions of Mary, in moving gestures and dramatic mimicry we see expressed the believer's relatedness to divine grace in joy and pain.

The Middle Ages regarded external beauty as a reflection of the divine harmony of the world; as such it elevated and liberated the person. Even the sweet smile of the "beautiful Madonna," her lovely, splendid garments, the gen-

tleness of "le beau Dieu" (Christ as the mild and handsome God) are a part of this concept of beauty. But at the same time the dark and painful qualities of Christ's passion, which are emblematic of human suffering, are included in devotion. The expression of the sufferer, whether it be Mary with the dead Jesus in her arms or Christ as the Man of

Sorrows, is desperate and distorted in pain. The image as a mode of expression for the soul is designed to educate and inform the believer by having him or her share the experience of suffering. The inwardness of the person takes in the devotional image as a part of the self. But every purely emotional experience has an individual cast to it. And so in the Western devotional image a space is opened up for the first time to individual artistic freedom of expression.

Part of the essence of the work of art in the West is the notion of its autonomy and uniqueness as formed by the hand of the artist. We see art as emerging from free individual creativity. Thus in the devotional image there is a potential for personal freedom, which assigns a central role to art as the conveyor of religious themes.

The great influence of art on men and women as their oldest and most personal means of expression has continually given rise to confrontations, as in the case of iconoclasm. From the standpoint of strict Byzantine canonical form the creative freedom of the artist is arrogance and a sin, because it distances people from the archetype. For the Western artist, however, it is the royal road to the self and hence an expression of one's dialogue with God.

When are images of Mary mere works of art, whose splendor and refinement seduce the believer into "worldliness and sensual lust"? When does the veneration of icons turn into idolatry? Between these two extremes the question of iconoclasm is a central theme running through Christian art down the ages. The biblical ban on images could scarcely prevail in the world of late antiquity, rich in images as it was. Hence the legends of the supernatural origin of the first icons are a necessary legitimization of the early Marian images. The old issue of images keeps coming up again and again. It begins with the early Byzantine controversy over iconoclasm, which dragged on for several centuries and was not decided in favor of the pro-image party until 787.

In the 11th century Bernard of Clair-

vaux fought the excessively rich ornamentation of the Late Romanesque cathedrals with their "heathen grimaces," as he called them, and depictions of demons. Stressing Christian prayer and mystical devotion, Bernard went to the swamps of Cîteaux and founded his Cistercian order, whose strictness and frugality are expressed in its buildings.

As Bernard saw it, Mary pointed the way for his movement of renewal. Turning to Mary is the purest, deepest, and most heartfelt devotional path to God. Mary became the central figure of the mystical and religious movements of the Middle Ages; she became the most important pictorial motif of Gothic art.

Three hundred years later in Italy Savonarola fought the seductive charm of the beautiful Madonnas from the world of Renaissance painting and sculpture as an anti-Christian work of the devil. Under the influence of Savonarola, Botticelli himself burned many of his paintings. Only a few decades later the iconoclastic circles around Luther and Zwingli destroyed the overly rich late Gothic pictorial ornamentation of the churches in northern Europe. This especially affected portrayals of Mary, since in relig-

ious painting they offered the greatest opportunity for narrative freedom and embellishment.

Whatever reasons the iconoclasts may have given, the vehemence of the struggle shows how much power people attributed to images.

In the case of Byzantine or early medieval art the issue was to permit or forbid representation. But the medieval reformers or the Reformation iconoclasts no longer called representation itself into question; rather they attacked the decadence and secularization of the images. Luther answered the old Christian question of the relative value of word and image by a sweeping rejection of the image and an exclusive stress on the word.

The Counter-Reformation rang in the spirit of the Baroque. Once again the image was given a central role in the cultic event, and in the knowledge of its effect on the human soul it became the bearer of pictorial representations of the tenets of faith. Vast ceiling paintings in Baroque churches proclaimed the heavenly cosmos.

The Italian Madonna types developed in the Early and High Renaissance were picked up again especially in the 19th century by classicists such as Anselm Feuerbach. Art as an ideal place of refuge from the banality of everyday life became a substitute for religion.

*Left:* Lippo Memmi (in Siena from to 1317 to 1347), *Madonna Enthroned* (painted ca. 1340, Altenburg, State Museum of Lindenau). The soft, tender delineation of the clothing and edging is characteristic of early Sienese painting. Mary's throne is likewise draped with a cloth of honor.

*Right:* Rogier van der Weyden (1399–1464), *Mary and Child* (Prado, Madrid). Here too Mary with the Child Jesus is seen in an architectural niche, thereby blending a sculpted altar and an architectural image. In comparison with Italian Madonnas the characteristic northern delight in concrete, fine details is plain to see.

## The Artistic Image

Individual, free artistic creation entered the realm of sacred art by way of the devotional image. Until the beginning of the 20th century the Marian image of the previous two hundred years was oriented toward the Italian High Renaissance, especially Raphael. The Renaissance freed art from the tightlaced canon of the medieval guilds and their close ties to the Church. Art became autonomous—and so did the artist, who uses art as a means of exploring nature, perspective, and anatomy. Art as science, science as art, art and religion seem to face each other as equals.

place of religion.

Artistic groups such as the "Nazarenes" (or "Brotherhood of Luke") in the years of early German Romanticism around 1800 strove, through reflection on the ties between religion and art, to revive an art that had become fossilized in academic forms. Yet no effort was made to awaken feelings of devotion through the portrayal of the Madonna, as was done, for example, in Gothic art. Instead the feeling of devotion was now itself made the subject of the image. In that way devotion and the enjoyment of art entered into a reciprocal relationship. Feelings of devotion while viewing art works and aesthetic pleasure

But at the same time the Marian piety of popular miraculous images and Marian apparitions is blossoming. It was precisely in the late 19th and 20th centuries through Marian dogmas, new pilgrimage sites, and miracle-working images that Mary became a central Christian subject. Miraculous images and their mechanical duplication are the new religious artifacts, no longer oriented to art and tradition but purely and simply portrayals of the miraculous apparition. Currently the artistic expression of religious devotion and Christian themes is left to the personal sensibility of the artist.

Idea, truth, and nature are concepts of the idealistic artistic interpretation of the 18th and 19th centuries that caused a profound alteration in the depiction of the sacred. The "ideal" art of the Academies, indeed culture itself, was now seen as the great educator of humanity. As early as the 19th century advancing this notion of art was seen as the task of the state, the monarchy, or rich patrons, and a service to all men and women. Art seemed to take the

while viewing sacred images make clear the transformation that occurred in the attitude toward religious images. The split between reason and faith that marks modern times also has its effect on the art of the present. Few 20th-century artists are still creating great sacred art. And if they are, then they do so as a personal way of expressing their own experience and their own language, their own style, free from all iconographic and formal traditions.

*Left:* Andrea della Robbia (1435–1525), *Madonna and Child with Angels*, the so-called *Madonna degli Architetti*, 1475, glazed terra cotta (Bargello Museum, Florence).

*Center:* Raphael (1483–1520), *Mary with the Christ Child and the Boy John in the Garden* (1507, Louvre, Paris).

*Right:* Anselm Feuerbach (1829–1880), *Mary with the Child Jesus between Angels Playing Music*, 1860, oil on canvas (Gemäldegalerie, Dresden).

# LUKE PAINTS THE MADONNA

Luke the painter is very closely bound up with the history of the Marian image. The pictures that the Apostle and Evangelist Luke is supposed to have painted of Mary were thought to have been created in a supernatural manner, and they are the archetypes of subsequent portrayals of Mary

and thereby authenticated it, or that Luke began the picture and that it was miraculously completed "without human hands."

The icon of the *Hodegetria,* Luke's "original image," is supposed to have been kept in the Hodegon church in Constantinople. Copied many times, it

solemn procession through the contaminated streets of Rome.

During the Renaissance the mystical, supernatural creation of the Lucan image, a story familiar to early Byzantine art, underwent a pictorial secularization in keeping with the spirit of the age.

The extremely numerous images of

and later of many miraculous images. The legend that Luke painted the Madonna is important, and not just for Byzantine art. The theme was picked up again in the Late Gothic, and it reflects in a new way the relationship between artist, depiction, and the rendering of transcendence.

Around the holiness of Mary's image legends began to spring up that ascribe its origin to supernatural powers, in order to document its identity with the divine archetype. "We know as little about the appearance of Christ as about that of his mother," St. Augustine sighed, "but the need to have authentic images is great."

One legend reports that Luke painted Mary in her lifetime; yet another that she blessed his painting from heaven

is the archetype of numerous pictures of the Madonna and until modern times it remained the basic way to depict the Mother of God.

Among the first so-called "Lucan images" is the icon in Santa Maria Maggiore in Rome, where she was venerated as "Salus populi Romani" (the salvation of the Roman people). This miraculous image is also called "Mary of the Snow," because the church of Santa Maria Maggiore, one of the four great Roman basilicas, was built, according to legend, on the spot where snow once fell in the middle of summer. As with many Lucan Madonnas, the picture has had miraculous powers attributed to it. Thus in the year 590, according to the *Legenda Aurea,* it is said to have banished the plague when it was carried in

Luke painting the Madonna that have emerged since the Late Gothic clearly highlight, for all their use of sacred attributes, the artistic process. Alertly perceiving the reality before him, the Apostle Luke depicts the Mother of God who is sitting as his model. The keen attentiveness of the artist is far removed from the mystical vision and supernatural origins of the early Lucan images.

In some of the pictures that show Luke the painter one can compare the realism of the portrait on the canvas with the Madonna herself. In some late Mannerist images, such as that by Jan Gossaert in Vienna's Kunsthistorisches Museum, the Madonna is again swept up on a cloud away from the earthly world. Nonetheless, this is no scene of a transcendent vision, but a superficial

*Left:* The Baroque painter Jacob von Schuppen again takes up the theme of Luke in the church of St. Charles, Vienna, but this time he makes it into a Baroque apotheosis, in which Mary, swept up from the earthly studio, is enthroned in the clouds of heaven.

*Center: Luke Paints the Madonna* (the bull nearby is his attribute). From the Book of Hours of Mary of Burgundy, Flemish, ca. 1470 (Austrian National Library, Vienna).

*Right:* The Madonna known as "Salus Populi Romani," 6th century, from the church of Santa Maria Maggiore in Rome. According to legend, it was finished by Luke or else by supernatural intervention, and hence venerated as a miraculous image. As far back as the early Middle Ages Luke had become the patron saint of the painters' guild. His role changed with the evolution of art. With the Renaissance and the increasingly powerful self-consciousness of the artist the motif of "Luke paints the Madonna" was likewise transferred from the sphere of mythical etiology into the real space of the studio.

*Page 222, left:* Maarten van Heemskerck (1498–1574), *Luke Paints the Madonna* (Frans Hals Museum, Haarlem). The artist takes the realism of the scene so far that the Madonna even seems to be making eye contact with the viewer.

*Page 222, right:* Lancelot Blondeel (1498–1561) shifts the scene to his own studio. The painting is now in the Municipal Museum of Bruges.

artistic device for making more graphic Mary's closeness to the divine in the earthly world of the studio.

The essential feature of these 15th-century "Lucan pictures" is that the appearance of the divine image is expressly transferred to sensory reality. The absolutely supersensory nature of the truth of the divine image is conceived in a new relationship between God and the world. If the miraculously painted Lucan archetype was given to humanity as a finished product, in these Renaissance examples the chief emphasis is laid on the creative process itself as an expression of what is most human. That is because in art humans touch the sphere of the divine process of creation. Luke, the painter of the Madonna and hence the symbol of the divinely

blessed artist in whose work the earthly and the heavenly fuse, is also the patron saint of the painters' guild (St. Luke's guild), which well into the 19th century was thought to represent the connection between art and religion. Luke became the symbol of the artist and the creative person in general. If one looks at one modern definition of art, "making the invisible visible," then the legends about Luke are a reflection of the mysterious creative process, which is ultimately inaccessible to rational scrutiny.

# THE DEVELOPMENT OF THE MARIAN IMAGE

**M**ary is one of the central themes of Christian art. The variety of representations and symbols of this rich iconographic language, but also of the possibilities for free artistic creation with it, has developed in the depiction of Mary as it has with scarcely any other topic of Western art.

The artistic rendition of the legends of Mary as part of Christian salvation history does not only show the complexity of the world of Marian beliefs and their meaning for Christianity. Beyond that, we see developing here a space for free creative options in art that go beyond the canonical tenets of faith.

If one looks at the New Testament descriptions of Mary, one finds scarcely any information to go by. Only Luke discusses Mary in a few sentences. The other evangelists mention her only in connection with a few events in the story of salvation, but never describe her as a person. That is why Luke appears as the painter of Mary in the legends of later centuries.

In the veneration of Mary and in the evolution of her image from the dignified "Theotokos," the Mother of God, through the sweetly smiling Gothic

*Above:* Among the earliest images in Christian history is this Italian catacomb painting from the end of the 3rd century (cemetery of St. Peter and Marcellinus, Rome; lunette from a wall tomb in the crypt of the Madonna). The tradition of Roman wall painting is clearly evident.

"Beautiful Madonna," all the way to the bourgeois Baroque woman, we see reflected the changes in the religious outlook of each period. No other figure of Christian iconography ties together so many legends, literary compositions, and customs from popular piety as those that make up the enormous variety of Marian themes. She is the Mother of God, the Bride of Christ, the Queen of Heaven, the symbol of wisdom on Solomon's throne. In relation to Wisdom, whose successor she is in the wisdom of creation, she is the simple, humble maiden. She spreads her protective mantle over believers, she is mother and Mater Dolorosa in one. This variety of iconographical aspects allows everyone to approach her in his or her fashion.

The genesis of the Marian image and the topics of Mary's life have had an equally powerful impact on the fine arts, music, and literature. The history of these topics embraces not only liturgical and ecclesiastical tradition, but also and above all popular piety. That piety finds expression both in everyday life and in the great pilgrimages to the miraculous Marian images or in the customs of Marian festivals.

Mary's role as advocate of human beings before God makes her a bearer of hope, protection, and comfort for humankind. She moves into the center of the tradition of Christian prayer. In this aspect she continues the tradition of the ancient goddesses, whether of Ceres, Demeter, Ishtar, or Isis.

The spread of Christianity in the Hellenistic-Egyptian world made a crucial contribution to the veneration of Mary, because there the need for a feminine cult figure was especially great. The native tradition of Demeter (Mary dressed in an ear of wheat), Venus, Isis, and many other female deities was extremely powerful. Despite the problems created by the biblical, i.e., historical documentation of Mary's life, all the ancient texts clearly demonstrate what needs and ideas in the broad reach of folk belief had to be taken into consideration. The primitive Christian Church, initially Jewish in character, found itself compelled to integrate the cultic practices of the great pagan mother goddesses into the veneration of Mary and there, in a sense, to bring them under control. In that way elements of ancient piety were passed on to the Christian West through the cult of Mary.

*T*he origins of the image of Mary are located in the time of confrontation between early Christianity and the still vital ancient pagan culture with its rich world of gods and images, with which strict Jewish tradition sharply clashed. Christianity too had its own commandment "to make no graven image of God." And in the early Christian communities this ran afoul of the first efforts to lend familiar pictorial expression to the new faith and to bring the divine closer to believers through images. The question of the priority of word or image runs through all the centuries of Christian doctrinal disputes. This apparent incompatibility has caused the dispute over iconoclasm to flare up again and again in Western culture.

In the 4th century, when a Christian cultic tradition began officially to take shape, the Roman empire was divided under Emperor Honorius (395) into Eastern Rome and Western Rome. The artistic evolution of these two kingdoms was destined to run altogether different courses. Not long afterwards at the Council of Ephesus (431) the question of the portrayal of God and divine iconography was given a theological foundation. The following centuries only modified and completed these theological foundations.

The special meaning of Mary had been indirectly dealt with by the Council of Nicaea within the framework of the doctrine of Christ's two natures. The Council decided against the Arian and gnostic conception of Jesus and in favor of the doctrine that Christ was at once true God and true man. In order to make it clear that Christ was from the beginning "of one essence" with God, Mary was designated "the Mother of God." That obviously elevated Jesus' mother to a venerable central figure in salvation history. No longer was Mary just an instrument of God—his maidservant. She became a figure who, by saying yes to the events of redemption, had made possible the salvation of the human race. As mediator between God and humans she was not just the helper in God's plan of salvation, but the advocate of all sinners and oppressed people.

As the Mother of God Mary also came to be seen as a symbol of God's house, the Church. In the conciliar decisions of the 4th and 5th centuries the divine nature of Christ was authenticated by his being taken up into heaven. Surrounded by angels, Mary remained the embodied Ecclesia, "the Church left behind by Christ on earth." In this early Byzantine period the basic types of representations of Mary were established. The first images show Mary enthroned in a dignified, strictly frontal pose, holding the Child Jesus as the boy Logos in the center of her lap. Christ likewise

appears in the clothing of a ruler, in his left hand the book, symbol of the Logos; his right hand is raised in blessing.

Only a few years after the Council there were thirty churches dedicated to Mary, and countless icons were being venerated as miraculous images. When early Christians were blamed for pagan idolatry because they worshiped images, theologians countered by citing Christ's salvific nature as well as the supernatural origins of the images. The saving events of the Incarnation also became the main legitimization for the theologically more central pictorial

*Above:* The Theotokos, flanked by angels; mosaic from the first quarter of the 6th century in Sant' Apollinare, Nuovo, Ravenna. Through Ravenna and Venice, which were Byzantine colonies, early Italian art was influenced by the language of Byzantine forms.

theme of Christ. Needless to say, whether the divine could be adequately represented in images has always been a recurrent problem in the iconoclastic dispute.

In this confrontation the legend of the divine, supernatural origin of the pictures, as in the legend of Luke's painting, proved decisive. As we have seen, the story was that Luke painted her portrait while the Mother of God was still alive. The picture was handed to him directly from heaven, not painted by human hands. Or Mary herself had completed the painting once it was started, or at least she had personally blessed it.

These legends carried over what was ultimately material from the traditions of classical antiquity into the Christian thinking of the Eastern Church. The Platonic notion of the archetype ("idea") in the divine, spiritual spheres, of which the earthly image is only a reflection (or shadow), was Christianized by the legend of the supernaturally painted pictures; and that formed the spiritual foundation for the veneration of icons. Now an image of the saints or Mary became the viewer's gateway for approaching the true archetype and its divine essence.

These notions, which are rooted in Platonism, run through the tradition of Byzantine painting to this day. That tradition obliges the artist to remain strictly bound to the archetype, once it has been recognized as true, through all further thematic repetitions. Every arbitrary alteration in the sense of Western artistic freedom would amount to a deviation from the divine source. And so for the Byzantine believer the image as a path to the holy and transcendent has the same status as the word of the Bible.

By way of explanation we may recall the process of painting itself. Apart from whatever artistic skill he may have, the painter, usually a monk, is asked to purify himself before beginning his work by days of prayer and fasting. This is in order to prove himself worthy of the encounter with the sphere of the divine. If the painter adheres to canonized, preestablished types of images, then even in this creative process the essence of the archetype will make itself felt. Hence the painting of a Madonna has the character of a devotional exercise.

Byzantine painting was robbed of countless examples of its best work by the many outbreaks of iconoclasm. In 730 Emperor Leo III banned the cult of images as pagan. The argument that as God Christ could not be represented, since "God is spirit, and those who worship him must worship in spirit and truth" (John 4.23), became the credo of the image-hating iconoclasts. However, in 787 the Second Council of Nicaea ended the controversy; and in 843 the Empress Theodora managed to integrate the veneration of images into the Byzantine Church once and for all: "When the images of Christ and his mother, of the angels and saints, are venerated, then the homage is directed to the archetype represented, not to the subject of the portrayal. The person is what is meant, not the material in which the person is portrayed. Thus icons are owed veneration (*proskynesis*), but not adoration (*latreia*), which is due solely to God, who cannot be represented" (L. Heiser). Hence in the Eastern Church the image of Mary acquired independence early on, and over the course of many centuries it became a formative element in Western art as well.

Byzantine art is marked by severe canonical forms, and this applies to more than the depiction of Christ and Mary. The glorification of the dynastic principle, which was also expressed in a strict ceremonial code, the formalization of court life, and its splendid display, makes use of severe, lofty figures, removed from all things earthly, to show the emperor and his court as representatives of God. The emperor was placed even higher than the supreme heads of the Church; and so the image of the emperor and empress left their mark on the image of Christ and Mary. The established Church of Constantinople gave bishops state power and supplied them with insignia, titles, and privileges. Hence in Byzantine art Christ himself was given the attributes and honors of the imperial court. Purple pillows and the nimbus of a ruler were just as much a part of all this as the representation of the apostles as the retainers of a celestial court. The imperial palace became "a shadowy reflection of the heavenly palace".

*Left:* This mosaic from the Chora monastery (Kariye-Camii) in Constantinople (Istanbul) from the first quarter of the 14th century shows the *Annunciation to Mary*. The subject is rendered here in a garden with a well. Mary comes forward to meet the angel in the attitude of an adorant.

*Right: Mary with the Child Jesus*, a circular mosaic from the same monastery.

*Below: Mary with the Child Jesus between Constantine and Justinian*, a lunette mosaic from the 10th century in the south vestibule of Hagia Sophia, Constantinople (Istanbul). One of the most impressive depictions of the Theotokos is the Mary shown here between Constantine, the first Christian ruler of the city, and Justinian, who built Hagia Sophia.

Byzantine painting remained indebted to this preestablished pictorial scheme for centuries.

227

Mary praying (mosaic from the Ursiana basilica, Ravenna, 12th century). In the Mediterranean basin Mary is linked to the female divinities Demeter, Isis, and Aphrodite. Formally speaking, the gesture of praying with both hands raised is borrowed by Christianity from the tradition of classical antiquity. Mary is depicted all by herself, thus stressing her autonomy.

*Page 229:* The Vladimir Madonna. Presumably painted in early 12th-century Byzantium, the icon came in 1161 to the cathedral of Vladimir in Kiev—hence the name Vladimirskaya. In the 14th century it was taken to Moscow, where it is now on display in the Tretyakov Gallery. This famous icon of the Mother of God corresponds to the type of the Maria Eleousa (also called the *Glykophilousa,* or "Sweetly Kissing"), which strongly emphasizes the tender mother-child relationship. This Madonna has often been copied and has become the archetype of numerous miraculous images.

Byzantine Christian art consciously turned away from the realistic spatial representation of late ancient art, from the here and now. The subject of the images is not the reflection of reality, but the legends of salvation and the rendering visible of the spiritual world. Thin, elongated bodies, accented only in their outlines, show not corporeal reality but emotion, which becomes visible only in gesture. The language of gestures and religious symbols is bound up with the gold ground, which reflects the spiritual world. Within this framework stands the Madonna Theotokos, presented like a Byzantine empress, an imperial ruler, powerful, but removed from things earthly.

Early Christian art, shaped by Byzantine-East Roman culture, can be seen above all in the depiction of Mary, whose main types were established between 400 and 700. These include the *Hodegetria* (the pathfinder), *Maria orans* (Mary praying), *Maria lactans* (Mary nursing), and the *Eleousa* (tender or merciful Madonna), to name just a few. The individual types of the Madonna merged with iconographic traditions of the cultures amid which early Christianity emerged. The goddess Isis, enthroned with the boy Horus before her, cannot be separated from the Theotokos. Thus the veneration of Mary fell on the fertile soil of a tradition of mother goddesses. Similarly, ancient representations of

*orantes,* people at prayer, have been taken over in the typology of *Maria orans.* One particularly impressive instance of this and one of the few examples of early book illuminations still preserved is the Rabbula Gospel from Syria (ca. 580). Here Mary is shown beneath the mandorla of the risen Christ.

At the same time as Mary's influence on the Church increased, the scanty traditional material about Mary in the New Testament was expanded and enlivened through the Protevangelium of James with its epic descriptions of the life of the Virgin, her parents, and many miraculous details about her engagement and much else. All this then became part of Christian folklore. In order to integrate the Marian element into popular piety, in the first centuries after Christ's birth Marian festivals, such as February 2, now known as Candlemas, were made into annual celebrations.

Many Marian prayers and icons, which assign the Madonna an important place in the liturgy, come from this same period of the 5th century. By now it was ancient tradition to call her Queen of Heaven, and as the all-embracing Mother of God, with the crescent moon, garment of stars, and sun crown, she was at the same time part of the cosmos and hence of nature. Here we can sense once more the tradition of the mother goddesses of the Middle

East and classical antiquity. Mary as the Mother of God became a sacred vessel, purified from all sin. Spotless in her conception and free from original sin, she is dramatically glorified in Western art as the Immaculate One, especially in the Baroque.

The influence of the powerful Byzantine empire stretched across Greece, the Balkans, Russia, and Italy all the way into the North. And so up until the beginning of the 13th century it left its mark throughout this region on the representation of Mary in art. Ravenna and Venice were Byzantine centers, whose iconography radiated out over many centuries. Many artists exiled by the iconoclasts left Byzantium for Italy, bringing their art, "la maniera greca," with them. The magnificence and universality of 12th- and 13th-century art shows that two great cultural tendencies, the Byzantine and the early Gothic from the North, fused into a powerful new unity. The extremely rich Italian image of the Madonna developed from the merging of the Byzantine mode of depiction—mystical, ecstatic, courtly—with the beginnings of the naturalistic grasp of reality in the Early Renaissance.

The image of Mary in the West has, therefore, been shaped largely by Byzantium. The power and splendor of the Byzantine empire held a great attraction for the imperial courts of the West and their ideas of an established church. Via the Byzantine centers of southern Italy, Ravenna, and Venice a lively exchange sprang up.

While in Byzantium the Second Council of Nicaea ended the second controversy over iconoclasm in favor of the "iconodules" (supporters of images) in 787, the courtly school of Charlemagne was developing. The argument over iconoclasm had less significance in the West, since Westerners had no direct encounter with the ancient world. Charlemagne saw in antiquity a model that he tried to emulate in his own

guage, also found in the decoration of Irish high crosses and portals, covers the image with a tissue of strictly regulated embellishment into which the figures are woven. In the Book of Kells, created around 800, the throne of the Madonna appears surrounded by angels.

Books illuminated in the Carolingian and Ottonian periods do not make the subject of Mary a central focus; instead, Christ as the ruler of the world is the main image of Christian iconography. Ottonian art adopts this type, especially in ivory miniatures and book illuminations, in which the scene of the Epiphany predominates. In the Pericope Book of Henry II or in the Hildesheim Psalter of Bernward Mary appears, flanked by angels, as the Queen of

left arm, the golden Madonna of Essen (980). Mary sits enthroned in dignity, staring off into space, as the Hodegetria; she knows about her approaching pain. Likewise in the later Imad Madonna (Paderborn, 1160) a growing sense of space clearly makes itself felt. This becomes evident from the gesture with which Mary hands Christ an apple, which symbolizes both the imperial orb and the new Eve.

The representations in the richly ornamented Romanesque cathedrals, such as that of Autun in France, are marked by the severity of Christ as the judge of the world, sitting enthroned in lofty power over the entrance portals of the church. Christ as the judge of the world, with his *majestas Domini* (majesty of the Lord), the great theme of the

architecture. The Carolingian court school, for example the Ada school, is indebted to the Byzantine formal canon, but we can recognize in it traces of the ancient depiction of space.

At the same time there grew up in Ireland a unique insular tradition of illuminated manuscripts, which reached a high point in the Book of Kells. Heraldic, ornamental formal lan-

Heaven. But, although Mary plays a role in Christian salvation history, she is portrayed as only a marginal figure. The early Gospels and pericope books, designed for use in the liturgy, mostly illustrate the life of Christ, his miracles, the passion and resurrection.

The first autonomous Madonna that has come down to us is the sculpture of a Hodegetria with the boy Logos on her

Romanesque period, undergoes a reinterpretation for the first time in Chartres. There Christ, now gentler and more human, becomes the compassionate Redeemer. This new mode of portraying Christ points to changes in piety that will put Mary in the center not just of devotional prayer but of the visual arts.

Page 230, left: The Coronation of Mary, a votive image in the Gospel book of Bernward of Hildesheim (bishop from 993–1022) ca. 1015. The Gospel book of the great medieval canon and master builder is dedicated to the Hildesheim Cathedral, a Marian church. The manuscript, with its extraordinarily rich ornamentation, introduces each chapter with a full-page illustration.

Page 230, center: The Mother of God Enthroned, from the Book of Kells, Ireland, ca. 800 (Trinity College, Dublin). The characteristically rich Irish ornamentation includes the heraldic figures, the folds of whose garments are drawn into the embellishment and conceived of as flat surfaces. The motif of the knot and the entangled lines symbolizes the path of life in Irish painting and in many other cultural contexts as well.

Page 230, right: Nicholas of Verdun (an important goldsmith, active in the second half of the 12th century): The Birth of Christ, panel from the Verdun altar, 1181, line and sunk enamel on gilded copper (Cathedral Chapter church, Klosterneuburg, Austria). The Verdun altar is one of the most important and precious artistic achievements of Romanesque art.

Each of the series of the fifteen images shows the salvation history of the Old (ante legem and sub lege) and New (sub gratia) Testament.

Left: The Golden Madonna of Essen, carved around 980, is the oldest preserved free-standing sculpture by a medieval goldsmith.

Right: Adoration of the Magi from the Golden Gospel of Henry III; Ottonian book illumination from Echternach, ca. 1050. The background with its rigid forms is a typical stylistic device of the Echternach school.

231

# GOTHIC

With the beginning of the 13th century profound changes were taking place in the spiritual tradition of Europe. These changes were accompanied by political uprisings, shifts in the center of power, and the breakdown of social traditions. The culture of chivalry blossomed and freed itself from the imperial courts (of the Ottos or the Hohenstaufen). In Italy as in the North the culture of the free city emerged, which gave the citizens new autonomy through guilds and newly acquired rights. People were unsettled by the after-effects of the Crusades and new concepts of the world.

In this period of upheaval Europe was struck by the black plague, which in some countries swept away roughly two-thirds of the population. Medieval people experienced this shattering event of the constant presence of death as a punishing response by heaven to their own sinfulness. Robbed of their old traditions and ideas, the uncertain people of the Gothic period looked for their answer in a deeply felt longing for salvation and an inward mystical quest for God with which they sought to participate in the cosmic event of salvation. This period saw the flowering of the devotional image, in which Mary represented the center of the Church's life.

If we compare the majestic enthroned Madonnas in the cultic images of Byzantine and later Romanesque art with the soulful devotional images of the Gothic, we can clearly see the yearning of believers to enter upon a heartfelt dialogue with Mary. They entrust the forgiveness of their sins to her mediation; through her comfort they experience relief from the harsh, painful realities of life. Thus the most important new creation of Gothic art is the *Pietà*, which shows the Mother of God with a painful facial expression as the Mother of Sorrows. For the first time the Gothic sees the realistic depiction of psychic and affective sharing of a religious experience as an important concern and shifts it into the center of the statement. Pain and deep emotion, joy and redemption, humility and sympathy mark the various types of Madonna, each in its own way.

A profoundly educational effect on the mind was now attributed to the religious image—and especially to the soulful devotional image. By suffering along with Mary believers were supposed to be moved, purified, and led to repentance. The cult images and representations of Bible history that had been valid up until now corresponded to the demands of the liturgy, but they could not meet the needs of extraliturgical, private devotion. So individual themes and figures were removed from the biblical narratives and coordinated with special feasts of the church year, such as Christmas, Easter, and the Marian festivals. A whole variety of new themes in the iconography of Mary came into existence.

The veneration of Mary in the Gothic period, then, was not satisfied with what we know about the mother of Christ from the Gospels and Apocrypha. Beyond that they drew their subjects from folk legends and Marian poetry, which had blossomed in this period. Mary's sweetness is described by medieval poets in a flood of Marian lyrics. Popular customs also joined in the Marian movement. Numerous Marian feast days were added to the calendar. With the rise of Marian mysticism and new forms of devotion, mystery plays were now composed, and new traditions of hymnology and prayer, such as the *Salve Regina*, emerged. In all prayers Mary was now characterized as Queen, as Virgin of the Universe and of the Kingdom of Heaven.

The coronation of Mary became a leading theme of the fine arts. Other important subjects were taken from the life of Mary with its many "stations": the sacrifice of Joachim, the answering of Anne's prayer, the meeting at the Golden Gate, the birth of Mary, the Presentation in the Temple, Mary's engagement and marriage, the Annunciation, the Visitation, the death and Assumption into heaven.

In this context Marian iconography was expanded by representations such as those of the *Madonna of the Protecting Mantle*, the *Death of Mary, Mary's Assumption into Heaven*, the *Coronation of*

for depicting salvation history and hence as a new point of reference to the earthly world. The individual panels are surrounded by portal-like arches, which refer to Mary's role as a symbol of the Church.

*Page 233, left: The Seven Heavenly and the Seven Earthly Joys of Mary* from the Book of Hours of Mary of Burgundy (second half of the 15th century), National Library, Vienna. Books of Hours (Livres d'Heures) are prayerbooks for lay people that list the prayers for each time of the day in a fixed order. In the Gothic period they were richly ornamented devotional works; their elaborate iconography especially centered on Mary.

*Page 233, right: Mary with the Christ Child* by Hans Memling (1435–1494) from the diptych of Martin van Nieuvenhove, 1487 (Memling Museum, Bruges). In the Middle Ages there were book illuminations and murals, but no independent panel paintings, which did not begin to develop until the 13th century. Only with the discovery of oil painting by the Van Eyck brothers in the early 14th century did it assume its central position in art.

233

Page 234: In the Cathedral of Chur in Switzerland is the important Late Gothic sculpted *Marian altar* of Jacob Ruß from the years 1486 to 1492. The three-paneled altar is capped by a powerful crest (*Gesprenge*), which once again shows the coronation of Mary. The art of sculpture enjoyed a particular blossoming in the Gothic period.

*Center:* Late Gothic Madonna from Weissenau, Ravensburg region (after 1485). As the Queen of Heaven, she stands upon the moon. The niche is lined with roses, the symbol of Mary.

*Right: The Coronation of Mary* from the Late Gothic winged altarpiece of the Maria Gail near Villach. The aestheticization of life through art, as expressed by the Beautiful Style around 1400, is exaggerated here in the form of billowing clothes and lush branches.

Above: *Coronation of the Virgin Mary.* This enameled plate, made around 1340 in Limoges, has a diameter of 23 centimeters (Louvre, Paris).

*Mary*, the *Madonna of the Rosary, The Seven Dolors and the Seven Joys of Mary*, as well as the *Pietà* and *Mater Dolorosa*.

## Cathedral Art

Still Mary had her most comprehensive impact on the art of the cathedrals. "The material church means the spiritual church" ("Ecclesia materialis significat ecclesiam spiritualem"), it says in the old Gothic stonemasons' books. In this way the visible became the symbol and reflection of the invisible. Every color had a higher significance. Light too, which shone through the high windows, symbolized the divine light as a cultic force. Every number hidden in the geometry of architecture was an image of higher harmonic proportions, which again were an expression of the harmony of the world. Since beauty is an expression of divine harmony, the divine cosmos can be made visible to the human eye by means of earthly beauty. Hence the idea comes to the fore that through symbols spiritual things can be realistically expressed in

earthly things. That way earthly reality, nature in its realistic representation, is given a place in religious painting that was unthinkable before. The Gothic artist applies himself devotedly to the tiniest detail of a flower, a dress, or the fold of a garment, because even the smallest thing is an image of the harmony in God's creation.

The cathedral is an all-embracing "total art work" that presents the Gothic idea of the sacred and secular and at the same time of familiarity with many-layered domains of symbolism. The deep knowledge that becomes visible in the Gothic cathedrals is one of the secrets of the stonemasons' lodges, the centers of medieval "science." The building of the cathedrals was also experienced as a way of serving God.

Gothic Scholasticism attempted, by contemplating the world, to verify the holy laws of God's plan of creation. In this context the cathedral was an image and an interpretation of the cosmos. In her role as mediator Mary embraced both the spiritual realm of the universe—the "cathedralis spiritualis"—as well as the earthly realm of the "cathe-

dralis materialis." She was the "Ecclesia." Hence most of the cathedrals are dedicated to Mary, referred to as Notre Dame de... or Our Lady of....

At this point reference must be made to the depictions of Mary as the Church in the fine arts. Many Gothic images (one thinks of the panel paintings of Jan van Eyck) show a larger than life-size Mary in a church interior, because "in the mystical perspective of the Middle Ages Mary beneath the cross became the archetype of Mother Church, the Ecclesia, because in the theology of the Mystical Body of the Church all Christians form part of the Body of Christ. At the same time they are considered spiritual children of the Mother of God, who in universal motherhood, praying and pleading beneath the bloody wounds of her Son, speaks up for her spiritual children" (J. Ströter-Bender).

The great arch over the entrance of most of the Marian portals shows the coronation of Mary as Queen of Heaven to reflect the equation of Mary and the Ecclesia. Christ is seen crowning a youthful Mary. Often enough the crown, symbol of royal dignity, is held

or brought by angels, which distinguishes her as the *Regina angelorum*, Queen of the angels. Beneath this scene are depicted the death of Mary and her bodily assumption into heaven. Around her deathbed stand the apostles, her beloved sons and brothers, while Christ receives her soul. The portal is divided by a central pillar, at which a free-standing Mary is installed as a separate figure. In the doorcasing of the portals are scenes from the life of Mary, particularly the Annunciation and Visitation. Amid this abundance of images the meaning and importance of the great Madonna figures on the portals of the great cathedrals are often pushed into the background. The finest examples are in Chartres, Amiens, Rheims, and Paris.

Mary enthroned with the Christ Child has had a secure place as a cultic image in the West. The free-standing Mother of God, at first bound up in the architecture but later breaking free from it, makes its triumphal entry with Gothic art and the great cathedrals. This created a new reality that was expressed in the rising tide of devotion to Mary. The thought that emerged from the art of the cathedrals and embraced all realms of art reflected in a new way the relation of the visible world to the world of the spirit and linked both in a wide-ranging symbolism. And so in sacred art the rendering of nature could also be interpreted as a part of religion.

Both northern Europe and Italy turned to the portrayal of reality. Still, for all the fine detail and naturalness of this portrayal, we still cannot speak of realism in the modern sense. Rather, the beauty of the things represented was viewed as the reflection of the divine and, by touching the soul of humans, as a path to it.

The gold ground as a divine background before which nature is depicted, as in the case of Stefan Lochner, for example, links the earthly and the heavenly in a characteristically Gothic unity. The meditations on beauty by someone like Bernard of Clairvaux or Hugh of St. Victor include light as a creative artistic power. The Gothic church windows, the radiance of the objects as well as the gold ground in paintings are aspects of a mysticism of light. In this connection Mary too, and her image in the beauty of medieval art, constitute a portion of the path of the faithful *through* her beauty. The aesthetic remains bound up with the religious experience of the individual. The medieval altarpiece and the art of the Late Gothic combine in their symbolic language the rendering of nature and religious themes.

The lily symbolizes Mary's purity; the rose is an image of her suffering. The moon and stars identify her as the Queen of Heaven. The apple, a symbol of the imperial globe and the rule of the world, also points to her victory over the Fall, which came through Eve's apple. There are various ways of alluding to Mary's purity, such as the "hortus conclusus" or the "Jesse tree," a pictorial form in which Mary likewise became a central figure, beginning in the 13th century.

The "hortus conclusus" (fenced-in garden), in which Mary is seen with the Christ Child, is full of flowers and plants and children at play. It symbolizes the Paradise to which Mary has returned as the new Eve. The walls enclosing the garden symbolize Mary's intact virginity.

In the painting by Rogier van der Weyden we see, as if lying there by chance, two apples on the clean and polished windowsill of the bourgeois house. They are symbols of the old and the new Eve. A candle is placed on the table as if it were an ordinary utensil, but it is conceived by the artist as a symbol of eternal light. The lily of the Annunciation, brought by the archangel Gabriel, is a symbol of Mary's purity. In many Dutch Gothic paintings it is casually placed in a vase alongside Mary and thus seemingly becomes a part of everyday life.

Mary's holiness, even when she is presented as a bourgeois wife without a halo, is shown in an allusive, cryptic fashion by the fact that, unlike all the other figures and objects, she casts no shadow. Her body is "not of this world." It is pure, without sin, and hence without a shadow.

*Above: Madonna in a Blade of Wheat Dress*, ca. 1450, painted by the Sterzing Master for the church in Sterzing. The interpretations of this theme go back, on the one hand, to the ancient myth of Demeter, where the blade of wheat appears as a symbol of fertility, and, on the other hand, to the Hebrew word Bethlehem, which means "house of bread." Konrad of Würzburg calls this image the "noble sheaf of virtue".

*Page 236:* Tilman Riemenschneider (ca. 1460–1531), shrine from the Marian altar in the church of the Lord God in Creglingen, Bavaria, ca. 1505–10.

*Page 239, left: Madonna,* a Gothic statue of painted stone, ca. 1450. The late form of a Beautiful Madonna in the original version (private collection).

*Right:* Jan van Eyck (1390–1441), *Madonna in a Church,* ca. 1426 (State Museums, Berlin). The theme of Mary as the Ecclesia is given especially realistic and beautiful treatment here. With a slight S-shaped posture Mary stands as the Beautiful Madonna in the nave of a Gothic church. Yet her stature is raised to supernatural levels, because her crown reaches up to the clerestory—a symbol of the equal status of Mary and the Church.

*Left:* The theme of the Madonna in a rose bower is also found in this terra cotta by Luca della Robbia (1400–1482), Bargello Museum, Florence. It may be cited here, with a view to the Early Renaissance, as an example of a contemporary Italian Madonna.

Gothic art turned in loving veneration to the beauty of this world as an expression of its divinity. Hence the radiance of silk is not just the reflection of materiality, but at the same time an expression of the splendor of divine light, and beyond that a symbol of a sovereign's dignity. The pearls that are woven into Mary's garments and that shine in between the rubies and the emeralds point beyond themselves. The Gothic idea of beauty reached its zenith in the later phase around 1400, in the "International" or "soft" style. The connections between the flourishing princely courts in places such as Paris, Prague, and Vienna led to such close artistic contacts and exchanges that in the "International style" the existing national differences were overcome for the first time.

The Madonna, also called the Beautiful Madonna, is distinguished by the soft and elegant fall of her draperies. Her body moves in a gentle S-curve. On her face is a youthful smile. The Beautiful Madonna is a sort of counter-image to the pain-twisted Pietàs and the broken bodies of Christ as the Man of Sorrows. Even the themes of the Passion take on a new beauty, a "relaxation, a blissful surrender to the sweetness of suffering, and hence a new ideal of beauty. At the same time we see here a more personal and intimate attitude, in which one has familiar conversations with the divine" (Dagobert Frey).

Here reference has to be made to the tradition of the Church Fathers, who strongly influenced both the Gothic and the Baroque. "In the woman of the Book of Revelation, threatened by the dragon and shining like the sun, the Church Fathers almost unanimously saw the heavenly archetype of the peo-

*Right: The Annunciation to Mary*, center panel of a triptych, ca. 1435, of Rogier van der Weyden (1399/1400–1464), Louvre, Paris. The artist renders space with what was at the time the modern instrument of perspective, and combines this with the Dutch love of detail. At the same time the apparently ordinary utensils conceal symbols of the Christian longing for salvation. The two apples on the mantelpiece refer to the old and the new Eve. The flower in the vase is the lily of the Annunciation, the medallion over the bed already points to the crucifixion.

*Left:* Jan Mostaert (ca. 1472–1555), *The Holy Family at Table*, ca. 1495–1500 (Cologne, Wallraf-Richartz Museum). The world of Gothic bourgeois life, as found in the free cities of the empire, is self-consciously introduced into representations of the Holy Family.

*Right: Mary on the Crescent Moon,* by the Master of the Life of Mary, a painter active in Cologne between 1463 and 1480. Here Mary is once again removed from everyday existence. The attributes of the crescent moon, sunburst, and halo symbolize her status as the Queen of Heaven, as do the colors: gold as the expression of the sacred world, red as the color of love and passion.

ple of God on earth. That is, this was the Church, persecuted by Satan and saved and preserved by God; from her—through baptism—new children were continuously being born. Not until the 12th century did writers begin to see in this heavenly apparition not the Ecclesia, but its representative, Mary, who gave birth to Christ, the ruler of the world" (H. and M. Schmidt).

In the Apocalypse of John a Queen of Heaven appears, clothed with the sun, with the moon beneath her feet and a crown of twelve stars on her head. For the interpreters of the Song of Solomon this was not only Wisdom, the "Sophia Maria" who sits on a throne of lions, but at the same time the Queen of Heaven, "outshining the sun and the stars." The moon too has to be seen in Early Gothic art as an attribute of Mary, although in Baroque depictions of the

Immaculate Conception it takes on a special emphasis. The moon was a symbol of ancient female deities, and thus Mary too, as "the star-studded Mother, the Princess of the Ages, the Ruler of the universe," stands beneath its sign.

In the Late Gothic the motif of the Madonna with the gloriole is given especially expressive treatment by Tilman Riemenschneider in his Volkach *Madonna of the Rosary.* Mary in a gloriole on the crescent moon is surrounded by angelic musicians. Two of them hold the crown over her head; thus she appears as "the woman of Revelation," clothed with the sun.

The Late Gothic has been described as a time of the "discovery of reality." But there is a difference from country to country in what the individual artists picked up from the nature around them. In Italy the exploration and real-

*There was no idyll of a happy life for Mary. Perhaps that is why she is so much the protecting
or at least the consoling mother of all those who have to suffer from violence.*

Dorothee Sölle

istic representation of *space* was expressed by the perspectivist construction of standpoint and vanishing point. Annunciation scenes in colonnades stretching into the distance were a preferred theme of Florentine art. The North adopted spatial perspective only with hesitation. On the other hand, it was extremely faithful in its rendering of *material objects*. Paintings by van Eyck, Bouts, Schongauer, and Memling revel in the radiance of pearls and diamonds, in the heavy fall of velvet and the moist glow of the dew on the flowers. The finest little folds and uneven surfaces are accurately depicted. One thinks of the unforgettable wrinkled hands of the *Three Kings* at prayer in the painting of the Nativity by Hugo van der Goes in the Uffizi.

In both cases—the Italian exploration of the world through the mathe-matical constructs of perspective or the loving use of detail in the North—behind the foreground of nature lies the glorification of God's world. With the Renaissance the representation of nature remained by and large the chief subject matter of art, but nature was now the object of the personal studies of the artist, who sought to approach the laws of nature with the interest of the scientist.

*Above:* Joachim Patinir (ca. 1475/80–1524), *Rest on the Flight into Egypt* (Prado, Madrid). Patinir is considered the first great representative of Dutch landscape painting, which over the centuries would shape painting in Holland. The theme of resting on the flight into Egypt was a favored opportunity to combine landscape painting with religious themes.

# RENAISSANCE

*Page 243:* Giotto (1267–1337), *Maestà* (Majesty), also known as the *Ognissanti Madonna.* In the early work of Giotto we can still sense the connection to his teacher, who was inspired by Byzantium. Yet here for the first time a feeling for space begins to emerge. Even the spatially ordered haloes of the angels cover up the ones standing behind them. The body of the enthroned Madonna is more forcefully modeled and stands out in her garb. This is a step toward the representation and exploration of real space that will characterize the Renaissance.

Cimabue (active between 1272 and 1302), *Maestà* (Madonna enthroned with the Christ Child), 1272–74 (Uffizi, Florence). Cimabue, Giotto's teacher, was still thoroughly indebted to Byzantine tradition. Here he shows the Madonna surrounded by angels, strictly arranged on a flat surface before the gold ground.

*I*n the history of ideas, modern times must be viewed as beginning in Early Renaissance Italy. The medieval orders of guilds and cities, which had provided the foundation for the cultural flowering of Gothic and had given the artist a secure role as a craftsman, were transformed with the emerging Renaissance. The preoccupation with antiquity assigned human beings a new role, and in the spirit of humanism they reflected on their own spiritual autonomy. In this way artists were set free from the world of the guilds, which they now felt to be constricting, to enter on an autonomous existence. Artists no longer saw themselves as craftsmen, but as explorers of the regular patterns of art and nature. In Christian art too artists offered new interpretations of religious themes, which were interspersed with ideas of art and beauty from classical antiquity.

The ideal image of the Renaissance is the free, self-conscious person, which finds its outstanding expression in the life form of the *uomo universale.* At the flourishing courts of Italian princely families, such as the Medici in Florence or the Sforza in Milan, this ideal of the "courtier," i.e., the *uomo universale,* was lived out. The Church was no longer the only source of commissions, as in the Middle Ages; now the independent connoisseur and Maecenas also came forward. Artistic self-understanding and innovation are very closely connected.

The first step away from the centuries-old dependence of Italian art on Byzantium was taken by Giotto in the 13th and 14th centuries. His teacher, Cimabue, who was still bound to the flat surfaces of Byzantine art, painted an enthroned Hodegetria, whose throne is fringed by a carefully arranged group of angels. Still faithful to Byzantine canonical forms, Cimabue's Madonna (*Maestà*) is trapped within ornamental lines on the surface. Giotto's Madonna also borrows the form of the enthroned, severe-looking Mother of God. But in her posture, the folds of her garment, and the volume of her body the beginnings of a three-dimensional concept of space are taking shape. And this trans-

forms the Madonna into something earthly, human, and autonomous. Above and beyond that, the this-worldliness and humanity of the figures are now shown through a personal, expressive language of gestures of a sort unknown in Byzantine art. In Giotto's *Lament over Christ*, at the Arena Chapel in Padua, Mary dramatically bends over the dead body of Christ. Even the angels observing the event are writhing in pain. Never before were human beings represented in such intense, spontaneous grief.

The early Sienese Madonnas, those of Simone Martini, for example, are placed in front of a dazzling gold ground and remain close to the Byzantine pattern. But here too the human expression is indicated though an animated language of gestures and lively shaping of the garments.

"Discovering reality" is the theme of the Renaissance as well, but it carries on the imitation of nature begun in the Gothic period in a new spirit. The exploration of space by means of perspective means taking a step toward the reality of human space. Through perspective the viewer is drawn for the first time into the structure of the picture. The "standpoint" of the observer determines the vanishing point of perspective.

Studies of perspective are an important element in Renaissance writings on the theory of art. In *Della pittura* Leon Battista Alberti does not only describe the laws of beauty, proportion, lighting, coloring, and perspective; he also categorizes the expressive forms of religious images. In Alberti's book the *prediche vulghare* of the wandering preacher Fra Roberto Caracciolo find a welcome. Here the various levels of meaning and the atmosphere of familiar events from the life of Mary are demonstrated: "Thus, for example, the five degrees of praiseworthy behavior of the Virgin at the Annunciation are enumerated and the proofs of their transposition into pictorial art are adduced—unrest, reflection, questioning, submission, and being marked by the honor of the Conception. Accordingly, gestures and facial expressions are matched in each of

Page 245, top: Michelangelo Buonarroti (1475–1574), *The Holy Family* (the Doni tondo), 1504 (Uffizi, Florence). Here Michelangelo takes up the *tondo* form of the Italian devotional picture. But several levels are bound together in the picture. In the foreground there is the scene in which Mary turns back to the child Jesus with an unusual twisting motion, in the background there are figures in the classical style that form the framework of the event.

the types of behavior" (Pochert).

The cheerful Madonna, lovingly turned to the child, experiences a Golden Age in Italian art. In particular the private devotional image or house altar picture develops special forms in Italy. This includes the tondo, small folding altars, and terra-cotta reliefs, which introduce the architectural elements so important in Italian painting. There are beautiful examples of this from the studios of the della Robbias.

The Italian Madonnas of this period—such as those by Masaccio, Fra Angelico, and, a few years later, Gozzoli and Lippi—glow with lovely youthfulness; and, despite the rich ornamentation, the forms show a moderation and restraint, compared with the "beautiful style" of the northern Pietàs. Still, with all the delight in gold borders, inlaid walls, and the touching gestures of mother and child, of Maria Eleousa, the preferred pictorial motif of this period, they retain a certain majesty.

An especially typical mode of portraying Mary in Italy is the *sacra conversazione*. The "sacred conversation" between Mary and the saints no longer simply depicts the Mother of God en-

*Left:* Simone Martini (ca. 1280/85–1344), *The Annunciation to Mary and Saints Ansanus and Julietta*, altarpiece on wood, 1330 (Uffizi, Florence). Martini painted the picture together with Lippo Memmi. The relation between Mary and the angel is matched by the interrelated lines of their clothes. The gold ground is still very much in the early Sienese tradition of surface representation.

*Right:* Il Parmeggianino (1503–1540), *Madonna with the Long Neck*, 1535 (Florence, Uffizi). The artist stresses the flowing outlines and body forms with Mannerist exaggeration, thereby distancing himself from the Renaissance ideal of harmonic proportions.

*Above:* Fra Filippo Lippi (ca. 1406–1469), *Mary with the Child and Two Angels* (Uffizi, Florence). The tender Madonna in front of a landscape breathes the freshness and clarity characteristic of the Early Renaissance.

*Right:* Domenico Veneziano (ca. 1400/10–1461), *Mary with the Child and Francis of Assisi, John the Baptist, Zanobius and Lucy*, ca. 1442–48 (Florence, Uffizi). The perspectival space, the central theme of the Renaissance, is stressed here through arches and niches.

throned with the child Jesus; now it adds a group of saints, representatives of the earthly world, who respectfully approach Mary. The Madonna as the embodiment of the celestial is no longer a distant queen of heaven. Majestically enthroned, she is drawn into the human world. In this way the ancient ideal of the noble, serene, calmly self-contained individual lives on in the elevated, dignified Madonna.

Just as Byzantine art first established the most important Madonna types for the Western world, the Gothic broadened the portrayal of Mary by adding a variety of themes. Thereafter new themes arose, but the older ones were also reinterpreted. Certain periods preferred specific types; still, most of the other types were preserved alongside them until the 19th century. The divine was experienced less in the glorification of the supernatural than in the harmonious regularity that encompasses humanity and the universe. The study of the objective laws of nature in connection with the Christian doctrine of salvation created a new human ideal. In the depiction of the Madonna the self-conscious, creative person of the Renaissance took over from the heartfelt, emotionally colored devotional form of mysticism in which the sufferings of Christ and the Madonna were the central theme. The Renaissance Madonna overcomes pain with severe dignity. She becomes a self-aware, tranquil figure. In his *Passion of the Lord* (ca. 1500) Geiler of Kaysersberg states that beneath the cross Mary did not fall into a swoon, but stood by full of strength. Gabriel Biel (ca. 1418–1495), who taught at the University of Tübingen, declares in one of his Sunday sermons: "While the disciples fled, Mary stood by upright. She stood unshakably and always paid heed to the dignity of her gestures."

Nature, i.e., the landscape, is symbolically portrayed in Early Gothic images through individual trees, animals, and mountains as the backdrop for scenes from the Bible. In the Late Gothic artists were already studying nature and depicting it realistically ("true to life"). Nevertheless, here too it was thought of only as a background and symbolic sup-

port for the visible as a messenger of the invisible. One especially favorite way of painting Mary was to show a vista through a window out onto a broad landscape. The Italian Renaissance was the first to make nature, in various ways, an object of study, a human habitat that could be visited and explored. Petrarch meditates on the beauty of nature as a series of givens perceived through the senses and reflecting his own facticity. If the gold ground was the spiritual level of the Middle Ages before which all events play themselves out, now the free glance of modernity breaks

through this level and, so to speak, opens up the world. It was the artists who did the first nature studies of botany and anatomy, but who also linked the beauty of nature to the beauty of art. Nature was no longer a symbol; it became landscape, but it was harmoniously connected to the human and the divine.

In the tradition of the cosmic deities Mary is related to nature above all in the portrayal of the *hortus conclusus* or of the rose bower. The Renaissance too related Mary to nature in a special way. Venetian painters in particular, such as Bellini and Titian, preferred to use broad Arcadian landscapes without any accessories to portray the Virgin and Child. The *Madonna of the Rocks* by Leonardo da Vinci brings Mary together in a unique way with the mysterious dark aspect of nature.

The scientific method used to fathom nature should not blind the modern observer to the fact that nature was understood as part of the divine and that its beauty, its light and darkness, were metaphysical categories. The divine is to be found in harmonic measure, which has the human being for its center. Raphael did paintings of Mary, such as the "Sistine" Madonna, that har-

critics to raise again the much-disputed question of images. Someone like Gottschalk Hollen (d. after 1484) argued against the iconoclasts of his day. He paid special attention to pictures of the Virgin Mary because she had rendered extraordinary service to the salvation of the human race. Mary, he said, as a human being without original sin, was the best expression of divine grace. In his *On the Images of Christ and the*

moniously unite all the goals of the Renaissance. The mild serenity of expression of the tranquil, self-possessed, dignified, majestic Madonna is bound up with the harmonic proportions of architecture or, in other pictures, with a landscape flooded by gentle light. The Raphael Madonnas became the ideal model for the following centuries up until the late 1800s.

Art and the technical possibilities made available by the knowledge of perspective and the laws of portrayal, along with the new color possibilities, gave the artist all sorts of opportunities for self-expression. To be sure, the wealth of paintings in both public buildings and private houses led many

*Saints* Hollen argues that not only are Marian images designed "to lead human beings to imitate [her]," but that by honoring Mary in them one also honors her Son, Jesus Christ. He also points once again to the divine origin of many paintings of Mary, because most of them were done by Luke. He specifically mentions the picture of Mary in Santa Maria Maggiore. Pope Sixtus IV confirmed the authenticity of Luke's work. How great the influence of this icon was can be seen by—among other things—the fact that the papal general Alexander Sforza, lord of Pesaro, had it copied around 1470 by Melozzo da Forlì and supplied with the following caption: "St. Luke painted this icon

*Left:* Leonardo da Vinci (1452–1519), *Madonna on the Rocks* (Paris, Louvre). This original version, painted between 1483–86, has been in the possession of the Kings of France since 1625. Mary embraces a small St. John who seems to bless Jesus seen next to an angel who is looking at the spectator. All this takes place in the warm twilight of a rocky cavern. A later, very similar version of this famous painting is in the National Gallery, London. (See also Mary's enlarged face on the book cover.)

*Right: Madonna della Vittoria* by Andrea Mantegna (1431–1506), 1496 (Paris, Louvre). In the Italian style of the "sacra conversazione" Mantegna has placed the "enthroned Madonna" in a niche made up of woven garlands. Nature here is subordinated to architecture and pictorial composition. The pedestal of the throne displays a relief with the motif of "Adam and Eve under the Tree of Sin." In this way the picture picks up again the rich traditional theme of Mary as the new Eve.

from life. The tablet is the authentic portrait. Alexander Sforza commissioned it. Melozzo painted it. Luke would say that it was his own work" (quoted from Schreiber).

Simonidis formulates the pictorial program of the High Renaissance and its artistic portrayal in the statement that "painting is silent poetry, poetry is painting that speaks." As Western art developed there were constant new struggles over the relative weighting of word and image. The Reformers

where it has no purpose; however, one sees few people striving to imitate her life in chastity, humility, and rejoicing over heaven's blessings."

The dispute over images lasted for centuries, and not just in Byzantium or the Renaissance. Within the Church criticism of the plethora of images was a subject raised even at ecumenical councils.

In the Middle Ages confidence in the power of Marian images to educate and work miracles was boundless. The

Italian Renaissance as directly as Albrecht Dürer. Dürer wrote a comprehensive treatise on the theory of art and did many studies of nature that are considered among the first autonomous portrayals of landscape in the North. The relationship of the artist to nature, to representation, and to landscape finds a characteristic expression north of the Alps, especially in the Danube school. The Madonna too, as we see her in paintings by Altsdorfer, is shown amid the proliferating, living greenery

  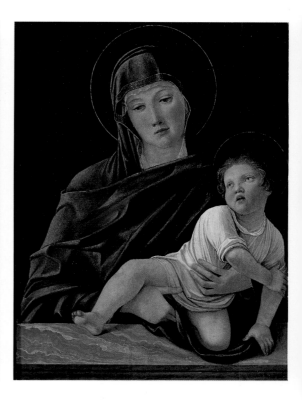

wanted to reshape worship services, to purify them from the late medieval clutter and the unrestrained use of images. In this context we recall Savonarola the preacher, who so moved Botticelli that the artist personally burned his own later paintings. Savonarola did not call for iconoclasm as such, but at the "bonfire of the vanities" in 1497 all offensive images that might distract believers from religion went up in smoke. In the spirit of the Reformation critical voices everywhere criticized not just the trade in indulgences but also the secularization of the portrayal of the saints. In his *Praise of Folly* Erasmus of Rotterdam wrote: "How many people one sees lighting candles to the Mother of God—and that in broad daylight,

richly ornamented images of the great monasteries violated the spirit of their own rules. The monks of Cluny, in particular, had embellished their churches with elaborate, often exotic, animal imagery. Bernard of Clairvaux was one of the earliest and harshest critics of this excess, which he saw as contradicting the ideal of monastic poverty, and he campaigned to reduce it. The Franciscans likewise limited the pictorial motifs in their churches to a few central ones. In the choir one could show only the Crucified, Mary, and John the Baptist. In the North the Gothic remained alive for a long time. Even when Renaissance forms were taken over, this was only in the realm of the decorative. Few artists confronted the thought of the

of trees. The Northern Reformation had a crucial influence on art; and Reformation spirituality influenced not only Dürer, but also the younger Holbein and Lucas Cranach. But this does not mean that artists had turned away from Christian themes, especially Mary. One of the greatest miraculous images, the Regensburg Madonna, was painted by Cranach, and Dürer's Madonnas are among the most important works of German art.

Around this time woodcuts and copper engravings flourished too. Both became important media for the dissemination of images. On the one hand this served Reformation propaganda; on the other it was the foundation for a great tradition of graphic art. This is the do-

*Above left:* The graphic art of the Renaissance, allied with the invention of printing, made possible the copying of engraved series, which greatly advanced the dissemination of thematic innovations. Albrecht Dürer did many series about the life of Mary with woodcuts or copperplate etchings. Both engravings shown here (*left*, the *Visitation*, *right*, the *Birth of Christ*) come from the 1511 series.

*Below left:* Likewise by Dürer is the pen-and-ink water color drawing of *Mary with the Many Beasts* (Albertina Graphic Collection, Vienna). Here Dürer transforms the "hortus conclusus," where Mary is seen surrounded by countless plants and animals, into an open rural landscape, so that symbolism and the rendering of reality fuse together.

*Right: Stuppach Madonna*, ca. 1518, by Matthias Grünewald (ca. 1470/75–1528), parish church of the Assumption in Stuppach near Würzburg. Grünewald once again picks up the motif of Mary in the rose bower.

*Page 248, left:* Hans Holbein the Elder, *Madonna* in the church of Bad Oberdorf in the Oberallgäu, 1493.

*Page 248, center:* Albrecht Altdorfer's (1480–1538) *Beautiful Mary of Regensburg* is a rendering of a 13th-century Byzantine icon (Diocesan Museum, Regensburg).

*Page 248, right:* Giovanni Bellini (ca. 1430–1516), *Mary with the Child* (the so-called Lochis Madonna), ca. 1470–80 (Bergamo, Gallery of the Carrara Academy).

*Left:* El Greco (1541–1604), *The Holy Family*, ca. 1594–1604 (Prado, Madrid). This unusual depiction of the Holy Family shows Elizabeth with the boy John alongside Mary.

*Right:* Lucas Cranach the Elder (1472–1553), *Rest on the Flight into Egypt*, 1504 (Gemälde-galerie, Berlin). The landscape, in which Mary is surrounded by angels and putti, is marked by large, rough trees, the rugged vegetation of the North.

main of the two great Passion cycles of Dürer, which treat the life of Mary thematically.

The Lutheran Reformation concentrated on the word of the Bible and hence led to a partial rejection of church images. But Luther fought against the outrages of the early 16th-century iconoclasts. As he saw it, the actual abuse lay not in the veneration of images, whose danger he dismissed, but simply in the notion that endowing images constituted good works. In his writing *Against the Heavenly Prophets* (1424–25) Luther opposed the banning of all images from inside churches, as

the iconoclasts demanded. Luther's criticism of Marian images (in his 1521 exposition of the Magnificat) takes aim at the fact that the painters portray the exalted Mother of God and not the poor despised person to whom God gives divine grace. Hence the Protestant image of Mary has to show that God turns to the lowly and unworthy human being. The images are not supposed to frighten, for example, as did the old depictions of Christ come to judge the world, but console. Hence, in Luther's view, pictures are not designed to visualize the transcendent but to make visible God's concrete action in

history. Since for Luther fantasy and pictorial imagination are part of human nature, the image has meaning as a metaphor for language. Beyond that, it can show allegorically things that are non-visual, such as death, hell, and even God. On the question of images Luther's fellow Reformers Zwingli and Calvin took a more radical stand. The controversy over images that Luther was engaged in concerned more than the destruction of religious works of art. When art was banned from the purely sacred space of the Protestant church, it carved out for itself its own autonomous space, which proved to be the

presupposition for a new artistic genre of landscape and genre painting.

The High Renaissance turned art into science and science into art. Liberal humanistic tendencies seemed to challenge the Church as much as the polemical writings and actions of the Reformers. The discovery of printing helped to spread among the people not only countless images of the Madonna and miraculous icons, but also many Reformation leaflets. The sobriety of Protestant faith placed the word of the Bible at the center of church activity. That reduced the portrayal of Mary to the few original scenes described in the New Testament. Among Protestants Mary is the model of the person who receives grace from God. She surrenders herself completely to the grace announced by Gabriel. As the handmaid of God she serves, and in the Passion she shares, the destiny of those who follow Christ. She stands on the side of humanity. But the veneration that the Catholic Church gives her is denied by Protestantism. The final phase of the Reformation—and of the Renaissance in Italy—is Mannerism, which by exaggerating the regular patterns of the Renaissance leads to an extreme sort of formal language. Now pushed over the limit, spaces, points of view, posture, and gestures seem to lose their expressive power and to become petrified into formalism.

251

*T*he Catholic Church formulated its answer to the Reformation at the Council of Trent (1545–1563). It had to take a clear position vis-à-vis Protestantism. Doctrinal decrees were issued—for example, concerning the sacraments, justification, the priesthood, and original sin—along with reform measures, on clerical celibacy, for instance. This fun-

The *Patrona Bavariae* (Patroness of Bavaria), 1594, by Hubert Gerhard (1550–1620) on the Marienplatz in Munich. Before the figure was placed on its pillar in 1638, it stood on the high altar of the Lady church. The Mary column is a typically Baroque form of Marian veneration.

damental theological and ecclesial reorganization stamped the whole further development of the Catholic Church.

The many statements made by the Church about images in the wake of Trent were concerned above all with Mariology. They aimed to restore the original meaning of religious representations. It was not a question of regulating artistic creation. Instead, the idea was to reevaluate, philosophically and religiously, the controversy over word and image that the Reformation had moved to the center. In the course of the 17th century the Jesuits took the lead in disseminating dogmatic and apologetical writings. The order had subordinated itself unconditionally to the pope through a special vow of obedience and had taken on the mission of advancing spiritual renewal by means of the *Exercises* and work in schools and universities. In the Counter-Reformation the pope's position grew stronger and combined once again with the absolutist courts of Europe to form an important power structure in the Christian West. The papacy and the courts became major clients of artists.

As a courtly stylistic epoch the Baroque represents the Counter-Reformation and absolutist feeling for life; it also continues the achievements of the Renaissance in its own way. As with the Renaissance, the currents of the Baroque came from Italy and spread not just through Catholic countries but in Holland as well, developing into the first "world style." Granted, the absolutist state structures of Europe at the time left their mark on their national autonomy and their own peculiar national styles—as in France under Louis XIV or Spain under Philip II. But they were all united in the potent shared language of the Counter-Reformation, the Baroque.

The spiritual confrontations of the Reformation escalated into the great religious war of the Baroque, the Thirty Years War (1618–1648), which left Germany and parts of neighboring countries in rubble and ashes. Thus art in this region could not participate in the great blossoming of Italy, France, and Spain. Only after many decades did

Germany and Austria reintegrate themselves into the international pattern, in the monumental church buildings of Fischer von Erlach in Austria, for example, or those of the Bavarian family of master builders, the Dientzenhofer.

In the world of the Baroque image ideas of humanism and its stress on classical antiquity blend with a didacticism in the use of emblems and a new emphasis on the pictorial. In this period Mariology experienced a new flowering. Some of the old apocryphal writings and the medieval Marian legends, which had found expression in the images of Mary, had their influence on iconography lessened by the dogmatic and apologetic texts of the Counter-Reformation.

We can see this, for instance, in Peter Canisius' (d. 1597) *De Maria Virgine incomparabili* or in Martin von Cochem's treatment of Mary in *The Great Life of Christ* of 1696, works shaped by the new dogmatic theology. Another pioneer of a new theocentric Mariology who helped revitalize popular piety and Marian pilgrimages was Francisco Suárez with his *Mysteria vitae Christi.* Catholic reform and Counter-Reformation as a powerful response to Luther's theses also served as the basis for the revival of images and trust in the pictorial representation of the saints and their martyrdoms.

The essential feature of Baroque religious art can be explained with terms from Baroque rhetoric. *Persuasio*—"enthusiastic power of conviction"—is supposed to lead to orthodox faith; while *compassio* is to lead the individual to sympathy. The didactic function of the Counter-Reformation images and the program behind them can be linked with the predominant contemplative technique of the day. This was presented by Ignatius Loyola in his *Spiritual Exercises* and spread by the Jesuits. The believer was to direct all of his or her energy to the chosen object of meditation. The event is to play itself out pictorially before the believer's inner eye. Starting with the sense of sight the meditation proceeds to what is heard and felt. Through absorption in mental prayer there finally occurs the union of

*Right:* Pietro da Cortona, *The Assumption of Mary* (church of Santa Maria in Valicella, Rome). The architecture of the Baroque, i.e., the Counter-Reformation, dramatically manifests itself in the great ceiling paintings. These present the Christian message of salvation in a *trompe l'oeil* artistic space as a visible truth. The individual figures, such as Mary, anxiously awaited by all of heaven, appear as part of *theatrum sacrum*.

*Left:* The *Immaculata of Aranjuez* by Bartolomé Esteban Murillo (1618–1682), ca. 1656–60 (Prado, Madrid). Mary floating up to heaven as the Immaculate Conception is one of the favorite themes of Baroque representation of Mary. With this Immaculate Conception, Murillo, a painter of Madonnas, mystical secrets, and visionary events, created the autonomous Baroque type of the girlishly innocent Madonna, linked to the atmosphere of the clouds surrounding her.

Peter Paul Rubens (1577–1640), *Mary Appears to Saint Ildefonso*, middle panel of the Ildefonso altar of 1630–32 (Vienna, Kunsthistorisches Museum). Saint Ildefonso, bishop of Toledo and champion of the doctrine of the Immaculate Conception, helped to shape Spanish piety with his visions of Mary. Rubens shows the saint kneeling before Mary during one of his visions. The group is irradiated by light and little angels. The powerful bodies are an external sign of inner greatness and emotion.

the observer with the object of contemplation. According to the Council of Trent, images could be useful for such meditative practice.

Thus the Baroque church interior becomes a "sacred theater" of salvation history, a splendid artistic synthesis. This "total art work" consists of the great altars, whose frames pass over into dramatically agitated figures that connect with the architecture, which in turn is drawn into the ceiling painting as a part of the whole. In keeping with the principle of *ordo*, the grand order of the Middle Ages, the century of the Baroque creates once again a unified cosmos of the heavenly and earthly world. In the ceiling painting the illusion of a perspective of endless space opens up a horizon to the believer in which vision, visualization, and rejoicing over the salvation event are integrated into the unity of faith.

Mary is the central theme of Baroque art. Its mighty altarpieces, the ceiling paintings and statuary, document the new Marian piety. Around this time popular religiosity and the great pilgrimages to miraculous images that were part of it gained in importance. Among the great themes of Marian representation were the Queen of Heaven, the Queen of Victory, and the Immaculate Conception. As reinterpreted in the Baroque, they became the most iconographically significant Marian types.

The Immaculate Conception had pride of place. Here the Baroque created its own peculiar Marian iconography. Its first convincing representation was the one that the Spaniard Bartolomé Esteban Murillo created for the Cathedral of Seville in 1650. The Immaculate Conception remained a preferred theme of Spanish religious painting. The picture shows the hovering figure of Mary without the Christ Child on the crescent moon as a cosmic Virgin, framed by angels. Attributes from the Litany of Loreto, such as the rose without thorns, the lily, the branch of olive and palm, indicate the Immaculate Conception. The special Baroque dynamic and dramatic attitude make Mary appear now as a radiant, potent Queen of Heaven.

According to church doctrine of the 14th and 15th centuries, Mary was born free of original sin. (In 1661 Pope Leo VII declared that the Immaculate Conception was a firm Catholic belief, and in 1854 Pius IX elevated it to a dogma.) But in the figure of the Immaculata, a central theme of the powerful Baroque altars, notions of Mary's purity as an expression of the mystical apparition of Sophia, God's wisdom, were also influential.

Modern Protestant mystics such as Jakob Böhme (1575–1637) shed new light on certain aspects of Western "sophology." "At a time when the representations of the Immaculate Conception were making their way into Catholic churches, Böhme wrote about the incarnation of holy Wisdom in the Virgin Mary: 'Before heaven and earth were created, she was a virgin, and wholly pure as well, without any stain; and this same pure, chaste Virgin entered matter in her incarnation and was her new human person in the holy element of God. Therefore she is the Blessed among all women and the Lord was with her, as the angel says'" (Ströter-Bender).

After the introduction of the feast of the Immaculate Conception for the whole Church in the year 1708 the portrayal of Mary as the victorious Queen of Heaven became one of the favorite themes of Baroque painting. The figure of Mary with the Christ Child as "victorious" (Victoria) presents her, with Baroque dramatic emphasis, standing on the globe, overpowering with her staff the Evil One in the shape of a dragon crouching at her feet. In sculpture the type of Mary Queen of Victory may be found in numerous "Mary pillars" in the centers of European cities and villages. They were erected as votive columns in thanks for Mary's protection in plague and war. The pillar as a symbol of dignity and power, comparable to the scepter, and an often-used motif in Baroque portraits, once again emphasizes Mary's royal dignity. Two great victories, in the sea battle of Lepanto against the Turks in 1571 and of the Catholic League over the Protestants in the battle of the White Mountain near Prague (1620),

Adam Elsheimer (1578–1610), *The Holy Family with the Boy John* (State Museums, Berlin). In this painting on copper Elsheimer combines the northern feeling for landscape with the mythology of classical antiquity in unique depth of feeling. Highly appreciated by his learned friends and the painters of the St. Luke Academy in Rome, Elsheimer displays a monumental composition that expresses itself even in this small-format painting. Mary and the boy John the Baptist are depicted near an angel, who looks sympathetically at both of them—in a landscape that wraps round the group like a grotto. Heaven is open only at a few points; from it light and many angels descend to Mary.

*Left:* Simon Vouet (1590–1649), *The Holy Family with Elizabeth and the Boy John* (Louvre, Paris). Vouet prepared the way for French classicism by taking over the Baroque ideal of the body and joining it to French discipline and delicacy.

*Right:* Rembrandt Harmensz van Rijn (1606–1669), *The Holy Family*, 1645, The Hermitage, St. Petersburg. Influenced by the chiaroscuro painting of Caravaggio and Elsheimer, Rembrandt transposes the religious event into the peace and quiet of everyday bourgeois existence. Mary as a simple wife looks down on the child in the cradle. The lighting and the unaffected rendering communicate a sense of silent devotion in an ordinary world.

*Below right:* Charles Lebrun (1619–1690), *Holy Family*, oil on canvas (Gemäldegalerie, Dresden). Lebrun was a student of Vouet and the director of the Gobelin factory in Paris. He mastered the strict classical formal language of the French Haute Époque.

Orazio Gentileschi (1563–after 1640), *Rest on the Flight*, 1628, oil on canvas (Louvre, Paris). The picture connects the naturalistic chiaroscuro painting of a Caravaggio to the Tuscan charm of Gentileschi. Without decorative accessories the scene shows the weariness of a hard journey. Joseph sleeps exhausted on the travel bags. No angel seems to be protecting the refugees. A threatening storm approaches on the horizon.

were attributed to Mary's help. With this began a new era for the Marian image, i.e., for the veneration of Mary. Bound up in the Baroque notion of history and God's grace, from now on the image of Mary would be linked to historical events. This gave a special vitality to the piety centered around the great miraculous images.

Murillo painted the Madonna at the handing over of the chasuble to St. Ildefonso (Prado, Madrid). Rubens picked up this theme in the St. Ildefonso altar (Kunsthistorisches Museum, Vienna). The portrayals of the great Donor Madonnas, which belong to the tradition of the *sacra conversazione*, are integrated into the *theatrum sacrum* of church painting.

The dynamic Baroque treatment of space with saints and other figures shows in their gestures the most expressive moment of excitement, in order to convey the strength of deep emotion, of ecstasy. Even the donors on the Madonna pictures no longer kneel motionless at her feet: they relate to Mary and the child with their pose and gestures, while she generally responds to this by her own posture.

With his renewal of altar painting Rubens begins a new chapter in the history of altar construction and monumental decoration of church buildings. The Gothic winged altar had stood isolated in the church interior; and even after the introduction of a single large altar panel, especially in Italy, it seldom had monumental proportions. Rubens raises the altarpiece to a size that dominated space; and, through the decorative architectonic elements surrounding it, he fixes it in a spiritual and formal unity embracing the entire space of the church.

In order to make the illusion of the presence of sacred reality on Baroque altars still more moving and convincing, sculptured figures, as if on a stage, are scenically arranged in three-dimensional space. Through purposeful lighting in the space around the altar the "earthly-spatial present" of the holy scene is given still more emphasis. One thinks of the great altarpieces of Bernini and Cortona in Rome. Moved by their true-to-life qualities and at the same time ecstatically removed, the believing observer is drawn into the elevating effect of the *theatrum sacrum*.

257

# THE 18TH CENTURY

*T*he language of Baroque art, despite all the national differences, united the European countries in the dramatic-emphatic gesture of the *grand siècle*. From the Early Renaissance, beginning in Florence, Italian art was the leading force. For the Baroque Rome was the center of artistic life in Europe, with its splendid buildings and works of art executed on commission from powerful popes with an appreciation for art and from the great Roman Academy of St. Luke.

With the gradual crumbling of ecclesiastical and absolutist power, i.e., with the 18th century, the dominant influence of France on European art and culture began. France had refined taste that knew how to combine elegance, power, and rationalistic enlightenment.

Franz Anton Maulpertsch (1724–1796), *The Holy Kin*, ca. 1750 (Austrian Baroque Museum, Belvedere, Vienna). In the Rococo the massive, dramatic Baroque forms dissolve into a light, courtly pose. The powerful darker colors metamorphose into glowing pastels.

This French preeminence, and not just in painting, would be decisive until well into the 20th century.

As the creative impulses of religion ebbed in the 18th century, classical mythology, which in the Baroque was still fused with the world of the Christian imagination, became an autonomous pictorial object. It was not religion but classical education that distinguished enlightened citizens of the 18th century, whose culture was shaped by "good taste" *(le bon goût)* and the ideal of the alert, critical mind *(esprit)*. The unquestioning Baroque representation of faith and power gave way in the 18th century to self-reflection in all areas of scientific and social life.

The idealized image of antiquity, its philosophy and art, became the standard for ethics and art, dignity and freedom. Ancient themes were taken up by both the late courtly art of Louis XVI and the art of classicism. Thus Winkelmann's formal canon of classicism places artists under a strict stylistic control that forces them to reflect constantly on their own statements. Just as the sciences specialize in individual areas, so art is differentiated in the individual kinds of painting, such as landscape, genre, still life, portraiture, etc. This set the stage for the "art for art's sake" that would mark the century that followed and completely redefine the relations between art and religion. Likewise for the academies of the 18th century religion was just one subject among others and no longer the primordial common ground beneath all art, as was taken for granted from the first icons all the way through the late Baroque.

When the fine arts are undergirded by religious responsibilities, they address every individual, regardless of status and class. But in the 18th century art began not only to split up into individual thematic groups, but with the various pictorial genres it also began to address the most varied groups of people. Art became secularized.

Strong as the French altarpieces of the 17th century were—as in Vouet or Le Sueur—the 18th century simply could not convey religious themes con-

vincingly with the gallant images of a Boucher or Watteau.

This development can also be seen in Spanish painting, which with its great Baroque artists such as Velázquez, Murillo, or Zurbarán influenced European religious painting and reformulated important themes and motifs such as the Immaculate Conception. But in the 18th century Spanish art too failed to find its way to its old artistic greatness in religious painting.

Secularization, Enlightenment, and the social upheavals of the French Revolution prepared the path for modernity in the 18th century. But once again the tradition of religious art enjoyed a final great blooming in Rococo. In those countries that had been destroyed by the Thirty Years War, after a delay of more than half a century, and not until after a rebuilding phase, a stage of late Baroque ripening was reached. This led in a rather conservative Germany and Austria to the great "total art work" of the mighty collegiate churches and monastic layouts of Fischer von Erlach, Hildebrandt, and in southern Germany, the Asam brothers.

Within the framework of the churchly total art work an important role was assigned to sculpture as the mediator between painting, mock architecture, plaster ornamentation, and architecture. The great sculptors like Ignaz Günther, the Asam brothers, or Maulpertsch created statues of the Madonna along the lines of the Rococo, which with courtly 18th-century facility take expressiveness to the point of ecstasy. The sensory was to be an expression of the supersensory, wiping out the boundaries between the real and the unreal, in order to unleash in the spectator a state of intoxicated religious enthusiasm. Thus the richly decorated interiors of Baroque and Rococo churches have the appearance of a feast for the senses. For the last time in Western culture the courtly art of the Rococo seems to unite with folk art and religious customs, especially pilgrimages, in a Marian confession of faith, in which all levels of the population can take part.

In late Venetian painting Italian art

experienced a flowering, which, along-side the famous vista painting, gives even religious panel painting a late Baroque splendor. In the ceiling paintings of Giovanni Battista Tiepolo, as in his Marian paintings (e.g., *The Veneration of Mary* in the Munich Pinakothek), Mary once again experiences a glorification in a burst of religious ardor and an understanding of her intercession that will be impossible for later generations of painters to represent in this way.

*Left: The Assumption of Mary,* altar by Egid Quirin Asam (1692–1750) in the monastery church of Rohr, Lower Bavaria (after 1717). Asam raises Mary's Assumption to a large-scale *theatrum sacrum,* which overcomes all the force of gravity in an upward-surging jubi-lation. Architecture, sculpture, ornament, and painting work together here in a grand synthesis, bound together by the lighting.

*Right:* Cosmas Damian Asam (1686–1739), *Adoration of the Shepherds,* 1724–27. A further example of the above-mentioned unity of architecture, sculpture, and painting is this ceiling fresco in the monastery church of Einsiedeln, Switzerland.

259

*T*he 18th century (which begins with the apotheosis of the Rococo), the century of the French Revolution, destroyed the old order and brought on a profound transformation in religious art as well. In art too the spirit of the goddess of Reason, evoked by the Revolution, led to secularization and division, but also to a thoroughly individualistic artistic freedom. Romantic artists in particular criticized this development as shallow, arbitrary, and decadent.

Romanticism at the beginning of the 19th century wanted to counter this situation by reflecting on religious tra-

tion was crammed with images of the Madonna and Christ. "I carried them around with me, cherished, and cared for them."

Still, this epoch of art, with all its sensitivity, did not create its own new image of Mary. Instead it harkened back to the formal language of the Gothic or imitated the time-honored Madonnas of Raphael. Thus the Madonnas of Romanticism remained anchored in historicism. Their transcendence was rather the mirror of their own ideals and sensitivity than a reflection of timeless religious reality. Thus Joseph von Führich described his

dence were at the disposition of their science and sensibility. In the various schools and tendencies of the age artists discovered nature, whether as a Romantic projection of their own search for God or—in the later decades of the century—as a reflection of the impressionistic, fleeting interplay of light and shadow. Historical painting, genre, animal painting, country idylls, elegant salon painting or art commissioned by the Church—in all the pictorial genres and themes there were individual Madonnas that stand out as works of art, such as J.A.D. Ingres' *Vow of Louis XII* from 1824, or Eugène Delacroix' *Vierge du*

dition. Recalling the evangelist Luke, the mythical painter of the first and "true" Marian image and patron of painting, in 1808 a group of German artists gathered around Friedrich Overbeck founded the "Lukas-Bund" (they were also called "Nazarenes," initially in mockery). Their goal was to reunite art and religion, so as to be able to get back to art's true source and original power.

The new piety of Romantic artists wanted to free itself from the chilly formal language of academically overloaded art, and to rediscover the unity of art, spirit, and religion through the forces of "heart, soul, and sensibility." Overbeck admitted that his imagina-

*Mary's Way over the Mountains* in the Vienna State Gallery as nature's homage to Mary. Nature, i.e., the landscape, the grasses, trees, and animals, does homage to Mary. The relationship between Mary and nature is different from what it was in the Middle Ages. Here we see reflected in Mary the Romantic experience of nature as the expression of the artist's own moods.

Both the Nazarenes and the Pre-Raphaelites sought to find renewal in a return to historical forms and types.

In their urge to explore the world the men and women of the 19th century were on a quest for the "earthly Paradise" in which nature and transcen-

*Sacré-Coeur*. But the expression of religious faith in 19th-century art finds a completely different language from that of the continuation of traditional religious iconography.

At the same time, along with this development in art the veneration of Mary in popular piety strongly increased. The Marian apparitions of Lourdes and the "miraculous medal," which got its start in Paris, were matched by the numerous new places of pilgrimage with miracle-working images.

If, in its historical efforts to reawaken religious art, the 19th century was able to express itself in a realistic representation of the world, then with the

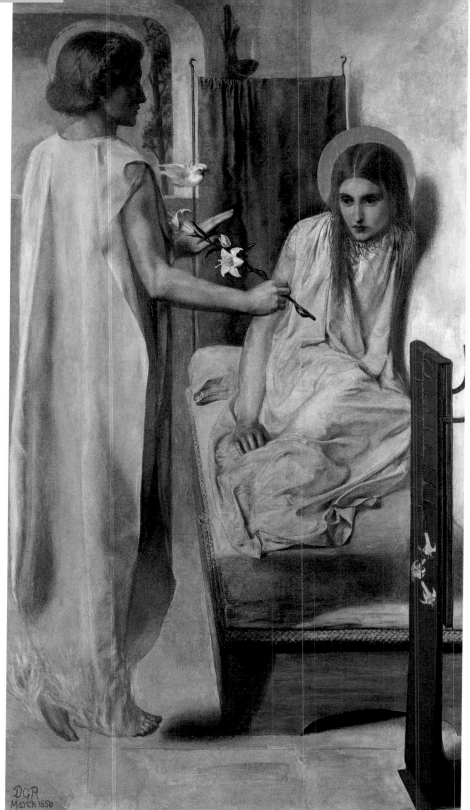

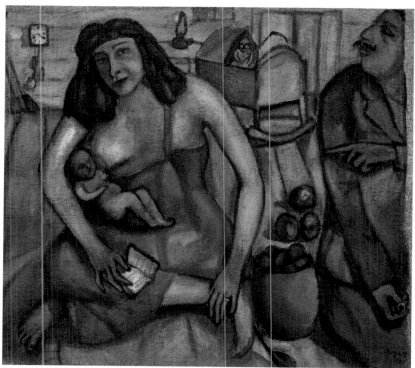

The 19th century opened up the possibility of every sort of personal artistic interpretation of religious themes.

*Page 260, left:* Paul Gauguin (1848–1903), *La Orana Maria*, 1891 (Metropolitan Museum of Art, New York). Gauguin transposes the Madonna into the world of the South Seas. Mary here is the symbol of each and every woman; only the halo marks her off as distinctive.

*Page 260, center:* Fritz von Uhde (1848–1911), *The Holy Family in the Workplace* (Gemäldegalerie, Dresden). Von Uhde interprets the theme outside of traditional iconography. The young Mary plays with a child who turns his back to the viewer. Only the title reminds us of the legend.

*Page 260, right: Birth of Jesus* by Gustave Doré (1832–1883), colored woodcut from the series of 230 illustrations for the Bible (German edition, Stuttgart, 1865).

beginning of early Cubism and abstract painting the situation was completely different. The shattering of the pictorial tradition demanded a new artistic language and confronted the viewer with a different mode of perceiving both hard reality and spiritual contents.

When religious themes are presented, then, as the few examples of this indicate (for example, Heckel's Madonna, Max Ernst, Rouault or Matisse), these are quite personal statements by the artist. They convince through their immediacy, and they show the religious theme from the point of view of the particular artist. The individual trends and directions in art, which followed

each other in rapid succession, came up with manifestoes and pronouncements by the artist that presented their own program, their own worldview, their own perception of reality. Artists such as Van Gogh and Picasso became involved in discovering new worlds outside of Europe. But, under these circumstances, there will never be a consensus for a common religious pictorial language if one goes looking for it in the traditional forms. And yet these very same 20th-century artists, in keeping with their own writings, took pains over *The Spiritual in Art* (as Kandinsky called his own theoretical piece). For Kandinsky and Mondrian spirit and matter

*Left:* Dante Gabriel Rossetti (1828–1882), *Ecce Ancilla Domini*, 1849–53 (Tate Gallery, London). Rossetti, a poet and painter, shifts the event to a sentimental poetic framework. Only the lily shows that this is an Annunciation.

*Right: The Holy Family*, from 1909, belongs to the early works of Marc Chagall (1887–1985), then still under Cubist influence. Later Chagall kept returning to the theme of the Madonna, for example in the *Village Madonna* of 1938–42 (Thyssen Collection, Lugano).

261

were not opposites but just parts of one spiritual energy: "The world rings out. It is a cosmos of beings whose activity is spiritual. Thus dead matter is living spirit," Kandinsky proclaims—a statement reminiscent of the mystical writings of the Middle Ages and one that is still valid for many of today's artists. Thus the current question of spiritual art is no longer to be answered by speeches about the preeminence of word or image or by the quest for new

stylistic forms for traditional iconographic themes, but by accepting the transformed perception of human beings through a transformed consciousness. The "religious" art that emerges from this will have to look for its own formal language for the transformed perception of the viewer.

1

4

5

6

7

8

9

10

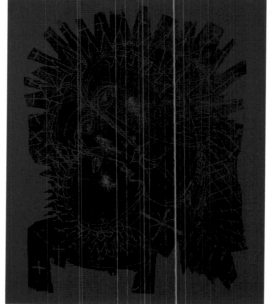

11

12

13

14

1. Korea, 20th century (Maryknoll Museum, New York).
2. Haiti, contemporary.
3. Wood statue, Zaire, contemporary.
4. West African wood figure, 19th century (Museum of Ethnology, Hamburg).
5. Salvador Dali (1904–1989), *Jour de la Vierge*, 1947, aquarelle on paper (private collection).
6. Ivory sculpture from China, contemporary (Maryknoll Museum).
7. Contemporary wooden sculpture from Africa.
8. Painted wooden figure from Melanesia.
9. Henry Moore (1898–1986), *Madonna and Child*, 1943–44 (Northhampton, St. Matthew's church).
10. *Mother of Divine Grace*, contemporary textile, Japan.
11. *Mother and Child*, silk painting on canvas, America, 20th century.
12. Ethiopia, 20th century.
13. China, 17th century (British Museum, London).
14. S.F. Overbeck, 1853 (Museum of Art and Cultural History, Lübeck).

263

## MARY'S LIFE

*Bible*
Scripture quotations are from the Revised Standard Version, Old Testament © 1952, New Testament © 1946 by the Division of Christian Education of the National Council of the Churches of Christ in the United States of America.

*Apocryphal Texts*
Willis Barnstone, ed., *The Other Bible.* San Francisco: Harper & Row, 1984.
Daniel-Rops, Henri, *Die Apokryphen Evangelien des Neuen Testaments.* Zurich: Verlag AG Die Arche, 1956.

## MARY IN LITERATURE

Lady Eve (p. 83); Arnstein Mary prayer (p. 83); Marian song of Melk (p. 83); Marian sequence of Muri (p. 84); Rhenish praise of Mary (p. 87); Reinmar von Zweter (p. 88); Konrad von Würzburg: "The Golden Forge" and "Mary, Mother and Virgin" (p. 89); "Hail, Mary" by Meister Boppe (p. 89); Liechtenthal Marian lament (p. 91); Heinrich von Meissen, "Marienleich" (p. 91); Hugo von Reutlingen: Marian petition (p.93); Johannes Tauler (p.94); Heinrich von Laufenberg (p. 94); from the prayerbook of George II of Waldburg (p. 95); contrafact from a manuscript from the Monastery of Neuberg (p. 96); Munich contrafact (p. 96); contrafact from Nuremberg (p. 97); Angelus Silesius (p. 99); hymn from the Augsburg songbook (p. 100); Pilgrim hymn of Fulda (p. 100); folksong (p. 100); petition to Mary from an Innsbruck print (p. 101); August Wilhelm Schlegel: sonnet (p. 104) "To the Assumption of the Virgin" (p. 105); "Star of the Sea, We Greet You" (p.107); Joseph Baron von Eichendorff: "Mary's I Longing" (p. 109): from *Deutsche Mariendichtung aus neun Jahrhunderten*, ed. Eberhard Haufe. © Buchverlag Union, Munich/Berlin, 1960.
"The Madonna of Stalingrad" (p. 119) from Arno Pötzsch, *Sein Wort geht durch die Zeiten.* © Verlag Junge Gemeinde, Leinfelden–Echterdingen, 1982.
"Lament of the Mother of God" and "Defiant Nightingale" (p. 104): from: *Friedrich Schlegel, Kritische Ausgabe,*

vol. V © Verlag Ferdinand Schöningh. Paderborn, 1962.
"Mary and the Women" (p.117): from: *Franz Werfel. Das Lyrische Werk*, ed. Adolf D. Klarmann. © S. Fischer Verlag, Frankfurt am Main, 1967.

The sources of some of the texts could not be located. We ask any holders of copyright to write to us at EMB Service, Museggstrasse 7, CH-6004 Lucerne, Switzerland. We will be glad to settle legitimate claims retroactively.

*Apokryphen zum Alten und Neuen Testament,* hrsg. v. A. Schindler, Zurich [5]1993.
*Beenken, Hermann:* Das 19. Jahrhundert in der deutschen Kunst, Munich 1944.
*Behling, L.:* Die Pflanze in der mittelalterlichen Tafelmalerei, Weimar 1957.
*Belting, H.:* Bild und Kult, Munich 1991.
*Bouquet, A. C.:* Everyday Life in the New Testament, London 1954.
*Bridges, Matthew:* B. V. M. in Purgatorio, London 1888.
*Bruder Philipps des Carthäusers Marienleben,* hrsg. v. Dr. Heinrich Rückert, Amsterdam 1966.
*Burckhardt, Titus:* Vom Wesen heiliger Kunst in den Weltreligionen, Zurich 1955 / Braunschweig 1990.
*Byron, George Gordon Noël:* Complete Poetical Works. Cambridge Edition, Boston – New York 1905.
*Calvocoressi, Peter:* Who's who in der Bibel. Aus dem Englischen v. A. Hausner, Munich 1990.
*Claudel, Paul:* Oeuvre Poétique, Paris 1957.
*Daniel-Rops, Henri:* The Book of Mary, translated by Al Guinan, New York 1960.
*Dante Alighieri:* Die Göttliche Komödie, übertragen v. Wilhelm Hertz, Frankfurt 1955.
*Das deutsche Gedicht vom Mittelalter bis zum 20. Jahrhundert,* hrsg. v. Edgar Hederer, Frankfurt 1959.
*Delius, W.:* Geschichte der Marienverehrung, Munich 1963.
*Drews, A. C. H.:* Die Marienmythen, Jena 1928.
*Dryden, John:* The Primer, London 1706.
*Des heiligen Ephraim des Syrers Hymnen De Virginitate,* hrsg. v. E. Beck, Louvain 1962.
*Frenzel, Elisabeth:* Stoffe der Weltliteratur, Stuttgart 1983.
*Frey, Karl:* Marienlegenden, Zurich 1926.
*Gebara, Ivonne / Lucchetti Bingemer, Maria:* Maria, Mutter Gottes und Mutter der Armen, Düsseldorf 1988 (orig. Petropolis 1987).
*George, Stefan:* Werke in 2 Bänden, Munich 1958.
*d'Ghéon, Henri:* Marie. Mère de Dieu, Paris 1939.
*Goedeke, Karl:* Grundriß zur Geschichte der deutschen Dichtung. Bd. I, Dresden 1884.
*Goethe, Johann Wolfgang von:* Faust, Leipzig o. J.
*Griechisch-deutsches Neues Testa-*

ment. Nach der deutschen Übersetzung Dr. Martin Luthers, Berlin–Frankfurt–Cologne 1888.

Guardini, Romano: Kultbild und Andachtsbild, Würzburg 1939.

Handbuch der Marienkunde, hrsg. v. Wolfgang Beinert und Wolfgang Petri, Regensburg 1984.

Harnack, Adolf v.: Chronologie der altchristlichen Literatur, Bd. II., Leipzig 1904.

Haufe, Eberhard: Deutsche Mariendichtung aus neun Jahrhunderten, Hanau 1961.

Heine, Heinrich: Werke in 2 Bänden, hrsg. v. Dr. Gunter Karpeles, Berlin o. J.

Herder, Johann Gottfried: Sämtliche Werke, Bd. XVII, Hildesheim–Zurich – New York 1994.

Heussi, Karl: Kompendium der Kirchengeschichte, Tübingen 1909.

Hoerni-Jung, Helene: Maria–Bild des Weiblichen, Munich 1991.

Housman, Laurence: Spikenard, London 1898.

Hunzinger, Johan: Herbst des Mittelalters, Stuttgart 1987.

Jantzen, Hans: Kunst der Gotik, Munich 1966.

Ders., Ottonische Kunst, Munich 1959.

Keller, Gottfried: Gesammelte Werke in 7 Bänden, Berlin 1900.

Klein, D.: St. Lukas als Maler der Madonna, Berlin 1933.

Des Knaben Wunderhorn, hrsg. v. A. von Arnim und Cl. Brentano, Halle 1891.

Kolb, Karl: Marien-Gnadenbilder. Marienverehrung heute, Würzburg 1976.

König, Robert: Deutsche Literaturgeschichte, Bielefeld 1879.

Kopp-Schmidt, Gabriele: Maria. Das Bild der Gottesmutter in der Buchmalerei, Freiburg – Basel – Wien 1992.

Der Koran, übertragen v. Lazarus Goldschmidt, Berlin 1916.

Kraut, Gisela: Lukas malt die Madonna, Worms 1986.

Krisz, R.: Die Volkskunde der altbayerischen Gnadenstätten, Munich 1955.

Küng, Hans: Das Christentum. Wesen und Geschichte, Munich 1954.

Die Kunst und die Kirchen, hrsg. v. R. Beck / R. Volp / G. Schmirber,

Munich 1984.

Lyrik des Barock, hrsg. v. M. Szyrocki, Reinbek 1971.

Mancinelli, Fabrizio: La vita della Madonna nell' arte.

Maria–für alle Frauen oder über allen Frauen? Hrsg. v. Elisabeth Gössmann und Dieter R. Bauer, Freiburg–Basel–Wien 1989.

Marienlexikon, 6 Bände, hrsg. v. Institutum Marianum Regensburg e. V., Remigius Bäumer, Leo Scheffczyk, St. Ottilien 1988–1994.

Marmy, Emile: Kleiner Wegweiser zu den Marienerscheinungen, übersetzt v. E. Nordmann, Freiburg i. Ue. 1990.

Mays, Cynthia Pearl: The World's Great Madonnas, New York 1947.

Medieval Age. Laurel Masterpieces of World Literature, hrsg. v. Angel Flores, New York 1963.

Mesters, Carlos: Maria, Mutter Jesu, Düsseldorf 1985 (orig. Petropolis 1977).

Miller, Elliot: The Cult of the Virgin, Grand Rapids 1992.

Mommsen, Theodor: Judaea und die Juden, in: Römische Geschichte, Bd. V, Berlin 1936.

Mulack, Christa: Maria, die geheime Göttin im Christentum, Stuttgart ⁴1991.

Mystische Zeugnisse aller Zeiten und Völker, hrsg. v. Martin Buber, Jena.

Neumann, Alfred: Alt- und neufranzösische Lyrik, Munich 1922.

Neumann, Erich: Die große Mutter, Darmstadt 1957.

Newman, John Henry (Kardinal): Oratory, London 1849.

Novalis: Werke in einem Band, hrsg. v. Uwe Lassen, Hamburg o. J.

Pelikan, Jaroslav: Mary through the Centuries, London–New Haven 1996.

Petrarca, Francesco: Die Gedichte, übersetzt v. Wilhelm Krigar, Hannover 1866.

Pochat, Götz: Geschichte der Ästhetik und Kunsttheorie. Von der Antike bis zum 19. Jahrhundert, Cologne 1986.

Pope, Alexander: Poetical Works, London 1966.

Des Priesters Wernher drei Lieder von der Magd (driu liet von der Maget), metrisch übersetzt v. Hermann

Degering, Berlin 1925.

Prudentius Clemens: The Poems, Vol. II, Washington 1962.

Reallexikon der deutschen Literaturgeschichte, Bd. II, „Mariendichtung", hrsg. v. Werner Kohlschmidt und Wolfgang Mohr, Berlin 1965.

Renaissance, Humanismus, Reformation, hrsg. v. Josef Schmidt, Stuttgart 1977.

Rilke, Rainer Maria: Ausgewählte Gedichte. Werke, Bd. I, Frankfurt 1955.

Schiller, Friedrich von: Sämtliche Werke in 14 Bänden, Bd. VI, Berlin –Leipzig o. J.

Schipflinger, Th.: Maria – Sophia. Eine ganzheitliche Vision der Schöpfung, Munich / Zurich 1988.

Schmidt, Heinrich und Margarethe: Die vergessene Bildsprache christlicher Kunst, Munich 1995.

Schreiner, Klaus: Maria–Jungfrau, Mutter, Herrscherin, Munich 1994.

Schreyer, L.: Das Bildnis der Mutter Gottes, Freiburg 1951.

Seine Mutter, unsere Schwester, hsrg. v. Wolfgang Bader, Munich–Zurich – Wien 1989.

Spee, Friedrich: Sämtliche Schriften, Bd. 2, hrsg. v. G. M. van Oorscht, Munich 1968.

Sperber, H.: Unsere Liebe Frau. 800 Jahre Madonnenbild und Marienverehrung zwischen Lech und Salzach, Regensburg o. J.

Stammler, W.: Wort und Bild. Wechselbeziehungen zwischen den Schriften und der Bildkunst des Mittelalters, Berlin 1962.

Ströter-Bender, Jutta: Die Muttergottes. Das Marienbild in der christlichen Kunst. Symbolik und Spiritualität, Cologne 1992.

Stubbe, A.: La Madonne dans l'art, Brüssel 1958.

Und Maria trat aus ihren Bildern, hrsg. v. Karl-Josef Kuschel, Freiburg–Basel–Wien 1990.

Warner, Marina: Alone of all her Sex, New York 1983.

Weinreb, F.: GottMutter. Die weibliche Seite Gottes, Weiler im Allgäu 1990.

Akademische Druck-und Verlagsanstalt,
Graz: 15 r, 22 or, 33 o, 41 ur, 47 o,
165, 169, 170 l.
Archiv für Kunst und Geschichte, Berlin:
26 ur, 32 l, 36 ur, 40 r, 53 r, 99, 126,
130, 135, 139 r, 143, 146 l, 147
(4/5/7/9/10/11/12/14/15/16) 171,
172, 175 l, 196 ml, 198 l, 214, 216,
217o, r, 219, 220 l, r, 221 l, m, r,
227 ol, u, 230 r, 231 r, 232/233 o,
233 ur, 235 l, 236, 237, 239 l, r, 240 l,
241, 242, 244 l, r, 245 ul, r, 246 l, r,
247 l, r, 248 m, r, 249 u, r, 250 l, r, 251,
253 l, 254, 256 or, 256 u, 257, 258,
260 m, r, 262 r.
Alinari Fratelli, Florence: 223 r.
Arborio Mella, Federico, Milan: 181 r.
Art Resource, New York: 10, 27 r, 174 r.
Badische Landesbibliothek, Karlsruhe:
76 o, u.
Baumli, Othmar, Meggen: 56, 97, 138 l,
190 o, u, 193, 195 ol, ul, 196 om, or,
203 r, 205 (9), 210.
Bayerisches Hauptstaatsarchiv, Munich:
43 ol.
Bayerisches Nationalmuseum, Munich:
103 l, 124 or, 145.
Bayerische Staatsbibliothek, Munich:
19 l, 54 u, 73 r, 96, 150 ol, or, 174 l.
Bayerische Staatsgemäldesammlung,
Munich
photo: Artothek, Peissenberg: 11, 22 l,
26 l, 37 r, 39, 137, 175 r.
Benediktinerkollegium Sarnen: 85 r.
Biblioteca Apostolica Vaticana: 63 r,
71 o, 148 u.
Biblioteca Medicea Laurenziana,
Florence: 87, 90, 92 u, 148 l.
Biblioteca Veneranda Ambrosiana, Mi-
lan: 34 l.
Biblioteka Jagiellonska, Crakow: 73 ol.
Bibliotheca Bodmeriana, Cologny/Ge-
neva: 20 l, r, 104.
Bibliothèque Nationale de France, Paris:
28 or, 64, 77, 80 r, 95, 159 l, 184 l.
Bibliothèque Royale Albert Ier, Brussels:
152 l, 153.
Bildarchiv Foto Marburg: 112, 213.
Birmingham Museums & Art Gallery:
139 o.
Bischöfliche Administration der Heiligen
Kapelle, Altötting: 205 (8).
Bodleian Library, Oxford: 86 r.
Böhm, Erwin, Mainz: 25 ul, 192 u.
Böhm, Osvaldo, Venice: 188 r.
Boltin Picture Library, New York: 29 r,
136 r, 262 (1), 263 (6 / 7 / 8 / 10 / 11 /
12).
British Library, London: 18 l, 28 m, 263
(13).
Bührer, Lisbeth, Lucerne: 47 r.

Bundesdenkmalamt, Wien
Foto: Eduard Beranek, Vienna: 223 l.
Caisse Nationale des Monuments Histo-
riques, Paris: 38 or.
Calouste Gulbenkian Foundation, Lis-
bon: 138 r.
Casa Ricordi, Milan: 158 or, ur.
Cermak Fotoverlag, Mariazell: 202 r.
Chartres, Cathedral Notre Dame: 191 u.
Chorherrenstift Klosterneuburg: 186 r.
Christiana Verlag, Stein am Rhein:
206 ur.
Cleveland Museum of Art: 44/45, 163.
Diözesan- und Dombibliothek, Cologne:
71 r.
Domkapitel, Aachen
Foto: Ann Münchow: 188 l, m, 191 or.
Domschatzkammer Essen: 231 l.
Dumbarton Oaks, Washington DC: 63 m.
EMB-Service für Verleger, Lucerne:
14 l, r, 15 l, 18 r, 19 r, 22 ur, 25 r,
26 or, 28 ur, 30 l, r, 35 ol, or, 40 l, 41 o,
43 u, 48 l, 49, 50 l, o, 52 or, 58, 61,
62 r, 63 o, 66, 67, 108, 125 l, r, 128 l, r,
131, 134 l, 140 r, 141, 142 u, 147 (8/
13/ 17), 164 l, r, 166 l, 168 l, u, 170 m,
178 m, 181 u, 183 l, 185 l, 186 l, 191
mr, 194, 195 r, 199 m, 202 l, 204 (3),
205 (4/ 6), 206 l, 207, 222 r, 226, 229,
230 l, 249 ol, or, 262 (2/ 3/ 4), 263 (9)
photo: J. Perret, Lucerne: 206 or.
photo: Tipo dec, Bukarest: 52 mr.
Faksimile Verlag, Lucerne: 38 l, 48 or,
230 m.
Frans Hals Museum – De Hallen, Haarlem: 222 l.
Franziskanerkloster, Werl
Foto: Helmuth Euler, Werl: 201 u.
Freies Deutsches Hochstift, Goethe-Mu-
seum, Frankfurt: 106 r.
Gebetsaktion Medjugorje, Hasle:
211 or, u.
Geiger Fotohaus, Flims-Waldhaus: 42 l.
Germanisches Nationalmuseum,
Nuremberg: 127, 144.
Hansmann, Claus & Liselotte, Munich:
182 ol, or, 183 r.
Held, Ursula, Ecublens: 68 l, 167, 224.
Hessisches Hauptstaatsarchiv, Wies-
baden: 83 m.
Honegger, Pascale, Pully: 147 (6).
Holy, Viktor & Sohn, Innsbruck: 217 l.
Ikonenmuseum Recklinghausen: 23 r.
Istituto Poligrafico e Zecca dello Stato,
Rom: 253 r.
Kantons- und Universitätsbibliothek, Fri-
bourg: 98.
Katholische Filialkirchenstiftung Herz
Jesu und Mariä, Wigratzbad: 211 mr
Photo: Fotostudio Bulmer,Wangen:
211 ol.

Kloster Andechs: 201 mr, ur.
König, Edm., Kunstverlag, Dielheim:
200 l.
Konrad Verlag, Weissenhorn: 85 l.
Kranich Foto, Berlin: 157 (3), 158 l.
Kröller-Müller-Museum, Otterlo: 140 l.
Kunsthistorisches Museum, Vienna:
42 r, 55.
„La Goélette", Prim'dias, Saint Ouen:
196 ur.
Landesmuseum, Zurich: 21 l.
Lensini, Fabio, Siena: 51, 149 or, 180 l,
185 r.
Leonard von Matt, Gemeinnützige
Stiftung, Buochs: 31 r, 32 o, 35 u, 225.
Loose, Helmuth, Autun: 23 l, 37 l, 189 l,
192 o, 218 l, r.
Ludwig Maximilians-Universität, Munich:
176.
Lutherisches Verlagshaus GmbH, Han-
nover: 119.
Maagd der Armen, Banneux: 209 l, r.
Mainfränkisches Museum, Würzburg:
178 r, 196 ul.
Martin von Wagner-Museum, Würzburg:
69 r.
MAS, Barcelona: 50 r, 187 l.
Metropolitan Museum of Art, New York:
48 ur, 182 u, 260 l.
Missio Bildarchiv, Aachen: 184 ur.
Monumenti Musei e Gallerie Pontificie,
Vatikan: 179 l.
Musée National d'Art moderne, Paris:
261 r.
Museo Castelvecchio, Verona: 125 m.
Museu de Montserrat: 201 o.
Museo del Duomo di Monza, Monza: 62 l.
Museum für Kunst- und Kultur-
geschichte der Hansestadt Lübeck:
263 (14).
Nationalmuseet, Kopenhagen: 181 ol.
Nationalgalerie (Narodni Galerie), Pra-
gue: 204 (1), 215.
National Gallery, London: 166 r.
National Gallery of Art, Washington: 29 l.
National Museums & Galleries of Mer-
seyside, Liverpool: 41 l.
Norfolk Museum (Castle Museum), Nor-
wich: 36 l.
NTV, Tokyo: 35 r.
Österreichische Galerie Belvedere, Wien
Foto Otto, Vienna: 114.
Österreichische Nationalbibliothek, Vi-
enna: 38 u, 71 ul, 73 or, u, 74 r, 80 l,
159 m, r, 161, 223 m, 233 ul.
Pedicini, Luciano, Naples: 28 l.
Pinacoteca di Brera, Milan: 173 l.
Pinacoteca Nazionale, Siena: 17.
Pinacoteca Nazionale, Bologna
Photo: Mario Berardi, Bologna: 199 l
Piskiewicz, Pascal, Toulouse: 205 (5).